Librarianship and
Information Work Worldwide
1998

Librarianship and Information Work Worldwide 1998

General Editor
Maurice Line

Editors
Graham Mackenzie
Paul Sturges

BOWKER
SAUR ●

London • Melbourne • Munich • New Providence, N.J.

British Library Cataloguing in Publication Data
A catalogue record for this title is available from the British Library

Library of Congress Cataloging-in-Publication Data
A catalog record for this book is available from the Library of Congress

Published by Bowker Saur, part of Reed Business Information Limited
Maypole House, Maypole Road
East Grinstead, West Sussex RH19 1HU, UK
Tel: +44 (0) 1342 330100 Fax: +44 (0) 1342 330101
E-mail: lis@bowker-saur.com
Internet Website: http://www.bowker-saur.com/service/

ISBN 1-85739-169-1

Cover design by John Cole
Typeset by The Castlefield Press, Kettering, Northants
Printed on acid-free paper
Printed and bound in Great Britain by Antony Rowe Ltd, Chippenham

Contents

About the editors

Maurice B. Line is a consultant specializing in strategic planning, staff development and the management of change. He retired in 1988 as Director-General, Science Technology and Industry, of the British Library. Before that he worked in five university libraries. He is a Professor Associate at Sheffield University. He has honorary doctorates from Heriot-Watt and Southampton Universities, and a fellowship from Birmingham Polytechnic. He was President of the UK Library Association in 1990, and was awarded the IFLA Medal in the same year. He has travelled widely on professional work. He edits *Alexandria* and has written over fourteen books and 334 articles and papers, covering a wide variety of topics from bibliometrics to library management; translations have appeared in 20 languages.

Graham Mackenzie read Classics at Glasgow. He was the founding Librarian at the University of Lancaster in 1963, establishing its Library Research Unit in 1967, and he was Librarian of the University of St Andrews from 1976 until he retired in 1989. A member of the Editorial Board of the *Journal of Documentation* since 1965, he has published widely, and retains a long-standing interest in consultancy work.

Paul Sturges is a Senior Lecturer in Information and Library Studies at Loughborough University and was Associate Dean (Research) in the School of Education and Humanities (1993–6). He is Chair of the Library Association's International Group (IGLA) and has held various other offices in the Library Association, Institute of Information Scientists and IFLA. He has lectured and spoken at conferences in many countries, and researched and written across the field of information and library studies. His recent published work includes articles on Africa, on the history of the British public libraries, and on legal and ethical issues in information work. He is joint editor (with John Feather) of the *International encyclopedia of information and library science*.

About the contributors

Raymond Astbury, following a career in public and college libraries, was for over thirty years a Principal Lecturer in the Department of Library and Information Studies of Liverpool Polytechnic/Liverpool John Moores University, specializing in public library, book trade, and community information studies. He is a Past-President of The Library Association of the United Kingdom and currently, in retirement, is editor of the *School Librarian*, the Journal of the School Library Association of the United Kingdom.

Barry Bloomfield retired from the British Library as Director of Collection Development in 1990. He had previously been Deputy Librarian, then Librarian, of the School of Oriental and African Studies, University of London, and Director of the India Office Library and Records, Foreign and Commonwealth Office. He is the author of bibliographies of the poets W.H. Auden and Philip Larkin, and the editor of the second edition of the *Directory of rare books and special collections in the United Kingdom and the Republic of Ireland* (1997).

J. Michael Brittain is Chair of Information Management, Victoria University of Wellington, New Zealand. He was, until recently, Professor of Information Management and Director of the Health Informatics Research Group (HIRG) at the University of South Australia. He has taught and researched at six universities in the UK, US, Australia and New Zealand in electrophysiology, criminology, information management, information needs assessment, research methodology, and medical and health care information systems. He has worked in the UK National Health Service/Department of Health, where he was the foundation Director of the NHS Information and Management Technology Education and Training Program. He is on the editorial boards of four international journals. He has written and edited books on health informatics, education and training in health informatics, integrated information systems in health, and published widely in professional journals.

Graham Cornish is Director of the Universal Availability of Publications Programme for the International Federation of Library Associations and Institutions (IFLA). After graduating from Durham University and Liverpool Polytechnic he joined the staff of the British Library, working in a variety of departments. He is also currently responsible for all aspects of copyright law within the BL. A prolific author of journal articles, he has also written several books on copyright law, national libraries and library co-operation. He is a fellow of both the Library Association and the Institute of Information Scientists.

Blaise Cronin was educated at Trinity College Dublin (MA) and the Queen's University of Belfast (PhD). He has been Professor of Information Science and Dean at Indiana University in the USA since 1991. He is concurrently the BLCMP Visiting Professor of Information Science at the Manchester Metropolitan University in the UK. From 1985 to 1990 he was Professor of Information Science and Head of Department at the University of Strathclyde in the UK. He is author/editor of more than 200 articles, books and technical reports, and has worked in 30 countries.

John Gilbert studied Natural Sciences at Trinity College, Cambridge University. He worked in the information departments of Unilever Research both in England and the Netherlands, before moving to Universiteit Maastricht (the Netherlands) in 1980 as head of the Scientific Information Department of the University Library. He became deputy librarian in 1987 and was appointed university librarian in 1992.

Alan Gilchrist joined Aslib in 1964 and left in 1977 to set up his own consultancy practice. Since then, he has carried out over 100 assignments in both the public and private sectors, and for international organizations; taking him to over 30 countries. He is a co-founder and Director of the CURA Consortium and GAVEL g.e.i.e., providing consultancy services in all aspects of information management from a European-wide base. He is the Editor of the *Journal of Information Science*.

Alex Klugkist studied Theology and Semitic Languages at the University of Groningen (the Netherlands). After a scientific career at this university and in Göttingen (Germany) he became director of the Student Admission Office of the Dutch Ministry of Science and Education in 1973. In 1976 he became Managing Director of the Faculty of Arts of the University of Groningen. From 1982 to 1990 he was deputy librarian of the University Library, and in 1990 he became University Librarian at Groningen.

Jennifer MacDougall is an independent researcher who has widely researched in the information, healthcare and public service sector in the UK and Republic of Ireland. Recent work includes Health Informatics in the *Journal of Documentation, Information for Health* (1995), *Marketing in the not-for-profit sector* (1997) and

Healthcare information services in Ireland in *Topics in Health Information Management*. She is currently working in the area of consumer health information in Ireland.

Beryl Morris established Hudson Rivers: Management and Training Consultants in 1972 and works with a variety of organizations in the academic, public and commercial sectors. In particular, she and her colleagues work with library and information managers and other staff in organizations which are undergoing change to help them respond to different circumstances and to feel more confident in their changing roles. Previously, she worked as a Chief Officer for the London Borough of Newham, with responsibility for Arts and Entertainment's, community centres, a major conference centre; catering and the borough's library service. Other posts have included Senior Lecturer at Manchester Polytechnic (now Manchester Metropolitan University); Assistant Polytechnic Librarian at the Polytechnic of East London and Management Adviser with the Industrial Society.

Guy St. Clair is the President of InfoManage/SMR International, a management consulting, training, and publishing company in New York City. He is the Editor and Publisher of two newsletters, *InfoManage: the international management newsletter for the information services professional* and *The one-person library: a newsletter for librarians and management*, both of which are published by InfoManage/SMR International. Guy St. Clair is the Guest Editor for the Bowker-Saur Information Services Management Series, for which he has written four books. A member of the Information Futures Institute and of the Spcial Libraries Association, Guy St. Clair was SLA's President in 1991–1992.

Jagtar Singh is Senior Lecturer in Library and Information Science at Punjabi University, Patiala. Having done his master's degree at the same university, he got his Ph.D. from Panjab University, Chandigarh. He previously has served as Lecturer at Jabalpur University, Jabalpur and Sagar University, Sagar. In 1992, he was awarded a Commonwealth Academic Staff Fellowship by the Commonwealth Scholarship Commission in the UK. His main areas of interest are information management, electronic publishing and preservation and conservation of digital information.

John Sweeney has been Head of Collection Development at the British Library Science Reference and Information Service since 1995. After graduating in chemistry he worked in various information posts before moving to the British Library in 1983. He is a member of the Institute of Information Scientists and the Circle of State Librarians and has been involved in committee work for both organizations. He previously contributed to the Bowker-Saur publication *Information Sources in Chemistry, 4th edition*.

Editorial advisory board

Foreword

Librarianship and Information Work Worldwide makes its seventh annual appearance with this volume. Reviews and personal comments confirm its value in presenting between two covers an overview of what is happening in the library and information world. We – the editors and publishers – believe that LIWW is still much too little known, even allowing for the fact that any new work takes time to get established. Coverage can never be complete; readers will always be able to point to references that the author has not found, and sometimes are not worth mentioning. But we believe that there are few serious omissions, and that the work gives a true picture of what has appeared in the literature (which may not of course always reflect what has been happening in practice).

Each volume has several regular chapters, covering the previous year in national, public, academic and special libraries, followed by chapters on other topics. Some of these appear every two or three years (e.g. bibliographic control, collections, or management – not always with the same title or slant), others less frequently than that. Because they do not appear every year, these chapters cover the last few years. In the present volume, two topics are covered for the first time: Health services information, and Research and consultancy. We also try to include in each volume one chapter on a particular region of the world, in this case South Asia.

As will be seen, there are more references to World Wide Web material in this volume. They will certainly continue to grow in number. While the increased amount of information available on the Web is welcome, its sheer volume and sometimes dubious value makes it very hard to achieve anything approaching good coverage; the material discovered by authors is more likely to be a good random selection. Unless and until better screening of Web material becomes a reality, it may as soon cause serious problems for the editors and authors of LIWW.

'Librarianship and Information Work Worldwide' is rather a mouthful. We have played around with other titles, but so far we have not found one that expresses succinctly what the work is. One solution might be to choose a snappier title as the main one and relegate *Librarianship and Information Work Worldwide* to a subtitle. Suggestions are welcome. Meanwhile, the initials *LIWW* are manageable, and the work has become known as such.

As ever, I would like to thank all our Editorial Advisers, who put a good deal of effort into guiding authors to sources they would otherwise be unlikely to find. And as ever, I invite suggestions for future topics and authors.

Maurice B. Line
September 1997

Editor's Note

It will be observed that all names beginning with 'van', 'te' or 'ter' (e.g. van den Hoogen, te Boekhorst) are filed in the References to each chapter under 'van' or 'ter', not under 'Hoogen' or 'Boekhorst'. We are aware that Dutch practice is to file such names under the last part, but English-speaking authors with Dutch names are known as 'van' or 'te'. Since readers will often not know whether authors cited are Dutch or not (we do not always know ourselves, since Dutch authors often write in English), we decided to follow the above practice, and hope that not too many Duth readers will be offended by it.

Maurice B. Line

Library and information science in context

1

Blaise Cronin

Introduction

The big picture

After almost three decades of scholarly and lay debate, there is still little agreement as to what the term 'information society' denotes. The ontological wrangle continues unabated, and Martin (1995) is not alone in wondering whether we are dealing with an idea or entity. Although Bell (1973) provided a path-breaking analysis of the conditions of post-industriality, many of his axial assumptions and inferences continue to be challenged. Poster (1990), for instance, accuses him of deploying the 'rhetoric of totalization' to assert rather than prove that knowledge and information 'are the leading variables of society', while Webster's (1995) book is a broadside against the theoretical, empirical, and methodological bases of Bell's elaborate critique. Contested though the construct of an information society may be, it nevertheless serves as a useful lightning rod for research and theorizing into the effects of large-scale informatization (Nora and Minc, 1980) – what Beniger (1986) terms 'the growing "systemness" of society' – on traditional economic structures and established social relations.

The subject exercises a fascination for scholars and, increasingly, for policy makers and politicians, as evidenced in the 1996 Ministerial Conference on the Information Society and the creation of the European Information Society Week, 6–10 May, 1996. A thoroughgoing and accessible analysis of the issues involved is provided in the *Economist's* recent review of cybernomics (Hitchhiker's, 1996). And serious thought is being given to the nature of the relationship between information and development, social as well as economic, particularly with regard to less developed countries (McConnell, 1995; Menou, 1993). The overall aim of this context-setting chapter, then, is to consider how the traditionally defined library and information science (LIS) field is adapting to the growing informatization of society – how librarians and information scientists are positioning themselves as players in an information society, characterized by metaphors such as 'Information Superhighway' and 'Worldwide Library'. It is personal in character and necessarily selective in scope. Its purpose, notwithstanding the North American bias, is to frame some of the issues, identify major change drivers, and consider the kinds of strategic responses being made by, and required of, the LIS field in the face of pervasive technologization and shifting social practices.

Education

Blurred edges

The disciplinary edges of library and information science are fuzzy. So, too, are the boundary lines that demarcate the information professions from other guilds, with whom they increasingly joust for jurisdiction and legitimacy (Abbott, 1983; Cronin, 1995; Cronin and Davenport, 1996; van House and Sutton, 1996). The once secure coordinates that defined the LIS field are now uncertain and constantly shifting, as work roles and technologies converge, creating a highly volatile information ecosystem, in which the library is only one element. The physicalist paradigm, which for so long moulded curricula and defined the work world of LIS graduates, has been found wanting in an age of 'formless data' (Negroponte, 1995). The concept of digital libraries, as Miksa (1996) notes, has thrown a spanner in the works, at least as far as curriculum development is concerned: 'Unfortunately, as a child of the modern library, current LIS education embodies the modern library almost completely in how it presents the idea of the library, in its curricular content, and in its research.' In particular, the rapid proliferation of wide area networks, software agents, electronic publishing and virtual libraries is challenging many of the traditional assumptions and models which have informed LIS thinking and practice.

Managing collections of bits calls for a different mindset than managing atoms: atoms, at least, seem to know their place. The age of post-physicalist librarianship has dawned, one in which fixity and stability seem almost anachronistic, but one that is replete with opportunities for the traditional LIS profession – provided there is a willingness to apply core skills and know-how well beyond the *locus classicus*, that is the traditional library, to electronic environments and media. In the words of the director of Copenhagen Public Libraries (Sørensen, 1996), 'the new library will not be judged by its collections but by its potential for connecting users with information'. Fashionable though this view be, there is still resistance to the new, as is demonstrated both by the public outcry (Shapiro, 1996) surrounding the opening of San Francisco's spectacular new public library (a 'mall for the mind') and by the negative reaction to the idea of 'hyperlibraries' in the context of the government commissioned review of the public library service in England and Wales (*Review*, 1995). It is worth speculating on how the profession will adapt to such a dramatic undercutting of the status quo (with its emphasis on place, physical formats and human mediation) and whether a new calculus of service effectiveness will emerge (*Books, bricks and bytes*, 1996). One notable recent attempt to understand the changing dynamic is *Buildings, books, and bytes: libraries and communities in the digital age*, the report of a study conducted in the USA by the Benton Foundation (1996) with financial support from the W.K. Kellogg Foundation.

Adaption, extinction or genetic drift?

During the late 1980s and early 1990s, the competitive dynamics of the library and information science field changed irrevocably, and not only in advanced industrial nations (Cronin, 1992). One effect of rapid technologization of LIS curricula has been a ramping up of the entry barriers in terms of capital expenditures and recurrent costs. A similar re-indexing of the field is noticeable with regard to human capital investments. Creating an information studies programme is no longer a relatively low cost option for an academic institution seeking to extend its portfolio of professional degree programmes. Pace-setting LIS schools and departments, at least in North America, have begun to recruit disciplinary 'outsiders' with an unprecedented aggressiveness. The retitled School of Information at the University of Michigan at Ann Arbor has an electrical engineer as dean, while the reconstituted programme at the University of California at Berkeley (School of Information Systems and Management) is directed by a theoretical economist. But it is not just the academic leadership that is undergoing change (Cronin *et al.*, 1997): the School of Library and Information Science at Indiana University at Bloomington, for instance, has 22 full-time professors on its faculty whose doctorates were earned in eleven different academic disciplines, including computer science, cultural anthropology, information transfer, law and psychology. The cost of staying 'in play' for some schools and departments has risen dramatically, and will inevitably accentuate the gap between first and second rank programmes. These change drivers make the choice facing some LIS parent institutions particularly stark: invest or exit. They also exacerbate the historic tensions between the academy, with its emphasis on research and scholarly production, and the world of professional practice, which stresses application and performance.

The altered structural dynamics of the broadly defined information studies marketplace, of which traditional LIS programmes constitute an important, if diminishing, subset, have triggered a variety of institutional response strategies (Cronin, 1993), the most common among them being the following:

- marriages of convenience (e.g. LIS departments are bundled in with cognate academic tribes to cut costs and/or create academic synergies);

- growth through acquisition (e.g. LIS programmes acquire parts of, or asset strip, other academic units);
- strategic coevolution (e.g. LIS and other departments jointly develop inter-disciplinary information studies programmes);
- internal growth (e.g. building an undergraduate programme; developing distance education modules);
- product portfolio diversification (e.g. new degree programme development).

While there is no one preferred option – much will depend on local conditions and wider political choices – it is fair to say that, as a general rule, programmatic restructuring and rapid retooling have become commonplace strategies, most notably in North America and the UK. Here, as elsewhere, incrementalism and parochialism have given way to a new planning ethos, one which stresses strategic advantage and competitive cooperation (Davenport and Cronin, 1994). But such change is not confined to the world of academia.

Co-prosperity initiatives

Forms of cooperation

A number of the trends sketched above find their echo in the sphere of professional practice, where a combination of unremitting budgetary constraints and dramatic growth in electronic access to remote collections has persuaded many librarians that collaborative approaches to resource procurement and management are required (DeLoughry, 1996). It is no accident that a stream of conference proceedings and monographs dealing with information economics and library fiscal management is beginning to appear on the market (Kingma, 1996; Mayère, 1997; Snyder and Davenport, 1997). The trend lines are graphically revealed in the Association of Research Libraries' time series data. From 1986 to 1994, ARL member libraries increased their serials expenditures by 93%, but acquired 4% fewer items. At the same time, monograph expenditures increased by 17%, but purchases fell by 22%. During this period, interlibrary lending (presumably including the supply of photocopies) increased by 50% and interlibrary borrowing rose by 99% (Kyrillidou *et al.*, 1995). The problem here is pretty clear: if remote access continues to replace acquisition, then production costs will rise, in turn driving up further the cost of remote access. It is a spiral, and ultimately self-defeating for all the parties involved. As McPherson (1996) observed, there is an amusing *reductio ad absurdum* in all of this: 'You can sell 600 copies of a monograph at $40 each or 60 copies at $3000 each. Or one copy which will fly around the country on Federal Express for $15,000.' It is hardly surprising, therefore, that the search for imaginative solutions has intensified, given the distortions exhibited in the present system of scholarly production and consumption. One vogue approach is to act in consort, suppressing institutional egos and purely local considerations in favour of collectivism.

Library consortia are by no means a new phenomenon, but their popularity is growing apace, as libraries struggle to adapt to structural changes in their fiscal and technological environments. The emerging electronic environment has destabilized the traditional access and delivery chain in scholarly communication by admitting new kinds of collaboration and partnering in the information industry. Flux and uncertainty in the supply side have compelled librarians to become more active players in the marketplace and to experiment with a variety of new alliances. An example of for-profit and not-for-profit interests converging is the agreement between Ameritech and the Universities of Chicago and Indiana to collaborate on the development of next generation Horizon software. The motive to collaborate is mutual self-interest (cost sharing/risk reduction), and there is every likelihood that we shall see an increase in co-prosperity initiatives of these kinds, as libraries and other players in the information marketplace seek to blur some of the traditional demarcations between their zones of operation. This, of course, has supply side simplications, as the vendor community has begun to realize (Miller, 1996).

The term 'consortium' connotes a range of cooperative forms (e.g. planned partnerships, outsourcing arrangements, co-development projects), but common to all is the principle of enlightened mutualism. The collaborating institutions may be of the same kind (e.g. academic or school libraries), but increasingly we are seeing the formation of multitype library consortia. In both the UK and the USA, consortia proliferated as a library-led response to developments in library automation during the late 1960s and early 1970s. These cooperatives offered a range of benefits to members, such as centralized processing, lower transaction costs and expanded content range. They were essentially not-for-profit clubs, funded by membership subscription and based on the principle of common pool resource management. Regionality was a defining feature as reflected in the names of the pioneers - or, in the recent case of the M25 Consortium of Higher Education Libraries in the UK, the name of an orbital motorway. BLCMP, in the UK, grew from a Birmingham-based cooperative cataloguing venture to become the market leader in library systems. VALA, in Australia, was a state-level pioneer based in Melbourne, Victoria. The Ohio College Library Center, which was established to serve academic institutions in the state of Ohio, has evolved into OCLC, the indisputable dynamo of the business, with 23,000 members in 63 countries and a turnover of more than $150 million. Other major utilities, such as the Western Library Network (WLN), with its 550 members in the Pacific Northwest, and the Research Libraries Group (RLG), with its 152 member institutions worldwide, have diversified from the core records business into cognate areas. For instance, the WLN Conspectus software is a widely recognized collection assessment and management system. The RLG's primary product is the Research Libraries

Information Network (RLIN), an online union catalogue of some 50 million items; this has been augmented by Ariel, a high quality transmission system for document images, and CitaDel, a fee-based document delivery service.

Contracting out services

Outsourcing is another response to budgetary pressures, and an option being considered by a growing number of libraries. A good illustration is the arrangement (announced mid-1996) between the Hawaii State Public Library System (HSPLS) and a number of suppliers of library automation, technical services, and both general and reference information. Five-year contracts were signed between HSPLS and Ameritech, Baker & Taylor, and Information Access Company to do what was once done internally. This is by no means an isolated example: Wright State University, a pioneer in this area, claimed savings of close to $250,000 through outsourcing of its cataloguing operations. Even if most librarians are not entirely comfortable with the idea of competitive tendering and outsourcing of (para)professional services and activities, we can expect budget-conscious administrators to promote such solutions. The implications of this trend, specifically for corporate information services, have been reviewed recently by Agada (1996).

A somewhat different picture obtains in the UK, where public librarians, in particular, have been strongly opposed to the idea of contracting out. In the last two years, there has been considerable debate as to the merits and feasibility of applying the principle of compulsory competitive tendering to public library services and operations. However, a much-heralded study by KPMG and Capital Planning Information, commissioned by the Department of National Heritage, concluded in late 1995 that the library service was not well prepared for competitive tendering and that the marketplace was as yet underdeveloped (KMPG/CPI, 1995). The issue of charging for (at least for certain categories of) service remains firmly centre stage, and it is highly probable that public sector libraries will be forced to differentiate between those facets of their portfolio that genuinely warrant the label public goods and those that really are more appropriately labelled either merit goods or private goods.

Buyer group formation

Another clear trend is the formation of joint buyer groups, which embody the principle of strength in numbers by altering the power balance between purchaser and commercial supplier. Examples in the UK are BIDS (Bath Information and Data Services), MIDAS (Manchester Information Datasets and Associated Services) and EDINA (Edinburgh Data and Information Access). This approach can be applied to monographs and serials, and also to software and database licensing agreements, where complex pricing/leasing models have become the norm. A good example of the genre is the CIC (Committee on Institutional Cooperation, 1996) in the USA, whose 12 members include major research universities such as Chicago, Indiana, Michigan, and Illinois. The CIC's combined library and information resource base gives it considerable muscle in negotiations with commercial publishers and database vendors. From the perspective of the user, whether a scholar at his workstation or a student logging on from her dorm, this ultimately translates into easier access to a much wider array of locally and remotely hosted information resources. The CIC consortium, established in 1958, is also aggressively pursuing multimedia electronic publishing, document delivery and cooperative acquisition initiatives, through CICNet Inc. and the CIC Centre for Library Initiatives. Although only one among many interesting consortial formations, the CIC is arguably *sui generis*, and thus worthy of special attention.

There is no comparable confederation of major academic institutions with a similar track record of multilateral cooperation or, arguably, equal potential for creating novel consortial initiatives. The CIC's objectives are laid out as follows (Committee on Institutional Cooperation, 1996):

> The Committee on Institutional Cooperation has always been governed by its three founding principles that no single institution can or should attempt to be all things to all people, that interinstitutional cooperation permits educational experimentation and progress on a scale beyond the capability of any single institution acting alone, and that voluntary cooperation fosters effective, concerted action while preserving institutional autonomy and diversity.

As an organization, it has interesting emergent properties. How might the CIC use its massive intellectual and physical capital base to forge a new generation of transsectoral alliances (e.g. joint ventures with software developers, systems suppliers, hardware vendors, telcos, cable companies, commercial publishers, manufacturing companies, etc.)? One example is the recently announced collaborative project with OCLC (1996) to build a Virtual Electronic Library, which will provide seamless desktop access for the CIC's 500,000 students and 35,000 faculty to the 60 million books and 550,000 serials, and numerous databases and digital 33 systems, owned or licensed collectively by the participating institutions. How else might the CIC exploit the economies of scale and scope which, along with its reputational edge, are its main sources of comparative advantage? Will the CIC take the lead in pioneering new kinds of joint acquisition programmes, interinstitutional resource sharing, collaborative archiving? Might it act as a stimulus for co-development initiatives involving historically autonomous university presses? As a phenomenon, the CIC is noteworthy because it has the potential to bring about a rewriting of some of the rules of the game which have heretofore defined trading relationships between libraries and also between libraries and their respective supplier/vendor populations.

Digital libraries

First generation blueprints for the digital library may still be somewhat fuzzy, but a battery of research projects is under way in both the USA – e.g. the National Science Foundation's Digital Library Initiative and the agency's (October 1996) announced funding opportunities in information technology, culture, and social institutions, and the UK – e.g. the Electronic Libraries (eLib) Programme. In other parts of the world, for example in the ASEAN (South-East Asian Nations) region, there is as yet little evidence of coordinated development activity (Reid, 1996). Undoubtedly, the Library of Congress has emerged as perhaps the most ambitious pioneer with its National Digital Library Program (begun in 1995 following the American Memory pilot project), which expects to commit $65 million to the digitization of five million items from its unique Americana collections over the next five years (Zich, 1996). Nonetheless, much fundamental research work remains to be done if the challenges of scaling, tagging, indexing, and deep semantic interoperability across large-scale federated databases are to be answered (Collier, 1996; Schatz and Chen, 1996), on top of which there are many issues relating to social infrastructures, data integrity, usability, and intellectual property rights management (Bishop and Starr, 1996), not to mention sustainable archiving – a topic that has been powerfully foregrounded thanks to the programmatic efforts of the Commission on Preservation and Access, both nationally and internationally (Conway, 1996).

There is little agreement as to the defining features of a digital library. The term sometimes connotes a common physical space which provides access to digitized information resources, both local and remote; at other times it implies a virtual library, with no physical context. There is debate as to whether a digital library ought to embody the defining features of the traditional, modern library (e.g. organization of materials, quality/authority control, mediation) or whether it should be a truly postmodern construct – a heterotopic assembly of digitized objects located in a more or less chaotic logical space where conventional notions of validation and archival permanence are of little or no consequence.

Consortial electronic publishing

But it is not just that the mode (digitization) and place (distributed) of storage are changing: the change effects ripple all the way along the classical scholarly production/distribution chain. It is clear that the roles of, and relationships between, players in the traditional chain are set to change dramatically, though precisely how and over what time frame remain hotly contested issues. 'This fragmentation within an embryonic market', to quote a report by DJB Associates (1996) on the future of electronic information intermediaries, characterizes the entire publishing chain. Everywhere there are examples of experimentation, stand-alone and collaboration – think of IDEAL, the online scientific journal library created by Academic Press, or Blackwell's Electronic Journal Navigator. Digitization alters long-established modes of production, distribution economics, licensing/ repurposing arrangements, and archiving policies, and is taxing the imaginations of commercial publishers, primary producers and institutional purchasers alike (Malinconico, 1996).

On the one hand we have statistics from the Association of Research Libraries (Mogge, 1996) which show a 257% increase in the number of electronic journals, newsletters, and newsletter-digests between 1995 and 1996; while on the other, there are cautionary findings from the summative evaluation of the TULIP project: postgraduate students are more likely than academic staff to use online systems, and journal readers have emotional ties to paper (Elsevier Science, 1996). The Elsevier report concludes as follows: 'A common view, which all TULIP participants share, is that the transition to a digital library will go slower than they had expected before starting the project.'

As the established model of scholarly publishing comes under increasing pressure, we can expect to see a new wave of electronic consortial publishing emerge, involving university libraries on the one hand, and bibliographic utilities, publishers, information systems suppliers, and telecommunications corporations on the other. Some of these initiatives will be led by primary producers (i.e. academic staff and their parent institutions). Some will be driven by existing commercial publishers; some will be launched by foundations and trusts. Others will be led by mediators and secondary publishers like ISI (Institute for Scientific Information) and utilities such as OCLC. Yet others will be driven by learned societies (e.g. American Mathematical Society; Institute of Physics) and professional associations (e.g. Association for Computing Machinery). One thing is sure: there will be much jostling for position, much experimentation and much soul-searching by both established players and new entrants.

Web-based publishing

The World Wide Web has been described (Gates, 1996) as the instantiation of friction-free capitalism. The medium offers direct contact between provider and consumer (be it on a business-to-business, business-to-customer, or customer-to-customer level). The Web concatenates established value chains, and the effect of bypass/disintermediation, coupled with extremely low entry costs, and immediacy of communication to a vastly expanded potential audience of like minds. In extreme cases, authors become do-it-yourself publishers/distributors. In similar vein, universities, acting alone or in consortia, have the potential to become primary publishers in their own right – forward integration. Of course, authors may still choose to have their works subjected to peer review before appearing on Web-based electronic journals, but we can expect to see personal archives and working papers proliferating on both personal and organizational home pages. As the ACM's imaginative Electronic Publishing Plan (Denning and

Rous, 1995) notes, 'authors are increasingly viewing their works as "living on the web" '. Given the competition for the coin of recognition, we can expect to see many scholars use the Web as a vehicle to promote their work and presence among their globally distributed peer communities. The Web is a flexible, inviting, expansive medium which, unlike conventional print-based scholarly publishing, can accommodate dynamic versioning and rolling (open) peer review. Almost certainly there will be changes in terms of components of the Web (browsers, search engines, protocols, scripting languages), but the fundamental features (flexibility, interconnectivty, modularity) will remain invariant.

For instance, if the Johns Hopkins University Press and the University Library can collaborate in making available via the Web the full text of scholarly journals in the humanities, social sciences and mathematics (Project Muse), what is to stop them and/or any other university from moving into territory once considered the privileged turf of commercial publishers? The idea of consortial university publishing is not new (Cronin, 1989), and the possibility of production scale ventures coming on stream should no longer be dismissed out of hand. Such uncertainty helps explain why cooperation and collaboration between even the most unlikely bedfellows have become relatively commonplace – think of the SuperJournal Consortium in the UK (which includes 21 publishers and two universities), or the Red Sage Electronic Journal Project, a collaborative effort between the University of California at San Francisco, AT&T Bell Laboratories (as was) and a variety of commercial publishers, or the JSTOR project, which brings together the Andrew W. Mellon Foundation, commercial publishers and university libraries, or, in a different vein, ISI and IBM's Electronic Library Pilot project, or OCLC and Elsevier Science's electronic publishing joint venture.

The Internet and LIS professionals

Demographics

The top nations in terms of the number of Internet hosts are all members of the Organisation for Economic Cooperation and Development (OECD). Only in the USA and a few other developed nations do users routinely have access to the Internet from their homes. Otherwise, access is provided almost entirely through universities, government agencies, and businesses (Cronin and McKim, 1997). Even assuming that a reliable telecommunications infrastructure and logistical support system exist, the prevailing culture, social structures, community values, and established rhythms of life in many less developed countries may retard or constrain uptake. In their review of computing in North Africa, Danowitz *et al.* (1995) acknowledge that Internet connectivity, in particular, could weaken the enforcement of prevailing social values and hinder censorship of ideas and opinions inimical to the powers that be. To illustrate the importance of cultural relativism, it is only necessary to compare information access policies in, say, Sweden or the USA with those of the People's Republic of China or Burma, where importing, owning or using a fax machine or modem without government permission is a crime punishable by up to fifteen years in jail. Not everyone, however, is as quite as enamoured of the US notion of democracy as the average American seemingly is, and not everyone is persuaded that the democracy augmenting capabilities of the Internet necessarily constitute an irresistible attraction. We have just begun to understand the cross-cultural significance of internetworking, and the sociopolitical consequences of global connectivity.

In the USA, the present administration is committed to connecting public schools, libraries and hospitals to the Internet as part of its National Information Infrastructure (NII) initiative. If public libraries have Internet connections, so the logic goes, local citizens and community groups will become electronically empowered. These policy thrusts have been boosted by a flurry of philanthropic activity: Ameritech, for example, recently donated $2 million to the Library of Congress in support of its digital library initiatives, while, also in 1996, the Pew Charitable Trusts and the William Penn Foundation, respectively, provided $2.8 million and $18 million grants to the Free Library of Philadelphia. Bill Gates, founder and chief executive officer of Microsoft Corporation, is already being spoken of by some as a latter-day Andrew Carnegie in the wake of recent grants and benefactions. In November 1995, Libraries Online!, a $3 million initiative involving the ALA, Microsoft Corporation, and the Centre for Technology in Seattle Public Library, was launched. Approximately a year later, Gates promised a further $10.5 million to provide computers and software for rural and city libraries as yet untouched by technology. All of these gifts, however, pale into insignificance alongside the recently announced $400 million gift to US libraries from the Gates Library Foundation. When it comes to fund raising and giving, no nation can compete with the philanthropic culture of the USA, though that does not mean that hard-pressed operating budgets cannot be supplemented in other ways. For instance, the library profession in the UK (via the Library Association and the Library & Information Commission) prepared a bid to the Millennium Commission to network all public libraries.

According to a recent survey by the National Commission on Libraries and Information Sciences (NCLIS), approximately 45% of US public libraries have some connection to the Internet (the 1997 projection was 76%), although such access is not equitably distributed (Bertot *et al.*, 1996). In many societies, pervasive networking may stimulate greater participation in the democratic process and, at the same time, add a further set of checks and balances on all levels of government. Networks can enable concerned citizens, local action groups, or disaffected individuals to challenge authority directly, to source important background information, and to mobilize support from like-minded, but often geographically dispersed, groups. But universal democracy comes with a price tag: the technology platforms that facilitate open exchange also support electronic eavesdropping and cyber-surveillance of dissident voices by, for example, government departments, national security agencies, or corporations. Indeed, in North America, the library and information professions have been highly visible in a variety of policy fora, and also highly effective in lobbying for unfettered access to information. This ideological opposition to censorship was evidenced powerfully during 1996 in the high profile case of the Communications Decency Act (CDA) in the USA, which sought to outlaw 'obscene' materials from the Internet, in the process requiring even more stringent legislation than currently applies to either printed or broadcast materials. In the course of the ongoing anti-lawsuit, the American Library Association alone has committed hundreds of thousands of dollars from its endowment funds to the campaign.

On the Web

Growth statistics for the World Wide Web are dramatic. Despite well-documented problems related to access, bandwidth, and responsiveness (Economics, 1996), the Web seems destined to become a truly significant site for global commerce, entertainment, distance learning, and diverse kinds of social interaction, particularly with the National Science Foundation's (NSF) provision of new funds for high-performance connections (Luker, 1996) and the current administration's promise of $500 million over the next five years to seed Internet II (Wilson, 1996). First generation Web search engines have been criticized for their limitations, notably the unacceptably high level of false positives resulting from searches. High recall and low precision are defining features of Web searches. That is only to be expected, however, given the heterogeneous, unregulated, dynamic, decentralized, hypertextual nature of the WWW. It is a mistake to make direct comparisons between the Web and the closed world of commercial online information retrieval systems. The number and sophistication of available search engines continue to grow, with Lycos, Alta Vista, InfoSeek and WebCrawler (automated) and Yahoo (manually indexed etc.) being among the most popular and effective. As more intelligence is built into harvesters, crawlers and spiders, the frustrations of Web-based searching will decrease. Indeed, the first 'peer-reviewed' search engine (Argos) has just been announced. Argos differs from first generation search engines by virtue of its selectivity of focus: it looks only at sites that a group of editors has deemed to be both scholarly and topical (Online, 1996). Other developments of note include the emergence of 'push services' which obviate the need for time-consuming surfing by pushing tailored/customized categories of information at Internet users on a subscription basis (Hafner and Tanake, 1996).

The online market is a mature business environment which brings together commercial vendors and knowledgeable customers, both intermediaries and end users, to trade access to highly structured, consistently updated and reasonably reliable data sets. The commercial online information business has invested considerable sums in developing sophisticated retrieval engines and ranking/ weighting algorithms, designing controlled vocabularies, imposing bibliographic structure, promoting common standards/record formats, and employing trained abstractors and indexers. In this world, the contents are often recognizable textual quanta (e.g. articles, abstracts, titles, bibliographic citations) or analogous packets of canned knowledge (chemical compounds, patents), and these quanta are labelled in such a way that they are maximally amenable to retrieval by searchers trained to extract such pre-formatted chunks. It is a controlled environment, with a high level of explicit, shared knowledge among suppliers and receivers. The Web, by comparison, is a chaotic and unbounded environment, in which the trivial and the serious commingle. Currently, its great appeal is as a browsable hyperspace in which unexpected gems may be discovered. As a novelty generator, the Web has attractions. As a globally distributed reference library, the Web also has enormous appeal. As a host to masses of grey literature, in the broadest sense, it has great attractions. As an alternative distribution channel for database providers, it has manifest value. Functional pluralism is certainly a defining feature of the Web.

A major problem with the Web is the lack of transparent structure and the absence of a universal and consistent classification scheme. It is debatable, however, whether Internet cataloguing initiatives, such as OCLC's NetFirst or the Catriona project funded by the British Library R&D Department, can work given the scale of the domain and the high maintenance/recurrent costs required to ensure that the record base is reliable. It may be that cataloguing and validation will be better left to local enterprise – to micro communities of practice. The picture is uncertain, but, as Jul (1996) says, there are really only two mistakes we can make: '1) thinking that cataloguing is *the* solution, and 2) thinking that it's not'.

Mediation, disintermediation and remediation

With the Internet, services that once necessitated a broker, intermediary or middleman can now be provided directly to the ultimate consumer (Gellman, 1996). New software (and successive upgrades) can, for example, be distributed directly without using wholesalers, retailers, dealerships or sales teams. Most of the operations and activities associated with high street banking can also be handled interactively via the Web, and there is no reason in principle why, for example, the entire home buying process could not be conducted without some of the traditional intermediaries. Bypass can thus translate into reduced operating costs for the manufacturer/service provider, which, in theory, should mean more competitive prices for the consumer/client. Books can be ordered via the Web from a virtual store with a virtual inventory, but one with a very real ability to satisfy almost any request. No longer is it necessary to go to a local bookshop in an effort to find what one wants from a necessarily constrained inventory. For at least some businesses and some clients, the Web promises a more immediate (and possibly more satisfying) form of consumption – sedentary and impersonal.

As far as the library and information services sector is concerned, we should be careful not fall into the trap of confusing changing modes of production/distribution with changes in the overall value chain, a point made cogently by Peters (1996):

> First of all, it is important not to mistake the distribution-chain for the value-chain. We believe that networks and networked information are creatively destroying the former, and that they are creatively reorganizing ('re-engineering' is an even better term) the latter. CNI (Coalition for Networked Information) believes that 'reintermediation' of actors (some old, many new) around different functions (again, some old, many new) is a more likely scenario for the value chain than is disintermediation.

The implications for librarians are thus clear: identify emerging roles and opportunities as, for example, Web publishers (Stover, 1996) in a reconfigured value chain where professional skills and expertise can be brought into play in such a way as to create fresh career opportunities (Hohman, 1996; Rosenthal and Spiegelman, 1996; Tate and Alexander, 1996). The uncertainty that the library and information science profession feels about its future has its mirror image in the uncertainties the general public feels about the place of the traditional library in the new information world order, as this telling quotation from the Benton Foundation (1996) study clearly indicates:

> Americans continue to have a love affair with their libraries, but they have difficulty figuring out where libraries fit in the new digital world. And many Americans would just as soon turn their local libraries into museums and recruit retirees to staff them. Libraries are thus at a crossroads, for they must adjust their traditional values and services to the digital age.

References

Abbott, A. (1983) *The system of professions: an essay on the division of expert labor.* Chicago, IL: University of Chicago Press.

Agada, J. (1996) Outsourcing of corporate information services: implications for redesigning corporate library services. *International Information and Library Review*, 28(2), 157–176.

Bell, D. (1973) *The coming of post-industrial society: a venture in social forecasting.* New York: Basic Books.

Beniger, J.R. (1986) *The control revolution: technological and economic origins of the information society.* Cambridge, MA: Harvard University Press.

Benton Foundation (1996) *Buildings, books, and bytes: libraries and communities in the digital age.* Washington, DC: Benton Foundation. Available at: http://www.benton.org/buildings.html

Bertot, J.C. *et al.* (1996) *The 1996 national survey of public libraries and the internet: progress and issues.* Washington, DC: NCLIS. Available at http://www.nclis.gov

Bishop, A.P. and Starr, S.L. (1996) Social informatics of digital libraries and infrastructure. *Annual Review of Information Science and Technology,* **31,** 301–401.

Books, bricks, and bytes (1996). *Daedalus,* **125**(4) [whole issue].

Collier, M. (1996) Towards a digital future. *Library Association Record,* **98**(12), 644–646.

Committee on Institutional Cooperation (1996) http://cedar.cic.net/cic/about.html

Conway, P. (1996) *Preservation in the digital world.* Washington, DC: Commission on Preservation and Access.

Cronin, B. (1983) *The transition years: new initiatives in the education of professional information workers.* London: Aslib.

Cronin, B. (1989) Research libraries: an agenda for change. *British Journal of Academic Librarianship,* **4**(1), 19–26.

Cronin, B. (1992) Information science in the international arena. *Aslib Proceedings,* **44**(4), 195–202.

Cronin, B. (1993) Educating librarians for an information society. In: P. Vodosek (ed.) *Bibliothek – Kultur – Information.* London: K.G. Saur, pp. 15–27. (Contributions to Library Theory and Library History, vol. 8).

Cronin, B. (1995) Shibboleth and substance in North American library and information science education. *Libri,* **45**(1), 45–63.

Cronin, B. and Davenport, E. (1996) Conflicts of jurisdiction: an exploratory study of academic, professional, and epistemological norms in library and information science. *Libri,* **46**(2), 1–15.

Cronin, B. and McKim, G. (1997) The Internet. In: *World information report 1997/98.* Paris: UNESCO, pp. 240–256.

Cronin, B. *et al.* (1997) Charting a new course: developing and implementing a new curriculum for a masters of information science degree. In: *Proceedings of the 30th Hawaii International Conference on System Sciences,* January 1997. IEEE Computer Society Press, vol. 2, pp. 12–22.

Danowitz, A.K. *et al.* (1995) Cyberspace across the Sahara: computing in North Africa. *Communications of the ACM,* **38**(12), 23–28.

Davenport, E. and Cronin, B. (1994) Competitive intelligence and social advantage. *Library Trends,* **43**(2), 239–252.

DeLoughry, T.J. (1996) Purchasing power: cost-sharing efforts help college libraries finance electronic acquisitions. *Chronicle of Higher Education,* 9 February, A21, A23.

Denning, P.J. and Rous, B. (1995) The ACM's electronic publishing plan. *Communications of the ACM,* **38**(4), 97–103.

DJB Associates (1996) *The future of electronic information intermediaries: a survey undertaken on behalf of UKSG and JISC/ISSC.* [np]: UKSG and JISC.

Economics (1996) of the Internet, The: too cheap to monitor? *Economist,* 19 October, 23–24, 27.

Elsevier Science (1996) TULIP: the final report. Available at http://www.elsevier.nl/locate/tulip/

Gates, B. (1995) *The road ahead.* New York, Penguin Books.

Gellman, R. (1996) Disintermediation and the Internet. *Government Information Quarterly,* **13**(1), 1–8.

Hafner, K. and Tanaka, J. (1996) A fix for info overload. *Newsweek,* 21 October, 49.

Hitchhiker's (1996) guide to cybernomics, The. *Economist,* 28 September, 3–46.

Hohman, J.M. 1996. Disintermediation and education. *Bulletin of the Medical Library Association*, **84**(4), 589–599.

Jul, E. (1996) Why catalog Internet resources? *Computers in Libraries*, **16**(1), 8, 10.

Kingma, B.R. (1996) *The economics of information: a guide to economic and cost-benefit analysis for information professionals.* Englewood, CO: Libraries Unlimited.

KPMG/CPI (1995) *Contracting out in public libraries.* London: KPMG.

Kyrillidou, M. *et al.* (1995) (eds) *AARL Statistics 1993–1994: a compilation of statistics from the one hundred and nineteen members of the Association of Research Libraries.* Washington, DC: Association of Research Libraries.

Luker, M. (1996) NSF's new program for high-performance Internet connections. *Communications of the ACM*, **39**(10), 27–28.

McConnell, P. (1995) (ed.) *Making a difference: measuring the impact of information on development.* Ottawa: International Development Research Centre.

McPherson, M. (1996) The economics of university investments in information resources. In: M.A. Butler and B.R. Kingma (eds) *The economics of information in the networked environment.* Washington, DC: Association of Research Libraries, pp. 53–55.

Malinconico, M. (1996) Electronic documents and research libraries. *IFLA Journal*, **22**(3), 211–225.

Martin, W.J. (1995) *The global information society.* 2nd rev. ed. London: Aslib.

Mayère, A. (1997) (ed.) *La société informationelle: enjeux sociaux et approches économiques.* Paris: Editions L'Harmattan.

Menou, M.J. (1993) (ed.) *Measuring the impact of information on development.* Ottawa: International Development Research Centre.

Miksa, F. (1996) The cultural legacy of the modern library for the future. *Journal of Education for Library and Information Science*, **37**(2), 100–120.

Miller, K. (1996) Library consortia change the rules. *Computers in Libraries*, **16**(10), 20–21.

Mogge, D.W. (1996) (ed.) *Directory of electronic journals, newsletters and academic discussion lists.* 6th ed. Washington, DC: Association of Research Libraries.

Negroponte, N. (1995) *Being digital.* New York: Knopf.

Nora, S. and Minc, A. (1980) *The computerization of society.* Cambridge, MA: MIT Press.

OCLC (1996) Information available at http://www.oclc.org/

Online (1996) *Chronicle of Higher Education*, 18 October, A23.

Peters, P.E. (1996) Cost centers and measures in the networked information value-chain. In: M.A. Butler and B.R. Kingma (eds) *The economics of information in the networked environment.* Washington, DC: Association of Research Libraries, pp. 137–142.

Poster, M. (1990) *The mode of information: poststructuralism and social context.* Chicago, IL: University of Chicago Press.

Reid, E.O.F. (1996) The Internet and digital libraries: implications for libraries in the ASEAN region. *Asian Libraries.* Available at http://www.mcb.co.uk/liblink/al/jourhome.htm

Review (1995) *of the public library service in England and Wales for the Department of National Heritage: final report.* London: Aslib.

Rosenthal, M. and Spiegelman, M. (1996) Evaluating use of the Internet among academic reference librarians. *Internet Reference Services Quarterly*, **1**(1), 53–63.

Schatz, B. and Chen, H. (1996) Building large-scale digital libraries. *Computer*, **29**(5), 22–26.

Shapiro, L. (1996) A mall for the mind. *Newsweek*, 21 October, 84–86.

Snyder, H. and Davenport, E. (1997) *Accounting for electronic services: a practical guide for managers*. London: Library Association.

Sørensen, B. (1996) Quoted in: Libraries ponder role in the digital age. *New York Times*, 20 April, B1, B4.

Stover, M (1996) The librarian as publisher: a World Wide Web publishing project. *Computers in Libraries*, **16**(9), 40–43.

Tate, M. and Alexander, J. (1996) Teaching critical evaluation skills for World Wide Resources. *Computers in Libraries*, **16**(10), 49–55.

Van House, N. and Sutton, S.A. (1996) The panda syndrome: an ecology of LIS education. *Journal of Education for Library and Information Science*, **37**(2), 131–147.

Webster, F. (1995) *Theories of the information society*. London: Routledge.

Wilson, D.L. (1996) Clinton's new Internet proposal could involve half a dozen agencies. *Chronicle of Higher Education*, 25 October, A29–30.34.

Zich, R. (1996) The Library of Congress National Digital Program Library. In: *Proceedings of the International Conference on Digital Libraries and Information Services for the 21st Century, KOLISS DL 96. September 10–13, 1996, Seoul*. Seoul: Korean Library and Information Science Society, pp. 176–185.

National libraries 2

Graham P. Cornish

Introduction

This chapter reviews material about national libraries which was published mainly in 1996. However, some items published in 1995 which were not included in the previous review have also been mentioned, as are some early 1997 references. As the previous review included such a variety of topics, some duplication of themes has been inevitable. An attempt has been made, however, to include different aspects and different national libraries. Again De Beer and Hendrikz (1996) have reviewed the literature on national libraries looking at both themes and individual countries. They draw attention to the rapid onslaught of technology and conclude that, despite the cost, 'major libraries are travelling into cyberspace'. This could mean that national libraries in less developed countries are left far behind. Some help for those drafting or revising their legislation is provided by Lor (1997), which can be used as a model and a tool of persuasion for more funding and enlightened laws.

Legal deposit

One of the most important features of many national libraries is that they are the primary point for receiving, storing and recording copies under various legal deposit arrangements. Legal deposit itself varies considerably from one country to another but the underlying concept is the same. Its previous link to copyright law, causing it to be called even today 'copyright deposit' causes more misunderstanding than almost any other misnomer in the library world. Although legal deposit arrangements most often cover print on paper, there is a considerable movement towards expanding their scope to ensure the conservation and recording of as much of a nation's cultural heritage as possible. Considerable interest in the deposit of electronic material has been shown in the literature for 1996 as it was in 1995, especially in the UK, and a number of studies on the topic were commissioned by the British Library Research & Development Department (now renamed the British Library Research and Innovation Centre). The report on preservation of digital material (Hendley, 1996) examines the problems of managing, preserving and resourcing the collection of digital material. 'Management' in this context includes all the usual library activities such as identifying what is to be collected, its acquisition (whatever that term means in the digital environment), storage, preservation and retrieval. The whole problem of identifying what is published (another term which needs to be redefined) is linked to the eligibility of documents to be subject to legal deposit in the first place. Other issues which the report highlights are the future computer needs of any library trying to preserve material which exists in an essentially volatile relationship between the producer (owner), intermediary (library) and user on the one hand, and manufacturers of the hardware in which to run it and the software which drives it on the other.

The question of the extra expense incurred by a library required to receive electronic material through legal deposit also has to be considered. The cost of maintaining and updating equipment will have to be found either from the library's existing funds or from additional resources provided by the government department concerned which, in the present global economic situation, is unlikely. These problems are being faced particularly by the Deutsche Bibliothek (Stephan,1996). Not surprisingly the situation worldwide is very chequered, with one or two countries having deposit for virtually every type of material, not just electronic and paper, while others have the same limitations as the UK in restricting deposit to print on paper only. A broad-based study of various countries (Hoare, 1996) shows just how uneven things are, although the selection of different countries would have given a different result. Concentrating on fourteen countries, eleven of which are in Europe and two in North America (the other being Australia) gives a rather biased view of the world. Some consideration of legislation and practice in eastern Europe and the CIS countries would have thrown more light on current practice, even if future developments may be rather slow to materialize in these areas.

If the problems of electronic deposit in general are complex those facing anyone trying to design a system for online databases are almost insuperable (Electronic, 1996). Legal deposit relies on the concept of a work being published and published in a particular country, neither of which is relevant to the online database situation where production and access are international. There are also problems connected with situations where the producer goes out of business or ceases to provide public access to the database. Further complications can be foreseen when access is no longer through a sole vendor or gateway, which may invalidate the concept of legal deposit anyway. National libraries may need to revise the concept of acquiring such works to mean providing access to them, but this in itself generates opposition from owners, as it may undermine their economic exploitation of the work by providing for free what owners charge for. This, in turn, requires the concept of deposit to be reconsidered as a form of contract which may be structured in such a way as to limit public access.

If deposit were thought of as a real option, then consideration of what version and how often such deposit took place would have to be redefined. The question of access versus delivery is explored in the Scandinavian context (Hedberg, 1996). Norway has had comprehensive legal deposit for several years; the experience gained there should enable others to design legislation and systems to avoid some of the pitfalls and benefit from areas of success. In Sweden the long tradition of openness raises all kinds of questions about access and availability, especially for electronic materials. These, in turn, lead the legislator, researcher or systems designer into many areas on the fringes of traditional librarianship such as International Standards Organization (ISO) standards for 'mark-up' languages and metadata which are essential to the structuring, indexing, retrieval and archiving of the documents.

This impacts on traditional cataloguing too: how to record and catalogue electronic items is still a matter for debate. This is a matter of considerable importance in France (Vayssade, 1996) where the law on legal deposit not only requires material in many different formats to be deposited but also gives the Bibliothèque nationale de France (BnF) the obligation to create a bibliographic record for each item so deposited.

Many of the problems associated with legal deposit of electronic documents are echoed in the findings of a working party set up by the National Library of Canada to look at the whole question of collecting electronic documents, especially under legal deposit regulations (Blair, 1996). This highlights especially the problems of selection. Traditionally legal deposit has included all materials in a particular class, but the electronic world enables individuals to be their own publisher. So just how national libraries are going to decide what is published, what constitutes publication and how to acquire the material they consider within their remit is a particular problem. Canada has already extended its legal deposit legislation in 1993 to include compact discs and videotapes but further legislation would be needed. Although the main reasons for deposit have been well documented over the years, it is always dangerous to make assumptions that everyone thinks the same way. Weiming and Ning (1996) give a short description of the National Library of China, its history and present services but point out in their essay that a primary function of their National Library is 'to preserve and disseminate information for the Communist Party of China' – perhaps not a view that would be echoed in other countries with different political systems. In the UK a consulation paper has recently been published (Department of National Heritage, 1997) on topics such as existing legal deposit arrangements, the need to extend legal deposit to non-print media, the costs of such a scheme, the implications for intellectual property rights, remedies for non-compliance, the idea of reducing the requirement to fewer copies, the disposal of unwanted copies and archiving. It will be very interesting to see what ensues, particularly with the recent change of government in the country.

Collections and access

With the increasing use of technology and the higher expectations it generates in users, the pressures on national libraries to make their collections more widely available without the necessity of physically visiting the library are becoming irresistible. The British Library has already demonstrated considerable skills in making one or two major elements in its collection available through the Internet but, in the words of Carr (1996), 'the challenge is to provide access to more than the tiniest tip of the vast iceberg' . The development of the new building at St Pancras offers great opportunities, but traditional methods of access must not be neglected at the expense of high technology which can often be seen as merely a gimmick, especially by those who do not have ready access to it. At the same time it must be remembered that there is, and for the foreseeable future will continue to be, vast quantities of material in conventional paper format. Such material must be collected and made available, just as the latest electronic documents need to be readily accessible.

This concept is behind the definitely low-technology mission undertaken by Cunningham (1996), because the National Library of Australia (NLA) has had in the past, and continues to perceive that it will have in the future, an important role in, and commitment to, the Pacific region, especially those smaller states with which it has strong commercial, cultural and political links. As a world resource centre of Pacific studies, the NLA considers it necessary to continue to build its collections relating to the region for the benefit of all those in the area, not just for Australians. By doing this, they ensure the preservation of much rare and often uncollected material for posterity. To enhance these collections Cunningham undertook a two and a half week trip identifying materials, contacting publishers and booksellers and talking with librarians in four territories – American Samoa, Western Samoa, Cook Islands and French Polynesia. In fact Cunningham actually sent home personally over 200kg of materials and bought up another 70kg for booksellers to send on to Australia later. Clearly the pioneering spirit is not dead in the Australian acquisitions community. The emphasis on providing access to paper documents in the traditional way is also underlined, paradoxically, by the new Bibliothèque nationale de France. Although one of the great high-tech library developments of the decade, the new building at Tolbiac will have a floor devoted to the Rare Books Department or Réserve which will also be enriched by the addition of 58,000 other books from the Department of Printed Books at the Richelieu site in central Paris (Coron,1996). Grunberg (1996) describes the library's audiovisual programme and points out that the new building is a wonderful chance to rethink the conservation of and access to multimedia information. One interesting question posed is whether multimedia items, which can be transmitted anywhere within the library, should be housed in a separate collection or in subject departments alongside more traditional tools.

The whole discussion about digital collections is often confused because there is a failure to distinguish between material which is acquired in digital form, usually directly from the publisher, and the digitization of existing material for the purposes of saving storage space, improving access and preservation. The arguments in favour of all or any of these reasons still need considerable refinement. The economics of digitization need to be thought through in the same way as those for microfilming had to be over 20 years ago. Large microfilm collections have never materialized in the ways predicted, and this may be true of the digital revolution as well. Certainly in Japan the development of the new Kansai building of the National Diet Library was deliberately postponed to give time to re-examine the potential of various technologies (Tsuruta, 1996). Other, very sensible, reasons for postponing the development are given, such as the evaluation of other digitization projects, some of which are government funded, the development of an electronic union catalogue and the design of a model for an electronic library.

The various techniques available need to be evaluated carefully, such as microfilm scanners or scanning original documents. Questions such as whether the scanning of a high quality photocopy will produce as good an image as scanning the original also need to be addressed. Although the possibilities of optical scanners are well known and the technology is improving, they still generate a considerable number of errors and their application to ideographic scripts such as Chinese, Japanese and Korean is still not fully explored (Tamura, 1996). Unlike the Japanese, the French have already progressed a long way with the digitization of a core collection for the BnF (Prytherch, 1996). It was foreseen that a core collection of electronic documents would be necessary to enable the BnF to offer a wide range of services and a considerably enlarged number of access points. The plan is to convert some 300,000 documents (books and journals) to electronic form over the next six to eight years. Two methods are being used: one involves scanning the paper documents using a line scanner which enables 8,000 pages a day to be processed. The second system can cope with 3,000–5,000 pages a day using microfilm technology.

The thorny problem of copyright has been dealt with by negotiating the necessary permissions from the appropriate French publishers who are also prepared to allow use of original photocomposition bands to store books in character mode. Game (1996) looks at some of the legal aspects of copyright law, moral rights and reproduction rights and how these have affected the BnF's digitization plans. An example of cooperation is provided by Dubois (1996) who describes how the BnF is allowed the free use of 10,000 images for digization and use at Tolbiac in return for providing digital copies for the Musée de l'Homme. Increasingly there is a need for co-operation between publishers and libraries to achieve workable systems for collection development and access, but some still see these two groups as in opposition, which does nothing for the improvement of library services.

The emergence of policies on the collection and availability of electronic materials raises the much explored theme of how comprehensive collections in any one library (or indeed any one country) need to be (Line, 1996). In the USA the establishment of the National Digital Library Federation (NDLF) raises more than one issue. The Federation consists of twelve major university libraries, plus the Library of Congress (LC), the National Archives and Records Administration, New York Public Library and the Commission on Preservation and Access. The initiative builds on the National Digital Library Program (NDLP) of LC, which one author (Lamolinara, 1996) has described as a 'metamorphosis of a national treasure'. The NDLF has as its first priority areas the discovery and retrieval of digital information; intellectual property rights management and economic models for the provision of digital information; and archiving of digital information. The initiative clearly recognizes that one national library cannot achieve all that needs to be done and must work closely in a group to realize its goals. At the same time NDLF is working towards a concept that the 'national library' is actually an aggregate of the collections of many libraries. This has always been the case in nearly every country, as no acquisitions policy, whether based on legal deposit or not, is exhaustive. The bringing together of university and public libraries, as well as the national archives and the national body responsible for preservation, make this a quite new and exciting development in the concept of the ' national library' (Hattery, 1996). Line (1995) discusses the role of paranational libraries, which he defines as large specialist libraries which can be 'considered a major part of the national resource'. He points out that in some countries, including the UK, such libraries have no officially recognized national function; but they contribute in two ways – on site and remotely, the latter being easier for them. He suggests that one way of giving these libraries recognition would be for them to receive legal deposit copies within their own subject fields, though he admits this is not as straightforward as it sounds. Funding is, as usual, a thorny issue: Line calls for the clarification of the functions and responsibilities of these paranational libraries as well as an assessment 'of which models prove most successful for countries of different sizes, types and stages of development'.

Universal Availability of Publications (UAP)

Advocates of UAP believe that all types of material should be available to all types of readers, wherever and whenever they require them, and in whatever format is necessary for the reader to be able to use them. Cornish (1996b) describes the role of national libraries in working towards the goal of UAP. The first step is to build the national collection, the next to preserve it, and the third to make it accessible. The collections and the information contained in them should be available to the whole population and not just to certain sectors of it. LC is particularly active in providing services to enable blind and visually impaired users to have the same access as sighted users. Cylke (1995) describes the National Library Service for the Blind and Physically Handicapped run by LC, in particular the responsibilities of its different divisions. The Service is run with as much staff involvement in the management process as possible. McNulty (1995) briefly describes recent automation projects implemented by the Service, all designed to improve access for handicapped users. New technology, adaptive equipment and electronic text have, in many cases, improved access for the visually impaired and a recent publication (News, 1996), which helps readers use electronic text, has been made available in print and braille formats.

Interlibrary loan (ILL) and document delivery

Interlibrary lending is an important component of UAP and any aids are welcome. Two new tools, which list the practices of libraries throughout the world, are of great help to those working in the interlibrary loan and document delivery scene (Barwick and Connolly, 1995, 1996). Malaysia has developed an easy interlending system and has produced various publications to enhance the system further (Jyoon and Ahmat, 1995). Cornish (1996a) looks at the present and future state of document delivery in South East Asia. Inevitably those countries in the region that have a significant volume of interlibrary lending are those which have achieved economic growth. In Russia the Russian State Library (formerly Lenin State Library) has suffered a reversal of fortune due to economic as well as political developments. Its previous coordinating role is no longer accepted and the previous ILL system has disintegrated (Cornish and Prosekova, 1996); sadly the authors do not foresee a quick solution. At the other end of the spectrum is the British Library whose document supply services deal with about four million requests a year from over one hundred countries (Wood, 1996). Rosenfeld (1996) provides more statistics on the Document Supply Centre's services and discusses the different provisions to different types of foreign customer. LC handles about 40,000 American requests per year, but as a last resort library, and it does not currently handle international requests (Wright,1996). However, it is looking to the future document delivery world with its National Digital Library, which will deliver not only text but pictures to its global users. The National Library of Canada handles 600 requests per day and is not concerned by a slight decrease in demand as it is encouraging more local and regional self-sufficiency through the use of new technology and resource sharing (Scott,1996). This Canadian resource sharing theme is developed further in the same publication by Evans (1996). Sweden too has a background of cooperation and interlending is decentralized, but the Royal Library promotes interlending and document supply; the role of BIBSAM (the Royal Library's Office for National Planning and Coordination) is described by Nilsson (1996).

Developments on the Internet

Most national libraries now have home pages on the World Wide Web and some have gone further along the information superhighway. Swab *et al.* (1996) describe the production of the home pages of the US National Agricultural Library (NAL), which are located at http://www.nal.usda.gov. Despite being highly rated as a World Wide Web site, NAL is continually improving its pages, adding new features and further developing the site. Examples of a couple of the pages are given in the article. NAL (ALIN,1996) has also produced some issues of its journal, *Agricultural Libraries Information Notes*, on the World Wide Web. Characteristics of the prototype are described and feedback from readers is sought. Comes (1996) briefly describes the enhancements, which were made to the printed form of the journal ready for the Internet prototype, along with the hardware and software used. Stetka (1996) describes the availability of NAL's Online Public Access Catalogue on the Internet, while Thompson (1996b) discusses the ideas behind the Agricultural Network Information Center (AgNIC). Elsewhere (Thompson, 1996a) he describes the launch of AgNIC and its goals, including the addition of various value added services.

Meanwhile, Gabriel (Gateway and BRIdge to Europe's national Libraries) continues to provide a single point of electronic access to information about European national libraries. Jefcoate (1996) provides the background to the project, describes its services and discusses its future management.

The national libraries of Australia and New Zealand attempted to develop an online information service, the National Document and Information Service (NDIS) Project. Australia's name for the new service was World 1 (Australia, 1996). This would have used many state-of-the-art technologies, including a client-server approach to allow access by different types of software including Web browsers; but alas, at the end of 1996 it was pronounced dead before its birth.

The Koninklijke Bibliotheek in the Hague has built an Advanced Information Workstation used for art research. Researchers can locate, read and process any electronic information on the Internet as well as on local and national networks (Niet and Wishaupt, 1996). LC, through its National Digital Library program, is now providing over 26 million records over the Internet and has a goal of digitizing five million items by the year 2000 (Thorin, 1995).

Bibliographic developments

Most national libraries have embraced automated cataloguing. Hernández (1995) describes the Spanish version, ARIADNA, a flexible system using fibre optic connections and containing over a million entries. The Bibliothèque nationale de France runs four databases which manage bibliographic and authority records (Guy,1996). Guy looks at the development of shared cataloguing and cooperation and stresses the need for adherence to international rules. One step in the right direction is that the British and Americans are working towards a joint authority file (Danskin, 1996). The British Library is also cooperating within Europe in the bibliographic field through Computerized Bibliographic Record Actions (CoBRA): Ede (1996) describes various initiatives. Zillhardt (1996) also looks at CoBRA, this time from the French viewpoint and Lehmann (1996) examines it from the German angle. Lehmann also describes other projects such as Metric and Flex, which have different scope but identical objectives. As he says, the EU Libraries Programme is a firm foundation on which to build and all the projects aim at 'preventing and overcoming division and fragmentation among European national libraries, adjusting imbalances . . . and avoiding isolated developments'. Meanwhile in the Republic of China (Taiwan) the National Central Library heads cooperation towards a national integrated online information network (Lin, 1996). Larsen and Nielsen (1996) describe the production of the Danish National Bibliography, which is shared by the Royal Library and the Danish Library Centre. DANBIB, the largest collaborative project between Danish libraries, a network of databases, aims to be the union catalogue for all Danish libraries.

LC, a leader in the cooperative cataloguing field, is aiming at more, better, faster and cheaper cataloguing (Tabb, 1996). A user's view of French bibliographic products (Lahary, 1996) which looks at quality, currency and comprehensiveness, emphasizes the need for standards in non-print media records. Whether to use, change or reject the subject headings used in the National Library of Poland is the subject of a Polish article by Sadowska (1995). The *Hungarian National Bibliography* was 50 years old in 1996, and its history is outlined from the first issue to the present computerized version (Bényei, 1996). Another anniversary in 1996 is the 95th one of the Biblioteca Nacionál José Martinez of Cuba, which is producing a CD-ROM of Cuban bibliographic information in celebration (National, 1996d).

Ping (1996) outlines the history and problems of bibliographic databases in the National Library of China. On 1 March 1996 the bibliographic database of Chinese monographs was opened to the public, and the library is currently working on the creation of three databases. The Cook Islands National Library and the Pacific Information Centre of the University of the South Pacific were working together to produce a national bibliography for the Cook Islands (Cook, 1996). Phase One, training, was completed but the project has now hit staffing and financial difficulties (C. Temata, personal communication). It is hoped that these can be resolved but the project may have to be scaled down. The NAL is also partway through a project – the retrospective conversion of 198,000 catalogue records for monographs and the process is described (Collins, 1996). Making these records available on the AGRICOLA database and ISIS, NAL's Online Public Access Catalogue, (which is now available over the Internet) will mean that library users worldwide have access to records about NAL's unique holdings. Access within a collection is discussed by Béguet and Hadjopoulou (1996) who describe the open shelves of the BnF. These reflect the library's arrangement, based on the Dewey Decimal Classification scheme, and the shelving is well signposted.

A wide view of bibliographic services is taken by Vitiello (1996). He looks at the purpose and structure of such services and the production of the records. He then examines the marketing aspect, concluding that if libraries seize their opportunities, national bibliographic services will have a 'fascinating future'.

New buildings

Despite the so-called paperless society national libraries are continually needing bigger and better premises. The ongoing saga of the new British Library building in London continues. Day (1995) looks at some of the arguments involved in the development of the St Pancras site and elsewhere continues to chart the progress of events and catalogue of disasters, concluding that the story still has 'some mileage left in the tank' (Day, 1996). Stoker (1996) follows a similar theme and regrets that the inefficiency and mismanagement during the planning stages may overshadow what will inevitably be a 'fine library'. The British Library insists that the move to St Pancras will take place on schedule (Move, 1996) and it posts news about the transfer of collections at http://portico.bl.uk/st-pancras/news/notice.html. In contrast to the new British Library, the planning, building and opening of a third library building at the National Library of Wales has gone very smoothly (Royal, 1996).

The new French and Japanese buildings have already been mentioned in the section above on **Collections and access**. The French opened their new building at Tolbiac, though the collection will not all be there until 1998, and some will not move at all. The process of producing signs to guide people round the inside of the new library is described by Tannières (1996). In Japan a design competition was held for the Kansai-kan building of the National Diet Library (Ministry, 1996) and the results are given elsewhere (Kokuritsu, 1996) while Nakamura *et al.* (1996) examine the concepts behind this library. In Denmark staff are playing a large part in planning a new building; Krarup *et al.* (1996) include a site plan and function diagrams in their report on the project. The National Library of Russia in St Petersburg is also involved with a new building, and staff and readers alike are looking forward to moving in the near future (Zäitsev, 1996). The Russian State Library in Moscow, however, is being restored and modernized, despite suffering from 'the shortage and irregular release of funds' (Montviloff, 1996).

Lest it be thought that Europe has the monopoly on the erection of new buildings for national libraries, the recently opened Biblioteca Nacionál of Argentina in Buenos Aires deserves comment (Jarak,1995). Its eight floors and 45,000 square metres house 700,000 monographs and 600,000 periodical volumes. Plans for networking all public libraries in Argentina with the Biblioteca Nacionál contrast with the authors' reminiscences about a former national librarian who was also a famous poet, demonstrating the vital marriage of culture and technology.

Less conventional literature

National libraries collect and provide access to all types of material, not just mainstream journals and monographs. One such category are ephemera, which can be so important for historians. Barnoud (1996) describes the French collection of leaflets or tracts. Meanwhile LC is promoting a quite different type of literature – 'the unwanted stepchildren of the literary mainstream' – science fiction (Stumbaugh and Johnson, 1996). Gaps in the collection have been filled and a discussion list set up on the Internet, which provides a scholarly forum for serious discussion of the genre.

The British Library holds 'probably the largest and most comprehensive central collection of unrestricted reports available for public use anywhere in the world': the collection is briefly described by Pilling (1996a). A much longer article by Campanile (1995) stresses the importance of grey literature for a research body like the Consiglio Nazionale delle Richerche and describes how the organization has become the Italian national centre for grey literature, playing an active role in the distribution of information. Shraiberg (1996) describes the grey literature databases produced by the Russian National Public Library for Science and Technology and points out that this material, once so hard to get hold of, is fast becoming more accessible thanks to modern technology. In New Zealand the focus has been on government information, but Atwool (1996) admits that it has not been easy to obtain agreement for a unified focus on government information because of competing policy issues such as health. However the National Library 'will continue to seek opportunities to add to the store of knowledge on government information and to achieve a unified focus on information as a national resource'.

In the UK the Patent Office Library is part of the British Library; Newton (1996) describes its collections and users and discusses the use of patent information on CD-ROM. Despite problems with the medium he believes it will play an important role for the next 20 years or so. Ashpitel (1996) looks at the library's patent research service, Patents Online, which is a fee-based service used mainly by remote users.

Reports from around the world

Although the term 'national library' is something that most readers will instantly recognize, it is by no means clear that the institutions which bear this title would be as easily recognized in their tangible manifestations if readers came across them in the various capital cities of the world. Indeed, the very term 'capital city' begs as many questions as it answers. While we learn in school the capitals of the world's countries, many of those countries have changed radically in their structure, and the rise of nationalist feeling has led to the creation or recognition, *de facto*, of libraries that did not previously carry this title. The contrasts can be seen very vividly in the literature of 1996; the differences are perhaps highlighted nowhere more dramatically than in a series being published in the *COMLA Newsletter*, particularly two articles on Oceania. In one (National, 1996b) the legal basis for the national library is described. This includes the standard duties of a national library, the preparation of the national bibliography and collecting and preserving Papua New Guinea publications. Like all national libraries PNG is short of funds and this is acknowledged in a tell-tale phrase '(technical staff . . . order (funds permitting) and process books)'. Nearby, the National Library of Australia (National, 1996a) is busy redefining its role in the light of technological developments such as the introduction of a World Wide Web server. Changes in thinking on the role of national libraries have also led to a reassessment of the National Documentation and Information Service (described more fully by Webb, 1995), and to the redirection of the collection development policy generally. Technology also permits the concept of the National Distributed Collection rather than physically housing everything in one building or location. As with other libraries, the magic words digitization and multimedia are playing a major role in influencing planning.

Redefining is a popular activity at present and is certainly being followed in Jamaica (Ferguson, 1996). The 'new' National Library of Jamaica grew out of the old West Indies Reference Library and is referred to in the article as one of the youngest national libraries in the world. Once again the question of definition raises its head. There are some 'new' countries which would claim their national library was younger than Jamaica's; but others would equally claim they are much older, depending on their political attitude. For example, when did the Slovak National Library become the national library of Slovakia? This institution, located in Martin, not Bratislava – remarks about capital cities seem relevant here – is old in foundation, but its 'national' role was somewhat diminished when Czechoslovakia was a single country. Now that the two halves are firmly independent, the Slovak National Library has a chance to demonstrate its national importance (Makulova,1996). Slovakia, like many countries, is a long way from developing a national strategy for library provision, but the National Library seems ready to take a lead.

Fragmentation in Europe has also brought other national libraries more into the limelight, some for the best of reasons, while others would have preferred the relative obscurity of former times. The National and University Library of Bosnia-Herzegovina and its collections were almost completely destroyed during the recent conflict in that country. A UNESCO mission (Plathe,1996) has attempted to assess the damage and draw up a programme for replacing the collection of Bosniana which has been lost during hostilities. At the same time the role of the National and University Library has been redefined in terms not only of function, but of geographical responsibilities in the light of the Dayton Accord. The recreation of the collection, beginning with records of what was formerly in existence there, is being considerably assisted by OCLC, which is participating in an international effort by a number of libraries with Slavonic collections to help in this process (Promenschenkel, 1996). A rather happier tale comes from another part of former Yugoslavia, though from a country whose very name is hotly disputed by one of its neighbours. The National Library of Macedonia (like the other national libraries in the region) doubles as the library for the university in the capital city. Despite considerable economic and social difficulties this particular national library is managing to fulfil the roles expected of a national library (Jankoska and Kostovska, 1996) and, as well as collection building and the production of bibliographies, has established an ASSN and ISBN centre, acts as a centre of consultation on preservation and restoration and is the focus for international activities such as interlibrary loans and membership of IFLA.

The mission of national libraries, as obliquely referred to above in relation to Papua New Guinea, is not necessarily uniform throughout the world. Indeed, in Lesotho (National,1996c) the main objectives include equipping teacher-librarians in high schools to offer an effective service and assist librarians in other library situations to improve their own services by organizing seminars and training. The varying mission statements (if that is not too grand a title for them in some instances) of national libraries is further emphasized by that of the Bibliothèque Nationale Suisse (Jauslin 1996a, 1996b) which is concerned only with the collection of Helvetica, i.e. Swiss publications. Even publications about Switzerland are not within its remit. Perhaps because of the federal nature of the Swiss constitution and its location in Bern rather than Basle, Zurich or Geneva, it is probably one of the least known national libraries in western Europe. This federalism also inhibits the introduction of any kind of legal deposit system, copies have to be requested and cannot be demanded. Nevertheless there is an extensive database of publishers and authors and automation generally is moving forward, concentrating on catalogues within the context of a new building recently opened.

The internal political structures of countries can cause many misunderstandings about the role and status of national libraries within the borders of what are perceived by outsiders as single nations. This problem is recognized and emphasized in a description of the National Library of Wales (Madden,1996) which begins 'Wales is a country of nearly three million inhabitants within the United Kingdom'. Although mainly descriptive, the article is an opportunity to make more people aware of the international importance of an institution which plays such a crucial role in the cultural and social life of Wales. This international significance is also clearly demonstrated by a description of the history and current policy in relation to the building up of German materials in the National Library of Scotland (Kelly,1996), which shows that these collections are of considerable value outside Scotland and could be of interest to German scholars elsewhere. The Anglo-German theme is continued in a detailed description for German readers and potential users of the British Library's plans for an electronic library (Labriga,1996). Such developments are of global significance, as some projects such as the Electronic *Beowulf* and the digitization of incunabula know no national boundaries once they are available though tools such as the World Wide Web. The internationalization of such projects is further underlined by an article describing similar developments in the Bibliothèque nationale de France for an Italian audience (Revelli,1996) and in another by Lang (1996) about the British Library written for French readers.

Although national libraries are concerned to collect what is published today for use tomorrow, it is in their nature to be concerned with the past, although not exclusively so. They do, after all, provide the national archive of recorded culture ('printed' no longer being a sufficient term). This was clearly appreciated by the founding fathers of the Biblioteca Nacionál of Mexico who decreed in 1833 that it should classify all new acquisitions and prepare indices to the collection which should be available for consultation in all rooms open to the public (Linea de Arenas,1995). How clearly this shows that descriptions of their own history can be enlightening, not just for students of library history, but for those studying cultural, political and social developments too. If the national library mirrors a major facet of national life then the chronicles of its collections, development and political support are all important. This is true of the Biblioteca Nacional in Lisbon, which celebrated its two hundredth anniversary on the somewhat unfortunate date of 29 February 1996 (Voos,1996), risking the charge from those with a certain sense of humour of being only 50 years old.

Unfortunately the existence of a long cultural and historical tradition in a country does not guarantee that the national library will necessarily reflect this adequately, if at all. The National Library of Bhutan, a country with a very long history, was established in 1967 (Kleemann and Kutsch,1996). Bhutanese written materials consisted mostly of Tibetan monastic texts, but now the national language has been reduced to a standard written form which makes publishing easier and gives the National Library something to collect of national significance. So far some 10,000 works have been collected, but the National Library suffers from its country's own geographical isolation and needs to build up international links. This can be contrasted with a country such as Cambodia, where the National Library dates back to 1924 and had a considerable collection representing the history of a people reaching back certainly to the 9th century in developed form. But the National Library has suffered so much since then that it is hard for it to function at the most basic level. After the 'evacuation' of most of the staff by the Khmer Rouge in 1975:

the notable garden area of the national library was used for keeping pigs and the library building for storage of food and as living-quarters for the pig-keepers. Books were pushed off the shelves to make room for cooking pots and some were evidently used to light fires or as cigarette papers (Sarak,1995).

Cambodia's neighbour, Laos, has fared rather differently (Phengphachan,1995) The National Library there is younger (founded in 1956) but has had the support of the government ever since. Most publishing in the early part of the Lao People's Democratic Republic was in the hands of government but there was, and is, no legal deposit system as such, so the National Library has relied heavily on donations from the former Soviet Union, Vietnam, Thailand, France and Australia. It is also difficult to produce a national bibliography with no definitive collection on which to base it. Since the introduction of a market-oriented economy things have become more difficult, and only about 30% of the collection has been catalogued so far. The National Library doubles up as the public library for Vientiane, but there have been no funds for collection building and the present collection consists of many books which are unwanted or in languages that most users cannot read.

One of Laos' neighbours, Myanmar (formerly Burma), fared rather better. Like Laos and Cambodia, Myanmar (Khin Maung Tin,1995) has a long and honourable cultural tradition and it is ironic that the beginnings of the National Library can be found in the establishment of a public library by the British commissioner of the local province. Sir Edward Bernard gave a large collection of books to form the public library in Yangon (Rangoon) and from this the present National Library has grown. It is rich in ancient manuscripts and palm leaves as well as more recent publications received through legal deposit and donations.

Formerly the Pasquier Library under French rule, Vietnam's National Library actively pursues international ties in general and book exchanges specifically (Hoang Thi Le Ha,1995). Unlike the components of the former Indochina and Myanmar, Thailand has no history of colonial rule. This has brought benefits in some respects, as the National Library can trace its history back to the 16th century when libraries in monasteries and religious places really developed. The present National Library dates from 1905 (Bhakdibutr,1995) and has extensive collections ranging from stone tablets and palm leaves right through to early manuscripts, books and the latest computer programs.

Future plans

Stephens and Jackson (1996) describe the British Library's aims for the year 2000. These include the new building already mentioned and improved user access to be brought about by modern technology. In China too plans for the future rely heavily on technology as the National Library transforms itself from traditional to modern library (Sun and Fan, 1996). The National Library of Medicine in the USA, which has long been involved with technology, also believes that new technology is the only way that their customers can keep abreast of the ever-increasing output of information (Smith and Mehnert, 1995).

However, technology is expensive: national libraries are increasingly feeling the financial pinch, and have to enter into commercial arrangements to find sources of funding. Arnold (1996) shows there are both advantages and disadvantages to such arrangements; along with other pertinent questions he queries whether the users' needs are always best served in this quest for money. He predicts that national libraries will become a mixture of free and fee-based services and that 'the blurring of lines between public good and commercial acumen will become more and more fuzzy' and perhaps 'ordinary users may suffer because the cure for financial pressure is worse than the disease'. Other authors feel that things are improving for users. Stephens (1996) writes about the challenge of the Citizen's Charter, which requires public services to publish their standards of service and report on their performance, and the British Library's *Code of service*, which he believes has led to the identification and solving of problems. Pilling (1996b) reports in more detail on customer service improvements at the BL's Document Supply Centre and concludes that improvements in the Centre's speed of service and relationship with customers have come about because of a Total Quality Management Programme at the Centre.

As well as good customer relations, national libraries nowadays need friends. Saunders Watson (1996) outlines the importance of these people who raise funds and promote a library's welfare for little reward other than knowing that they are helping 'a great and respected national institution'. The role of one of these institutions has recently been questioned. Weech (1996) reports that a recent list of priorities refers to LC as a library of the people rather than a national library and that this has produced some confusion about its national role.

Conclusion

National libraries continue to respond to the opportunities and challenges of new technology, digitization projects and the legal deposit of electronic material being good examples. They are increasing their efforts to make their collections more accessible, whether by digitization, availability on the Internet, improved cataloguing, interlibrary loans or by cooperation on national and international levels. Despite reduced funding in many cases, national libraries are alive and kicking and in good shape to meet the opportunities and challenges of the next millenium.

References

ALIN (1996) on the WWW. *Agricultural Libraries Information Notes.* **22**(1–3), 16.

Arnold, S.E. (1996) National libraries. Leveraging intellectual assets. In: *National Online Meeting Proceedings – 1996. Proceedings of the 17th National Online Meeting, New York, 14–16 May 1996*, ed. M.E. Williams. Medford, NJ: Information Today, pp. 5–12.

Ashpitel, S. (1996) Patents online at the British Library. *Law Librarian*, **27**(2), 84–85.

Atwool, M. (1996) 'You can't eat information': government information and the information policy role of the National Library of New Zealand. *Government Information Quarterly*, **13**(3), 311–322.

Australia (1996) and New Zealand plan NDIS online. *Library Association Record*, **98**(2) [Library Technology, supplement **1**(1), 6].

Barnoud, M. (1996) Littérature éphémère et sources de l'histoire: les tracts à la Bibliothèque national de France. *Bulletin des Bibliothèques de France*, **41**(3), 26–29.

Barwick, M.M. and Connolly, P.A. (1995) (eds) *A guide to centres of international lending.* 5th ed. Boston Spa: IFLA Offices for UAP and International Lending.

Barwick, M.M. and Connolly, P.A. (1996) (eds) *A guide to centres of international document delivery.* 5th ed. Boston Spa: IFLA Offices for UAP and International Lending.

Béguet, B. and Hadjopoulou, C. (1996) Les collections en libre accès de la Bibliothèque nationale de France: organisation par départements et usage de la Dewey. *Bulletin des Bibliothèques de France*, **41**(4), 40–46.

Bényei, M. (1996) A kurrens magyar nemzeti bibliográfia ötven éve. *Könyvtári Figyelő*, **6**(42), 391–402.

Bhakdibutr, C. (1995) Library and information services in Thailand: a country report. In: Gould S. and Watkins J. (1995) (eds), pp. 77–85.

Blair, R. (1996) La gestion des documents électroniques: le point de vue de la Bibliothèque nationale du Canada. *Documentation et bibliothèques*, **42**(3), 127–133.

Campanile, A. (1996) Development trends of the C.N.R.'s scientific research as a result of the production of grey literature. In: *Grey exploitations in the 21st century. Second International Conference on grey literature, Catholic University of America, Washington D.C., USA, November 2–3, 1995. GL'95. Conference Proceedings.* Amsterdam: Transatlantic/Grey Literature Network Service, pp. 107–125.

Carr, J. (1996) Les collections patrimoniales de la British Library: une politique d'ouverture au public. *Bulletin des Bibliothèques de France*, **41**(3), 57–59.

Collins, D.S. (1996) Cataloguing retrospective conversion. *Agricultural Libraries Information Notes*, **22**(6–8), 1–2.

Comes, J. (1996) Putting ALIN on the Internet. *Agricultural Libraries Information Notes*, **22**(1–3), 17.

Cook (1996) Islands National Bibliography. *PIC Newsletter*, (45–46), 3.

Cornish, G.P. (1996a) Developing document delivery in South East Asia now and in the future. *Interlending & Document Supply*, **24**(4), 19–24.

Cornish, G.P. (1996b) The role of national libraries in achieving universal availability of publications (UAP) and the supply of international loan and document supply services. In: Watkins, J. (1996) (ed.), pp. 27–33.

Cornish, G.P. and Prosekova, S. (1996) Document supply and access in times of turmoil: recent problems in Russia and eastern Europe. *Interlending & Document Supply*, **24**(1), 5–11.

Coron, A. (1996) La réserve des livres rares à la Bibliothèque nationale de France: constitution d'une nouvelle collection. *Bulletin des Bibliothèques de France*, **41**(3), 20–25.

Cunningham, A. (1996) Polynesian pathways: the National Library of Australia Pacific acquisition trip, 1995. *Australian Academic and Research Libraries*, **27**(2), 124–131.

Cylke, F.K. (1995) National Library Service for the blind and physically handicapped. In: C.D. Missar (ed.) *Management of federally sponsored libraries; case studies and analysis*. New York: Haworth Press, pp. 109–128.

Danskin, A. (1996) The Anglo-American Authority File – completion of Phase 1. *Select Newsletter*, (17), 11.

Day, A. (1995) Turning point for the British Library? *Library Review*, **44**(2), 38–43.

Day, A. (1996) The British Library: the cost is counted. *Library Review*, **45**(8), 6–16.

De Beer, J. and Hendrikz, F. (1996) National libraries around the world 1994-1995: a review of the literature. *Alexandria*, **8**(1), 3–33.

Department of National Heritage *et al.* (1997) *Legal deposit of publications: a consulation paper*. London: Department of National Heritage.

Dubois, J. (1996) Un exemple de coopération nationale; la Bibliothèque du Musée de l'homme et la Bibliothèque national de France: la numérisation des images et les problèmes de droits. *Bulletin d'Informations de l'Association des Bibliothécaires Français*, (172), 93–97.

Ede, S. (1996) Libraries and technology in the European Union: soldering the connections. *Information Technology and Libraries*, **15**(2), 117–122.

Electronic (1996) Publishing Services. *The legal deposit of on-line databases*. London: British Library Research and Development Department. (British Library Research & Development Report 6244).

Evans, G. (1996) Trends in interlending loan in Canada: lessons from two resource sharing surveys. In: Watkins, J. (1996) (ed.), pp. 83–87.

Ferguson, S. (1996) Defining a role for a new national library in a developing country: the National Library of Jamaica, 1980-1990. *Alexandria*, **8**(1), 65–74.

Game, V. (1996) La constitution d'un fonds d'images et d'ouvrages numérisés par la BNF. *Bulletin d'Informations de l'Association des Bibliothécaires Français*, (172), 89–92.

Gould, S. and Watkins, J. (1995) (eds) *From palm leaves to PCs: library developments in South East Asia. Papers from the UAP Workshop held in Bangkok, January 1995*. Boston Spa: IFLA Programme for Universal Availability of Publications.

Grunberg, G. (1996) The audiovisual programme of the Bibliothèque nationale de France. *Alexandria*, **8**(3), 181–188.

Guy, M. (1996) The Bibliothèque Nationale de France and authority files: advances and perspectives in co-operation. *International Cataloguing and Bibliographic Control*, **25**(3), 59–62.

Hattery, M. (1996) Computers in Libraries 96: mastering electronic information. *Information Retrieval & Library Automation*, **31**(10), 1–4.

Hedberg, S. (1996) Authorities and electronic publishing: an overview of the efforts to apply library legislation and established organizational patterns to electronic publications. *Alexandria*, **8**(2), 135–142.

Hendley, T. (1996) *The preservation of digital material*. London: British Library Research and Development Department. (British Library R&D Report 6242).

Hernández, N. (1995) Der Faden der Ariadne. *Bibliothekdienst*, **29**(3), 482–487.

Hoang Thi Le Ha (1995) Library services in Vietnam. In: Gould, S. and Watkins, J. (1995) (eds), pp. 97–101.

Hoare, P. (1996) *Legal deposit of non-print material; an international overview, September–October 1995.* London: British Library Research and Development Department. (British Library R&D Report 6245).

Jankoska, S. and Kostovska, V. (1996) The St Clement of Ohrid National and University Library: Macedonia's national library. *Alexandria,* 8(2), 117–134.

Jarak, V. (1995) Dove convergono tutte le luci del paese. [Interview with Héctor Yánover]. *Biblioteche Oggi,* 13(7), 20–25.

Jauslin, J-F. (1996a) Une Bibliothèque nationale dans un ètat fédéral. *Bulletin d'Informations de l'Association des Bibliothécaires Français,* (172), 19–23.

Jauslin, J-F. (1996b) The Swiss National Library and its environment. *Information Technology and Libraries,* 15(2), 113–117.

Jefcoate, G. (1996) Getting the message from Gabriel. *Library Technology,* 1(2), 33–34.

Jyoon, C.L. and Ahmat, A. (1995) Country report from Malaysia. In: Gould, S. and Watkins, J. (1995), pp. 41–62.

Kelly, W.A. (1996) The German collections in the National Library of Scotland. *German Studies Library Group Newsletter,* (20), 2–11.

Khin Maung Tin, U. (1995) The current situation of libraries in Myanmar. In: Gould, S. and Watkins, J. (1995), pp. 63–76.

Kleemann, G. and Kutsch, M. (1996) Bücher auf dem Dach der Welt. *Bibliotheksdienst,* 30(1), 17–18.

Kokuritsu (1996) kokkai toshokan kansaikan sekkei konpe ga shuryo. [Results of Kansai-kan of the National Diet Library design competition]. *Biblos,* 47(9), 22–23.

Krarup, K. *et al.* (1996) Det kongelige Bibliotek i Havnefronten: om bygning af et nyt Nationalbibliotek. *DF-Revy,* 19(1), 7–15.

Labriga, P. (1996) Die Britische Nationalbibliothek auf dem Weg zur elektronischen Bibliothek. *Bibliotheksdienst,* 30(6), 1035–1043.

Lahary, D. (1996) Les produits bibliographiques de la BnF; point de vue d'un utilisateur. *Bulletin d'Informations de l'Association des Bibliothécaires Français,* (172), 74–79.

Lamolinara, G. (1996). Metamorphosis of a national treasure. *American Libraries,* 27(3), 31–33.

Lang, B. (1996) La British Library et les services destinés aux bibliothèques. *Bulletin d'Informations de l'Association des Bibliothécaires Français,* (172), 16–18.

Larsen, S.B. and Nielsen, E.K. (1996) Les choix du Danemark. *Bulletin d'Informations de l'Association des Bibliothécaires Français,* (172), 62–66.

Lehmann, K-D. (1996) European National Libraries and the CoBRA Forum of the EU Libraries Programme. *Alexandria,* 8(3), 155–166.

Lin, S.C. (1996) The development of national online networking in the Republic of China – the role of the National Central Library. *Information Technology and Libraries,* 15(2), 65–79.

Line, M.B. (1995) The role of paranational libraries in national information provision. *Information Development,* 11(4), 225–228.

Line, M.B. (1996) National self-sufficiency in an electronic age. In: *Electronic documents and information: from preservation to access. 18th International Essen Symposium, 23–26 October 1995,* eds A.H. Helal and J.W. Weiss. Essen: Universitätsbibliothek Essen. pp. 170–193.

Linea de Arenas (1995) The National Library of Mexico. *Focus on International & Comparative Librarianship,* 26(1), 16–20.

Lor. P.J. (1997) *Guidelines for Legislation for National Library Services.* http://www.nlc-bnc.ca/ifla/VII/s1/gnl/index.htm

McNulty, T. (1995) National Library Service of the Library of Congress: new electronic information projects. *Library Hi Tech News,* (125), 17–18.

Madden, J.L. (1996) Llyfrgell Genedlaethol Cymru: the National Library of Wales. *Alexandria,* 8(1), 51–63.

Makulova, S. (1996) National library and information research policy in Slovakia. In: *European library & information research policy; proceedings of a seminar held at the Hotel Russell, London, 7–9 December 1994,* eds D. Haynes and R. Cotton. London: British Library Research and Development Department. (British Library R&D Report 6249), pp. 67–72.

Ministry of Construction, Japan. (1996) Kansai-kan of the National Diet Library (provisional name), design competition. *National Diet Library Newsletter,* (98), 12–15.

Montviloff, V. (1996) Russian State Library. *UNISIST Newsletter,* 24(1), 4–5.

Move (1996) on time, not on budget. *Library Association Record,* 98(8), 387.

Nakamura, Y. *et al.* (1996) Kokuritsu kokkai toshokan kansaikan koso ni taisuru ichi kento. [An examination of the concept of the Kokuritsu Kokkai Toshokan Kansaikan (National Diet Library, Kansai Library, Japan)]. *Toshokan-Kai [Library World],* 48(2), 56–61.

National (1996a) libraries of the Commonwealth. Part 1: Oceania. *COMLA Newsletter,* (89), 3–5.

National (1996b) libraries of the Commonwealth. Part 1: Oceania. *COMLA Newsletter,* (90), 7–11.

National (1996c) libraries of the Commonwealth. Part 2: Africa. *COMLA Newsletter,* (90), 17–22.

National (1996d) Library CD-ROM project, The. *IFLA Journal,* 22(3), 261.

News (1996) from the National Library Service: new guide helps readers use electronic books. *Library of Congress Information Bulletin,* 55(5), 113.

Newton, D. (1996) Experience of a national patent library as an intermediary of using patent information on CD-ROM. *World Patent Information,* 18(1), 15–18.

Niet, M. de and Wishaupt, M. (1996) Art in the Web: the advanced information workstation as a tool for art research. *Art Libraries Journal,* 21(1), 8–10.

Nilsson, K. (1996) Interlending and document supply in Sweden: the role of the Royal Library. In: Watkins, J. (1996) (ed.), pp. 75–81.

Phengphachan, B. (1995) Libraries in the Lao People's Democratic Republic (Lao PDR). In: Gould, S. and Watkins, J. (1995) (eds), pp. 37–39.

Pilling, S. (1996a) The National Reports Collection at the Document Supply Centre. *Laser Link,* (Spring/Summer), 9.

Pilling, S. (1996b) Putting the customer first: total quality and customer service at the British Library Document Supply Centre. *Interlending and Document Supply,* 24(2), 11–16.

Ping, F. (1996) Chinese bibliographic databases in the National Library of China. *International Cataloguing and Bibliographic Control,* 25(2), 29–31.

Plathe, A. (1996). PGI staff mission to Bosnia and Herzegovina 30 January – 7 February 1996. *UNISIST Newsletter,* 24(1), 7–11.

Promenschenkel, G. (1996) OCLC helping to rebuild National Library of Bosnia. *OCLC Newsletter,* (220), 16.

Prytherch, R. (1996) Information handling at the new French national library. *Information Management Report,* (January), 12–14.

Revelli, C. (1996) La Bibliothèque nationale de France. *Biblioteche Oggi*, **14**(2), 30–37.

Rosenfeld, M. (1996) Le British Library Document Supply Centre; les services proposés aux clients étrangers. *Bulletin des Bibliothèques de France*, **41**(6), 60–65.

Royal (1996) visit for expanding National Library of Wales. *Library Association Record*, **98**(7), 354–355.

Sadowska, J. (1995) Hasla przedmiotowe Biblioteki Narodowej. Przejmowac? Zmeniac? Odrzucac? [Subject headings of the National Library. Take over? Change? Reject?]. *Bibliotekarz*, (4), 12–15.

Sarak. S. (1995) National Library of Cambodia. In: Gould, S. and Watkins, J. (1995) (eds), pp. 33–35.

Saunders Watson, M. (1996) Friends of national libraries. (Guest editorial) *Alexandria*, **8**(2), 83–84.

Scott, M. (1996) Role of the National Library of Canada in interlending and document supply. In: Watkins, J. (1996) (ed.), pp. 47–53.

Shraiberg, Y. (1996) New types of and access to grey literature databases generated by the Russian National Public Library for Science and Technology. In: *Grey exploitations in the 21st century. Second International Conference on grey literature, Catholic University of America, Washington D.C., USA, November 2–3, 1995. GL'95. Conference Proceedings.* Amsterdam: Transatlantic/Grey Literature Network Service, pp. 56–62.

Smith, K.A. and Mehnert, R. (1995) National Library of Medicine. In: C.D. Missar (ed.) *Management of federally sponsored libraries; case studies and analysis.* New York: Haworth Press, pp. 129–146.

Stephan, W. (1996) Die Deutsche Bibliothek: the national archive for electronic media? In: *Electronic documents and information: from preservation to access. 18th International Essen Symposium 23–26 October 1995. Festschrift in honor of Patricia Battin*, eds A.H. Helal and J.W. Weiss. Essen: Universitätsbibliothek Essen, pp. 132–140.

Stephens, A. (1996). National libraries and the citizen's charter. (Guest editorial) *Alexandria*, **8**(1), 1–2.

Stephens, A. and Jackson, M. (1996) Working towards the millenium: the British Library's plans for the year 2000. *New Library World*, **97**(1126), 33–37.

Stetka, J. (1996) ISIS on the Internet. *Agricultural Libraries Information Notes*, **22**(1–3), 14.

Stoker, D. (1996) Planning disasters for the twenty-first century. *Journal of Librarianship and Information Science*, **28**(3), 129–131.

Stumbaugh, C. and Johnson, E.A. (1996). Raising science fiction's profile at the Library of Congress . . . and beyond. *RQ*, **35**(3), 298–302.

Sun, B. and Fan, G. (1996) *The National Library of China towards the 21st century.* [Paper presented at the 62nd IFLA General Conference, Beijing (118-NAT -1-E).]

Swab, J.N. *et al.* (1996) NAL home page on the World Wide Web. *Agricultural Libraries Information Notes*, **22**(1–3), 1–5.

Tabb, W. (1996) Plus, mieux, plus vite, moins cher. Le *leadership* de la Bibliothèque du Congrès dans le catalogage pour les années quatre-vingt-dix et au-dela. *Bulletin d'Informations de l'Association des Bibliothécaires Français*, (172), 52–56.

Tamura, K. (1996) Denshi toshokan to shiryo no denshika [Digital library and digitization]. *Yakugaku Toshokan [Pharmaceutical Library Bulletin]*, **41**(2), 131–137.

Tannières, F. (1996) Orienter, informer, identifier . . . trois actions pour un métier: signaléticien. *Bulletin d'Informations de l'Association des Bibliothécaires Français*, (171), 11–15.

Thompson, R.E. (1996a) Agricultural Network Information Center. *Agricultural Libraries Information Notes*, **22**(1–3), 1, 6–10.

Thompson, R.E. (1996b) The Agricultural Network Information Center (AgNIC) concept. *Agricultural Libraries Information Notes*, **22**(1–3), 10–13.

Thorin, S.E. (1995) The Library of Congress's National Digital Library Program. In: *Hands on hypermedia and interactivity in museums; selected papers from the Third International Conference on hypermedia and interactivity in museums (ICHIM '95. MCN '95), San Diego, California, October 9–13, 1995*, ed. D. Bearman. Pittsburgh, PA: Archive & Museum Informatics, pp. 21–25.

Tsuruta, S. (1996) Denshi toshokan wo mezasu gyosei no doko-kokuritsu kokkai toshokan wo chushin to shite. [The involvement of administrative agencies towards the digital libraries – mainly concerning the National Diet Library,]. *Yakugaku Toshokan* [*Pharmaceutical Library Bulletin*], **41**(2), 155–162.

Vayssade, C (1996) Entre mission et service: l'offre bibliographique de la BnF. *Bulletin d'Informations de l'Association des Bibliothécaires Français*, (172), 72–74.

Vitiello, G. (1996) The production and the marketing of National Bibliographic Services in Europe. *Alexandria*, 8(2), 97–116.

Voos, C. (1996) 200 Jahre Nationalbibliothek in Portugal. *Bibliothekdienst*, 30(10), 1641–1645.

Watkins, J. (1996) (ed.) *Interlending and document supply: Proceedings of the Fourth International conference. Papers from the conference held in Calgary, June 1995*. Boston Spa: IFLA Programme for Universal Availability of Publications and Office for International Lending.

Webb, K. (1995) National Library of Australia. *LASIE*, 26(1–3), 39–43.

Weech, T.L. (1996) La Bibliothèque du Congrès et la coopération entre bibliothèques. *Bulletin d'Informations de l'Association des Bibliothécaires Français*, (172), 58–61.

Weiming, J. and Ning, A. (1996) The National Library of China. *Alexandria*, 8(2), 143–147.

Wood, D. (1996) The British Library's role in interlending and document supply. In: Watkins, J. (1996) (ed.), pp. 63–74.

Wright, C. (1996) The Library of Congress: last-resort lending in the digital age. In: Watkins, J. (1996) (ed.), pp. 55–61.

Zaïtsev, V.N. (1996) La Bibliothèque nationale de Russie; le nouveau bâtiment. *Bulletin des Bibliothèques de France*, **41**(5), 92–96.

Zillhardt, S. (1996) CoBRA; une action concertée entre bibliothèque nationales. *Bulletin des Bibliothèques de France*, **41**(1), 66–9.

Academic libraries 3

John D. Gilbert and
Alex C. Klugkist

Strategy

Formulating a well-balanced mission for academic libraries is not an easy matter (Hipsman, 1996). On the one hand they have to fulfil their traditional tasks of information supply and document delivery; on the other they have to adapt to the new possibilities of information technology, and consequently to prepare for new tasks in the process of scholarly communication (Crawford and Gorman, 1995; Eberhart, 1995; Charkin, 1996; Hamaker, 1996; Hardy, 1996; Krysiak, 1996). The library has to develop into an information centre providing access to information that is available not only locally, but also nationally and worldwide; by developing and applying new techniques and methods libraries can help to advance education and research (Erens, 1996a, 1996b; Palmer, 1996; Rouhet, 1996).

In other words, the library finds itself in an environment of change, which implies changing roles and responsibilities (Probst, 1996). Guidelines for evolving effective strategies under such conditions have been set out by Tuten and Jones (1995), Allen (1996), and Heery and Morgan (1996). The environment of change is characterized by:

- greater access to a range of information;
- increased speed in acquiring information;
- greater complexity in locating, analysing and linking information;
- constantly changing technology;
- lack of standardization of both hardware and software;
- continuous learning for users and library staff;
- substantial financial investment in technology (Creth, 1996).

In addition, changes in higher education can influence libraries. Drake (1996) and Stoffle (1996) mention reduction in finances, increase in the demand for higher education, changes in higher education as a result of new information and telecommunication technology and a shift in emphasis from teaching to learning.

In this changing environment libraries have to find ways of securing their future existence. It is essential for them to determine their place and role in the university setting: a library is part of a larger entity and has to contribute to its results. The library has to be highly visible and should be valued as essential to the teaching, learning and research activities of the university. Libraries should adopt the concept of 'the teaching library and the librarian as a teacher' (Creth, 1996). Librarians will be change agents and carriers of innovation by virtue of the experience and knowledge they bring to the enterprise (Stoffle, 1996).

Creth (1996) holds that there are sufficient new opportunities for libraries: user education, knowledge management, organization of networked information resources, electronic publishing and curriculum development, information policy development. In order for the library to fulfil a new function within the entity, a number of conditions have to be met. Strategic planning and strategic thinking should be fundamental concepts that librarians incorporate into their daily activities. Much more attention has to be paid to the strategic planning of the university and its faculties, so that the library strategy can be geared to them. Partnerships are essential with technologists and especially with faculty. Changes in organization and culture are essential, as is the training of library staff.

The awareness that the library is part of a larger entity has implications for quality assessment. Attention should be paid to qualitative aspects such as integration and liaison, relevance of learning materials, availability and accessibility, user support and evaluation, and feedback (Sykes, 1996). According to Pritchard (1996), the quality of the library must be judged by the quality of the outcomes of the institution of which it is part.

Organization and management

The changing environment has implications for library organization (Lee and Clark, 1996; Riggs, 1996; Stoffle *et al.*, 1996; St. Clair, 1996). Characteristic descriptions of the present organization are: bureaucratic, functionally oriented, inflexible, arrogant, isolated, focused on internal quality and stability, and made up of mutually competitive departments, oriented towards acquiring, processing and storing physical objects. If they are to survive, libraries have to undergo radical, revolutionary organizational change (Stoffle *et al.*, 1996). In short, libraries have to become the opposite of what they are now, whether one calls this 'entrepreneurial librarianship' (St. Clair, 1996) or 'organizational development' (Lee, 1996). A library organization which can thrive in an environment of change is characterized by a focus on customers and their requirements, and a translation of this in the organization, willingness to take risks, quest for quality, and continual improvement and evaluation. Boissé (1996) describes two models for a 'flattened organization'. The search for quality, improvement and evaluation is explicitly manifest in Total Quality Management focused on customer and staff (Brophy and Coulling, 1996; Pauleweit, 1996). Ultimately, one can opt for certification (Ellis and Norton, 1996; Pauleweit, 1996), whereby ISO 9000 implementation can be integrated into a broader framework of Total Quality Management (Johanssen, 1996).

Whether or not one opts for quality management or certification, a number of things are essential if one is to transform the library, namely: clear definition of goals (mission statement) and involvement and commitment of the staff. The role of management is crucial in this respect: encouraging staff, stimulating cooperation, opening up communication and giving a good example. To realize this, management must be prepared to change, to look critically at its own work, and to develop and communicate shared values. Johanssen (1996) shows how the interpersonal, informational, and decision roles of management are essential in the implementation of ISO 9000.

Staff structure and development

Crowley (1996) describes the need to redefine the status of the librarian in higher education: unless librarians secure peer status through adherence to core academic standards, the emerging era of electronic information will see a diminution in the librarian's influence over library affairs. Rapid developments in computer technology demand that the familiar role of librarians must undergo immense change if they are to avoid being displaced by other intermediaries. Morgan (1996) lists the following factors which libraries have to consider in the (re)organization of their activities:

- breakdown of hierarchical staffing structures;
- participative decision-making models;
- greater emphasis on accountability and performance;
- insistence that departmental objectives support institutional strategies;
- widespread financial constraints;
- ability to negotiate effectively with institutional managers;
- recognition that change has become a way of life;
- greater emphasis on teamwork;
- flexibility in working arrangements;
- devolution of responsibilities and budgets;
- individual time management.

Similar trends are described in two books. In Bluck's chapter (1996) in Oldroyd's book on staff development in academic libraries, he reports four key areas of change, of which two relate specifically to subject librarians. They will have a major role as mediators and facilitators of resource-based open learning, with responsibilities for first-line instruction and supervision of students. Furthermore they will be expected to master skills for navigating electronic databases and showing others how to do so. The remaining two areas of change are tailoring services more closely to the needs of customers and organizing the library with a greater emphasis on teamwork. The latter theme is also dominant in *Humanistic management by teamwork* (Baldwin and Migneault, 1996). The benefits of this new approach are that it makes greater use of the talents of individuals organized in teams and that it is based on the principle of mutual respect, regardless of position.

There is a parallel between the training needs of modern librarians and the perception of their professional role and status in the era of the virtual library. This is often characterized as the era of networking, hence the emphasis on the need to develop IT skills. Morgan (1996), however, warns not to focus too much on IT skills. People- and service-based skills are also essential, for it is people within the academic community who are the significant players. IT is merely a means to an end.

Hyams (1996) concludes that librarians as information professionals should be flexible and should update their knowledge and skills continually to take advantage of the changes. Walton *et al.* (1995) recommend the following areas of training for library staff: IT skills, network navigation, customer service and interpersonal skills, support of management of change, teamworking, quality improvement programmes, learner support and management techniques. Libraries should devote 5% of their time to staff development and training.

Digital libraries

The coming of the electronic library impinges on library strategy; it means a shift from library automation to information strategies and virtual library services. Some librarians believe they have already implemented the virtual library; others believe that the virtual library represents a distant objective or threat. Harris (1996) sees networking as the dominant factor. The virtual library provides access to multiple information resources and allows users to manipulate them to meet their individual needs (Broering, 1995).

In the past, library automation relied heavily on a core bibliographic file, the catalogue. Nowadays, libraries subscribe to all sorts of databases, including full text and multimedia (Harris, 1996). There is a change of focus from the economic life cycle of a single (automated) system to the development of strategies to coordinate systems and services with varying life cycles. Dempsey and Heijne (1996) see the systems of the future as building blocks: the major challenge lies in their effective integration.

Covi and Kling (1996) define digital libraries from a user's point of view as collections of electronic resources and services for the delivery of materials in a variety of formats. Members of faculty tend to use digital libraries to supplement, not to replace, traditional modes of communication: e-mail, interlibrary loan, OPACs and electronic bibliographies have found their way to the end user. According to Broering (1995) the librarian should focus on system integration and single-menu access. The fastest growing responsibility for librarians is their instructional role: teaching users about computers, information access skills, and navigation of the Internet.

Kochtanek (1996) sees the coming of personal digital libraries: a powerful desktop computing device, linked to information servers housing massive amounts of information in digital format. Supported by personal information management software, the end user has a personal library, tailored to his own complex information needs, at his disposal. Carbonell (1996) suggests we should develop not only digital libraries, but also digital librarians.

Cooperation with computing centres

One of the issues raised by the digitization of library sources and services is the cooperation of libraries with computing departments.

There are already more than a thousand libraries administering large numbers of electronic documents. The World Wide Web provides some good starting points, e.g. UC at Berkeley (Regents University of California, 1996) or Stanford University (McClung, 1996). The collections in these and other directories are substantial and professional.

Focus is shifting from the application of new technology towards management of stable services. The cooperation between libraries and computing centres has likewise shifted focus. It is vital that libraries define their own quality standards. In order to do so they must be able to define the quality of services that the IT infrastructure of the institution must meet: for example, the uptime for http servers providing access to the electronic library needs to be as good as, or better than, that required for OPACs. The conference of the European Library Automation Group (1996) on the quality of electronic services revealed a multitude of problems in establishing a service which runs for 24 hours a day, seven days a week. Current cooperation is a mix of innovative projects and steady services. Lippincott (1996) describes the conditions for partnership, whereas D.W. Koehler (1996) describes the challenges and problems in merging Web technology with administrative computing.

Web technology is the common ground of libraries and computing departments. Libraries focus on enlargement of IT knowledge within their organizations (Hastings and Tennant, 1996), while the IT community increases its efforts in information retrieval technology and hypermedia (Association for Computing, 1996).

Another major trend is cooperation in programmes that go beyond individual institutions. Programmes such as the Digital Library Initiative, eLib, and those of the Research Libraries Group and UKOLN encompass a great number of universities and other institutions. Both IT and library staff are involved in these programmes. This seems to be the general perspective: cooperation between libraries and computing centres is seen as being 'a natural thing to do'.

In Gilbert's introduction to the national initiative in the Netherlands, he (1995) calls for more cooperation between the digital library programmes of the various countries.

Financial planning

The digital revolution has not eased the financial pressure on libraries. On the contrary, research libraries are encountering more and more obstacles to sound financial planning. There are several reasons for this. The first is that, in most countries, library budgets have been frozen because of economic problems or, for instance, decreasing numbers of students and researchers.

A second factor is the explosive price increase of books and especially journals (Carrigan, 1996). Publishers raise the prices of printed scientific information and of information stored electronically by 10% or more each year. The overall quantity of information is still growing, but libraries can afford to purchase less and less of it. If publishers continue to raise their prices and do not develop other less expensive ways of providing information, universities and research institutions will intensify the search for alternative ways of scholarly communication.

A third factor is the necessity for libraries to offer new facilities and services in addition to maintaining their present-day services. The new services are often related to the digital library, e.g. providing access to information elsewhere in the world, offering better search and retrieval methods, and providing more and better user support and instruction.

The result is a complicated budget allocation situation (Griebel, 1996) and many libraries have been forced to reassess their budgets. Evans (1995) surveyed 101 academic libraries: the results indicate that libraries have responded to increased costs for resource materials by enlarging this part of the budget and decreasing the budget allocation for salaries.

Angiletta (1995) has reviewed the financial difficulties of the past 20 years in academic and research libraries in the USA. The budget situation in German university libraries is described by Griebel (1995a, 1995b) and Waetjen (1996), that in the UK by T. Graham (1996), and that in Greece by Raptis and Sitas (1996).

One response to budget cutting is the generation of extra revenue for fee-based services (Coffman, 1995; McDaniel and Epp, 1995). Many libraries in the USA, and more and more in Europe, are active in the field of fund raising in order to counterbalance the negative effects of decreasing finances. It is also a good means of proving the library's scholarly and cultural potency in society. Myers and Carnes (1995) describe how to be successful in fund raising and how to organize fund raising campaigns. Burlingame (1995) has edited a book on library fund raising on the basis of case studies. Wilkinson (1996) writes on income generation in UK academic libraries. Poll (1996) does the same for German ones.

Acquisitions policy

The pricing of academic books and, especially, of serials (and the emergence of electronic publications) will have severe consequences for scholarly communication in the near future. As a result of the incredible prices demanded by publishers, more journals are being cancelled and fewer books are being bought. It is difficult to stipulate a minimum level of acquisitions, although Clouston (1995) and Wise and Perushek (1996) postulate standards for library acquisitions for large university library systems. Diedrichs (1996a) discusses acquisitions management in changing times. Werner (1996) reviews criteria for the selection of serials acquisition.

Many library users and librarians expect a serials crisis before the end of this millennium. They think the serials market will be reorganized, but exactly how is unclear (Echt, 1996). Odlyzko (1995) thinks that we are on the verge of a drastic change from printed journals to electronic ones, and that the change is likely to be sudden. The effects on printed journals, publishers, and libraries will be profound.

There are no clear solutions for the impending crisis. The reasons for this are closely connected with the changes in scholarly communication between researchers. In many disciplines alternative information circuits have developed, such as bulletin boards, newsletters, printed or electronic preprints, and reports. According to Covi and Kling (1996), however, library users do not yet see electronic publishing as a replacement of the traditional publishing cycle, which provides a quality-filtering process between author and reader.

More and more serials are offered in a networked environment (Davis, 1996; Malinconico, 1996). In the near future printed journals might be substituted by electronic ones, but it is impossible to predict whether this will be a solution for the problems mentioned above (Brown, 1996; German, 1996).

Whatever the case, budgeting nowadays involves not only purchase of printed books and serials, but also licences for electronic resources (Johnston and Witte, 1996). Libraries have to be active in the marketplace for both electronic information and printed information (Rowley, 1996b). West (1996) states that the Internet is changing the economics of the information distribution system. According to Barker (1996) pricing strategies will have a direct impact on alternative media. Many publishers offer electronic versions of journals, mostly in combination with subscriptions to the printed ones and on the basis of add-on prices. There are different policies, different licences, different contracts, different formats, different data structures, and different delivery media. It is in the interests of the users to standardize these points.

Diedrichs (1996b) sums up the individuals with whom an acquisitions librarian may need to interact and sets out how financial relationships with them can be established and enhanced. Library acquisitions formulae, by which the allocation of acquisitions funds for books and periodicals can be determined, are described by Evans (1996). A special issue of *Acquisitions Librarian* (**8**(16), 1996) deals with the function and impact of approval plans.

Some people argue that librarians will soon be replaced either by commercial publishers, who will take over their function of document delivery, or – even worse – by 'interfaces'; others think that librarianship and librarians will maintain the status quo. The truth may lie somewhere in between these two extremes (Leonhardt, 1996).

A probable scenario for academic libraries will be the maintenance of a core collection of printed serials, directly accessible on open shelves, and facilities for remote access to more specialized serials stored electronically on document servers in the library, at the publisher or the serials agent. Libraries might increasingly set up consortia for this purpose.

Nisonger (1996) reviews the subject of library acquisitions. The electronic newsletter edited by Tuttle (1996) is important for those who want to be regularly informed about pricing issues. Electronic Data Interchange (EDI) may simplify the life of acquisitions librarians. The journal *Library Administration and Management* devotes a special issue (**10**(3), 1996) to this subject. See also Wiessner (1995, 1996).

Collection management

The questions as to which material a university library has to acquire and who has the final say are not easily answered. The wishes of researchers, the needs of students and the professional knowledge of librarians all have to be combined. Qualified collection development requires cooperation and partnership (Shaughnessy, 1995; Bogey, 1996; Brophy and Coulling, 1996; Johnson, 1996) and has strong links with acquisitions (Kemp, 1996). The quality of collections is a popular topic. Dobson *et al.* (1996) give a comprehensive approach to collection evaluation for interdisciplinary fields. Lambert and Taylor (1996) do the same for the journals collection. Wood (1996) describes Conspectus as an instrument for collection analysis and development. Pastine (1996) presents a guide to collection development bibliography. Pierce (1995) treats the weeding and maintenance of reference collections. Voorbij (1996) describes the collection development situation in the Netherlands. Line (1996b) discusses the importance of national self-sufficiency in the electronic era.

Automated systems have the capacity to provide the statistical data necessary to manage library collections, but this capacity is utilized inadequately (Atkins, 1996). Examples are given of a library in the USA producing statistical data from its library system to plan a major serials cancellation project and to negotiate with the teaching faculty about the necessary reduction in the serials budget. The consequences of new automation technology for acquisitions and collection development are explained by Bazirjian (1995).

To what extent can librarians explain or defend their collection development policy? Snow (1996) argues that drawing up collection development policies is a waste of time, because they quickly become outdated and irrelevant. Librarians should instead concentrate on the selection and evaluation of their collections. Martin (1995) offers step-by-step guidance on how to plan, develop, defend, and implement collection budgets. Henschke (1996) writes about how to anticipate and provide for the need for literature and information in research libraries.

There is a close relationship between collection management and scholarly communication. Atkinson (1996) and Tonta (1996) connect this issue with the development of digital libraries and the consequences for library functions. Hitchingham (1996) examines the implications of electronic publishing for the traditional functions of collection management. Electronic resources have to be integrated into the collection development policies (Vogel, 1996). Libraries apply similar collection–development criteria to Internet resources as they do to print publications (Emerson, 1995). Several authors consider the relationship between electronic resources and collection development (Chaudhry, 1996; Demas *et al.*, 1995; Enderle, 1996; Kelly, 1996; McCarthy, 1996; Skinner, 1996; Stolt, 1996). Miller and Lundstrom (1996) deal with the relationship between CD-ROMs and collection development.

The more electronic databases become available, the more money has to be spent on access to them (Carpenter, 1996; Holleman, 1996). The acquisition of CD-ROMs has become part of the collection development policy of all research libraries. The same is or will be the case for acquiring licences. The way site licences take shape varies from information provider to information provider and much literature is devoted to this topic (Olivieri, 1996; see also the articles about the UK Pilot Site Licence Initiative in *Serials*, 2(9), 1996).

New media

In view of their popularity, CD-ROMs deserve special attention. The number of titles available in this format continues to increase. By the end of 1996 20,000 commercial titles were available worldwide, 45% more than a year before; of these 4,000 can be characterized as multimedia. This fact illustrates that the content of CD-ROMs is changing, from bibliographic data to full text and multimedia. At the same time, the number of CD-ROM drives is also increasing; almost 90% of PCs sold now have such a drive (Galante Block, 1996). The proportion of libraries offering CD-ROMs doubled from 38% in 1991 to 75% in 1994 (Mehta, 1996).

With the coming of the Digital Versatile Disc (-ROM) capacity is now 30 times that of the first CD-ROM (Bell, 1996). Silver Platter was due to bring out an edition of the Union Catalogue of Belgian Research Libraries in February 1997.

End users are demanding WAN access to CD-ROMs, with home access as the ultimate step. Although this is being worked on, there is increasing competition for CD-ROM. Suppliers can opt to offer access through the Internet protocol TCP/IP. There are several alternatives for this: ERL-technology, WWW, Z39.50, remote log-in (Mehta, 1996). Moreover CD-ROMs are becoming available which are accessible from various PC-platforms (Ling, 1996). The choice between the various possibilities is determined by factors such as price comparison, the need for platform independence, quality requirements (e.g. user interface, local network quality) and the availability of qualified personnel for maintaining a local CD-ROM service.

As a result of cross-licensing, more suppliers are able to offer the same databases. This enables libraries to limit the number of suppliers and hence the number of different interfaces. Graphic interfaces (e.g. Windows) are replacing character-based interfaces; this increases the user friendliness for accessing chemical formulae and structures, tables, and figures (Mehta, 1996). The CD-ROM is evolving from a static into a dynamic medium; hybrid CD-ROMs can be updated with fresh information straight from the Internet (Martin, 1996). This is perhaps a solution for the dilemma which Finn (1996) describes, namely the choice which publishers have to make between CD-ROM and the Internet.

CD-ROMs aside, electronic publications are still a relatively new category within library collections. The main problems with regard to electronic publications are the lack of academic status and the question of authenticity and integrity. Although suggestions have been made as to how these obstacles can be removed, there is no clear view how electronic scientific communication can best be organized (Lancaster, 1995a, 1995b; Okerson and O'Donnell, 1995; Tenopir, 1995; Bide, 1996; Giles, 1996; Neubauer, 1996). Neither is it clear whether the method should be the same for all disciplines.

There is also discussion about economic issues (King and Griffiths, 1995), but it is clear that there could be advantages for both publishers (Clark, 1995) and libraries (Task Force on Archiving of Digital Information, 1996). It all boils down to the search for a method of payment which guarantees returns for the publisher and is acceptable to the academic community. H. Koehler (1996) has made proposals from a publisher's viewpoint.

In the electronic era it is clear that libraries will have to provide 'on-demand services' and they will be assessed on their ability to do so (Leskien, 1996b). The user must get what he wants when he wants and in the desired form. This means a redesign of library procedures which up to now have been based primarily on print collections. It also means the acquisition and maintenance of hardware and software, for access to external and even internal materials. Menil (1996) considers the library should be responsible for the education of users in the application of such hardware and software so that they are able to search and acquire information independently.

Libraries will be forced to cooperate with parties which could be their competitors, e.g. in the field of resource sharing (Dannelly, 1995: Leskien, 1996b). Dannelly stresses that a condition for resource sharing is the existence of a collection to be shared. However, it is not yet clear who should store which electronic material and where this should be stored, nor what the costs will be. But libraries cannot afford a passive approach as this will weaken their ability to compete. Libraries will also have to address the problem of storing electronic documents. Not only do they have to guarantee access, they must also be able to guarantee authenticity and integrity. (Brichford and Maher, 1995; Task Force on Archiving of Digital Information, 1996).

Conservation and preservation

A university library that cherishes its collections provides for their preservation and conservation and – just as important – for making them available for study. Mere possession must not be a university library's main object: its goal should be to aid and stimulate academic teaching and research. Only when its collections are really used for education and inquiry does the library meet its mandate. In addition, libraries traditionally fulfil other more general social and cultural functions (Miksa, 1996).

Therefore, conservation and preservation are issues of ever-increasing importance for libraries (Fletcher, 1996). In this field not only do professional and technical methods (Guerra *et al.*, 1995; Hanus *et al.*, 1995; Havermans, 1995; Neuheuser, 1996) and storage conditions (Foot, 1996) deserve attention, but also management and conceptual items have to be the focal points of the librarian's interest (Leskien, 1996a). Several authors point out the necessity for special care and techniques for the storage and conservation of cartographic materials (Burtseva, 1996; Duchemin, 1996; Otto, 1996).

Preservation policies and practices in British libraries are dealt with by Eden and Feather (1996) and Feather *et al.* (1996). During the JISC/British Library Workshop, organized by UKOLN and held at the University of Warwick on 27 and 28 November 1995, several interesting papers were presented on the topic of the long-term preservation of electronic materials. The European Commission on Preservation and Access (ECPA) organized its first conference on preservation in 1996 in Leipzig (Lusenet, 1996; Schmidt, 1996).

It is clear that preservation of electronic material is as important as that of printed material (Lievesley, 1996; Long, 1996: Mackenzie Owen, 1996; Marcum, 1996). Printed material has better prospects for preservation for many years than electronic material (Lehmann, 1996). If digital material is not to be lost to coming generations, the data will have to be transferred regularly to new storage devices (Reinitzer and Kroller, 1996).

LIBER has published useful information about preservation activities in Canada (Turko, 1996), Russia, Ukraine and Hungary (Kovacs, 1996). Feldmann (1996) deals with the preservation and accessibility of old and precious works in libraries in Westphalia.

Library buildings

It has always proved difficult to achieve consensus between librarians and architects when designing new library buildings. They do not always share standards and values about the academic libraries of the future. A complicating factor today is that the internal layout and equipping of academic library buildings must take into account new developments in IT, and be as user-friendly as possible (Cirillo and Danford, 1996). Architects and librarians should recognize that printed collections will remain a primary function of libraries for the foreseeable future; flexibility in shelving and compact shelving are important. Printed and electronic media must coexist. IT has not reduced library space requirements (Foote, 1995; L.A. Wilson, 1995). Bennaciri (1995) discusses the standards for the allocation of space for academic library buildings.

Kurak and Cikatricisova (1996) review the developments in the design, construction and renovation of library buildings during the last 20 years. Examples from different countries are provided. Melot (1996) describes the architecture and layout of fifteen newly built libraries and some under construction such as the Library of Alexandria, the British Library and the Bibliothèque nationale de France. Criteria and procedures for the assessment of library buildings by the Library Committee of the German Wissenschaftsrat (German Academic Advisory Council) are given by Frankenberger (1995).

In many academic libraries there is a great demand for extension stacks. When the shelves cannot contain all the volumes the library owns and some of the collection has to be transferred to branch stacks, the items to be placed there should be selected carefully. Silverstein and Shieber (1996) developed a method for decision-making in such a situation. Hawthorne and Martin (1995) present case studies of how additions to academic library buildings should be planned.

Bosch (1996) reviews their work. Rare books and archival documents demand special building measures (Baynes-Cope, 1996).

Several countries are developing a national policy on new library buildings. In Hungary, for example, a survey of library space in the eighteen most significant universities was commissioned by the Hungarian Ministry of Culture and Education, in order to determine future priorities for development, sites for new buildings and building costs (Urban, 1995). A similar study was undertaken in Poland (Jopp, 1995).

Access versus holdings

One of the key issues facing libraries is that of ownership versus access. Digitization makes the issue even more vital. Will libraries still need to store collections of printed material locally in the next millennium or will access to scholarly information in electronic form or by interlibrary loan and document delivery services fully meet the needs of future generations of students and researchers (Kingma and Irving, 1996; Prestamo, 1996)? Will the process of scholarly communication be predominantly electronic or will the supply of information from books and journals in their traditional printed form continue to be the best way to disseminate knowledge? And, will a newer world information order arise resulting in greater justice in the global flow of information (Evans *et al.*, 1996; Skreslet, 1996)? The 18th International Essen Symposium (23–26 October 1995) was dedicated to the theme 'Electronic Documents and Information: From Preservation to Access' and treated many issues in this domain (Helal and Weiss, 1996).

Today, a great deal of information in electronic form is accessible to students and researchers, provided they have the right equipment and the appropriate licences. Technically, access to all kinds of electronic resources over open networks is improving every year. Often, however, electronic information is more expensive than printed information, and large amounts of money have to be spent on the technical infrastructure (Bennett *et al.*, 1996; Hawbaker and Wagner, 1996, Saffady, 1996).

Allen (1996) gives a survey of the budgets of academic libraries in the USA and Canada for products and services providing access to information. A cost–benefit analysis can clarify the relationship between periodical ownership versus full-text online access or versus electronic journals (Beardman, 1996; Collins and Howell, 1996; Hawbaker and Wagner, 1996; Ketcham and Born, 1996).

The user is not concerned with the physical location where electronic information is stored, as long as the library can guarantee quick access and good performance. The user should not be aware of the fact that he is accessing information stored on a document server outside his own library (Mandel, 1996).

Today, access to information is as important as the holding and possession of information was in earlier days. This not only applies to recently published books and serials, but also to rare books and manuscripts (Snyder, 1996). Networked information systems will supply more and more scholarly information and therefore their influence on scholarly communication is not to be underestimated (Dempsey and Heijne, 1996; Nicholson, 1996). Line (1996a) gives a realistic view of how libraries can find a balance between access and ownership.

Interlending, document delivery, resource sharing, networking

Good collection management and efficient sharing of resources on the basis of interlibrary loan are still foundations of library services (Lapelerie, 1996). Nowadays, however, the world of information is developing in the direction of a 'global city' in which all kinds of information are available to all its inhabitants (Jacquesson, 1995; White, 1995). Scientific data have become more accessible than ever before, thanks to improvements in the quality of catalogues and retrieval systems, the organization of interlibrary loan and document delivery, and the quality of the IT infrastructure. Those who want to be regularly informed about new literature related to these issues are referred to the section 'Bibliographies of interlending and document supply' in the journal *Interlending and Document Supply*.

Library users who find information in catalogues and databases from all over the world will expect their libraries to be able to obtain this information and deliver it to them. Nationwide and worldwide accessibility of information demands an intensified sharing of resources, not only of printed material, but also of electronically stored information. The quality of interlibrary loan and document delivery will become increasingly important (Jurow *et al.*, 1995; Lenzini, 1996). Ferguson *et al.* (1995) discuss aspects of staffing, technology and budgeting related to document delivery. Price *et al.* (1996) review electronic document request and delivery research. The importance of library networking for cooperation and resource sharing is dealt with by Klugkist (1995), Lievesley (1995), Chaudhry (1996), Cornish (1996), Costers (1996), Degkwitz (1996), and Simpson (1996).

Baker and Jackson (1995) dedicate a double issue of the *Journal of Library Administration* to the topic of resource sharing. Economic decision models, consortia agreements, copyright dilemmas and technological advance are discussed. Convergence of reference and resource sharing was the central theme of the OCLC Symposium ALA Midwinter Conference in January 1996 in Dublin, Ohio (American Library Association, 1996). Huston-Somerville and Wilt (1995), Huston-Somerville *et al.* (1996) and Ruppert and Sühl-Strohmenger (1996) consider the relation between electronic information and resource sharing.

According to S.E. Ward (1996) commercial information services will become increasingly active in the field of document delivery and libraries will be faced with the challenge of fundamentally reappraising the needs for document provision. Clement (1996) carried out a pilot project to investigate commercial document suppliers in terms of speed, efficiency, quality, and cost-effectiveness.

Cataloguing, indexing and information retrieval

Where does the future of cataloguing lie? Most librarians agree that cataloguing as a bibliographic tool and finding list will remain important. Several authors pay attention to modern developments in the field of cataloguing and indexing, for example, Foskett (1996), Hädrich (1996), Havekost and Wätjen (1995), O'Connor (1996), Rowley (1996a, 1996b) and M.L. Ward (1996).

Some think that cataloguing may be replaced by new search and retrieval tools and by the development of metacatalogues. Such discussions are perhaps somewhat premature when one considers that many university libraries with large collections are still in the process of converting their card catalogues into online catalogues. In the UK, the Follett Implementation Group on Information Technology (FIGIT) recently commissioned a study to assess the justification for a national programme of retrospective cataloguing in the higher education sector. Chapman (1996) gives an outline of this study and the main recommendations; attention is paid to the national benefits, costs and funding of such activities (see Sweeney, 1996).

The building of online catalogues, together with the development of associated bibliographic services, is still one of the librarian's important tasks. It is not realistic to suppose that in the near future we will no longer need such catalogues (Vitiello, 1996), but with the introduction of new and better search engines the level of cataloguing activities may be questioned (Harmon, 1996). Cataloguing, indexing and classification techniques have a strong relationship with those for information retrieval; Ellis (1996) reviews the state of the art.

A topical issue is the cataloguing of digital material. Several authors write about the cataloguing of electronic journals, serials and computer files (Dodd, 1996; Geer, 1996; Kellum, 1996; Soper, 1996). Wallace (1996) advises on how to optimize serials access in the online catalogue. Xu (1996) deals with the impact of automation on job requirements and qualifications for cataloguers and reference librarians in academic libraries. The outsourcing of cataloguing services is being taken into consideration by more and more libraries; it has advantages and disadvantages (Dunkle, 1996; Johnston, 1996; K.A. Wilson, 1995). Other possibilities are cataloguing by paraprofessionals, for example by paraprofessional copy cataloguers (Rider, 1996) or by teleworking (Black and Hyslop, 1996).

OPAC developments

For many years the OPAC has held a prominent place in academic libraries. With the advent of the graphical user interface (GUI) the OPAC is in danger of becoming outdated (Harbord, 1996). Fortunately, a new generation of OPACs is being developed, based on Z39.50 or WWW or both; the OPAC is developing from a finding list for local holdings into an interface between the library's users and its services, including resources outside the library itself.

Tomaiuolo (1996) discusses both advantages and possible disadvantages of the GUI, including possible adverse affects on health. Overall the advantages prevail. Use of PCs instead of dedicated terminals can present security problems; Schuyler (1996) offers solutions, on the basis of CD-ROM technology. In a special issue of *Library Hi Tech* devoted to the empowerment of persons with disabilities, McNulty (1996) pays attention to graphic interfaces. The popularity of the GUI forms a threat to visually handicapped users. Modifications are being studied. This issue is also discussed by Edwards (1996), and by Chalfen and Farb (1996) in relation to the Americans with Disabilities Act of 1990. Sulaiman and Meadows (1995) studied the possible use of icons in OPACS, in view of their multilingual or language-independent character. Molnar and Kletke (1996) studied voice recognition as a possibility for user interfacing; as yet, this technology cannot compete with a graphical interface. Despite drawbacks, the advantages of graphical interfaces predominate: they are quicker, easier and more accurate than text-based interfaces. Moreover, under the influence of Windows, diversity is decreasing.

Online catalogues should offer facilities to handle spelling errors (Drabenstott and Weller, 1996). Intelligent user interfaces should improve the quality of formal and subject retrieval facilities in the online catalogue (Huibers and van Linder, 1996; Recker *et al.*, 1996). LeBlanc (1995) examines the intrinsic value of browsing a library collection, either in the stacks or in the library's online catalogue, and discusses in this respect the cost-benefit of classification and shelf-listing.

The call for standardization and interoperability is widespread. In the UK the NOPAC (Network OPAC) has been developed for remote access by users of the JANET research network. According to M. Graham (1996) the search terms have to be adapted to the catalogue searched, but it is possible to transfer a search strategy from one catalogue to another, or to build up a personal file of relevant references. NOPAC has a graphic interface. In the Netherlands, Pica (URL) has developed a graphic interface, Web-OP(A)C, for its library network which permits searching of individual library catalogues and of the union (national) catalogue. In such cases, there is a degree of uniformity in software and network architecture. However, the requirements go further and call for interoperability of systems with different interfaces.

The answer could lie in technical protocols such as Z39.50 and WWW. Schneider (1996) explains how Z39.50 enables realization of two of librarians' wildest dreams: one-stop shopping and a simple (single) user interface. Smith (1995) describes the role of Z39.50 in the ONE project (OPAC Network Europe) and sees it as a step towards a European information network. Dekkers (1996) discusses Z39.50 in relation to the typically European problems of multiplicity of languages and character sets.

Some express their doubt as to the future value of Z39.50. Although national libraries in USA, UK and Canada have built Z39.50 servers into their catalogues, Casale (1996) wonders whether the future could lie with retrieval systems based on the Internet. Place and Dijkstra (1995), however, see Z39.50 and WWW as complementary ('the best of both worlds'): Z39.50 specifically for database searching and HTTP (WWW) for document delivery. The strength of HTTP lies in its combination of HTML and the Common Gateway Interface. The latter is sometimes associated with 'statelessness': web servers have no knowledge of who makes requests and whether they have been preceded by other requests. Arfield *et al.* (1995) solved this problem with the aid of URLs in developing a WWW OPAC at Loughborough University.

Molnar and Kletke (1996) feel that the OPAC goes a long way in determining user satisfaction: however, a good interface cannot compensate for a poor database (Tomaiuolo, 1996). Gluck (1996) distinguishes 'relevance' and 'user-satisfaction' in the evaluation of information systems.

While discussion prevails as to whether catalogues will lose importance with the development of WWW search engines, initiatives are being taken for the (distributed) cataloguing of the Internet itself. Nicholson and Steele (1996) describe a distributed, Z39.50-based approach in the UK. They see a role for libraries in the development of a distributed catalogue of Internet EIOs (electronic information objects), including Z39.50 OPACs.

Internet directories, home pages

Cataloguing the Internet is a monumental task. The net continues to double in size approximately every twelve to fifteen months. Between January and July 1996 the number of hosts increased from 9,472,000 to 12,881,000. More and more users are connected to the Internet via access providers, whereas previously the majority of users had institutional/organizational access.

In addition to the efforts made at cataloguing the Internet, libraries are taking initiatives in building discipline/subject-oriented directories or guides of Internet resources (Ensor, 1996; Sloan, 1996). These sometimes contain metadata (descriptions of databases and documents): so-called quality-controlled, subject-access gateways to networked information (Porat and Zehavi, 1996).

The University of Wisconsin at Madison has developed campus standards and guidelines for the design, style and content of WWW pages (McClements and Becker, 1996). Oslo University's Informatics Library makes the institutional publications accessible electronically on the WWW, using PostScript or HTML formats (Strange, 1995). This trend is evident elsewhere. Michigan University explored the use of image capture by electronic media scanners and made available sample images of ancient papyri from one of the world's largest collections (Gagos *et al.*, 1996).

The home page of the Engineering College Library of the University of Cincinnati has evolved into a teaching tool for electronic information retrieval (Byers and Wilson, 1995). Hypermedia library guides for academic libraries on the WWW are reviewed by Cox (1996). The library of the University of Maryland at Baltimore is using a WWW browser as user interface for all of the library's electronic resources. The University Library at Indiana University-Purdue University Indianapolis has built a multiplatform, multimedia integrated workstation using a WWW browser as an interface (Koopman and Hay, 1996).

Scholar workstations

For the modern library the challenge is the development of a transparent and campus-wide supply of bibliographic information to the library user, while maintaining traditional services. The need for patrons to select (bibliographic) information sources and to manage the information found across a variety of networks is apparent from the extensive use of information databases and management tools (Baumgras, 1995; Combs, 1996a, 1996b; Kaufman, 1996; Tomaiuolo, 1996). Libraries wishing to facilitate research and education will need to design information environments and offer intermediary services that assist the end user in managing information, enabling data exchange between various programmes (Mess, 1995; Palmer, 1996). Ideally, staff and students should have access to 'scholar workstations' at or near their workplaces, providing such an environment (Heck and Baker, 1995) and facilitating information searching, storage, retrieval, transfer, and processing (Mendelsohn, 1995).

How can the library provide a virtual environment in which users are seamlessly led to the best resources for their needs? In other words: how do we build the ideal scholar workstation? As already mentioned, one approach is the implementation of information-retrieval protocols like Z39.50, which shield the user from having to learn the complications of various search engines. Dempsey (1996) considers Z39.50 'a crucial building block of future distributed information systems'. Another approach is the exploitation of the graphical user interface (GUI) by the database (search engine) provider. Although the interfaces to bibliographic information sources were originally exclusively character based, the majority of providers utilize Windows when upgrading their databases and their search engines. The preference of the end user for the GUI has already been mentioned (Tomaiuolo, 1996).

A third approach is the exploitation of the Web, since it provides an enormous amount of information resources such as bibliographic and full-text databases, and library catalogues (Day and Armstrong, 1996; Garlock and Piontek 1996) on the one hand, and a potential structure for building electronic distance education and virtual learning platforms (including 'shared spaces') on the other (Dumont, 1996; Jorn *et al.*, 1996). One can choose from a variety of Web search engines to find relevant sites and resources (Duval and Main, 1996). Several projects aimed at constructing Web interfaces which give access to Z39.50-based sources are in progress. In the further development of the scholar workstation, libraries should cooperate with each other and with faculty and computer centres (Clark, 1996; Day and Armstrong, 1996; Dempsey and Heijne, 1996; vander Meer and Poole, 1996; Will, 1996).

Digital formats

As more and more electronic documents become available, the lack of standardization becomes more frustrating to users trying to access and obtain such documents. Developments are rapid. Wusteman (1996) gives an extensive review of electronic journal formats. Along with others (Premium, 1995; Dempsey *et al.*, 1996), they conclude that ASCII and bitmaps formats are still widely used for the distribution of journals, but that their share will decline in favour of other formats, such as PostScript, Portable Document Format (PDF), Standard Generalized Markup Language (SGML) and Hypertext Markup Language (HTML).

Problems of PostScript are that not everyone has the proper PostScript printer and that not all computer platforms have viewers available (Heijne, 1996). PDF is a version of PostScript with additional hypertext features for online presentation and browsing of documents. An important disadvantage of formats with a fixed structure is that such documents can only be viewed with the proper software (Heijne, 1996). Novell has developed the Envoy format, which offers similar functionality to PDF (Portable, 1996).

How durable are the formats currently used? Will we be able to read these documents in, say, 30 years' time? Even standardized formats like SGML may not be entirely 'future-proof' (Wusteman, 1996). HTML is a simple application of the SGML standard and, like PDF, focuses on display. So far, however, there is no (international) conformity on the use of HTML.

SGML is a system-independent language and has its emphasis on content structure rather than appearance, which makes consistent and precise display difficult (Cole and Kazmer, 1995). Implementation of SGML in libraries will pose questions concerning its compatibility with library systems. If additional processing is required to make SGML viewable on a library's system, they pose the question whether libraries will be entitled to make such changes to copyrighted materials.

For images a number of formats is used (JPEG, TIFF and PNG) (Wusteman, 1996). As multimedia support of World Wide Web browser increases, electronic journals will incorporate multimedia. Formats to be used in this perspective are MPEG, AU, VRML and Java.

Copyright

Argument still continues on the matter of copyright of digital materials. It all devolves on the question as to whether there is analogy between digital and analogue information products. Libraries say yes, in order to achieve free availability; publishers say no, in order to safeguard their profits.

Risher (1996) defends the publishers' position and accentuates the role of copyright in encouraging creativity. Digital material differs from printed material. Risher is specially concerned about 'browsers' which make a complete copy of electronic files for replication on a computer screen. She holds that digital 'browsing' is not the same as casually leafing through a few pages of a book in a library. In the worst case publishers, as copyright owners, could forbid the browsing of digital works by library users.

Gasaway (1996) defends the libraries' position and hopes that libraries will have the same rights to access copyrighted works in the digital environment as they have in the analogue world. She fears that the public's rights will be sacrificed to the more powerful commercial interests of publishers' groups. Her fundamental argument is that users of new technologies should enjoy the same privileges that library patrons currently have. As for the browsing of electronic works, Gasaway argues that the incidental reproduction in a computer in connection with lawful use is not the same as making copies on the computer's hard drive or a floppy disk.

The discussion on the balance between public good and economic interests is likely to continue with respect to the digital library.

Meredith (1996) focuses on several attempts in the intellectual property arena by the US government, the European Union and various publishers' organizations and gives the publishers' view of document supply in the electronic world. Hoeren (1996) gives an overview of intellectual property and copyright law, which are also treated by Okerson (1996). Love (1996) points out the dangers of the treaty proposed by the World Intellectual Property Organization (WIPO) for the protection of the rights of database owners and vendors.

Experience with Internet information resources and services suggests the demise of the classical, paper-based process of scholarly communication, and of the related professions and institutions. Network-based processes are rapidly becoming established. Peters (1996) discusses this in the context of the relation between authors and readers of intellectual works.

The European Copyright User Platform (1996), a concerted action supported by EBLIDA, the European Bureau of Library and Documentation Associations, and funded by the European Commission DG XIII/E-4, has proposed regulations for the lawful use of printed and electronic journals.

Reference services

Libraries are becoming increasingly aware of the importance of their relationship with users. One area of consideration is that of reference services. The current reference environment is an interplay of options (print vs. electronic), where education has become a routine responsibility for reference librarians, where users will be frequently assisted beyond library walls, and where changes in user attitudes and expectations are creating increased demands, which often lead to staff burn-out (Crook, 1995).

Brandt *et al.* (1996) see an enhanced role for the librarian as systems designer/ tool builder: many of the traditional reference inquiries will be handled by improved interfaces and help systems that librarians will play a primary role in developing. It will change the reactive reference scenario of the past into a proactive, 'just-in-time' mode. Simple mediated reference services will become even less important as networks become faster, systems more intelligent, and interfaces easier to use.

Snyder (1995) argues that 'reference work' is not distinct from bibliographic instruction. It is the only way for libraries to reach some of their primary clientele and is an indispensable part of a professional job. Reference and information desk services continue to be important, but as specialized additions to the basic instruction function. Instruction services need to be located in a special department, reporting to as senior an officer as possible within the library organization (Kohl, 1995). The goal is to create independent professionals who can operate effectively and creatively on their own. The teaching mission has become so important, that libraries need to be reorganized if they are to facilitate independent users.

Benchmarking will increase the likelihood of significant process improvement in reference services (Buchanan and Marshall, 1996). The quality of reference services can also be influenced by interpersonal relationships between librarians and users. Radford (1996) argues for a new model of the librarian–user reference interaction that recognizes the vital importance of relational messages that are communicated in the reference encounters together with the factual information.

User education and the teaching library

Higher education and research are influenced by information technology (Day *et al.*, 1996). New IT and new forms of education, such as problem-oriented education and computer-aided education, will play an important role in coming years. Academic libraries will become teaching libraries which should equip students with lifelong learning skills (Daragan and Stevens, 1996; Stoffle and Williams, 1995). The library should direct its teaching activities not only towards students (Orr *et al.*, 1996) but also towards academic staff (Luey, 1996) and towards its own employees (Beheshti, 1996; Roselle, 1996). Academic librarians have to develop new teaching information skills (Duff, 1996; Morgan, 1996). Other authors have also addressed these issues (Carty *et al.*, 1996; DeSieno, 1995; Moore, 1995; Stephens, 1996). According to Pacey (1995) a library should teach user education in such a way that the library becomes self-explanatory in its user service; see also Thomasson and Fjällbrant (1996). The introduction of new techniques and methods is important (Nardi and O'Day, 1996).

Educating for the Internet is a task that modern librarians have to fulfil (Bunnell, 1996; Burrows, 1995; Kaczor and Jacobson, 1996). The same is true for multimedia (vander Meer and Rike, 1996). In this context, it is important to study the information-seeking behaviour of students (Hsieh-Yee, 1996) and staff of universities.

Using 'cyberspace' for user instruction is a modern approach in the academic world, for which the term Networked Learner Support (NLS) has been coined (Levy *et al.*, 1996). Instruction on the Internet could be realized by creating a 'hypertext library guide', incorporating a library tour, detailed guides to the library for particular faculties, details of services, and feedback to allow readers to ask questions and register complaints (Cox, 1996). Konrad and Stemper (1996) see instruction via the Internet as a natural extension of existing bibliographic instruction programmes.

According to Oliver (1996), instruction in the use of Interactive Information Systems (IIS) leads to a basic knowledge of the search systems but fails to provide the knowledge and understanding required for a successful use of the more powerful reaches of the IIS. He suggests there is a need for specific instructional strategies that are aimed at developing an understanding of the information base as well as of the programme and its interface.

Lee (1996) argues that today's students differ from their predecessors, and benefit from other forms of library instruction. Stimulation, variety, preference for concrete, specific information, the desire to learn leading-edge technology and personal contact are important items. The trend toward computer-assisted instruction (CAI), online tutorials, and distance learning does not negate their need for personal contact. They are impressed by people and organizations which they feel 'care about them'. One way to improve personal contact is to train students in giving library instruction to fellow-students (Stelling, 1996).

Quality assurance

User orientation can be decisive in determining the quality of a library's level of service. Performance measurement has long been recognized as a means of quality assurance in the world of academic libraries (Poll and Te Boekhorst, 1996). The way in which performance is measured, however, is changing. The accent is shifting from the monitoring of internal processes to the assessment by the library's customers (van den Hoogen, 1996a). This is partly due to the rapid changes in the area of information technology, notably the Internet and WWW. Nitecki (1996) concludes that access to information rather than the size and ownership of a collection will become the key quality feature in the eyes of the users. Te Boekhorst (1996) sees IT as a threat and an extra argument to look at performance from the user's viewpoint.

Quality of service is very much a subjective matter (van den Hoogen, 1996b). Nitecki (1996) expresses the need for a method of comparing the performance of academic libraries, one which is both user-based and widely accepted. He proposes the SERVQUAL method, which has its origins in marketing and in which the customer determines the level of quality. If the method were to be used by more academic libraries, normative measures could be developed, thus facilitating benchmarking of library service quality. Mutual comparison would also be possible if libraries were to adopt the ISO 9000 certification (Melling, 1996). As yet, however, few academic libraries have adopted this approach (te Boekhorst, 1996).

Other examples of the measurement of quality of service can be found in the literature. Frowein and Kramp (1996) give a checklist for quality measurement and improvement. Doyle (1995) has studied the possibility of measuring the evaluation by students with the aid of a Perception of Library Service Questionnaire. The Library of Monfort University has incorporated performance measurement in a decision support system (S. Ward, 1996).

Final remarks

The literature reflects the growing but uncertain influence of IT on the academic library environment, with the emphasis on environment. The Internet and the web affect the process of scholarly communication. Paradoxically, the more library services migrate to the end users and their workstations, the greater the demand will become for more user-friendliness in 'information handling'. This manifests itself in areas such as interfacing, information retrieval, user education, and standardization. Simply put: the more IT, the greater the focus on persons, both end users and staff.

Acknowledgements

The authors would like to express their thanks to colleagues at Maastricht and Groningen who helped to select and review the literature.

References

Allen, F.R. (1996) Materials budgets in the electronic age. A survey of academic libraries. *College and Research Libraries*, **57**(2), 133–143.

American Library Association (1996) *The future is now: the convergence of reference and resource sharing. Proceedings of the OCLC Symposium ALA Midwinter Conference, January 19, 1996 – Dublin, OH.* Dublin, Ohio: OCLC.

Angiletta, A.M. (1995) Collection development in the large American research library: at an end or at the beginning? In: A.H. Helal and J.W. Weiss (eds). *Information superhighway: the role of librarians, information scientists and intermediaries. 17th International Essen Symposium, 24–27 October, 1994.* Essen: Universitätsbibliothek Essen, pp. 337–348.

Arfield, J. *et al.* (1995) Developing a World-Wide Web OPAC. *Vine*, (99), 32–37.

Association for Computing (1996) First ACM international conference on digital libraries. http://fox.cs.vt.edu/DL/96

Atkins, S. (1996) Mining automated systems for collection management. *Library Administration and Management*, **10**(1), 16–19.

Atkinson, R. (1996) Library functions, scholarly communication and the foundation of the digital library: laying claim to the control zone. *Library Quarterly*, **66**(3), 239–265.

Baker, S.K. and Jackson, M.E. (1995) (eds). *The future of resource sharing.* New York: Haworth. [Also published as *Journal of Library Administration*, **21**(1–2), 1–202.]

Baldwin, D.A. and Migneault, R.L. (1996) *Humanistic management by teamwork: an organizational and administrative alternative for academic libraries.* Englewood, CO: Libraries Unlimited.

Barker, J. (1996) Academic journals: pricing strategies, alternative media and the maximization of value. *Serials*, **9**(1), 27–34.

Baumgras, J.L. (1995) Chemical structures at the desktop. *Journal of the American Society for Information Science*, **46**(8), 623–631.

Baynes-Cope, A.D. (1996) Creating buildings for rare books and archival documents. *Restaurator*, **17**(1), 22–24.

Bazirjian, R. (1995) (ed.) *New automation technology for acquisitions and collection development.* New York: Haworth Press. [Also published as *Acquisitions Librarian*, (13/14), 1995.]

Beardman, S. (1996) The cost-effectiveness of access versus ownership: a report on the virtual library project at the University of Western Australia Library. *Australian Library Review*, **13**(2), 173–181.

Beheshti, J. (1996) Ein systematisches Trainingsprogramm für den Umgang mit den neuen Technologien in den Informationsberufen. *Bibliothek*, **20**(1), 40–49.

Bell, A.E. (1996) Next-generation compact discs. *Scientific American*, **275**(1), 28–33.

Bennaciri, S. (1995) Les normes des bâtiments des bibliothèques universitaires. *Revue de la Science de l'Information*, **1**(2), 69–85.

Bennett, P. *et al.* (1996) Charging, paying and copyright – information access on open networks. *Serials*, **9**(1), 49–56.

Bide, M. (1996) How can we create universally acceptable standards for electronic publishing? In: Neubauer, K.W. (1996) (ed.), pp. 94–101.

Black, L. and Hyslop, C. (1996) Cataloging from home: telecommuting at the Michigan State university libraries. *International Cataloguing and Bibliographic Control*, **25**(2), 37–39.

Bluck, R. (1996) Staff development for subject librarians. In: M. Oldroyd (ed.) *Staff development in academic libraries: present practice and future challenges*. London: Library Association Publishing, pp. 94–106.

Bogey, D. (1996) Collection development. *Library Journal*, **121**(14), 145–149.

Boissé, J.A. (1996) Adjusting the horizontal hold: flattening the organization. *Library Administration and Management*, **10**(2), 77–81.

Bosch, A.W. (1996), Review of planning additions to academic library buildings: a seamless approach. *Journal of Academic Librarianship*, **22**(2), 148–149.

Brandt, K.A. *et al.* (1996) Reflections on reference services. *Journal of the American Society for Information Science*, **47**(3), 210–216.

Brichford, M. and Maher, W. (1995) Archival issues in network electronic publications. *Library Trends*, **43**(4), 701–711.

Broering, N.C. (1995) Changing focus: tomorrow's virtual library. *Serials Librarian*, **25**(3–4), 73–94.

Brophy, P. and Coulling, K. (1996) *Quality management for information and library managers*. Aldershot: Aslib Gower.

Brown, D.J. (1996) (ed.) *Electronic publishing and libraries: planning for the impact and growth to 2003*. London: Bowker-Saur.

Buchanan, H.S. and Marshall, J.G. (1996) Benchmarking reference services: step-by-step. *Medical Reference Services Quarterly*, **15**(1), 1–14.

Bunnell, N. (1996) The Internet and learning. *Technical Services Quarterly*, **13**(3–4), 5–22.

Burlingame, D.F. (1995) (ed.) *Library fundraising: models for success*. Chicago: American Library Association.

Burrows, T. (1995) Educating for the Internet in an academic library: the scholar's centre at the University of Western Australia. *Education for Information*, **13**(3), 229–242.

Burtseva, J.F. (1996) State and perspectives of the scientific conservation of cartographic materials. *INSPEL*, **30**(2), 162–166.

Byers, D.F. and Wilson, L. (1995) *Library instruction using Mosaic*. [Paper presented at the 16th National Online Meeting, New York, 2–4 May 1995.]

Carbonell, J. (1996) Digital librarians: beyond the digital book stock. *IEEE Expert: Intelligent Systems and their Applications*, **11**(3), 11–13.

Carpenter, K.H. (1996) Competition, collaboration, and cost in the new knowledge environment. *Collection Management*, **21**(2), 31–46.

Carrigan, D.P. (1996) Commercial journal publishers and university libraries: retrospect and prospect. *Scholarly Publishing*, **27**(4), 208–221.

Carty, J. *et al.* (1996) Towards a strategy for supporting distance-learning students through networked access to information: issues and challenges in preparing to support the doctorate in education. *Education for Information*, **14**(4), 305–316.

Casale, M. (1996) Searching for a common language. *Library Manager*, (14), 22–23.

Chalfen, D.H. and Farb, S.E. (1996) Universal access and the ADA: a disability access design specification for the new UCLA library online information system. *Library Hi Tech*, **14**(1), 51–56.

Chapman, A. (1996) Retrospective catalogue conversion: a national study and a discussion based on selected literature. *Libri*, **46**(1), 16–24.

Charkin, R. (1996) The process of scholarly communication: the state of the art - a commercial publisher's perspective. *Serials*, **9**(3), 299–300.

Chaudhry, A.S. (1996) Exploiting network information resources for collection development in libraries. *IFLA Journal*, **22**(3), 191–198.

Cirillo, S.E. and Danford, R.E. (1996) (eds). *Library buildings, equipment, and the ADA: compliance issues and solutions. Proceedings of the LAMA Buildings and Equipment Section Preconference, June 24–25, 1993. New Orleans, Louisiana.* Chicago: American Library Association.

Clark, P. (1996) Disciplinary structures on the Internet. *Library Trends*, **45**(2), 226–238.

Clark, T. (1995) On the cost differences between publishing a book in paper and in the electronic medium. *Library Resources and Technical Services*, **39**(1), 23–28.

Clement, E. (1996) A pilot project to investigate commercial document suppliers. *Library Acquisitions: Practice and Theory*, **20**(2), 137–146.

Clouston, J.S. (1995) How much is enough? Establishing a corridor of adequacy in library acquisitions. *Collection Management*, **19**(3/4), 57–75.

Cole, T.W. and Kazmer, M.M. (1995) SGML as a component of the digital library. *Library Hi Tech*, **13**(4), 75–92.

Coffman, S. (1995) Fee-based services and the future of libraries. *Journal of Library Administration*, **20**(3/4), 167–186.

Collins, T. and Howell, B. (1996) Journal accessibility factor: an examination of serials value from the standpoint of access and delivery. *Collection Management*, **21**(1), 29–40.

Combs, J. (1996a) EndNote Plus 2: enhanced reference database and bibliography manager from Niles and Associates, Inc. *Library Software Review*, **15**(1), 49–59.

Combs. J. (1996b) ProCite 3.1 for Windows: professional and personal bibliographic management from Personal Bibliographic Software, Inc. *Library Software Review*, **15**(2), 119–131.

Cornish, G.P. (1996) Resourcing academic libraries: is IT the answer? Electronic document delivery services. *New Review of Academic Librarianship*, **2**, 83–90.

Costers, L. (1996) The role of library cooperatives in a changing world. In: *International Summer School on the Digital Library, Tilburg, 4–16 August 1996*, eds J.G.B. van Luyt-Prinsen and E. Meijer. Tilburg: Ticer B.V.

Covi, L. and Kling, R. (1996) Organizational dimensions of effective digital library use: closed rational and open natural systems models. *Journal of the American Society for Information Science*, **47**(9), 672–689.

Cox, A. (1996) Hypermedia library guides for academic libraries on the World Wide Web. *Program*, **30**(1), 39–50.

Crawford, W. and Gorman, M. (1995) *Future libraries: dreams, madness and reality.* Chicago: American Library Association.

Creth, S.D. (1996) The electronic library: slouching toward the future or creating a new information environment. (Follett Lecture Series). http://www.ukoln.ac.uk/follett/creth/paper.html

Crook, M. (1995) Carolyn Tenopir discusses electronic reference services. *OCLC Newsletter*, (215), 22–23.

Crowley, B. (1996) Redefining the status of the librarian in higher education. *College and Research Libraries*, **57**(2), 113–122.

Dannelly, G.N. (1995) Resource sharing in the electronic era: potentials and paradoxes. *Library Trends*, **43**(4), 663–678.

Daragan, P. and Stevens, G. (1996) Developing lifelong learners: an integrative and developmental approach to information literacy. *Research Strategies*, **14**(2), 68–81.

Davis, C. (1996) Serials in a networked environment. *Serials Librarian*, **28**(1/2), 115–122.

Day, J.M. *et al.* (1996) Higher education, teaching, learning and the electronic library. A review of the literature for the IMPEL2 project: Monitoring organisational and cultural change. *New Review of Academic Librarianship*, **2**, 131–204.

Day, P.A. and Armstrong, K.L. (1996) Librarians, faculty, and the Internet: developing a new information partnership. *Computers in Libraries*, **16**(5), 56–58.

Degkwitz, A. (1996) Resource sharing: serials acquisition based on supra-regional collection emphases. *Serials Librarian*, **29**(1–2), 205–218.

Dekkers, M. (1996) *Z39.50 and multi-national/multi-lingual environments.* [Paper presented at the Distributed indexing/searching workshop.] http://www.w3.org/pub/WWW/search/9605-Indexing-Workshop/papers/Dekkers@Pica.html

Demas, S. *et al.* (1995) The Internet and collection development: mainstreaming selection of Internet resources. *Library Resources and Technical Services*, **39**(3), 275–290.

Dempsey, L. (1996) Towards distributed library systems: Z39.50 in a European context. *Program*, **30**(1), 1–22.

Dempsey, L. and Heijne, M. (1996) Scientific information supply: building networked information systems. *Electronic Library*, **14**(4), 317–332.

Dempsey, L. *et al.* (1996) On behalf of FIGIT. eLib standards guidelines Version 1.0. http://ukoln.bath.ac.uk/elib/wk_papers/stand2.html

DeSieno, R. (1995) The faculty and digital technology. *Educom Review*, **30**(4), 46–48.

Diedrichs, C.P. (1996a) Acquisitions management in changing times. *Library Resources and Technical Services*, **40**(3), 237–250.

Diedrichs, C.P. (1996b) Off to see the Wizard: demystifying your financial relationships. *Library Administration and Management*, **10**(2), 105–109.

Dobson, C. *et al.* (1996) Collection evaluation for interdisciplinary fields: a comprehensive approach. *Journal of Academic Librarianship*, **22**(4), 279–284.

Dodd, D.G. (1996) Grass-roots cataloging and classification: food for thought from World Wide Web subject-oriented hierarchical lists. *Library Resources and Technical Services*, **40**(3), 275–286.

Doyle, C. (1995) The perceptions of library service questionnaire (PLSQ): the development of a reliable instrument to measure student perceptions of and satisfaction with quality of service in an academic library. *New Review of Academic Librarianship*, **1**, 139–159.

Drabenstott, K.M. and Weller, M.S. (1996) Handling spelling errors in online catalog searches. *Library Resources and Technical Services*, **40**(2), 113–132.

Drake, M.A. (1996) Information, librarians and learning: the challenge ahead. *Follett Lecture Series*, (Mar.). http://www.ukoln.ac.uk/follett/drake/info_libs_learning.html

Duchemin, P.Y. (1996) Caring for map collections. *INSPEL*, **30**(2), 107–123.

Duff, A. (1996) The literature search: a library-based model for information skills instruction. *Library Review*, **45**(4), 14–18.

Dumont, R.A. (1996) Teaching and learning in cyberspace. *IEEE Transactions on Professional Communication*, **39**(4), 192–204.

Dunkle, C.B. (1996) Outsourcing the catalog department: a meditation inspired by the business and library literature. *Journal of Academic Librarianship*, **22**(1), 33–44.

Duval, B.K. and Main, L. (1996) Microcomputer applications in the library. Searching the net: general overview. *Library Software Review*, **15**(4), 242–251.

Eberhart, G.M. (1995) (ed.) *The whole library handbook 2: people, materials, guidelines, technology, operations, funding, staff development, issues, diversity, the internet, librariana: current data, professional advice, and curiosa about libraries and library services.* Chicago: American Library Association (continuation of: *The whole library handbook*, 1991).

Echt, R. (1996) Scholarly journals at the crossroads. *Serials Librarian*, **28**(3–4), 355–360.

Eden, P. and Feather, J. (1996) Preservation in libraries and archives in the UK: towards a national policy. *Library Review*, **45**(8), 33–40.

Edwards, A.D.N. (1996) The rise of the graphical user interface. *Library Hi Tech*, **14**(1), 46–50.

Ellis, D. (1996) *Progress and problems in information retrieval.* 2nd ed. London: Library Association Publishing.

Ellis, D. and Norton, B. (1996) *Implementing BS and ISO 9000 in libraries.* 2nd ed. London: Aslib.

Emerson, P.R. (1995) Making the Internet easier to use. *College and Undergraduate Libraries*, **2**(2), 133–137.

Enderle, W. (1996) Shared digital collection development: the first steps to the virtual library. *European Research Libraries Cooperation*, **6**(4), 367–382.

Ensor, P. (1996) Web organization: use of the Library of Congress classification. *Technicalities*, **16**(3), 11–12.

Erens, B. (1996a) How recent developments in university libraries affect research. *Library Management*, **17**(8), 5–16.

Erens, B. (1996b) *Modernizing research libraries: the effect of recent developments in university libraries on the research process.* East Grinstead: Bowker-Saur. (British Library Research Series).

European Library Automation Group (1996) Berlin page of ELAG 96 – Papers and Links. http://hub.ib.hu-berlin.de/~elag96/

European Copyright User Platform (1996) *Position on user rights in electronic publications.* Den Haag: ECUP.

Evans, J.E. (1995) Cost analysis of public services in academic libraries. *Journal of Interlibrary Loan, Document Delivery and Information Supply*, **5**(3), 27–70.

Evans, J. et al. (1996) BIODOC: access versus holdings in a university library. *Interlending and Document Supply*, **24**(4), 5–11.

Evans, M. (1996) Library acquisitions formulae: the Monash experience. *Australian Academic and Research Libraries*, **27**(1), 47–57.

Feather, J. et al. (1996) *Preservation management: policies and practices in British libraries.* Aldershot: Gower.

Feldmann, R. (1996) Making the old and precious libraries in Westphalia accessible. *European Research Libraries Cooperation*, **6**(2), 148–161.

Ferguson, A. *et al.* (1995) Document delivery: staffing, technology, and budgeting implications. *Serials Librarian,* **25**(3/4), 319–325.

Finn, R. (1996) Electronic science – scientific publishers are offering more products, including journals, databases, bibliographic abstracts and full-text articles on CD-ROM and the World Wide Web. *Scientist,* **10**(16), 19–21.

Fletcher, M.P. (1996) Transformation in the library bindery through increased preservation awareness. *Serials Librarian,* **28**(3/4), 343–348.

Foot, M.M. (1996) Housing our collections: environment and storage for libraries and archives. *IFLA Journal,* **22**(2), 110–114.

Foote, S.M. (1995) An architect's perspective on contemporary academic library design. *Bulletin of the Medical Library Association,* **83**(3), 351–356.

Foskett, A.C. (1996) *The subject approach to information.* 5th ed. London: Library Association.

Frankenberger, R. (1995) Das Verfahren zur Beurteilung von Bauvorhaben für Hochschulbibliotheken durch die Arbeitsgruppe Bibliotheken des Wissenschaftsrates. *ABI-Technik,* **15**(4), 385–400.

Frowein, C. and Kramp, A. (1996) Vanuit de klant bekeken, onderzoek naar de kwaliteit van de dienstverlening. *Open,* **28**(12), 266–268.

Gagos, T. *et al.* (1996) Scanning the past: a modern approach to ancient culture. *Library Hi Tech,* **14**(1), 11–22.

Galante Block, D. (1996) The returns of CD-ROM. *CD-ROM Professional,* **9**(6), 62–69.

Garlock, K.L. and Piontek, S. (1996) *Building the service-based library web site: a step-by-step guide to design and options.* Chicago: American Library Association.

Gasaway, L.N. (1996) Libraries, educational institutions, and copyright proprietors: the first collision on the information highway. *Journal of Academic Librarianship,* **22**(9), 337–344.

Geer, B. (1996) Training aid in cataloging gopher sites and electronic serials. *Serials Librarian,* **28**(3/4), 337–342.

German, L. (1996) Surviving the serials crisis. Are e-journals an answer? A report of the program sponsored by the ACRL Journal Costs in Academic Libraries Discussion Group. *Library Acquisitions,* **20**(2), 199–200.

Gilbert, J.D. (1995) Wetenschappelijke informatievoorziening in digitale stroomversnelling: tijd voor herontwerp bibliotheekstelsel? *Open,* **27**(11), 330–334.

Giles, M.W. (1996) From Gutenberg to gigabytes: scholarly communications in the age of cyberspace. *Journal of Politics,* **58**(3), 613–626.

Gluck, M. (1996) Exploring the relationship between user satisfaction and relevance in information systems. *Information Processing and Management,* **32**(1), 89–104.

Graham, M. (1996) A graphical user interface: the case for the British library network OPAC. *Managing Information,* **3**(1), 34–37.

Graham, T. (1996) Funding arrangements for UK Universities and their libraries. *New Review of Academic Librarianship,* **2**, 27–40.

Griebel, R. (1995a) German university library budgets: model and reality. *Library Management,* **16**(7), 3–8.

Griebel, R. (1995b) Etatsituation der wissenschaftlichen Bibliotheken 1995. *Zeitschrift für Bibliothekswesen und Bibliographie,* **42**(6), 561–603.

Griebel, R. (1996) University library budgets. Model and reality. *New Review of Academic Librarianship,* **2**, 59–68.

Guerra, R.A. *et al.* (1995) Procedure for simultaneous deacidification and sizing of paper. *Restaurator,* **16**(4), 175–193.

Hädrich, G. (1996) Unreglementierte Gedanken zur Weiterentwicklung des Regelwerks für die alphabetische Katalogisierung. *Zeitschrift für Bibliothekswesen und Bibliographie,* **43**(5), 471–488.

Hamaker, C.A. (1996) Redesigning research libraries: first step toward the 21st century. *Journal of Library Administration,* **22**(4), 33–48.

Hanus, J. *et al.* (1995) Influence of boxing materials on the properties of different paper items stored inside. *Restaurator,* **16**(4), 194–208.

Harbord, E. (1996) From golden retriever to GUI – recent OPAC developments at Newcastle. *Library Review,* **45**(2), 10–14.

Hardy, S. (1996) The process of scholarly communication: The state of the art - a learned society publisher's perspective. *Serials,* **9**(3), 301–306.

Harmon, J.C. (1996) The death of quality cataloging: does it make a difference for library users? *Journal of Academic Librarianship,* **22**(4), 306–307.

Harris, H. (1996) Retraining librarians to meet the needs of the virtual library patron. *Information Technology and Libraries* **15**(1), 48–51.

Hastings, K. and Tennant, R. (1996) How to build a digital librarian. http://www.dlib.org/dlib/november96/ucb/11hastings.html

Havekost, H. and Wätjen, H.J. (eds.) (1995) *Aufbau und Erschliessung begrifflicher Datenbanken: Beiträge zur bibliothekarischen Klassifikation: eine Auswahl von Vorträgen der Jahrestagungen 1993 (Kaiserslautern) und 1994 (Oldenburg) der Gesellschaft für Klassifikation.* Oldenburg: Bibliotheks- und Informationssystem der Universität Oldenburg.

Havermans, J. (1995) Effects of air pollutants on the accelerated ageing of cellulose-based materials. *Restaurator,* **16**(4), 209–233.

Hawbaker, A.C. and Wagner, C.K. (1996) Periodical ownership versus fulltext online access: a cost-benefit analysis. *Journal of Academic Librarianship,* **22**(2), 105–109.

Hawthorne, P. and Martin, R.G. (1995) (eds.) *Planning additions to academic library buildings: a seamless approach.* Chicago: American Library Association.

Heck, J. and Baker, G. (1995) The scholar's workstation project at the University of Tennessee. *Library Hi Tech,* **13**(3), 55–66.

Heery, M. and Morgan, S. (1996) *Practical strategies for the modern academic library.* London: Aslib.

Heijne, M.A.M. (1996) Documentformaten onderzocht. *Open,* **28**(7/8), 170–172.

Helal, A.H. and Weiss, J.W. (1996) (eds). Electronic documents and information: from preservation to access. *18th International Essen Symposium, 23–26 October, 1995.* Essen: Universitätsbibliothek Essen.

Henschke, E. (1996) Ermittlung und Deckung des Literatur- und Informationsbedarfs wissenschaftlicher Bibliotheken. *Zeitschrift für Bibliothekswesen und Bibliographie,* **43**(3), 299–303.

Hipsman, J.L. (1996) Strategic planning for academic libraries. *Technical Services Quarterly,* **13**(3/4), 85–104.

Hitchingham, E. (1996) Collection management in light of electronic publishing. *Information Technology and Libraries,* **15**(1), 38–41.

Hoeren, T. (1996) Intellectual property and copyright law in the European Union and other major jurisdictions: a bird's eye view. *Serials,* **9**(3), 269–276.

Holleman, C. (1996) Collection issues in the new library environment. *Collection Management,* **21**(2), 47–64.

Hsieh-Yee, I. (1996) Student use of online catalogs and other information channels. *College and Research Libraries*, **57**(2), 161–175.

Huibers, T.W.C. and van Linder, B. (1996) Intelligent information retrieval agents. In: *Proceedings of the 18th BCS IRSG annual colloquium on information retrieval research: 26–27 March 1996*. Manchester: Manchester Metropolitan University/Information Retrieval Specialist group, British Computer Society.

Huston-Somerville, M. and Wilt, C.C. (1995) (eds.) *Networks and resource sharing in the 21st century: re-engineering the information landscape*. New York: Haworth Press.

Huston-Somerville, M. *et al.* (1996) Networks and resource sharing in the 21st century. *Bolletina AIB*, **36**(3), 339–340.

Hyams, E. (1996) The information professional in the year 2000. *New Library World*, **97**(1129), 31–35.

Jacquesson, A. (1995) *L'informatisation des bibliothèques: historique, stratégie et perspectives*. Nouvelle édition. Paris: Électre-Éditions du Cercle de la Librairie.

Johanssen, C.G. (1996) ISO 9000: a managerial approach. *Library Management*, **17**(5), 14–24.

Johnson, P. (1996) An exercise in partnership – library faculty liaison. *Technicalities*, **16**(2), 12–14.

Johnston, B.J. and Witte, V. (1996) Electronic resources and budgeting: funding at the edge. *Collection Management*, **21**(1), 3–16.

Johnston, J.L. (1996) Outsourcing: new name for an old practice. *Law Library Journal*, **88**(1), 128–134.

Jopp, R.K. (1995) Neue wissenschaftliche Bibliotheken in Polen. *ABI-Technik*, **15**(3), 251–261.

Jorn, L.A. *et al.* (1996) Designing and managing virtual learning communities. *IEEE Transactions on Professional Communication*, **39**(4), 183–191.

Jurow, S.R. *et al.* (1995) *Benchmarking interlibrary loan: a pilot project*. Washington DC: Association of Research Libraries, Office of Management Services.

Kaczor, S.A. and Jacobson, T.E. (1996) Bibliographic instruction for the Internet: implications of an end user survey. *Research Strategies*, **14**(4), 214–233.

Kaufman, D. (1996) Citation 7: a datafile manager and bibliographic citation generator. *Library Software Review*, **15**(2), 113–118.

Kellum, C. (1996) Cataloging computerfiles as serials. *Serials Librarian*, **28**(3–4), 331–336.

Kelly, J.A. (1996) Collecting and accessing 'free' Internet resources. *Journal of Library Administration*, **22**(4), 99–110.

Kemp, J.H. (1996) Common ground: intersections in the work of acquisitions and collection development librarians. *Collection Management*, **21**(3–4), 103–120.

Ketcham, L. and Born, K. (1996) Projecting the electronic revolution while budgeting for the status quo. *Library Journal*, **121**(7), 45–51.

King, D.W. and Griffiths, J.M. (1995) Economic issues concerning electronic publishing and distribution of scholarly articles. *Library Trends*, **43**(4), 713–740.

Kingma, B.R. and Irving, S. (1996) The economics of access versus ownership: the costs and benefits of access to scholarly articles via interlibrary loan and journal subscriptions. *Journal of Interlibrary Loan, Document Delivery and Information Supply*, **6**(3), 1–76. Also published as a monograph, New York: Haworth Press.

Klugkist, A.C. (1995) Open library networking and interlibrary cooperation. In: A.H. Helal and J.W. Weiss (eds). *Information superhighway: the role of librarians, information scientists and intermediaries. 17th International Essen Symposium, 24–27 October 1994*. Essen: Universitätsbibliothek Essen, pp. 276–286.

Kochtanek, T.R. (1996) *Personal digital libraries.* [Paper presented at the 17th National Online Meeting 1996, New York.]

Koehler, D.W. (1996) Administrative computing meets the Web: discover the possibilities. http://ukoln.bath.ac.uk/fresko/net_info/koehler.html

Koehler, H. (1996) Pricing considerations for electronic products in a network and requirements for a billing system – from a publisher's viewpoint. In: Neubauer, K.W. (1996), (ed.) pp. 119–124.

Kohl, D.F. (1995) As time goes by . . . revisiting fundamentals. *Library Trends,* **44**(2), 423–429.

Konrad, L. and Stemper, J. (1996) Same game different name: demystifying Internet instruction. *Research Strategies,* **14**(1), 4–21.

Koopman, A. and Hay, S. (1996) Large-scale application of a Web browser. *College and Research Libraries News,* **57**(1), 12–15.

Kovacs, L. (1996) Libraries and archives in Russia, the Ukraine and Hungary. Preserving man's memory and material past. *European Research Libraries Cooperation,* **6**(2), 162–188.

Krysiak, E. (1996) The process of scholarly communication: an Eastern European angle. *Serials,* **9**(3), 291–298.

Kurak, J. and Cikatricisova, V. (1996) Kniznice buducnosti. [Libraries of the future]. *Kniznice a Informacie,* **28**(6), 268–277.

Lambert, J. and Taylor, S. (1996) Evaluating a journals collection in an academic library. *Serials,* **9**(3), 317–321.

Lancaster, F.W. (1995a) Evolution of electronic publishing. *Library Trends,* **43**(4), 518–527.

Lancaster, F.W. (1995b) Attitudes in academia toward feasibility and desirability of networked scholarly publishing. *Library Trends,* **43**(4), 741–747.

Lapelerie, F. (1996) Le prêt entre bibliothèques universitaires scientifiques, existe-t-il? *Bulletin des Bibliothèques de France,* **41**(4), 56–73.

LeBlanc, J. (1995) Classification and shelflisting as value added: some remarks on the relative worth and price of predictability, serendipity, and depth of access. *Library Resources and Technical Services,* **39**(3), 294–302.

Lee, C.A. (1996) Teaching generation X. *Research Strategies,* **14**(1), 56–59.

Lee, S. and Clark, M.E. (1996) Continued organizational transformation: the Harvard College Library's experience. *Library Administration and Management,* **10**(2), 98–104.

Lehmann, K.D. (1996) Das kurze Gedächtnis digitaler Publikationen. *Zeitschrift für Bibliothekswesen und Bibliographie,* **43**(3), 209–226.

Lenzini, R.T. (1996) Delivery of documents and more: a view of trends affecting libraries and publishers. *Journal of Library Administration,* **22**(4), 49–70.

Leonhardt, T.W. (1996) The alarmists versus the equilibrists: reexamining the role of the serials professional in the information age. *Serials Librarian,* **28**(3/4), 187–195.

Leskien, H. (1996a) Konzeption bestandserhaltender Massnahmen und Geschäftsgänge. *Bibliothek,* **20**(2), 253–256.

Leskien, H. (1996b) Dienstleistungen der Bibliotheken bei Zugang und Distribution elektronischer Publikationen. In: Neubauer, K.W. (1996) (ed.), pp. 46–54.

Levy, P., *et al.* (1996) Networked learner support. *Library Association Record,* **98**(1), 34–35.

Lievesley, D. (1995) Creating sustainable networked research resources. *Proceedings of the UK Office for Library and Information Networking (UKOLN) Conference: networking and the future of libraries 2, Bath, 19–21 April 1995.* London: Library Association Publishing in association with UKOLN, pp. 100–109.

Lievesley, D. (1996) Maintenance and preservation of large databases. *European Research Libraries Cooperation*, 6(4), 472–482.

Line, M.B. (1996a) Access versus ownership: how real an alternative is it? *IFLA Journal*, 22(1), 35–41.

Line, M.B. (1996b) National self-sufficiency in an electronic age. In: A.H. Helal and J.W. Weiss (eds). *Electronic documents and information: from preservation to access. 18th International Essen Symposium, 23–26 October, 1995.* Essen: Universitätsbibliothek Essen, pp. 170–193.

Ling, P. (1996) CD-ROM and multiplatform performance: the hybrid road. *CD-ROM Professional*, 9(5), 38–49.

Lippincott, J. (1996) Collaboration: partnerships between librarians and information technologists. http://ukoln.bath.ac.uk/fresko/net_info/lippincott.html

Long (1996) term preservation of electronic materials. A JISC/British Library Workshop as part of the Electronic Libraries Programme (eLIB), organized by UKOLN at the University of Warwick on the 27th and 28th November 1995. Boston Spa: British Library Research and Development Department. (British Library R&D Report 6238) [Also available at http://ukoln.bath.ac.uk/elib/wk_papers/]

Love, J. (1996) A primer on the proposed WIPO treaty on database extraction rights. *Information Policy Notes.* A newsletter available from listproc@tap.org. 29 October, 1996.

Luey, B. (1996) The librarian's role in teaching academic authors about publishing procedures and ethics. *Serials Review*, 22(1), 39–46.

Lusenet, Y. de (1996) Die Europäische Kommission für Bestandserhaltung (ECPA) organisierte ihre erste Konferenz in Leipzig. *Zeitschrift für Bibliothekswesen und Bibliographie*, 43(5), 510–513.

McCarthy, C.K. (1996) Collection development in the access age: all you thought it would be and more. *Journal of Library Administration*, 22(4), 15–32.

McClements, N. and Becker, C. (1996) Writing Web page standards. *College and Research Libraries News*, 57(1), 16–17.

McClung, P.A. (1996) Digital collections inventory report. URL: http://palimpsest.stanford.edu/cpa/reports/mcclung/

McDaniel, E.A. and Epp, R.H. (1995) Fee-based information services: the promises and pitfalls of a new revenue source in higher education. *Cause/Effect*, 18(2), 35–39.

Mackenzie Owen, J. (1996) Preservation of digital materials for libraries. *European Research Libraries Cooperation*, 6(4), 435–452.

McNulty, T. (1996) Libraries and the empowerment of persons with disabilities. *Library Hi Tech*, 14(1), 23–26.

Malinconico, M. (1996) Electronic documents and research libraries. *IFLA Journal*, 22(3), 211–225.

Mandel, C.A. (1996) Enduring access to digital information. Understanding the challenge. *European Research Libraries Cooperation*, 6(4), 453–464.

Marcum, D.B. (1996) The preservation of digital information. *Journal of Academic Librarianship*, 22(6), 451–454.

Martin, K. (1996) Hybrid CD-ROMs. Digital publishing comes of age with the advent of CDs that update directly from the Net. *MacUser*, 12(22), 160–164.

Martin, M.S. (1995) *Collection development and finance: a guide to strategic library-materials budgeting.* Chicago: American Library Association. (Frontiers of Access to Library Materials, 2).

Mehta, A. (1996) Are CD-ROM LANs a thing of the past? *Computers in Libraries*, **16**(8), 64–68.

Melling, M. (1996) The University of Central Lancashire Library: ISO 9000 as part of a total quality programme. In: (ed.) K. Pauleweit *Qualität und Leistung – Bibliotheken auf dem Prüfstand, Beiträge zum Qualitätsmanagement in Bibliotheken*. Berlin: Deutsches Bibliotheksinstitut, pp. 95–106.

Melot, M. (1996) (ed.) *Nouvelles Alexandries: les grands chantiers de bibliothèques dans le monde*. Paris: Electre.

Mendelsohn, L.D. (1995) The chemist's workstation. *Journal of the American Society for Information Science*, **46**(8), 609–641.

Menil, C. (1996) Die soziale Funktion der Bibliotheken im Zeitalter der elektronischen Publikationen. In: Neubauer, K.W. (1996) (ed.), pp. 125–133.

Meredith, B. (1996) Document supply in the electronic world: the publishers' view. *Interlending and Document Supply*, **24**(3), 6–11.

Mess, J.A. (1995) Design considerations for creating a chemical information workstation. *Journal of the American Society for Information Science*, **46**(8), 632–637.

Miksa, F. (1996) The cultural legacy of the 'modern library' for the future. *Journal of Education for Library and Information Science*, **37**(2), 100–119.

Miller, R.H. and Lundstrom, Th. (1996), CD-ROMs in the electronic library: completing the collection management cycle. *Collection Management*, **20**(3/4), 51–72.

Molnar, K.K. and Kletke, M.G. (1996) The impacts on user performance and satisfaction of a voice-based front-end interface for a standard software tool. *International Journal of Human-Computer Studies*, **45**(3), 287–303.

Moore, M.G. (1995) The 1995 distance education research symposium: a research agenda. *American Journal of Distance Education*, **9**(2), 1–6.

Morgan, S. (1996) Developing academic library skills for the future. *Library Review*, **45**(5), 41–53.

Myers, M.J. and Carnes, L.W. (1995) Academic library campaigns: suggestions for fundraisers. *Bottom Line*, **8**(4), 13–16.

Nardi, B.A. and O'Day, V. (1996) Intelligent agents: what we learned at the library. *Libri*, **46**(2), 59–88.

Neubauer, K.W. (1996) (ed.) *Elektronisches Publizieren und Bibliotheken*. Frankfurt am Main: Klostermann. [Also published as *Zeitschrift für Bibliothekswesen und Bibliographie. Sonderhefte*, 65, 1996.]

Neuheuser, H.P. (1996) Gesundheitsvorsorge gegen Schimmelpilz-Kontamination in Archiv, Bibliothek, Museum und Verwaltung. *Bibliothek*, **20**(2), 194–215.

Nicholson, D. and Steele, M. (1996) CATRIONA: a distributed locally-oriented Z39.50 OPAC-based approach to cataloguing the Internet. *Cataloging and Classification Quarterly*, **22**(3–4), 127–142.

Nicholson, H. (1996) Journals of the future: orderly shelves versus networked information. *Serials*, **9**(3), 233–238.

Nisonger, T.E. (1996) Authorship in library acquisitions: practice and theory. *Library Acquisitions*, **20**(4), 395–420.

Nitecki, D.A. (1996) Changing the concept and measure of service quality in academic libraries. *Journal of Academic Librarianship*, **22**(3), 181–190.

O'Connor, B.C. (1996) *Explorations in indexing and abstracting: pointing, virtue and power*. Englewood, CO: Libraries Unlimited. (Library and Information Science Text Series).

Odlyzko, A.M. (1995) Tragic loss or good riddance? The impending demise of traditional scholarly journals. *International Journal of Human-Computer Studies*, 42(3), 71–122.

Okerson, A.S. (1996) The current national copyright debate; its relationship to the work of collections managers. *Journal of Library Administration*, 22(4), 71–84.

Okerson, A.S. and O'Donnell, J.J. (1995) *Scholarly journals at the crossroads: a subversive proposal for electronic publishing*. Washington, DC: Association of Research Libraries; Office for Scientific and Academic Publishing.

Oliver, R. (1996) The influence of instruction and activity on the development of skills in the usage of interactive information systems. *Education for information*, 14(1), 7–17.

Olivieri, R. (1996) Site licences: a new economic paradigm. *Serials*, 9(2), 137–142.

Orr, D. *et al.* (1996) Teaching information literacy skills to remote students through an interactive workshop. *Research Strategies*, 14(4), 169–193.

Otto, H. (1996) Restoration of maps. *INSPEL*, 30(2), 158–161.

Pacey, P. (1995) Teaching user education, learning information skills; or, towards the self-explanatory library. *New Review of Academic Librarianship*, 1(1), 95–104.

Palmer, C.L. (1996) Information work at the boundaries of science: linking library services to research practices. *Library Trends*, 45(2), 165–191.

Pastine, M. (1996) Guide to collection development bibliography. *Collection Management*, 21(3/4), 157–178.

Pauleweit, K. (1996) (ed.) Qualität und Leistung – Bibliotheken auf dem Prüfstand, Beiträge zum Qualitätsmanagement in Bibliotheken. Berlin: Deutsches Bibliotheksinstitut.

Peters, P.E. (1996) From serial publications to document delivery to knowledge management: our fascinating journey, just begun. *Serials Librarian*, 28(1/2), 37–56.

Pica (URL) http://www.pica.nl/docs/en/products/webopc.html

Pierce, S.J. (1995) (ed.) *Weeding and maintenance of reference collections*. New York: Haworth Press.

Place, T.W. and Dijkstra, J. (1995) *Z39.50 or WWW: which way to go?* [Paper presented at the Second Electronic Library and Visual Information Research Conference, De Montfort University, Milton Keynes, UK, May 1995.]

Poll, R. (1996) Possibilities of income generation in German academic libraries. *New Review of Academic Librarianship*, 2, 73–82.

Poll, R. and Te Boekhorst, P. (1996) *Measuring quality: international guidelines for performance measurement in academic libraries*. München: Saur.

Porat, L. and Zehavi, O. (1996) Building academic sites in the Internet. *Information and Librarianship*, 22(1), 21–27.

Portable (1996) document formats. *Digital Publisher*, 1(1), 13–18.

Premium (1995) production of electronic materials through international and uniform methods, http://www/nic.surfnet.nl/surfnet/projects/premium/premium.eng/home.html

Prestamo, A.T. (1996) Virtuality and the future of the printed word: challenges and implications for academic libraries. *Technical Services Quarterly*, 13(3/4), 39–70.

Price, S.P. *et al.* (1996) An overview of electronic document request and delivery research. *Electronic Library*, 14(5), 435–448.

Pritchard, S.M. (1996) Determining quality in academic libraries. *Library Trends*, 44(3), 572–594.

Probst, L.K. (1996) Libraries in an environment of change: changing roles, responsibilities, and perception in the information age. *Journal of Library Administration*, 22(2/3), 7–20.

Radford, M.L. (1996) Communication theory applied to the reference encounter: an analysis of critical incidents. *Library Quarterly*, **66**(2), 123–137.

Raptis, P. and Sitas, A. (1996) Academic libraries in Greece: a new perspective. *Libri*, **46**(2), 100–112.

Recker, I. *et al.* (1996) OSIRIS (Osnabrück Intelligent Research Information System) – ein hyperbase front end system für OPACs. *Bibliotheksdienst*, **30**(5), 833–848.

Regents University of California (1996) Digital collections (DL SunSITE). http://sunsite.Berkeley.EDU/Collections

Reinitzer, S. and Kroller, F. (1996) Langfristige Erhaltung digitaler Dokumente: Datenmigration oder Kulturverlust. *ABI-Technik*, **16**(3), 278–282.

Rider, M.M. (1996) Developing new roles for paraprofessionals in cataloging. *Journal of Academic Librarianship*, **22**(1), 26–32.

Riggs, D.E. (1996) Editorial. Creating and managing change: some controversy, some level-headedness. *College and Research Libraries*, **57**(5), 402–404.

Risher, C. (1996) Libraries, copyright and the electronic environment. *Electronic Library*, **14**(10), 449–452.

Roselle, A. (1996) The case study method: a learning tool for practising librarians and information specialists. *Library Review*, **45**(4), 30–38.

Rouhet, M. (1996) (ed.) *Les nouvelles technologies dans les bibliothèques*. Paris: Electre.

Rowley, J. (1996a) *The basics of information systems*. London: Library Association Publishing.

Rowley, J. (1996b) Libraries and the electronic information marketplace. *Library Review*, **45**(7), 6–18.

Ruppert, H.A. and Sühl-Strohmenger, W. (1996) Kooperation beim Angebot von elektronischer Fachinformation und die Erwartung der Nutzer in Universitäten. *Zeitschrift für Bibliothekswesen und Bibliographie*, **43**(5), 423–440.

Saffady, W. (1996) The availability and cost of online search services. *Library Technology Reports*, **32**(3), 337–340.

St Clair, G. (1996). *Entrepreneurial librarianship: the key to effective information services management*. New York: Bowker-Saur.

Schmidt, W.R. (1996) Choosing the preserve: towards a cooperative strategy for longterm access to the intellectual heritage. International conference, March 1996, Haus des Buches, Leipzig. *ABI-Technik*, **16**(2), 183–186.

Schneider, K.G. (1996) Z39.50: beyond your wildest dreams. *American Libraries*, **27**(6), 86.

Schuyler, M. (1996) Toward a GUI-based OPAC. *Computers in Libraries*, **16**(9), 26–28.

Shaughnessy, T. W. (1995) (ed.) Perspectives on quality in libraries, *Library Trends*, **44**(3), 459–678.

Silverstein, C. and Shieber, M. (1996) Predicting individual book use for off-site storage using decision trees. *Library Quarterly*, **66**(3), 266–293.

Simpson, D.B. (1996) Electronic resources: a new set of questions for resource sharing efforts. *Collection Management*, **21**(1), 57–64.

Skinner R. (1996) Collection bits: the Internet as a library resource. *Collection Management*, **21**(3/4), 121–138.

Skreslet, P.Y. (1996) A newer world information order: reaching for greater justice in the global flow of information. *Alexandria*, **8**(2), 85–96.

Sloan, S. (1996) The Virtual Pathfinder: a World Wide Web guide to library research. *Computers in Libraries*, **16**(4), 53–54.

Smith, N.A. (1995) One – OPAC Network in Europe: taking a further step towards a Europe-wide information network. *Program*, **29**(4), 427–432.

Snow, R. (1996) Wasted words. The written collection development policy and the academic library. *Journal of Academic Librarianship*, **22**(3), 191–194.

Snyder, H.L. (1996) Providing access to rare books and manuscript collections and services in a time of change: the electronic revolution. *IFLA Journal*, **22**(2), 115–120.

Snyder, L. (1995) The human touch: its future in a world of bibliographic instruction technology. *Catholic Library World*, **65**(3), 17–18.

Soper, M.E. (1996) Cataloging electronic journals; the University of Virginia experience. *Serials Librarian*, **28**(3/4), 263–268.

Stelling, P. (1996) Student to student: training peer advisors to provide BI. *Research Strategies*, **14**(1), 50–55.

Stephens, K. (1996) The role of the library in distance learning: a review of UK, North American and Australian literature. *New Review of Academic Librarianship*, **2**, 205–234.

Stoffle, C.J. (1996) The emergence of education and knowledge management as major functions of the digital library. (Follett Lecture Series) (Nov.). http://www.ukoln.ac.uk/follett/stoffle/paper.html

Stoffle, C.J. and Williams, K. (1995) The instructional program and responsibilities of the teaching library. *New Directions for Higher Education*, (90), 63–75.

Stoffle, C.J. *et al.* (1996) Choosing our futures. *College and Research Libraries*, **57**(3), 213–225.

Stolt, W. (1996) Managing electronic resources: public service considerations in a technology environment. *Collection Management*, **21**(1), 17–28.

Strange, B. (1995) Katalogisering av elektroniske dokumenter og Internettressurser ved Informatikbiblioteket. *Synopsis*, **26**(6), 337–343.

Sulaiman, M. and Meadows, J. (1995) Icons and OPACs. *New Library World*, **96**(1121), 11–14.

Sweeney R. (1996) Retrospective conversion of library catalogues in UK institutions of higher education: a quantitative analysis. *Library Review*, **45**(2), 52–57.

Sykes, J.M. (1996) SCONUL and quality assurance. *Library Review*, **45**(5), 17–22.

Task Force on Archiving of Digital Information (1996) *Preserving digital information: final report and recommendations, May 1996.* http://www.rlg.org/ArchTF/

Te Boekhorst, P. (1996) Qualitätsmanagement und wissenschaftliche Bibliothek, ein unüberbrückbarer Gegensatz? In: Pauleweit, K. (1996) (ed.), pp. 173–180.

Tenopir, C. (1995) Authors and readers: the keys to success or failure for electronic publishing. *Library Trends*, **43**(4), 571–591.

Thomasson, G. and Fjällbrant, N. (1996) EDUCATE: The design and development of a networked end user education program. *Education for Information*, **14**(4), 295–304.

Tomaiuolo, N.G. (1996) End user perceptions of a graphical user interface for bibliographic searching: an exploratory study. *Computers in Libraries*, **16**(1), 33–38.

Tonta, Y. (1996) Scholarly communication and the use of networked information resources. *IFLA Journal*, **22**(3), 240–245.

Turko, K. (1996) Preservation activities in Canada. A unifying theme in a decentralised country. *European Research Libraries Cooperation* **6**(2), 117–147.

Tuten, J.H. and Jones, B. (1995) *Allocation formulas in academic libraries.* (Clip note #22). Chicago: Association of College and Research Libraries.

Tuttle, M. (1996) *Newsletter on serials pricing issues.* Ed. M. Tuttle<tuttle@gibbs.oit.unc.edu> [Subscribe to <prices@listserv.oit.unc.edu>].

Urban, L. (1995) Az egyetemi konyvtarak fejlesztesenek terigenyei. [Space requirements of the development of university libraries]. *Konyvtari Figyelo*, **41**(3), 406–418.

van den Hoogen, H.J.M. (1996a) Quality management at a university library, plan and execution at the University of Limburg. In: Pauleweit, K. (1996), pp. 130–138.

van den Hoogen, H.J.M. (1996b) Quality and customer orientation. In: Pauleweit, K. (1996), pp. 139–149.

vander Meer, F. and Rike, G.E. (1996) Multimedia: meeting the demand for user education with a self-instructional tutorial. *Research Strategies*, **14**(3), 145–158.

vander Meer, P. and Poole, H. (1996) The connection between library use and use of campus computer applications. *Electronic Library*, **14**(4), 339–346.

Vitiello, G. (1996) The production and the marketing of national bibliographic services in Europe. *Alexandria*, **8**(2), 97–116.

Vogel, K.D. (1996) Integrating electronic resources into collection development policies. *Collection Management*, **21**(2), 65–76.

Voorbij, H.J. (1996) Are Dutch academic libraries keeping up with research material? The coverage of foreign academic publications in Dutch libraries. *Alexandria*, **8**(3), 189–204.

Waetjen, H.J. (1996) Financing higher education libraries in Germany. *New Review of Academic Librarianship*, **2**, 11–26.

Wallace, P.M. (1996) Optimizing serials access in the online catalog. *Serials Librarian*, **28**(3–4), 269–274.

Walton, G. *et al.* (1995) Training needs for staff competencies in a quality library service. Relevance of the IMPEL Project. *LIBER Quarterly*, **5**(4), 389–401.

Ward, S. (1996) Systeme zur Entscheidungsunterstützung und Leistungsindicatoren. In: Pauleweit, K. (1996), pp. 107–129.

Ward, M.L. (1996) The future of the human indexer. *Journal of Librarianship and Information Science*, **28**(4), 217–226.

Ward, S.E. (1996) Document delivery: the perspective of industrial information services. *Interlending and Document Supply*, **24**(2), 4–10.

Werner, A. (1996) Serials acquisition: selection. An overview of criteria. *Serials Librarian*, **29**(1/2), 153–162.

West, R. (1996) Changing costs of information in the networked world. *British Library Journal*, 25–30.

White, H.S. (1995) *At the crossroads: librarians on the Information Superhighway*. Englewood, CO: Libraries Unlimited.

Wiessner, M. (ed.) (1995) *Electronic Data Interchange (EDI). Beiträge zur elektronischen Kommunikation zwischen Buchhandel und Bibliothek*. Berlin: Deutsches Bibliotheksinstitut. (DBI-Materialien, 144).

Wiessner, M. (1996) Impact of EDI on the acquisitions process. *Library Administration and Management*, **10**(3), 155–160.

Wilkinson, J. (1996) External funding sources: income generation in UK academic libraries. *New Review of Academic Librarianship*, **2**, 69–72.

Will, B. (1996) California: library information technologies. *Library Hi Tech*, **14**(2/3), 57–67.

Wilson, K.A. (1995) Outsourcing copy cataloging and physical processing: a review of Blackwell's outsourcing services for the J. Hugh Jackson Library at Stanford University. *Library Resources and Technical Services*, **39**(4), 359–383.

Wilson, L.A. (1995) Building the user-centered library. *RQ*, **34**(3), 297–302.

Wise, K. and Perushek, D.E. (1996) Linear goal programming for academic library acquisitions allocations. *Library Acquisitions*, **20**(3), 311–327.

Wood, R.J. (1996) The Conspectus: a collection analysis and development success. *Library Acquisitions*, **20**(4), 429–454.

Wusteman, J. (1996) Electronic journal formats. *Program*, **30**(4), 319–344.

Xu, H. (1996) The impact of automation on job requirements and qualifications for catalogers and reference librarians in academic libraries. *Library Resources and Technical Services*, **40**(1), 9–31.

Public libraries 4

Raymond Astbury

Public libraries are currently undergoing a process of transformation as they adapt to the impact of a complex of changes and developments in the postmodern environment: ideological and political; cultural and social; economic and technological (Black and Muddiman, 1997).

Public libraries and the business ethos

Public librarians are facing the dilemma of having to choose between mission and market (Blokland, 1996). Reforms, which governments are implementing across the whole spectrum of public sector organizations in many parts of the world, embrace their structure, financial management, commercial practices, planning and reporting, human resources management and industrial relations (Willard, 1995).

The international literature of librarianship indicates that librarians have adopted the management strategies and techniques of the business sector and the language of commerce wholesale (Seay *et al.*, 1996). The library's public, formerly identified as readers/users/patrons/clients, is now increasingly referred to as customers.

A British researcher has published a critique of the management changes in the public library which questions the validity and appropriateness of applying the values, strategies, methodologies and terminologies of the private sector, and of introducing the ethos of the new managerialism, to an institution whose *raison d'être* is to respond to the needs of citizens and communities as much as to the wants and demands of customers (Usherwood, 1996).

The application of performance indicators is generally pervasive within the library world. German public librarianship, for example, is preoccupied with discussions about the introduction of new methods in public sector management (public libraries in Germany are often the first public sector organizations to experience the application of the new management techniques); about the restructuring of public libraries to create flatter, smaller, more flexible administrations (paralleling the fitter and leaner, downsized organizations of the commercial world); and about performance indicators and performance measurement (Borchardt, 1995, 1996).

A three-year project measuring public library performance is in progress in Norway (Nilsen, 1996). In the USA, a management specialist has singled out public libraries as one of the few local government services which engages in performance measurement and which does so more meaningfully than most of the other services (Altman, 1996a; Ammons, 1995).

Over 90% of the librarian respondents to a survey in Britain thought that the setting of output or outcome standards or measures had increased during the past five years (Usherwood, 1996). This trend will now intensify because the Department of National Heritage's Public Library Review report, *Reading for the future* (1997), requires every library authority in England to produce by April of each year a Public Library Plan for the coming year which must include key performance indicators and targets.

From Australia to the People's Republic of China practices such as benchmarking and assessment processes for the comparative measurement of library systems are being consolidated (Xiaoqin, 1996; Prestell, 1997, personal communication).

Value for money for taxpayers and customers is the motive declared by the governments which are most active in promoting and imposing the implementation of management reforms and restructuring in the public sector. This was the phrase used by the City Council of Wellington, New Zealand, when implementing the recommendation of a management consultant which requires the library staff to be cut from 146 full-time equivalents to 93 over a two-year period. The Council claims that downsizing will improve rather than worsen services to the public due to the introduction of new technology, including self-service issue systems and remote access to the library's online public access catalogue (OPAC) (Altman, 1996b).

In Britain, the Audit Commission, a statutory body whose members are appointed by government, but which is independent of both national and local government, has undertaken a value-for-money study of the public library service. In the early stages of this study the researchers were surprised by the sheer range and diversity of the activities undertaken by public libraries and by the difficulty of obtaining reliable evidence of the effectiveness of the service, especially in respect of all the purposes served. They were 'unclear where exactly public libraries see their mission and priorities' (Kennedy, 1997). However, within their differing cultural contexts, librarians are in fact engaged in a process of redefining (if to date inconclusively) the key missions and priorities of the public library in order to present a more sharply focused image of the service to the politicians and to the public (Hare, 1996; Scheepstra, 1996; Skot-Hansen, 1996).

Usherwood (1996) advocates a 'social process audit', which assesses social costs and benefits, as being more appropriate to an institution which the UNESCO *Public library manifesto* of 1994 proclaims as a 'living force for education, culture and information' whose services should be provided on the basis of equality of access for all. The British Library has awarded a grant to Sheffield University to undertake such a social audit of a sample of libraries in urban and rural areas. Research already completed, distinct from this grant award, in a community which experienced the almost total temporary closure of the library service during an eight-week strike by the staff, reveals that for the great majority of users 'the public library is a service of inestimable value, enhancing quality of life and, for many people, fulfilling an essential need that no other pursuit or activity satisfies' (Proctor *et al.*, 1996).

Compulsory competitive tendering (CCT)

In several countries governments require local authorities to put their services, including library services, out to tender. This policy is variously referred to as market testing, compulsory competitive tendering, contracting out, or outsourcing. The stated objectives of CCT are to achieve better services at less cost, or better services at the same cost, or the same services at less cost. The process involves a division between the purchaser (the library authority) and the provider of the service (the contractor).

In the UK the contracting out of book supply and servicing requirements has been a feature of the public library scene for many years and has resulted in the provision of cost-effective services. But CCT may require the commercial providers (or the inhouse library staff if they are allowed to bid for the contract) to deliver the service directly to the public under contract to the local authority. Thus individual departments or branch libraries, or indeed the whole of the library service, might be delivered by staff employed by the commercial provider.

In the UK, after several pilot schemes for public library service delivery were carried out and reviewed, a consultant's report concluded that CCT for public libraries was feasible but neither appropriate nor cost effective (Department of National Heritage, 1995). The most recent government statement on CCT for public libraries confirms that it does not intend – for the present – to require local authorities to introduce CCT for library services (Department of National Heritage, 1997).

Two local authorities in the UK (both of them in London) have contracted out library services: Wandsworth tendered its bibliographical services to a successful inhouse bid; from 1994 Brent tendered two branch libraries, also to a successful inhouse bid. Neither of these authorities has subsequently extended CCT in the library service.

The charitable trust model for public library management is also favoured by the British government. The London Borough of Hounslow has decided to devolve the whole of its Leisure Services Directorate, which includes library services, to an independent charitable trust. In this model, the local authority remains the main funding body, sets objectives and monitors the service, but the law does not permit the local council to have a majority of elected representatives on the board of the non-profit company running the trust.

There is a prototype for this model in the Netherlands, where most of the public libraries are funded by local government but organized as private foundations or trusts, though some of the larger libraries are directly under local authority control. The library boards of the trusts usually lay down policy in broad terms while delegating freedom of management to the library director.

In Sweden there has been a vigorous and highly contentious debate within the library profession and among politicians on the issue of CCT for public libraries (Thomas, 1993, 1996). Different types of contractor have been used: a business group; a group of booksellers in cooperation with the library and local voluntary education associations (a partnership approach); a local bookseller; the Workers' Educational Association; the National Association of Tenants Savings and Building Society (HSB); and in one case a Liberal Party organization. Some other examples involved the members of Friends of the Library groups and other voluntary organizations providing library services without pay. Workers and voluntary associations have played a role in the origin and early development of public libraries in Sweden, building societies have not; and the appropriateness of involving groups with political affiliations in direct delivery of services has been questioned.

Research in Sweden indicates that CCT has not resulted in reduced costs or better services. Indeed, it has been shown that in the key areas of purchasing procedures and accounting, the management is inefficient (Thomas, 1996). About ten library services, mostly branch libraries, are still being provided by outside contractors, but the implementation of CCT as a lively political issue has receded.

By contrast, an emotive, sharply polarized, and highly politicized debate about CCT is in progress in the State of Victoria, Australia (Garner, 1995; Anderson, 1996). The Victorian Local Government (Competitive Tendering) Act 1994 requires each local government authority to market test not particular services but a percentage of its total budget: in 1994/5, 20%; in 1995/6, 30%; in 1996/7, 50% (King, 1996; Pryor and Lee, 1996). Very little research trialing was undertaken prior to these targets being set. There has since been a case study about the outsourcing of non-core services in one library system (Macvean, 1996). Victoria is the only state government which has as yet introduced CCT for library services (Martin, 1997, personal communication).

A more pragmatic view on this question of the outsourcing of services is presented by those librarians who stress that, though public libraries are still multipurpose agencies providing educational, cultural, recreational and informational services, they must now identify and prioritize their core or basic activities within this broad spectrum. At a time of financial cutbacks, with the public demanding multimedia materials, access to the Internet and more customized services, more rationalization, cooperation and outsourcing of non-core activities to specialized companies would make public libraries more efficient and effective (Scheepstra, 1996).

In the Netherlands many libraries are currently moving away from the traditional system whereby local authorities provide the library management with an annual revenue based upon the estimate of expenditure. It will be replaced by a new kind of contract arrangement (budget financing), whereby the local authority agrees a contract with the library board, ensuring the provision of finance over the specified period of some three or four years, based upon the library's achievement of agreed targets. This system facilitates more flexible management, but also necessitates more accurate costing of services. If the library does not meet its targets, the finance provided by the local authority will be reduced. However, if it exceeds its target, it is most probable that the finance will not be increased (Riesthuis-Groenland, 1996, personal communication).

Public libraries and economic development

Librarians in most countries do not anticipate that they will be able to fund the public library as a main player in the digital age from tax revenue. Indeed, often they have an increasingly difficult task in funding their current range and level of provision solely from the income generated by taxes. The competition between local authority services for funding is intensifying. Public librarians have to work harder to convince local politicians of the service's value to the community. At the Public Library Association (PLA) of America's Public Policy for Public Libraries Section (PLA, PPPLS) meeting in March 1996, a city manager from California revealed how city managers in the state perceived libraries not as essential 'public good' agencies but 'as cost centers and discretionary services that drain the municipal general fund' (Engel, 1996).

An international comparison of public library statistics reveals that of the wide range of services provided 'the predominance of the book media, the inter-library lending features, and the strong children's service are universal' (Hanratty and Sumsion, 1996). The same source indicates that per capita expenditure (with the caveat that differing accounting conventions and range of services can significantly distort the comparisons) is highest in the Scandinavian countries, followed by Canada, New Zealand, and the Netherlands at the second level, the UK and USA at the third, with Australia, France and Germany coming below these countries. Membership percentages range from 6% to over 50%.

In the USA in the early 1990s public library services had to weather the economic recession and during 1994 they had to absorb the effects of a nationwide freezing of income from tax revenue. By contrast, public library budgets are currently 'relatively healthy across the board'. However, these budgets are stretched to meet current demands on public library services just at a time when the libraries are having to meet the sharply rising technology-related costs of their efforts to establish themselves as electronic centres in the community (St. Lifer, 1996, 1997).

It is against this background that librarians have begun to address the issue of the 'value' of the public library in terms of the ways in which libraries contribute to the economic development of the local community. It is known that the presence of libraries in local communities has an impact upon the public's use of commercial retail outlets (Usherwood, 1996). An Australian management consultant asserts that politicians and librarians greatly underestimate both the current and potential economic value of public libraries and suggests that currently for every A$1 of cost there is at least A$2 of benefit created (Haratsis, 1995).

The question that some librarians are now beginning to address is: 'What kind of dollar impact does your public library have on your community?' (Mielke, 1996). The PLA has contracted researchers to develop a cost-benefit analysis model to facilitate assessment of the economic benefits that derive directly and indirectly from investment in libraries and their services. Similarly, a firm of consultants in New Zealand is developing a cost-benefit methodology for assessing the value of library outputs (Coopers and Lybrand, 1996).

Economists globally have identified small businesses as a growth sector for economic regeneration and employment opportunities and it has been suggested that public libraries should prioritize their services to business in this sector (Waters, 1996). The role of the library in the economic development of rural communities and their potential as information providers within cooperative networks in the community in the digital age is beginning to be discussed in the professional literature of the developed and developing economies (Walzer and Gruidl, 1996; Waters, 1996; Xiaoqin, 1996). In China, public librarians have evolved the strategy of feeding key readers in rural areas with information for economic and agricultural development which is then cascaded down to the illiterate peasants (Xiaoqin, 1996). Thus the role of the library in economic development can involve a wide range of activities from the encouragement of literacy to the provision of specialized business services (Scheepstra, 1996). However, even in countries with highly developed economies and library systems, many libraries still do not provide focused information services for the business community (PLA, 1996).

Against a background of financial constraints, the perceived need to provide new and 'value added' high-cost services, to maintain high-quality book and multimedia provision and to implement social justice policies for the delivery of specialized services to minority groups, raises the question of which services might be defined as core or basic and which might be categorized as fee based. This is becoming an increasingly divisive issue within the library profession in various parts of the world.

The American Library Association (ALA) policy is opposed to fees, but the PLA's Fee-Based Services Committee document, *Fees for public libraries: an issue statement*, which has been accepted by the PLA board, attempts to address decisions about fees policies on grounds of pragmatism rather than principle. This caused considerable controversy when it was presented at the 'Price is right' programme at the PLA Conference, Portland 1996 (Berry, 1996; Engel, 1996). Elsewhere, an ideological commitment to the 'no charge' principle, because of the fear that fees for special services might gradually spread to core services, is thought by some commentators to hinder the development of a possible symbiosis between 'fee and free' services which might primarily be to the benefit of the latter (Kristensen, 1996). In Chinese public libraries fees are charged for selective dissemination of information (SDI) services, newspaper cuttings services, and for special events and training sessions in libraries (Xiaoqin, 1996).

Fundraising campaigns and commercial sponsorship programmes for library buildings and services are more typical of the library scene in the USA than anywhere else. The political technique of library organized public referenda, either to challenge local authority plans to cut the library's tax revenue, or as a means of validating the raising of capital or revenue finance by the issue of public bonds, is unique to the USA (Hall, 1996). The number of library systems in the USA engaging in fundraising is rising and currently about half of them do so. These libraries raised 25% more money in 1996 than in 1995. Even so, income generated by fee-based services and fundraising accounts for only a very small percentage of the revenue income of libraries and is less than that generated by the combined income from fines, rental collections, and cost recovery charges (St. Lifer, 1996, 1997).

Overall, the statistics relating to the British public library indicate that the last decade was one of stability or gradual decline, with expenditure reaching a plateau in real terms in 1994–5. Income generation has increased by 60% over ten years and by 25% over the past five years, with income from fines and fees accelerating in the past two years. However, income from fines and fees still only averages £1 per library user per annum over the whole of the UK. Income from audio, and especially from video rental collections, has risen even more dramatically, but the figure is still small in absolute terms (Robertson, 1996; Sumsion *et al.*, 1996). Income generation accounts for a greater proportion of the annual budget in some countries, for example, in the Netherlands where 20% of income consists of subscriptions and lending charges.

Despite the statistical evidence which indicates a general financial stability in the British public library environment over a decade, the professional literature and public press continues to refer to a 'funding crisis' in the system. This perception is engendered by the fact that budgets have been and continue to be stretched by the provision of new services and in meeting increased public demands. There has been a large reduction in the number of service points open less than ten hours a week, a significant reduction in the number of libraries open more than 45 hours a week, creeping deprofessionalization of the service with a reduction of 16.1% in professional staff per head of population over ten years, and a continuing decline, compensated for by an increase in the number of unqualified library assistants. A minority of library authorities has suffered highly publicized severe cutbacks; present indications are that expenditure cuts planned for 1997–8 will, if realized, result in a further general erosion of the service, with some authorities experiencing severe cuts (Sumsion, 1996; Sumsion *et al.*, 1996; Daines, 1997a).

Legislation, reorganization and restructuring

The UNESCO *Manifesto* 1994 asserts that, 'The public library shall in principle be free of charge.' This principle is everywhere under challenge. Traniello (1994) discusses the role of European library legislation in codifying and regulating the principle of free basic library services for end users and in granting discretionary powers to local authorities to levy charges. There is no uniformity in Europe in respect of charging for basic and other services, irrespective of the existence or absence of library legislation. However, a current trend is the introduction of registration or subscription charges for membership of a public library. Registration fees are charged in the Netherlands and Belgium and increasingly so in France and Germany. In Germany, with the exceptions of Frankfurt, Nurnberg, Leipzig and Dresden, most of the metropolitan public libraries require users to pay a registration fee (Kamp, 1996, personal communication).

In the UK the government has recently reaffirmed its existing statutory commitment to the provision of free book lending and book reference services to end users (Department of National Heritage, 1997).

Finland is exceptional in Europe in that its library legislation of 1992, while not making it compulsory for local authorities to provide a public library (though all currently do so), obliges libraries to allow the borrowing and reference use of all kinds of materials, print, audio-visual, sheet music, etc., free of charge. A new Finnish Library Act is in preparation and is expected to become law during 1997. It confirms this provision and also for the first time makes it mandatory for local authorities to establish and maintain public libraries, which will be categorized as one of the basic services at the local level. Libraries may charge end users for accessing the Internet but at present none do so. Internet services are now available in 60% of Finnish public libraries (up from 15% in 1995). The government's three-year project *Towards the Finnish information society* includes a budget of ten million FIM for 1996. Another government-funded project, *The house of knowledge*, encourages public libraries to introduce and promote the public use of networks for the provision of cultural material (Haavisto, 1996, personal communication; Laatu, 1996, personal communication).

Historically, Swedish library authorities have provided public library services free of charge without national library legislation. However, the first Swedish Library Act passed the legislature in December 1996 and under its terms local authorities are required to provide public libraries, with free borrowing and reference use of printed materials, including books borrowed from other libraries (the interlending system in Sweden includes the university sector), with a strong recommendation that the borrowing of audio-visual materials and access to the Internet should also be free to end users (Östling, 1996, personal communication).

The Library Association of Ireland consistently opposes charges to end users for library services, but the Irish government leaves the decision about charging book borrowers to the local authorities. Twenty-seven of the 32 library authorities do require adult book borrowers either to pay a registration fee or to pay a fee per book issued; some require them to do both. Some authorities exempt old age pensioners and the unemployed/unwaged. Twelve authorities require children to pay a registration fee and one requires them to pay a fee per book issued (Irish Library Council, 1996; Ronayne, 1996, personal communication).

Klinec (1991) indicates that in central and eastern Europe the process of transition to a market economy, combined with reductions in funds for public libraries, is creating a situation in which charges are imposed on end users for formerly free public library services. Most public libraries in central Europe are experiencing reduced numbers of users, book issues, book and periodical acquisitions, service points, trained and untrained staff, and reduced income. Wherever library staff are classed as being part of the cultural sector their rates of pay tend to be lower than the national average.

New public library legislation is in preparation or progressing through parliament in several countries, including Latvia and Slovenia. In Hungary a new Library Act is at an advanced stage and should very shortly become law. It strategically reorientates the national library service within the new market economy. Under the terms of this new statute, anyone may use all the documents in public libraries free of charge, but in order to borrow books readers from fourteen years of age upwards must pay a registration fee. The amount of this fee is decided by the local authority, but the Act recommends that it should not be more than the average price of the printed materials acquired in the previous year. Registered users must also pay for borrowing audio-visual materials and for accessing the Internet.

Eronica and Semskov (1993) assert that in the new Russia only radicals remain the ardent supporters of free-of-charge services. However, the Federal Library Law passed in December 1994 stipulates (Article 7, 'Rights of Library Users') that basic library services must be free of charge to the end users, but readers are asked on registration to pay the cost of the registration card. A more serious issue for librarians in Russia is the long delays they are experiencing, in common with other public sector workers, in the payment of their relatively low salaries (Roberts, 1996, personal communication).

As new legislation directly or indirectly affecting public libraries is planned, the issue of free or user-pays basic or core library services is debated afresh and laws tend to be drafted to make charging policies more permissive. In Canada, for example, most provinces do not at present have user charges for basic library services. Alberta law does permit libraries to charge for borrowing materials (Calgary and Edmonton do so) but not for using the library. Quebec law allows libraries to charge for membership, but the amount charged varies from library to library. Newfoundland regulations do not prohibit charging, but libraries do not currently charge users (Robinson, 1997, personal communication).

In Ontario, the Local Control of Public Libraries Act of 15 January 1997 guarantees free access to libraries, free use of materials in libraries, free borrowing of printed materials by residents, and free borrowing of special format materials for residents with disabilities. In parallel with this library law, the Municipal Act (amended under a Savings and Restructuring Act of 30 January 1997, whose intention is to achieve public sector savings through restructuring) now gives greater autonomy to the municipal library boards for the management and funding of libraries (Langford, 1996; Larmer, 1997; Mushinski, 1997). But at the same time provincial funding for municipal libraries is being phased out, so that whereas in 1995–96 the province contributed $30 million towards the operating costs of Ontario's 1,000 libraries, by 1997–98 this will be reduced to $18 million, and in the following year it will disappear. The more autonomous municipalities face the challenge of raising funds from taxes or other sources to make up the shortfalls in their library budgets (Riley, 1997). However, the province will continue to fund partnership initiatives, the province-wide network of shared resources, and the telecommunication links connecting Ontario's libraries to each other and to the global networks (Ontario, 1997).

In the so-called underdeveloped and developing countries membership charges are sometimes introduced essentially in order to ration scarce print resources. In Zimbabwe, this is the case in Bulawayo Public Library, and even applies to a library set up by donations through Book Aid International in Gwanda (Olden, 1995; Kristensen, 1996).

Less than half the 26 states within the Union of India have enacted library legislation, though model statutes have been published in the professional journals to encourage them to do so. The key factors are the unwillingness of the state governments to take on the financial responsibility for the provision of public libraries and the absence of a groundswell of public demand. Outside the state and municipal library structure of provision, there is a number of religious and charitable organizations which provide library services in return for a small membership charge (Subbarao, 1995).

In the UK a major reorganization of local government is underway which, if the current proposals are realized, will result in the existence of 208 public library authorities by comparison with the previous 167. In England a number of new unitary authorities will be created by abolishing some county councils and by some other counties losing territory; public library authorities will be replaced by unitary authorities in Scotland and Wales; Northern Ireland will either continue to have five Education and Library Boards or these will be reduced to three (Daines, 1996b). One of the key issues in this reorganization is whether or not all the new unitary authorities will have the critical mass of population to maintain high quality library services.

Within these reorganized authorities, departmental restructuring, an existing trend in local government is continuing. Library departments are being merged into large directorates of, for example, leisure and amenities or culture or education. Usherwood (1996) suggests that it would be more appropriate for libraries to become part of directorates or departments with a broad information provision role, embracing parts of the education and arts and culture functions of the local authority. Within the large new directorates staff may be required to operate across former departmental boundaries. The head of the library service may be a librarian who also manages programmes outside the library sector or a non-librarian who is responsible for a range of services including libraries. Within such a corporate culture management abilities become as or more important than professional skills (Kinnell, 1996). These trends of departmental mergers and the development of interchangeable management skills are noticeable in a number of countries from Norway (Nilsen, 1995) and Sweden (Haggstrom, 1995) to the USA (Klenitz, 1996).

Closures of school libraries in some states of the USA and the need to maximize cost effectiveness in providing local library services is motivating mergers between school and public libraries. There is a certain irony in this accelerating trend as historically the public library in the USA strove to free itself from association with the schoolhouse and some communities have done so only very recently (Goldberg, 1996). In a number of countries reduced expenditure on school and college libraries is placing more pressure on public libraries as students make greater use of their services.

In the UK legislation which frees schools from the financial and management control of local authority education departments, combined with financial pressures upon the currently reorganized local authorities, makes schools library services, whether provided through education or public library departments, especially vulnerable. The government's local management of schools (LMS) policy means that schools are free to buy in to the local authorities schools library services (SLS) or to purchase services elsewhere (Heeks, 1996). Some SLS have persuaded sufficient numbers of schools to buy in to their services in order to remain viable within the customary local authority framework; some have closed down and others have set up as 'stand-alone' business units (*School Librarian*, 1996).

Public libraries and the information society

In Queensland, Australia, a Libraries Working Group of the Cultural Ministers Council has commissioned a series of reports which together provide comprehensive and detailed coverage of a range of themes, including information about the users and use made of public libraries, and issues relating to the positioning of the public library within the education, cultural, and digital environments (Broadband Services Export Group, 1995; Catlin, 1996; Mercer and Smith, 1996). In February 1997 the federal government announced that A$2.2 million had been allocated to support a number of projects to enhance public access to online services, such as the Internet, in public libraries and other public institutions. This is the first time federal funding has been provided for public libraries (Prestel, 1996, personal communication).

The wide-ranging and important Benton Foundation survey in the USA (Benton, 1996a), financed by the W.K. Kellogg Foundation, compares the opinions of library leaders with those of the public about the future of the public library in the digital age. The public agreed with the view of the majority of librarians that the library of the future should be a hybrid institution providing both digital and printed resources and with a strong commitment to bridging the gap between the 'information haves and have-nots' by the provision of equal and free access to information. But the 18–24 years old age group are the least enthusiastic about maintaining the public space of library buildings into the future and about the role of the library in a digital age, preferring the money they pay in library tax to be used instead for the purchase of digital information for accessing in their homes. Non-users are the least enthusiastic about paying increased taxes for public library services.

Moreover, there are significant contradictions and ambivalencies (especially when the views of the respondents in the main survey are compared with those of the participants in focus groups) in the respondents' views about the function of libraries, about the role of librarians in the digital age, and about the public willingness to pay increased taxes to enable the public library to provide the range of services which the majority perceive as desirable. The report highlights the fact that Americans continue to have a 'love affair' with their public libraries, but also emphasizes that many would also be willing to have them functioning merely as information archives and museums staffed by volunteer retirees.

Libraries are perceived to be at a crossroads in their history as to whether they have a central place in the electronic society or remain on the margins and whether they remain able to attract the funds to provide the print resources and the range of programmes still required by many of the public. At issue is the very idea of a public culture. The whole nexus of public institutions and community networks needs to define their relative and collective roles in forming alliances and resource-sharing networks in the expanding information marketplace.

The American Library Association (ALA) is vigorously promoting the idea that the 100,000 public libraries in the USA are the nation's information infrastructure.

This campaign is being waged under the slogan 'Equity on the Information Superhighway' and was launched at a summit meeting, 'A Nation Connected', in February 1966. This provided the model for summit meetings across the nation at which librarians and experts from the public and private sectors discussed the key issues surrounding the protection of the public interest in citizens having equality of access to information in the digital age (Turock, 1996).

The United States National Commission on Libraries and Information Science *Final report* (Bertot, 1996) reveals that American public libraries have made significant progress in connecting to the Internet. Between 1994 and 1996 Internet connectivity increased 113% overall from 20.9% to 44.6%, and by March 1997 it is projected that Internet connectivity may exceed 90%, though only about half these libraries will provide public access services. In general libraries do not charge for their public access Internet services. The Commission expresses concern at discrepancies in provision, especially the lack of current and projected provision in libraries serving smaller communities (Bertot *et al.*, 1996). McClure *et al.* (1996) outline the possible roles of public libraries in the provision of Internet/National Information Infrastructure based services.

The implementation of the Telecommunications Act of 1996 and the public interest issues involved in ensuring that all American citizens have equal access to information in the digital age are addressed in a series of Benton Foundation publications (Benton, 1996b). The American government's goal of connecting every library and school to the Information Superhighway by the year 2000 was furthered by the Federal-State Joint Board of the Federal Communications Commission's endorsement in November 1996 of key ALA proposals. It voted in favour of discounts for telecommunication services, ranging from 20% to 90% for libraries and schools, with even greater discounts for those in rural and low-income communities (Flagg, 1996). Other issues relating to the Information Superhighway include censorship, intellectual property and copyright. Public library policy documents which regulate the age at which minors unaccompanied by adults may access Internet services and which require adults to agree not to access obscene or violent material together with the use of cyber blocking software, are becoming more common (Bedfordshire Libraries, 1996).

In the USA, the ALA is a lead plaintiff in a case challenging the legality of the Communications Decency Act (CDA) 1996 which prohibits the transmission of 'indecent' material, defined in very broad terms, on the Internet. The Supreme Court will finally rule on this issue in the spring of 1997 (American Civil Liberties Union, ACLU, 1997a). But at least eleven states have passed Internet censorship legislation in the past two years and others have bills under consideration or pending, affecting a wide range of online speech and content (ACLU, 1997b). ACLU takes action against those libraries using software which either blocks out material without specifying what has been censored or which prevents adult users, or minors with parental permission, from modifying or switching off the programme while surfing the Web (ACLU, 1997c).

In Singapore the government took the lead in developing a strategic plan, the Library 2000 Vision, to create a network of national, public, academic, school and special libraries. All the publicly funded libraries will be linked in a computer network, with their resources accessible from homes, offices and libraries. Their collections will be developed within a coordinated strategy and their services will be market orientated (Sabaratnam, 1996).

In December 1995, 53% of the UK library authorities had some form of Internet connection, but typically this is very limited. Only 17% offer Internet access to the public, and at only 0.4% of the service points at which it is provided is it free of charge (Ormes and Dempsey, 1996).

A UK survey of the members of EARL (Electronic Access to Resources in Libraries), a consortium of UK public library authorities, flagged up three issues of particular concern to libraries: user policies relating to censorship and the availability of illegal material on the Internet, with respondents being unenthusiastic about the use of 'net nanny software'; copyright and intellectual property rights infringement; and what respondents identified as a major issue – the principle of providing services (or a level of service) free at the point of delivery as opposed to introducing charges to offset costs not covered in base budgets (EARL, 1996).

In November 1996 Information For All, a company jointly set up by the Library Association UK and the Library Commission, submitted a bid for a grant from the Millennium Commission to fund a national programme for the networking of 4,000 public libraries, giving everyone in a local area free access to local and international information. A broadband communications network would connect the smallest and most remote libraries to others in their area and through the Internet to all other libraries and online sources (Information For All, 1996). The bid was not successful on this occasion, but it will be put forward again in a modified form (Library Association, 1997).

The British government acknowledges that public libraries have a key role to play in providing and organizing electronic materials for use, and in helping and training users to navigate the Information Superhighway. After the millennium has been celebrated, part of the Millennium Fund will be used for the development of information and communication technology (ICT) and public libraries would be one of the beneficiaries. The government also places emphasis on sponsorship from and partnerships with the private sector and advocates an expansion of the Input Output Centre libraries in the UK whereby the private sector funds the cost of 'user pays' computer centres within public libraries, and the library receives a commission for the private use of a public space (Department of National Heritage, 1997).

On the wider European scene, a special edition of *Cordis Focus*, the Commission of the European Communities: Community Research and Development

Information Service, contains a special feature on the Directorate General XIII Telematics for Libraries programme (Iljon, 1996). Research and development in the libraries sector of the telematics applications programme is aimed at facilitating access to library resources and promoting the interconnection of libraries with each other and with the information and communications infrastructure. The ultimate aim is to enable users to have remote access to information through the application of telematics services throughout European libraries.

Synopses of the library projects, including a number led by public libraries, have been issued (European Commission DG XIII-E4, 1996a). There is a generic Telematics for Libraries Website which systematically guides the user to almost all the sources of information on library projects and other European documents concerned with information policy (http://www2.echo.lu/libraries/en/libraries.html). However, to date the public library projects are perceived as being too fragmented within the overall programme. To support more involvement by public libraries, DG XIII-E4 has launched two new initiatives: the Public Libraries in the Information Society study (PLIS); and PUBLICA, the concerted action for public libraries initiative.

The PLIS study has resulted in five case studies of public libraries which are models of innovation; eleven national case studies; a study on regional cooperation in Italy; two analytical studies of the main barriers holding back innovation in public libraries in the information society; and guidelines and questionnaires for carrying out the studies. The study stresses that the great majority of public libraries in the countries of the European Union are lagging behind the pace of change in the evolving information society. A workshop report has been published which presents the preliminary results and recommendations of the study (European Commission DG XIII-E4, 1996b). A final report will be published in 1997 and there is also a Website which provides extracts from all of both the country and the individual library studies (http://www2.echo.lu/libraries/en/plis.html). PUBLICA is a consortium of seven public libraries whose role is to encourage the information provision role of the public libraries and their greater involvement in the DG XIII-E4 library programmes (European Commission DG XIII-E4, 1996a).

The fastest growing public library network in Europe is in Portugal where a programme for the creation and development of municipal libraries, based upon the principles of the UNESCO *Manifesto*, was initiated in 1987, with 50% funding being provided by the government and 50% by the relevant municipality. At the end of 1996, 125 of the 275 municipalities had contracted with the government to found public libraries. Fifty-six libraries had already been inaugurated and the remainder were under construction. In 1997 a medium-term programme to complete the network over the whole country will be launched (Moura, 1996, personal communication).

Public libraries and lifelong learning

There has been a significant growth in open and distance learning modes in all kinds of environments – educational, library, home, workplace, business. There is an increasing public demand for libraries to provide not only the multimedia learning packages and the hardware and software required to use them, but also the professional support needed by independent learners.

In the UK the government-sponsored Open for Learning Project 1992–95 demonstrated that large numbers of people were willing to take advantage of open learning opportunities provided in libraries for a wide range of self-development and vocational ends (Allred, 1995).

The DG XIII-E4 Public Libraries and Adult Independent Learners (PLAIL, 1996) project 1994–6, and the ongoing Libraries Integrated System for Telematics-based Education project (LISTED) (European Commission DG XIII E4, 1996a) are concerned with the development of new roles for librarians and with the development and application of new technology in the delivery of Open and Distance Learning (ODL).

The PROLIB-ODL study in 1995 concluded that public libraries could play a major role in cooperation with other agencies, in the delivery of ODL to Europe's citizens. The findings of this study are recorded in the Final Report (Brophy *et al.*, 1996) which provides an overview of the current involvement of EU public libraries in the provision of ODL and examines the potential for the development of this role by libraries.

The north-south divide

By the year 2025 it is estimated that more than 90% of the world's population growth will have occurred in the developing or currently underdeveloped nations. The developed nations' share of the world population at that time will be only 16% (Magpantay, 1996). In large areas of the world there is currently no access to printed sources of information, either through lack of funds or illiteracy, or both, and it will be very many years before the vast majority of the people in underdeveloped countries is able to access electronic information. A monograph by Olden (1995) and the review article by Benge (1996), which it inspired, are a starting point for an exploration of the reasons for the current poor state of African public libraries in general. A selection of other current studies is concerned with the analysis of information needs and with the development of appropriate theoretical foundations and the implementation of practical, relevant strategies to meet them through library and information services (Garcha and Buttlar, 1996;

Onwubiko, 1996; Sturges and Chimseu, 1996; Ward, 1996). Alemna (1996) identifies the common elements in national library and information policies in developing countries, but notes that there has been limited achievement in terms of their implementation. Lor (1996) charts the information dependence factor in Africa and discusses its implications for bibliographical cooperation and the availability of publications.

The South African Institute for Librarianship and Information Science (SAILIS, 1995) carried out a survey which revealed the poor condition of many public libraries. They lack investment in buildings, materials and trained staff, whilst there is restructuring at provincial and municipal levels of government. This report stimulated controversy in the professional literature (Malan, 1996; Morrow, 1996; Vijoen, 1996; Kenvyn, 1997).

In India only very slow progress has been made in the development of rural libraries since India gained its independence from British rule 50 years ago (Vashishth, 1995). There persists the fundamental challenge of convincing communities that information can be a vital resource for community development (Ferguson, 1995). No public library in India provides public access Internet services. The British Council in New Delhi has been providing a service from 1 April 1997. There is a number of embryonic local networks being developed in major cities. The most advanced of these is DELNET (Delhi), with 40 libraries participating in the network, but the information provided is minimal. The National Informatics Centre (NIC), which is part of the government's Planning Commission, runs a networked service of statistical and government information called GIST (General Information Service Terminals) that does have some public terminals, and has experimented with public library access. However, the information on this service tends to be out of date.

Conclusion

In the rapidly developing multimedia and electronic environment, with more information being made available only in non-printed and digitized forms, public libraries internationally are increasingly restricting services that are free to end users to core or basic services, essentially book lending, book-based reference services, and computer databases produced inhouse. In addition many are charging registration fees. The crucial issue which has to be addressed by politicians and professional librarians is how to facilitate the genuinely equal and open access to information for all citizens which is a prerequisite for the creation of free and economically developed societies.

References

Alemna, A.A. (1996) *Issues in African librarianship*. Accra: Type Co. Ltd.

Allred, J. (1995) *Improving access to open and flexible learning: open learning in public libraries: the evaluation report*. London: John Allred (Information for Learning) for The Library Association.

Altman, E. (1996a) Take a bow, PLA. *Public Libraries*, **35**(1), 12.

Altman, E. (1996b) Dispatch from down under. *Public Libraries*, **35**(6), 340.

American Civil Liberties Union (1997a). ACLU background briefing Reno v. ACLU: the road to the Supreme Court. http://www.aclu.org/news/n10936b.html

American Civil Liberties Union (1997b). The threat of state censorship bills. http://www.aclu.org/issues/cyber/censor/stbills.html

American Civil Liberties Union (1997c). ACLU cyber-liberties update. 8 January. http://www.aclu.org/iss...updates/jan8clu.html#fla

Ammons, D.N. (1995) Overcoming the inadequacies of performance measurement in local government. *Public Administration Review*, **55**(1), 37–47.

Anderson, C. (1996) Contracting out in public libraries: the DNH study. *Australasian Public Libraries and Information Services*, **9**(1), 57–61.

Bedfordshire Libraries/CableTel (England) (1996) World Wide Web Station. Rules and advice.

Benge, R. (1996) Library provision in Africa 20 years on: a review article. *Journal of Librarianship and Information Science*, **28**(3), 171–175.

Benton Foundation (1996a) *Buildings, books and bytes: libraries and communities in the digital age. A report on the public's opinion of library leads' visions for the future*. Washington: Benton Foundation.

Benton Foundation (1996b) http://www.benton.org/Policy/Uniserv/

Berry, J.N. (1996) PLA stacks the deck for fees. *Library Journal*, **121**(7), 6.

Bertot, J.C. *et al.* (1996) *1996 National survey of public libraries and the Internet: progress and issues*. Washington, DC: National Commission on Libraries and Information Science.

Black, A. and Muddiman, D. (1997) *Understanding community librarianship: the public library in postmodern Britain*. Aldershot: Avebury.

Blokland, H. (1996) Summary. *Bibliotheek en Samenleving Library and Society*, (1), 32.

Borchardt, P. (1995) *IFLA Public Library News: Newsletter of the Section of Public Libraries*, **13**(3).

Borchardt, P. (1996) *IFLA Public Library News: Newsletter of the Section of Public Libraries*, **13**(3).

Broadband Services Export Group (1995) *Networking Australia's future*. Canberra: BSBG.

Brophy, P. *et al.* (1996) *Open distance learning in public libraries*. Luxembourg: European Commission, DG XIII E4. (EUR 16904 EN).

Catlin, I. (1996) *State of the nation: Australia's public libraries*. Queensland: Cultural Ministers, Libraries Working Group.

Coopers and Lybrand (1996) *Valuing the economic costs and benefits of libraries: a study prepared for the N strategy*. Auckland: New Zealand Library and Information Association.

Daines, G. (1997a) *Survey of public library authority budget plans for 1997/8*. London: Library Association, Public Libraries Committee. [An edited summary of a privately circulated survey carried out by the Society of Chief Librarians (SCL).]

Daines, G. (1997b) *New library authorities*. London: Library Association.

Department of National Heritage (1995) *DNH study: contracting out in public libraries.* London: KPMG/CPI.

Department of National Heritage (1997) *Reading the future: public libraries review.* London: DNH.

EARL (Electronic Access to Resources in Libraries) (1996) *Policy issues/public access strategies. Preliminary report.* London: EARL Special Interest Group.

Engel, D. (1996) The price is right: pricing strategies for public libraries. *Public Libraries*, **35**(4), 251–252.

Eronica, E.A. and Zemskov, A.L. (1993) *On the way from free of charge socialism to fee-based democracy.* [Poster session paper presented at the 59th IFLA General Conference, Barcelona.]

European Commission, Directorate General XIII E-4 (1996a) *Synopses of projects supported by the European Commission for the application of telematic systems in libraries.* Luxembourg: European Commission, Directorate General XIII E-4.

European Commission, Directorate General XIII E-4 (1996b) *Telematics for libraries concertation meeting: public libraries and the information society proceedings. Meeting held in Luxembourg on 8 July 1996.* Luxembourg: European Commission Directorate General XIII E-4.

Ferguson, S. (1995) Resource mobilization for the implementation of the rural community resource centre (RCRC). In: *Libraries as rural community resource centres. Papers and proceedings of the Workshop on rural community resource centres*, ed. C.P. Vashishth. Delhi: B.R. Publishing.

Flagg, G. (1996) FCC Joint Board endorses deep discounts for libraries, schools. *American Libraries*, **27**(11), 11.

Garcha, R. and Buttlar, L.J. (1996) Profiling African libraries: automation in Ghana, Kenya and Nigeria. *Library Review*, **45**(6), 25–32.

Garner, B. (1995) Neither a borrower, nor a lender be. *Australasian Public Libraries and Information Services*, **8**(4), 173–177.

Goldberg, B. (1996) Public libraries go back to school. *American Libraries*, **27**(11), 54–55.

Haggstrom, B-M. (1995) *IFLA Public Library News: Newsletter of the Section of Public Libraries*, **13**(4).

Hall, R.B. (1996) Back in the black: library campaigns pay off. *Library Journal*, **12**(11), 37–39.

Hare, G. (1996) The state of public libraries. *Public Library Journal*, **11**(6), 151–154.

Hanratty, C. and Sumsion, J. (1996) *International comparison of public library statistics.* Loughborough: Loughborough University, Library and Information Statistics Unit.

Haratsis, B. (1996) Justifying the economic value of public libraries in a turbulent local government environment. *Australasian Public Libraries and Information Services*, **8**(4), 165–173.

Heeks, P. (1996) Service to schools. In: M. Kinnell and P. Sturges, (eds). *Continuity and innovation in the public library: the development of a social institution.* London: Library Association Publishing, pp. 131–146.

Iljon, A. (1996) Interview with Mrs Ariane Iljon, Head of Unit XIII\E-4, responsible for the Libraries Programme. *Cordis Focus*, 17, 23 December, 11–12.

Information For All (1996): the public library millennium bid raising public awareness. London: Library Association.

Irish Library Council (1996) *Public library statistics 1988–1994: an analysis of national trends in relation to Irish public libraries: public library authority statistics 1994.* Dublin: ILC.

Kennedy J. (1997) Looking at value for money. *Library Association Record*, **99**(1), 32–33.

Kenvyn, D. (1997) South Africa: a new start for libraries. *Library Campaigner*, (55), 8–9.

King, J. (1996) Specifying a library service for CCT. *Australasian Public Libraries and Information Services*, **9**(1), 39–51.

Kinnell, M. (1996) Managing in a corporate culture: the role of the chief librarian. In: M. Kinnell, and P. Sturges (1996) (eds). *Continuity and innovation in the public library: the development of a social institution.* London: Library Association Publishing, pp. 167–186.

Klenitz, L. (1996) Ten reasons for librarians to don different hats. *Public Libraries*, **35**(1), 13–14.

Klinec, P. (1991) *Impact of political and economic changes upon public libraries in Czech-Slovakia.* [Paper presented at the 57th IFLA General Conference, Moscow (49-PUBL-2-E).]

Kristensen, K. (1996) The no-charge principle – a hindrance to public library activities? *Scandinavian Public Library Quarterly*, **29**(4), 10–12.

Langford, M. (1996) Remarks to OLTA Session #611 at the Ontario Library Association Superconference, 9 February. http://www.sols.on/.ca/lcib/english/dirola. html.

Larmer, S. (1997) Newsfronts. *Feliciter*, **42**(4), 7.

Library Association (1997) Down but not out for the count. *Library Association Record*, **99**(3), 121.

Lor, P. (1996) Information dependence in southern Africa: global and subregional perspectives. *African Journal of Librarianship and Information Science*, **6**(1), 1–10.

McClure, C.R. *et al.* (1996) Enhancing the role of public libraries in the national information infrastructure. *Public Libraries*, (July/August), 232–235.

Macvean, C. (1996) Outsourcing noncore library activities: a case study of a Victorian public library. *Australasian Public Libraries and Information Services*, **9**(2), 83–90.

Magpantay, J.A. (1996) The emerging electronic age: a background paper. In: B. Turock (ed.) *Envisioning a nation connected, 1996.* Washington, DC: ALA, p. 7.

Malan, C. (1996) Unity needed to meet growing demand in time of change. *Library Association Record*, **98**(10), 511.

Mercer, C. (1995) *Navigating the economy of knowledge: a national survey of users and non-users of state and public libraries.* Queensland: Cultural Ministers Libraries Working Group.

Mercer, C. (1996) Rich aunt or poor cousin?: policy dilemmas for publicly funded libraries. *Australasian Public Libraries and Information Services*, **9**(1), 5–15.

Mercer, C. and Smith, M. (1996) *2020 vision: towards the libraries of the future.* Queensland: Cultural Ministers Council, Libraries Working Group.

Mielke, L. (1996) Managing for cybersurvival. *Public libraries*, **35**(6), 341–342.

Morrow, V. (1996) On the brink of collapse? *Library Association Record*, **98**(7), 333.

Mushinski, M. (1997) Minister's letter to clients: 15 January. http://www.sols.on.ca/lcib/english/legltr.html

Nilsen, S. (1995) *IFLA Public Library News: Newsletter of the Section of Public Libraries*, **13**(4).

Nilsen, S. (1996) *IFLA Public Library News: Newsletter of the Section of Public Libraries*, **15**(6).

Olden, A. (1995) *Libraries in Africa: pioneers, policies, problems.* Lanham, MD and London: Scarecrow Press.

Ontario, Ministry of Citizenship, Culture and Recreation (1997). *Fact sheet. Local Control of Public Libraries Act 1997.* Ontario: Ministry of Citizenship.

Onwubiko, C.P.C. (1996) The practice of Amadi's 'barefoot librarianship' in African public libraries: constraints and proposals. *Library Review*, **45**(4), 39–47.

Ormes, S. and Dempsey, L. (1995) *Library and Information Commission public library Internet survey. First public report.* http://www.ukoln.bath.ac.uk/public/lic/html.

Proctor, R. *et al.* (1996) *What do people do when their public library service closes down?: an investigation into the impact of the Sheffield libraries strike.* London: British Library R&D Department. (R&D Report 6224).

Pryor, C and Lee, T. (1996) Compulsory competitive tendering: the issues. *Australasian Public Libraries and Information Services*, **9**(1), 53–55.

Public Libraries and Adult Independent Learners (1996) *Final report of the PLAIL Project.* Wales: Clwyd County Council Library & Information Service on behalf of the PLAIL Project (LIB-PLAIL/3-2081).

Public Library Association of America (1996) *Public library data service statistical report.* Chicago: PLA.

Riley S. (1997) Libraries check out changes. *Ottawa Citizen*, 6 January, 8.

Robertson, S. (1996) *Fines and charges in public libraries in England and Wales.* 9th ed. Sheffield: Central Library.

Sabaratnam, J. (1996) *Planning the library of the future – the Singapore experience.* [Paper presented at the 62nd IFLA General Conference, Beijing (006-PUB-3-E).]

St. Lifer, E. (1997) Public libraries budgets brace for Internet costs. *Library Journal*, **122**(1), 44–47.

St. Lifer, E. *et al.* (1996) Public libraries face fiscal challenges. *Library Journal*, **121**(1), 40–45.

Scheepstra, D. (1996) *Public libraries and economic development: is it wishful thinking or will the public library survive anyhow?* [Paper presented at the 62nd IFLA General Conference, Beijing (006-PUB-2-E).]

School Librarian (1996) **44**(4) [Special issue on schools library services in the UK].

Seay, T. *et al.* (1996) Measuring and improving the quality of public services: a hybrid approach. *Library Trends*, **44**(3), 464–465.

Skot-Hansen, D. (1996) The local library – its profile and anchorage. *Scandinavian Public Library Quarterly*, **1**(96), 4–10.

South African Institute for Librarianship and Information Science (1995) *Republic of South Africa: collapse of provincial and public library information services.* SAILIS.

Sturges, P. and Chimseu, G. (1996) The chain of information provision in the villages of Malawi: a rapid rural appraisal. *International Information and Library Review*, **28**(2), 135–156.

Subbarao, C.V. *et al.* (1995) (eds) *Preparing libraries for the 21st century. Seminar papers: Fortieth All India Library Conference, Goa University Library, Goa, 5–8 January, 1995.* Delhi: Indian Library Association.

Sumsion, J. (1996). Staying in the top flight. *Bookseller*, 29 November, 20–26.

Sumsion, J. *et al.* (1996) *LISU Annual library statistics 1996: featuring trend analysis of UK public and academic libraries 1985–95.* Loughborough: Loughborough University, Library and Information Statistics Unit. (LISU Public Library Statistics Report no. 19).

Thomas, B. (1993) Public responsibility for public libraries. In: *IFLA Seminar. Revision of the UNESCO public library manifesto '72 Report. 17–20 August, Guimaraes, Portugal.* IFLA Section of Public Libraries.

Thomas, B. (1996) Contracting out of public libraries. [Paper presented at the 62nd IFLA General Conference, Beijing (057-MGT-3-E).]

Traniello, P. (1994) *Review of library legislations in central Europe. Workshop on reforming library legislation in central Europe: needs and expectations. Strasbourg, 1–8 November 1994.* Strasbourg: Council of Europe, 1994 (CC/Lib.Leg (94)3).

Turock, B. (1996) (ed.) *Envisioning a nation connected: libraries define the public interest in the information SuperHighway.* Chicago: ALA. [The proceedings of the summit are available at the ALA's Website http://www.ala.org/]

Usherwood, B. (1996) *Rediscovering public library management.* London: Library Association Publishing.

Vashishth, C.P. (1995) Over-view of rural libraries in India. In: *Libraries as rural community centres. Papers and proceedings of the workshop on rural community centres,* ed. C.P. Vashishth. Delhi: B.R. Publishing, p. 63].

Vijoen, J.H. (1996) Acting, democratically, to publicise true plight. *Library Association Record,* **98**(10), 511.

Walzer, N. and Gruidl, J. (1996) Role of small public libraries in community economic development. *Illinois Libraries,* **78**(4), 50–55.

Ward, D. (1996) The changing role of mobile libraries in Africa. *International Information and Library Review,* (128), 121–133.

Waters, R.L. (1996) Economic development: the public library must be a player. *Public Library Quarterly,* **45**(4), 33–36.

Willard, P. (1995) Public sector reform in Australia. *International Information and Library Review,* **27**(4), 359–373.

Xiaoqin, L. (1996) Public libraries and economic development in China. [Paper presented at the 62nd IFLA General Conference, Beijing (029-GENPUB-1-E).]

Special libraries 5

Guy St. Clair

Introduction

Special libraries exist in large numbers throughout society, and they exist wherever an organization, institution, business, enterprise, or other societal entity believes that information is required for the successful achievement of the organizational mission. Because all of society at the end of the 20th century is characterized by change, special librarianship, too, is so characterized. Change and change management have become the critical focus of emphasis in special librarianship, and with the acceptance by information workers that change is both inevitable and desirable, specialist librarians and the organizations their libraries support are working hard to move information services into this new era of information management. In fact, change and change management continue to be major subjects for discussion at all professional conferences in which special librarians participate, including the 62nd IFLA General Conference held in Beijing, China, in 1996 (McGarry, 1996).

With respect to the methodologies of information delivery, this last decade of the 20th century might well be called 'the practitioner age', for information services practitioners of all kinds – particularly special librarians – are doing everything they can to devise, create, or otherwise initiate practices that will enable their information customers to have the highest levels of information delivery that they can provide within the frameworks in which they must work.

At the same time, this period in the history of information services management might also be characterized as 'the age of the information customer', for at no time in the history of librarianship and information services has the authority of the customer been so recognized and so respected. Here again, special librarians particularly are working hard to consider and respond to the authority of the customer, for they have learned – through experience and through their own history – that in the field of specialized librarianship 'the dissatisfied information customer' is an oxymoron. The very survival of the library is dependent on its success in delivering the information products, services, and consultations that information customers require and expect. National and international trends in specialized librarianship indicate that future information workers will be more concerned than they have been in the past with connecting their work with the specific needs of their information customers, and that these trends will continue.

Specialist librarianship: concepts

For many in the field, special libraries are best defined as what they are not. Special libraries are not public libraries or academic libraries, although these may include special libraries as components of an organizational framework. A departmental library in a university, for example, might be considered a special library, as might, say, the local history section of a public library. By and large, however, special libraries exist to support the work of a parent institution:

> A special library is characteristically a unit or department of an organization primarily devoted to other than library or educational purposes. . . . A special librarian is first an employee, a staff member of the parent organization, and second, a librarian. 'Special' really means library service specialized or geared to the interests of the organization and to the information needs of its personnel (Ferguson and Mobley, 1984).

This concept is included in the definition of specialized librarianship that is built into the Strategic Plan of the Special Libraries Association, the international professional organization in the USA that supports the work of special librarians. For SLA and its members, a special library is defined there as 'an organization that provides focused, working information to a specialized clientele on an ongoing basis to further the mission and goals of the parent company/ organization'. Special librarians are 'information and research professionals who provide focused, working information to a specialized clientele on an ongoing basis to further the mission and goals of the parent company or organization' (Special Libraries Association, 1989).

   That special libraries are different from other libraries has been established for many years. As early as 1982 Edward G. Strable had identified several characteristics which distinguish special librarianship from other types of library work. His distinctions for special libraries were summarized as follows:

> While the major goals of other kinds of libraries may encompass education, recreation, aesthetic appreciation, or scholarly research, the traditional major goal of special libraries has been, and continues to be, providing information for immediate and utilitarian purposes. The information function must always take priority over technical processes. The special library's users do not expect to be instructed, they expect to be informed. . . . In every case, the common characteristic

is an orientation to information and library materials which are specialized rather than generalized in character (Strable, 1982).

Thus we find, in that branch of information services known as 'specialized' librarianship, in which information materials and information delivery are provided for the exclusive use and 'private advantage' of the organization which provides financial support for the library, that the focus has always been slightly different from that of other types of librarianship (Ashworth, 1979). With the introduction of enabling technology into the information process – as well as changes in what might be called the 'philosophy' of information delivery – that focus and that difference have been considerably enhanced. Special libraries exist to provide specific information that is used to enable the organization to achieve its organizational mission, and when that information is better delivered by an external agency, as often happens, a management decision is made to outsource the library function or parts of it. In extreme cases, a decision is made to close the special library altogether. The closing of special libraries is a subject of much attention in the profession (Matarazzo, 1990). The outsourcing of special library services, particularly when linked to the closing of a special library, likewise causes much consternation and distress in the specialist library community (Wordsworth and Williams, 1993; Prusak, 1994).

Certain management themes are prominent in the minds of the practitioners of special librarianship and are continually being given serious attention:

- the management of information services vis-à-vis organizational management (St. Clair, 1995b; St. Clair, 1996a; St. Clair, 1996b; St. Clair, 1996c);
- quality management initiatives in information delivery (ACLIS/Australian Council of Libraries and Information Services, 1996; Brockman, 1992; St. Clair, 1997a; Spiegelman, 1992; Spiegelman, 1994);
- public and private sector involvement in information services management (Albrecht, 1994; St. Clair, 1994; St. Clair, 1996f; St. Clair, 1996h);
- customer focus and the role of customer service in information delivery (St. Clair, 1993b);
- strategic planning in information services management (Ferriero and Wilding, 1991; Asantewa, 1992; Hayes, 1993; St. Clair, 1993a; St. Clair, 1994);
- change management in the information services environment (Riggs, 1987; St. Clair, 1993a; St. Clair, 1995);
- performance evaluation and effectiveness measures in information delivery (Griffiths and King, 1991; Queensland Department of Education Virtual Library, 1993; Powell, 1994; Sweeney, 1996);
- the development and implementation of organizational information policy (Orna, 1990; St. Clair, 1993; Hasenyager, 1996);
- interrelationships between information content specialists and information technology specialists (Knowledge, 1996; Campbell and Prime, 1997; St. Clair, 1997a).

These themes and issues provide a continuous counterpoint to the profession's equal attention to sources and methodologies for information delivery.

Trends in specialist librarianship

The magnitude of change currently experienced by every information services professional is multiplied for the specialized librarian, and the last decade of the 20th century is presenting the information services profession with a host of challenges. First, these have to do with the relationship between the information customer and the specialist librarian: a reorientation of library services to mission-critical information; the re-engineering of information services; the focusing of information services to reflect the customer perspective; the information-independent (or nearly independent) organization; and the disintermediation of information. A second major trend that we are seeing in specialist librarianship is a move toward identifying and codifying the particular competencies required for success as a special librarian. The Special Libraries Association has considered this matter so critical for its members' edification that it has published a formal Competencies Statement to guide them and their employers as they consider the role of the specialist librarian in their organizations. An additional direction is the growing interest in the role of the specialist librarian as knowledge manager and the movement in information services management at large to the development of an integrated information/ knowledge management function within organizations and businesses. Linked to this is yet another consideration, one which has been anticipated for some time, the growing number of one-person libraries in the specialized library community. In fact, this combined attention to the authority of the customer, the competencies of practitioners, increased attention to knowledge management, and the increasing numbers of single-staff practitioners have led to the identification of a new management trend in information services, the employment and utilization of the insourced information specialist/consultant.

Running as a sort of theme through all of this important activity is the work of the Special Libraries Association, the international professional organization for specialized libraries and information services workers. SLA's initiatives encapsulate and draw attention to these trends, as well as to several others (like its influence in the international information services arena) which taken together position specialist librarianship as a powerful and critical player in the information services marketplace.

Customer service in special librarianship

In addressing customer service, it must first be recognized that this is a broad subject, although it was not given much attention prior to the late 1980s. One of the special library manager's first duties is the reorientation of library services to mission-critical information, and the best example for this is in the work being done at Coopers & Lybrand, the large accounting firm, where Foy is working to reinvent information services. Reinvention – and nothing less – is called for simply because the information needs of the customers are changing, and the information services operation must go along with whatever changes are taking place in the environment. At Coopers & Lybrand, this change means that the company's many corporate libraries are being reorganized into a group of information delivery agencies, with various layers of service. These operations, designed to provide customers with exactly what they need, are not called 'libraries' because the term evokes a perception of information that is not appropriate to the services that these agencies will provide. Such activity is not unusual in the special libraries environment today, and more and more information services operations are being reorganized and recalibrated as the organization's management and its specialized librarians realize that to meet the information customers' needs and to match their expectations, drastic measures are needed (Matching, 1995).

It is, of course, this emphasis on customer service that is leading the drive for the re-engineering of information services:

> We are entering an era where businesses and professions are re-engineering and restructuring as a consequence of the exponential leap in information technology. This re-engineering and restructuring, some believe, will lead to vast improvements in customer-valued productivity, optimization of businesses, and competitiveness ... library managers must re-engineer their libraries or information centers to deliver information using the most cost-effective electronic tools and products available in the industry ... the library or information center must seek to exist as a borderless service, a place where information can be sought wherever it exists and used immediately by local or remote customers ... only real time information will be valued as a competitive tool (Piggott, 1995).

Such demands on the specialized librarian mean that additional training and education are required. This 'new' work positions the specialized librarian to play an important role in the determining of organizational information policy, for there is seldom anyone else in the organization who has the special librarian's understanding of the differences between information and information technology.

Davenport, who is a strong advocate of an advanced level of process re-engineering (he calls it 'process innovation'), identifies information technology as an 'enabler' in this important activity. He provides a workable distinction between information ('the thing being manipulated') and information technology ('the thing doing the manipulation'). He also makes the point that in the ongoing confusion between information and information technology, 'information always seems to get the short shrift in the analysis' (Davenport, 1993). Meg Paul, who manages a company that provides library consultancy services for the special libraries community in Australia, regards the customer focus as a question of survival:

If a library does not meet the needs of its clients, the value and integrity of the information it provides is not recognized and the library is not able to prove its cost effectiveness. When this happens, the library will cease to exist as clients withdraw their support. The clients are the stakeholders and those librarians who do not heed their needs and listen to them will face extinction or radical upheaval (Information, 1994).

And what advice does Paul offer to prevent that radical upheaval? This, too, reflects an important trend that is now being given serious attention in special librarianship:

An astute librarian should realize that even an excellent service needs advocates within the organization. ... There are always occasions when you will need advocates to lend support in internal political situations and these will usually be clients who value your services. Your clients become your insurance policy (Information, 1994).

The rise of the information-independent (or nearly independent) organization and the disintermediation of information are, in fact, two sides of the same coin, and they are trends which must be watched carefully as special librarians attempt to adapt to the changing needs of the information marketplace. End-user information gathering is now a fact in many organizations where librarians formerly were responsible for providing information. While organizational libraries and other information providers are going to continue to have work, much attention is being given to those organizations where end users are taught to use the system themselves and to go their own way in tracking down what they want to know. The information-independent organization is not necessarily a threatening situation. The concept has not come about to downsize, save resources, cut staff, or for any of those other usual reasons that an information services unit takes off in a new direction. At Bankers Trust, in New York, for example, and at other companies and organizations that are incorporating the information-independent 'direction' into their organizational management philosophy, it is done simply because it is the best way to move information through the organization (Information, 1993).

When the information 'independence' no longer requires the services of a specialized librarian, then the professional information workers get nervous. Fitzsimmons has identified what he calls 'disintermediation'. This is a structural change that is now taking place in the information 'food chain,' as it were, which frequently does away with the person who serves as a mediator between the information and the user of the information. In the creation and delivery of information in the past, Fitzsimmons points out, a mediator was required and, whether gatekeeper or interpreter, that person played an important and very crucial role in the information transfer process. Now the picture has changed and the many component information services workers, the authors, the aggregators, the resellers, the distributors, the specialized librarians, the desktop publishers, and even the end users, are now interacting all over the place, without mediation. This means that specialized librarians must rethink their roles and if necessary learn new skills, if they expect to be part of the information delivery process (Looking, 1994).

Competencies for special librarianship

In 1991–92, the first formal steps to address the issue of competencies for specialized librarianship were undertaken in the work of SLA's Presidential Study Commission on Professional Recruitment, Ethics and Professional Standards, known as the PREPS Commission. Underlying the work of the Commission was the premise that special librarianship is a unique branch, despite the great diversity within special librarianship itself.

As part of a study of standards for special libraries, the PREPS Commission recognized the role that standards play, but also that broad disparities exist within specialized librarianship:

> Standards are important. In addition to enhancing our professionalism, they allow for some type of measurement of success, which every organization needs in one fashion or another. While attempts have been made to 'value' the information services professional and measure success in that fashion, the measures used do not work well in every environment or even in the same environment every time (Special Libraries Association, 1992).

Building on the fact that each specialist librarian works for an organization with its own set of standards and values, and that no formal set of standards would be likely to be acceptable in all environments, the PREPS Commission recommended that SLA reorient its focus on standards for special libraries to emphasize, instead, standards and competencies for special librarians.

In 1996 SLA published *Competencies for special librarians of the 21st century* (Special Libraries Association, 1996). This important document addresses both professional competencies (defined as those 'relating to the special librarian's knowledge in the areas of information resources, information access, technology, management and research, and the ability to use these areas of knowledge as a basis for providing library and information services'), and personal competencies (those which 'represent a set of skills, attitudes, and values that enable librarians to work efficiently, to be good communicators, to focus on continuing learning throughout their careers, to demonstrate the value-added nature of their contributions, and to survive in the new world of work').

Knowledge management and the integration of information

One of the most significant trends in special librarianship today has to do with a new understanding of what constitutes 'information services,' of what is meant by 'information services management,' and how the broader profession of information services management relates to specialized librarianship. It does not matter whether the special librarian is employed as an information manager, information provider, information specialist, or indeed, as an information counsellor (as these information workers have sometimes been described). In fact, anyone who is connected to information, who provides information in any form, is part of information services today. Orna (1990) pointed out that within the organization or enterprise, information will be found everywhere, 'not just in formal repositories like libraries or information systems, and not just in those functions where people spend a lot of time reading, writing, or interacting with computers'. For Orna, the 'touchstone' for identifying information is simply: 'Is this something that people need to know and apply in their work, to achieve their, and the enterprise's objectives?' The list of items that meet her criteria is long, and includes such things as customer records, financial records, internal information, external information, technical information, and information about the environment in which the enterprise operates.

Much of the 'new thinking' in special librarianship connects to the emerging discipline of information resources management (IRM). Described as a movement in the government to manage information and make it available to the people of the United States, in reality IRM is not only about government information but about any kind of information services management that involves large blocks of information. IRM looks at information in management terms that almost literally matches up with the competencies required for success in special librarianship (regardless of the information entity under discussion). The 'principles' of IRM, as they are called, make it clear that serious special library management – when linked to IRM – is built on a useful and socially responsible foundation:

- Information is a resource. Like other resources it has value and can be managed.
- Information gains value with use.
- Since information gains value with use, it should be available to the broadest possible audience.
- Information should be organized to meet the needs of the user; organizations should be organized around the flow of information.
- Work will be fundamentally transformed if: information is managed as a resource; information is organized for dissemination; work is organized around information flow (Megill, 1995).

This trend toward the integration of information, leading as it does toward the management of a broader-based commodity than a library and its contents, has serious implications for special librarians. In fact, according to Remeikis, a leader in the field of knowledge management (but originally a specialist librarian): 'There are many, many people working as special librarians who are qualified to be knowledge managers in their organizations . . . connecting knowledge management and special librarianship seems to make a lot of sense' (Knowledge, 1996).

Remeikis defines knowledge management as: The creation, capture, exchange, use, and communication of a company's 'intellectual capital' – an organization's best thinking about its products, services, processes, market, and competitors. Closely related to a company's other information activities, knowledge management involves gathering internal information, such as financial and marketing data, and combining it with related external data, such as competitive intelligence. It goes beyond simple records management in that the information captured may include ongoing discussions, corporate stories, and other facts not typically documented (Knowledge, 1996).

One-person librarianship

Until 25 years ago, one-person librarianship as a recognized branch of specialized librarianship and information services did not exist. Today, there are more than 1,000 members in the Special Libraries Association's 'Solo Librarians' Division, and it has been estimated that over half of all those who call themselves 'librarians' work alone. As we look at how companies and organizations organize information, it must be recognized that more and more organizations will move toward single-staff information delivery by the beginning of the 21st century because it is cost-effective to do so. Since librarians and other information providers are now comfortable with the use of technology, they can free themselves from the time-consuming clerical tasks that formerly inhibited the successful delivery of information services and products in single-staff libraries (St. Clair, 1997b).

The Solo Librarians Division of SLA and other organizations like Aslib in the UK have taken initiatives for the training of one-person librarians. Important work is also being done in Germany, where the leaders of the library and information services profession, working with the Deutsches Bibliotheksinstitut, have created a national body to study one-person librarianship. The group has been instrumental in the creation of a commission on one-person librarianship and has worked with several of Germany's library schools in establishing the study of one-person librarianship in the training programmes for librarianship, information studies, etc.. The prospect for the growth of an influential programme of studies in the area of one-person librarianship looks very good.

If the programme succeeds, it will be replicated elsewhere (OPLs, 1995). The first book on the subject stated

> It is probably safe to assume that the number of one-person library operations will grow, as management comes to realize that one excellent, efficient, and enthusiastic librarian or information specialist is preferable to two or more who do not provide the same level of service for users. It is these committed, enthusiastic librarians who will bring to the profession a level of service that their employers cannot help but appreciate, because they will bring to the parent organization, the employing corporation, hospital, society, or teaching facility, good library service, which is all they wanted in the first place (St. Clair and Williamson, 1986).

The insourced information specialist/consultant

Much attention has been paid in recent years to the outsourcing of those functions within an organization that are not part of the organization's core competency. These could include the hiring of a short-term research team, for example, to determine the validity of pursuing a particular course of action before resources are committed to it, or the hiring of an external project management team to implement the activity, so that internal resources are not used. Little has been said, however, about those situations wherein organizational managers hire and add to staff the same types of employees for permanent research- or project-related tasks. As managers and department chiefs realize that they need information, even though the organization at large might not require the services of a permanent library or information centre, they realize that an individual unit of the organization might very well need a person who is an information specialist and who can perform all functions connected with the management and delivery of information. When that unit's manager decides to hire a person to do this work, with his or her tasks limited to that work, the unit is insourcing. It has been defined as follows:

> the establishment of a departmental or other limited-sphere information management function in which the employee or employees who perform the function not only acquire the information that is required for the department to achieve its stated mission, but serve the department as information counsellors, mediators, analysts, and interpreters. In the department, an agreed-upon information policy defines the scope of the information management function, and all information specifically identified as falling within the agreed-upon range of services is requested through the information management employee, who is generally referred to as an 'insourced information specialist' (Berner and St. Clair, 1996a).

Insourcing emphasizes the relationship between the information specialist/ consultant and the specifically defined customer base. Because the specialist is a member of the departmental team, he or she is in a position to know intimately the requirements of the people in the department who are going to be using the information being provided. Because of that knowledge, the information specialist/consultant has responsibility for determining how the information will be obtained, what the best search strategies will be, the appropriate formats for searching, and, once the information has been received, responsibility for analysing and interpreting the information before it is delivered to the departmental customer. It represents an almost idealized version of the quality perspective in information delivery, for it provides the best opportunity yet for a personal and immediate interaction between the parties involved in the information transaction. Significantly, in the insourcing arrangement, the information function is no longer characterized merely as a 'support' function and the role of information in the unit's operation is acknowledged as critical to the unit's success.

Examples are found in a number of environments. In a large manufacturing enterprise, for example, the engineering and design staff might have an information 'point person' assigned to specific projects, so that the information function can be focused on the specific needs of that project team. Historically, of course, marketing departments in many businesses have often operated their own information gathering and analysis units, as have multinational businesses, government agencies, or research organizations with information needs that involved security and privacy issues. The new attention to insourcing, however, is notable in that it looks at information management in terms of its critical role and accepts that role as a normal operational function, not as a separate 'stand-alone' function to be turned to when necessary. As such, of course, it relates directly to the quality customer service model, for the very concept of insourcing establishes the critical link between the value of the information provided by the information consultant and use of that information by the information customer.

Professional associations, networking, and collaboration

The Special Libraries Association with its headquarters in Washington, DC, is an organization of some 15,000 specialized librarians and other information services professionals throughout the world. It is clear that the SLA is leading specialized librarianship in three areas: networking, collaboration, and the exploration of international information issues. Similar groups bring specialized librarians together to discuss mutual concerns, for example, such groups as the 'specials' (as they are called) of the Australian Library and Information Association, or the Special Libraries Interest Group of the South African Institute for Librarianship and Information Science, or the Beratungsdienst Wissenschaftliche Spezialbibliotheken of the Deutsches Bibliotheksinstitut. Many special librarians also belong to organizations that connect with the subject speciality or discipline with which their parent organizations are concerned. Thus specialized librarians are to be found at the meetings of the American Chemical Society, because it is to their advantage – as information services practitioners – to be familiar with the professional activities of their information customers. It has been suggested that through these collaborative activities the specialized librarians are able to make their most effective contribution to their parent organizations. Bender (1995) states that we are now living and working in 'the network society.' He points out that 'while the Internet may be the electronic tie that binds us into a professional network', it is the developing of alliances and the growth of relationships that enable special librarians to do their best work. He advocates:

- boundaryless behaviour, 'the ability to overcome mental and physical barriers to cooperation and sharing';
- speed, 'the ability to adapt quickly to change';
- stretch, 'the ability to set our sights high and to perform better than traditional expectations';
- simplification, 'the need to operate as efficiently and cost-effectively as possible'.

Two specific efforts of SLA are noteworthy: the planning now being done for the Second Worldwide Conference on Special Libraries, to be held in England in the year 2000, and the creation of the Freedom Forum/SLA International Library Fellowship. The Freedom Forum facilitates the development of journalism libraries in areas in which they have not existed before, and the Fellowship will send librarians to Freedom Forum sites in Europe and Asia to study and conduct research in special librarianship. As the specialized library community moves toward the development of policies and implementation methodologies for the borderless exchange of information, these are significant efforts.

Conclusions and implications

With enabling technologies now permitting more customization and less standardization in information delivery, the authority of the customer in the information transaction assumes dynamic potential for specialized librarians and other information practitioners. There will be important new opportunities for information transfer, and as special librarians seek and find connections with information services colleagues in other parts of the world, the quality of information they can provide for their customers will be heightened. The quantity of information grows too, of course, but that, too, provides a wonderful opportunity for special librarians, as they become known in their organizations as information consultants and become available to work with information customers in filtering out the useful from the useless.

If there is a cloud hanging over special librarianship, it has to do with societal changes relating to librarianship at large and how specialist librarians will be positioned in the future as the result of these changes. In several countries, specifically Canada, New Zealand, Australia, South Africa, and the USA, efforts are being made to separate librarianship from the educational professions with which it has traditionally been associated. In several countries, the governing authorities are encouraging librarians to affiliate with other cultural institutions, such as museums. Special librarians, information workers whose information focus is quite different from that of those who work in traditional library fields, are very concerned about librarianship being seen as part of the cultural community, just as they were concerned when librarianship was seen as part of the educational community (Report, 1997). Robert L. Klassen, who directs the US Office of Library Programs, now part of the US Department of Education but soon to be part of a new, independent agency, the Institute of Museum and Library Services, does not feel that special librarians will lose anything with this new direction:

> Special libraries are included in the Library Services and Technology Act of 1996. Of course they are, for the whole focus of the legislation is to create a programme of library services that looks at community-based information needs, and special libraries and the organizations that support them are part of the community. Obviously special libraries and their librarians and managers must determine themselves what information is proprietary and what can be shared, but that is not a responsibility that they would shirk. Again, remember what the legislation does. It has been passed to set up a mechanism for creating linkages. We want to link all information in the community that should be linked, to insure equal public access to information (*That*, 1997).

What is happening, in this and in the other changes that are being hurled fast and furious at special librarians, is that the new emphasis on the authority of the customer and the utilization of enabling technology gives them – regardless of where in the world they work – a vehicle for raising the standards of information delivery, for offering information services they were unable to offer in the past, and for enhancing their own roles in the organizations in which they are employed. The current special libraries scene is a busy one, and change is having its impact on the work done by specialist librarians, but these are not negative forces. They are bringing special librarianship into a future that looks, from this perspective, very bright indeed.

References

Abram, S.A. (1993) Sydney Claire, SLA Professional Award Winner 2005: transformational librarianship in action. *Special Libraries*, **84**(4), 213–215.

Abram, S.A. (1996) Adding value . . . *InfoManage*, **3**(3), 6–8.

ACLIS/Australian Council of Libraries and Information Services (1996) *Benchmarking, best practice, and quality management: what's it all about?* Canberra, ACT: Australian Council of Libraries and Information Services.

Albrecht, K. (1994) *The northbound train: finding the purpose, setting the direction, and shaping the destiny of your organization.* New York: American Management Association.

Asantewa. D. (1992) *Strategic planning for special libraries.* Washington, DC: Special Libraries Association.

Ashkenas, R. *et al.* (1995) *The boundaryless organization: breaking the chains of organizational structure.* San Francisco, CA: Jossey-Bass.

Ashworth, W. (1979) *Special librarianship.* London: Clive Bingley.

Australia Department of Finance (1995) *Quality for our clients: improvement for the future.* Canberra, ACT: Australia Department of Finance.

Barker, J. (1993) *Paradigms: the business of discovering the future.* New York: HarperBusiness.

Barrier, M. (1992) Small firms put quality first. *Nation's Business*, **80**(5), 22–32.

Bender, D.R. (1995) *The network society: 1995 state-of-the-association address.* Washington, DC: Special Libraries Association.

Berner, A. and St. Clair, G. (1996a) Insourcing: the evolution of information delivery. *The One-Person Library*, **14**(4), 1–5.

Berner, A. and St. Clair, G. (1996b) Insourcing II: reinventing the OPL's job. *The One-Person Library*, **14**(5), 1–5.

Berner, A. and St. Clair, G. (1996c) Insourcing: positioning the information function where it counts. *InfoManage*, **3**(11), 6–8.

Besant, L.X. (1993) Transformational librarians and entrepreneurial librarians: are they different? *Special Libraries*, **84**(4), 218–219.

Block, P. (1993) *Stewardship: choosing service over self-interest.* San Francisco, CA: Berrett-Koehler.

Brockman, J. (1992) Just another management fad? The implications of TQM for library and information services. *Aslib Proceedings*, **44**(7/8), 283–288.

Campbell, C. and Prime, E. (1997) Reaching the promised land: an interview with Eugenie Prime. *Information Outlook*, **1**(1), 14–16.

Choo, C.W. (1995) *Information management for the intelligent organization: the art of scanning the environment.* Medford, NJ: Information Today (ASIS, American Society for Information Science, monograph series).

Clausen, H. (1995) ISO 9000 and all that: is the information sector ready for the big quantum leap? *Online Information 94 Proceedings.* London: Learned Information, pp. 34–36.

Cundari, L. and Stutz, K. (1995) Enhancing library services: an exploration in meeting customer needs through total quality management. *Special Libraries*, **86**(3), 188–199.

Davenport, T.H. (1993) *Process innovation: reengineering work through information technology.* Boston, MA: Harvard Business School Press.

Dinerman, G. (1996) The information professional: a portrait of progress. *SpeciaList*, **19**(5), 1, 11, 14.

Drabenstott, K.M. (1994) *Analytical review of the library of the future.* Washington, DC: Council on Library Resources.

Dupper, M. (1996) (ed.) Special libraries and librarians. *Innovation*, **12**, June [special issue].

Duston, B. (1993) IT in the OPL: the fugitive user. *The One-Person Library*, **10**(2), 3–4.

Dysart, J. and Abram, S. (1997) What is your information outlook? *Information Outlook*, **1**(1), 34–36.

Ettorre, B. (1995) Managing competitive intelligence. *Management Review*, **84**(10), 15–19.

Fahey, L. and Narayanan, V. (1996) *Macroenvironmental analysis for strategic management*. St. Paul, MN: West Publishing.

Ferguson, E. and Mobley, E. (1984) *Special libraries at work*. Hamden, CT: Shoe String Press.

Ferriero, D. and Wilding, T.L. (1991) Scanning the environment in strategic planning. In: *Masterminding tomorrow's information – creative stregies for the 90s*. Washington, DC: Special Libraries Association.

Franklin, B. (1994) The cost of quality – its application to libraries. *Journal of Library Administration*, **20**(2), 67–74.

Gohlke, A. (1996) Reinvention effort provides model for libraries. *Library Benchmarking Newsletter*, **3**(1), 1–2.

Griffiths, J.-M. and King, D.W. (1991) *A manual on the evaluation of information centers and services*. New York: American Institute of Aeronautics and Astronautics.

Hammer, M. and Champy, J. (1993) *Reengineering the corporation: a manifesto for business revolution*. New York: Harper Collins.

Hammer, M. and Stanton, S.A. (1995) *The reengineering revolution*. New York: Harper Collins.

Hasenyager, B.W. (1996) *Managing the information ecology: a collaborative approach to information technology management*. Westport, CT: Quorum Books.

Hayes, R.M. (1993) *Strategic management for academic libraries: a handbook*. Westport, CT: Greenwood.

Hayes, R.M. and Walter, V.A. (1996) *Strategic management for public libraries*. Westport, CT: Greenwood.

Horton, F.W. Jr. (1994) *Extending the librarian's domain: a survey of emerging occupation opportunities for librarians and information professionals*. Washington, DC: Special Libraries Association.

Information (1993) independent organization, The: Carol Ginsburg's bold approach. *InfoManage*, **1**(1), 1–4.

Information (1994) interview, The: Meg Paul talks about information in Australia, and about the satisfied customer as advocate. *InfoManage*, **1**(5), 1–4.

Jurow, S. and Barnard, S.B. (1993) (eds). *Integrating total quality management in a library setting*. New York: Haworth Press. Also published as *Journal of Library Administration*, **18**(1/2), 1993 [whole issue].

Kahaner, L. (1996) *Competitive intelligence*. New York: Simon and Schuster.

Knowledge (1996) management: the 'third era' of the information age? Lois Remeikis at Booz-Allen & Hamilton thinks it is. *InfoManage*, **3**(10), 1–4.

Lawes, A. (1995) Ann Lawes: thinking about the information manager as change agent. *InfoManage*, **3**(1), 1–4.

Looking (1994) to the 21st century: Joe Fitzsimmons and UMI take on the big issues. *InfoManage*, **1**(3), 1–4.

Matarazzo, J.M. *et al.* (1990a) *Valuing corporate libraries: a survey of senior managers*. Washington, DC: Special Libraries Association.

Matarazzo, J.M. (1990b) *Corporate library excellence*. Washington, DC: Special Libraries Association.

Matarazzo, J.M. and Drake, M.A. (1994) *Information for management: a handbook.* Washington, DC: Special Libraries Association.

Matching (1995) corporate information services to corporate information needs: at Coopers & Lybrand Trish Foy is reinventing information services. *InfoManage*, 2(11), 1–4.

McGarry, D. (1996) IFLA 1996 – the challenge of change: libraries and economic development. *Special Libraries*, 87(4), 322–335.

Megill, K.A. (1995) *Making the information revolution: a handbook on federal information resources management.* Silver Spring, MD: Association for Information and Image Management.

Mount, E. (1995) *Special libraries and information centers.* Washington, DC: Special Libraries Association.

OPLS (1995) in Germany move to enhance status: formal steps taken to structure one-person librarianship as 'a distinct discipline' in information services. *The One-Person Library*, 12(2), 1–7.

Orna, E. (1990) *Practical information policies: how to manage information flow in organizations.* London and Brookfield, VT: Gower.

Orna, E. (1993) Why you need an information policy – and how to sell it. *Aslib Information*, 21(5), 196–200.

Peters, P.E. (1995) Information age avatars. *Library Journal*, 120(5), 33–35.

Piety, J. (1997) What makes you a *special* librarian? *Information Outlook*, 1(1), 32–33.

Piggott, S.E.A. (1995) Why corporate librarians must re-engineer the library for the new information age. *Special Libraries*, 86(1), 11–20.

Powell, A. (1994) Management models and measurement in the virtual library. *Special Libraries*, 85(4), 260–263.

Prusak, L. (1994) Corporate librarians: a soft analysis, a warning, some generic advice. In: M. Matarazzo, and M.A. Drake (eds). *Information for management: a handbook.* Washington, DC: Special Libraries Association.

Queensland Department of Education Virtual Library (1993) *Measuring quality and productivity: performance measures for non-school libraries.* Queensland: QDEVL.

Report (1997) *of the information services management/special librarianship delegation to the Republic of South Africa.* Spokane, WA: Citizen Ambassador Program People to People International.

Riggs, D.E. (1987) Entrepreneurial spirit in strategic planning. *Journal of Library Administration*, 8(1), 41–52.

St. Clair, G. (1993a) Benchmarking, total quality management, and the learning organization: new management paradigms for the information environment, *Special Libraries*, 84(3) [special issue].

St. Clair, G. (1993b) *Customer service in the information environment.* London: Bowker-Saur.

St. Clair, G. (1994) *Power and influence: enhancing information services within the organization.* London: Bowker-Saur.

St. Clair, G. (1995a) Coming back into the information community. *InfoManage*, 2(2), 5–6.

St. Clair, G. (1995b) *Entrepreneurial librarianship: the key to effective information services.* London: Bowker-Saur.

St. Clair, G. (1996a) *Beyond the paradigm shift: bringing inevitable and desirable change to information services.* [Keynote address for the New Zealand Institute of Management's Absolutely Positive Management Conference, Wellington, NZ, 3 May.]

St. Clair, G. (1996b) *Entrepreneurial librarianship: the key to effective information services management.* [Spring Colloquium for the University of Texas at Austin Graduate School of Library and Information Services. Austin, TX, 21 March.]

St. Clair, G. (1996c) The information audit: a powerful management tool for special librarians. *SpeciaList*, **19**(2), 5–6.

St. Clair, G. (1996d) *Information policy: the ethical framework.* [The Second Annual Ethics Lecture in Library and Information Science, presented by the Wayne State University Library and Information Science Program and the Center for Academic Ethics, Detroit, Michigan, 15 February.]

St. Clair, G. (1996e) Managing those expectations: an employee's place in the information services industry. *Information World Review*, (120), 51.

St. Clair, G. (1996f) *Maximizing your influence in a global information environment.* [Keynote address for the Motorola InfoPro Conference '96, Fort Lauderdale, FL, 20 March.]

St. Clair, G. (1996g) *One-person libraries: Checkliste als Orientierungshilfe für den Berieb von OPLs.* Dt. übers. und Bearb.: Evelin Morgenstern. Berlin: Deutsches Bibliotheksinstitut.

St. Clair, G. (1996h) *Power for information services managers: playing the organization like a musical instrument.* [Address for the Annual Alice Rankin Distinguished Lecturer Program, New Jersey Chapter, Special Libraries Association, Warren, NJ, 16 April.]

St. Clair, G. (1996i) Those mythical end-users. [Editorial]. *Library Manager*, (16), 43.

St. Clair, G. (1996j) TQM and libraries: the battle isn't won yet. *Library Manager*, (17), 14–15.

St. Clair, G. (1997a) *Total quality management in information services.* London: Bowker-Saur.

St. Clair, G. (1997b) *Twenty-five years of one-person librarianship: identity, trends, and effects.* [Keynote address for the Annual Conference of Arbeitsgemeinschaft der Spezialbibliotheken e.V./Sektion 5 im Deutschen Bibliotheksverband, Berlin, 6 March.]

St. Clair, G. and Williamson, J. (1986) *Managing the one-person library.* London: Bowker-Saur.

Senge, P. (1990) *The fifth discipline: the art and practice of the learning organization.* New York: Doubleday.

Special Libraries Association (1989) *Strategic Plan.* Washington, DC: SLA.

Special Libraries Association (1992) Presidential Study Commission on Professional Recruitment, Ethics and Professional Standards [The PREPS Commission]. *Report.* Washington, DC: SLA.

Special Libraries Association (1996) Special Committee on Competencies for Special Librarians. *Competencies for special librarians of the 21st century: executive summary.* Washington, DC: SLA. http://www.sla.org

Spiegelman, B.M. (1992) Total quality management in libraries: getting down to the real nitty-gritty. *Library Management Quarterly*, **15**(3), 10–13.

Spiegelman, B.M. (1994) Total quality management: how to improve your library without losing your mind. In: J.M. Matarazzo and M.A. Drake. *Information for Management: a Handbook.* Washington, DC: Special Libraries Association.

Stevenson, H.H. and Jarillo, J.C. (1990) A paradigm of entrepreneurship: entrepreneurial management. *Strategic Management Journal*, (11), 17.

Strable, E.G. (1982) Special libraries: what's the difference? *Illinois Libraries*, (62), 215–217.

Sweeney, D. (1996) (ed.) *Position descriptions in special libraries.* Washington, DC: Special Libraries Association.

That (1997) much-anticipated change in American librarianship is now going to happen – and Bob Klassen is supervising the job. *Info Manage*, **4**(3), 1–4.

Thompson, L. Jr. (1994) *Mastering the challenges of change.* New York: American Management Association.

Urgo, M. (1996) Information services and information technology: can management make the partnering make sense? *InfoManage*, 3(9), 6–8.

White, M.D. and Abels, E.G. (1995) Measuring service quality in special libraries: lessons from service marketing. *Special Libraries*, 86(1), 36–43.

Wickware, M. (1996) When the theoretical meets the ideal: a graduate student's response to insourcing. *One-Person Library*, 14(7), 4–5.

Woodsworth, A. and Williams, J.F. II (1993) *Managing the economics of owning, leasing and contracting out information services.* Brookfield, VT: Ashgate.

Collections

6

John Sweeney

Finance

Financial problems and how to cope with them have, not surprisingly, dominated the published literature during the review period. Very few libraries can now buy everything they want and the gap between desire and reality in collection development is exacerbated by the fact that literature prices, especially for serials, have risen far beyond the general rate of inflation. Libraries have tried to cope with this problem by increasing their reliance on remote supply, by cooperative arrangements with other libraries and by greater dependence on electronic sources. While these approaches are often necessary (and, when properly handled, can even be innovative) they are not without problems of their own. Many collection development policies are now formulated with financial constraints in mind.

How can libraries cope with financial cut-backs? They can try to live within their reduced budgets and prioritize their needs. More positively, they can seek other sources of funding such as sponsorship. A greater reliance on donations can help to relieve the financial burden. Libraries can also move towards access rather than ownership; but the obvious danger of this approach is that other libraries and information sources may be doing the same. In this context cooperation between libraries becomes important to coordinate collection development policies.

Why do libraries exist at all and what are their benefits to society? An excellent paper (Carrigan, 1995) emphasizes the benefits libraries confer on their users, and hence the central importance of collection development. Benefits can either be confined to the individual user (e.g. the gardener who can grow better roses because appropriate literature is held in the public library) or can be wider as a result of work done by the user (e.g. medical research). The return on investment in libraries can however be difficult to quantify: if it were not libraries might attract more funding. Use of individual items is not necessarily the best measurement of benefit because not all uses are positive: many items are scanned and rejected as irrelevant to the users' interests. Hence it is better for the user to have comprehensive collections available on open access so that literature can be scanned without the need to obtain (and pay for) large numbers of items through document delivery services. Available resources should be used to develop both collections and support for them, for example, by funding increases in staff numbers to enable the library to stay open longer.

A paper presented at the 17th International Essen Symposium (Angiletta,1995) discusses how funding crises in US libraries have affected their collection development programmes. The effects of cuts in Finnish universities and the subsequent questioning of the values of libraries are discussed by Kytömäki (1996). One consequence of reduced funding will be prioritization of material to be acquired. An exercise by Shropshire County Libraries to prioritize library spending, including acquisitions spending, is described by Beech (1996). The steps taken in Shropshire will, alas, be depressingly familiar to all librarians who have to cope with reduced budgets – prioritization, purchase of paperbacks rather than hardbacks, stock management efficiency and the elimination of multiple copies even when they are needed. While these steps can mitigate the worst effects of funding shortfalls for a time, they can be counterproductive if they give the impression to the fundholders that the library has coped, and can therefore handle further reductions. The role of price in the selection of literature is the subject of a survey of public libraries in the 200 largest US cities described by Robinson (1995). This found that, interestingly, user demand ranked as more important than price in selection. This may be because price is less important for the type of material generally bought for public libraries than that bought for other types of library; a similar survey of academic libraries might well show a different response:

> Most public library selectors believe that the price of an item does not weigh heavily in making a selection decision. There is little of that spirited price resistance encountered, for example, in academic librarians when they speak of periodical price increases (Robinson, 1995).

Price rises did however result in fewer duplicates being selected as well as fewer non-book items: with serials this is to be expected given the ongoing financial commitment involved. Other articles on the impact of cuts on library acquisitions are by Read (1995), Sumsion (1995), Merrifield (1995) and O'Brien (1995). A recent book on finance and collection development is by Martin (1995).

With funds from their paymasters becoming increasingly limited it is not surprising that libraries are looking at other sources of funding. These can range from sponsorship through schemes of the 'friends of the library' and 'adopt-a-book' type, to agreements with publishers (either directly or via agents) to obtain printed and/or electronic material on advantageous terms. Most librarians would probably not go as far as Michael Olson of the Widener Library at Harvard in seeking sponsorship for his participation in the Boston marathon, but it shows how some imagination can have a positive impact on library funding (Carpenter,

1995). Not all free sources of material are necessarily advantageous: donations in particular are notorious for their unreliability, leading to gaps in serial runs and painful decisions on whether to purchase if the free supply dries up. Sometimes, indeed, the staff resource needed to deal with donations costs more than the price of the serials. The problem is particularly acute in the Third World where many libraries are dependent on such supplies, resulting in uneven coverage and gaps in holdings. This is discussed by Mills (1994) with particular reference to Pacific countries. An article on the Kenya Polytechnic Library (Odini, 1994) puts forward as an interesting idea the possible introduction of a library development levy. The financial problems of serials are particularly acute and are discussed below in **The problem of serials.**

Cooperation – can it overcome financial constraints?

Financial pressures on libraries can make cooperation between them seem attractive. What better way, after all, than to share resources so that each library can be certain that non-core material can be cancelled in the knowledge that another library will take it? The reality is less simple. A group of libraries may agree to cooperate over collection development and will certainly do so for a time, but eventually one or more participants will withdraw because of increased financial pressures. Librarians do not make the key financial decisions in their organizations, and the people that do may not regard continuation of library cooperation agreements as their highest priority. Boissé (1995) has appropriately described library cooperation as a remedy but not a panacea. He presents eleven postulates to be borne in mind when envisaging cooperation:

- Library cooperation is easy when money is plentiful.
- Library cooperation is easier to launch with someone else's money.
- The more meaningful it is, the more difficult it will be to implement.
- Library cooperation is easier to establish in a hitherto unexplored area.
- The more democratic the organization you create, the more difficult the decision-making.
- Your own library will never be the same.
- Be prepared to lose some autonomy.
- Success will be dependent on the success of delivery systems.
- Once established, a library cooperative never ceases to exist.
- Do not boast too much about the success of cooperatives.
- The proof is in the implementation.

While some of these points can be disputed (does a library cooperative never cease to exist?) they are all important and cannot be ignored. Point ten in particular is a warning not to give those who hold the purse strings any opportunity to cut budgets. A better approach is to show that more information can be made available for the same cost.

Voorbij (1996) emphasizes that cooperation in collection development still needs adequate funds to work properly – it cannot be seen as an excuse to cut funding to the cooperating libraries:

> Without adequate funds, local collections become restricted or are stripped down to their bare essentials. More and more, libraries are obliged to cancel even core periodicals. In this situation, cooperative collection development will be hindered and can better be described as shared poverty: this is reason enough to be concerned about the adequacy of the aggregate collection of Dutch libraries (Voorbij, 1996).

Coordination of collection development can change its emphasis from being supplier oriented towards a greater responsiveness to users' needs. An example from South Africa is described by Adams (1994) in which a computerized book selection system for Cape Provincial Library Service was extended to all the participating libraries. A proposed scheme for coordinatiing collection development among academic libraries in Taiwan (Liu, 1994) has as its goal the reduction in the overload of interlibrary loans within the participating libraries.

Serials put a particular strain on acquisitions budgets, and a study at Iowa State University shows the potential for cooperative collection development for geology serials (Zipp, 1995). A Finnish study describes the use of a questionnaire sent to 54 research libraries to assess the potential for cooperative collection development (Wilén, 1995). An interesting recent example of cooperation is the LAMDA project in which nine supply libraries in London and Manchester provide document delivery services to academic libraries in the two cities. Scanning technology is used to transmit documents as laser printout via JANET (Blunden-Ellis, 1996).

Networks and cooperative arrangements are the subject of several papers, for example, in London and South-East England (Nyffenegger, 1996; Sykes, 1996), China (Wang, 1996; Zhu, 1996), Taiwan (M.H. Yang, 1995), Belgium (Borm, 1995), France (Deschamps, 1996), Denmark (Jensen, 1995), Europe and the South Pacific (Dierickx and Evans, 1996), Indiana (Topp, 1996) and on an international scale (Tzeng, 1995). The achievements and limitations of LINC in promoting library cooperation in the UK are discussed by Burch (1996) while *APT (1995) Review* describes a study for LINC of library cooperation in the British Isles. This emphasizes the need to set up actual cooperative arrangements rather than merely to promote the concept of cooperation, and recommends that cooperating libraries agree on common standards of provision. This is particularly important between different types of libraries which in the past may have seen themselves as having different roles, for example, public and academic libraries. The strengthening of regional library systems is recommended in order to expand their activities across the full range of cooperative library and information services and to act as a channel of communication between their members and national bodies. This is admirable in theory, and many regional library systems are already actively involved in such cooperative schemes; but it is the needs of individual library users that are paramount. The regional library system can alert members to, and promote the use of, national information systems covering particular topics; but there is little point in continuing to promote such systems if there is no demand for them. The review also recommends that development of regional library systems be undertaken in conjunction with the creation of mechanisms for strategic regional planning. Another recommendation is that links between the Information and Library Services Lead Body and the Advice, Guidance and Couselling Lead Body are set up, as these bodies are responsible for the development of Scottish/National Vocational Qualifications in their fields. Hence staff working in library cooperation can benefit from the standards which these bodies are promoting. Plaister (1996) provides a useful review of the report.

Collection development

Policies and practice

The days when collection development policies were largely independent of financial considerations are long over. Increasing financial pressures and technological developments mean that policies will be different from those of even ten years ago: access versus ownership will now have greater importance, as will the need to consult users. Any collection development policy must therefore be dynamic while providing sufficient continuity. It follows that a written policy in particular must be constantly revised. Snow (1996) considers written policies unnecessary because they become irrelevant and outdated; selection and collection evaluation should be given precedence. Written policies are useful, but do need updating to cope with advances in the subject (for example, computing) and also new directions in the library's collecting activities: for example, a library may find it necessary to start collecting environmental aspects of its core subjects. Greater flexibility in collection development policies (Hazen, 1995) is necessary in order to serve library users better, 'Library orthodoxy has congealed around a number of purportedly self-evident truths, among them a universal need for collection development policies.' He goes on to suggest as a solution the creation of discipline-specific resource maps that would cover all the resources appropriate to each field. Traditional collection development policies do nevertheless have a valuable and necessary part to play in clarifying the goals of the library or information centre. Rather than do away with them, a better approach is to keep them under constant review and revision to achieve the flexibility that is indeed required.

Truesdell (1994) describes three criteria that can be used to evaluate the effectiveness of access: costs, turnaround time and fill rate. The methodology used at the University of Arizona Library to formulate policy is the subject of a paper by Brin and Cochran (1994) in the same issue. Evaluation of collection development is a process distinct from the evaluation of a library's collections (Carrigan, 1996) and the latter cannot be substituted for the former.

Changes in collection development since 1965 are reviewed by Reid (1996), who also covers the question of access versus holdings, as does Angiletta (1995). Another conference which dealt with collection development policies was that held jointly by the National Acquisitions Group and the UK Serials Group in May 1995 (Horseman, 1995). Pankake (1996) describes collection development at the University of Minnesota. The principles used in building up library stock to optimum levels for different types of library are given by Vasilchenko (1996).

Vision statements are a popular way of expressing the ultimate aims of an organization, and although they can appear to state the obvious – no organization is ever likely to adopt a negative vision statement – they are important in reminding library staff and users of the central importance and goals of libraries. Nowhere is this more important than with acquisitions, for it is these which ultimately define worth. Schmidt (1995) addresses this issue in an article which puts forward several different vision statements with different approaches. The more visionary and snappy and the less conventional these are, the greater is their impact.

The developing role and future of collection development is the subject of a paper by Flowers *et al.* (1995) with reference to the Fondren Library at Rice University. In a significant reorganization the distinction between public service and selection has been blurred, but this is a positive step as it brings selectors more into contact with users and their needs. Collection development departments are increasingly being organized along team lines, but with individuals being given responsibility for selection (Johnson, 1996a). The future of collection developers in a future environment dominated by networked electronic information is discussed by Buckland (1995). Even if networked electronic information leads to a reduction in local collections there will still be a need for collection developers to provide the expertise required to deal with the new sources. Perhaps this is analogous to the situation in online searching, where the move to more end-user and CD-ROM searching has brought about changes in the role of the information specialist rather than its abolition. Collection developers should work closely with acquisitions departments to ensure the smooth selection and acquisition of material for the library. Strategies for working together can be drawn up, including the setting of priorities and the boundaries of responsibilities, and defining mutual expectations (Cargille and Cargille, 1996).

Finance is of course a major constraint on collection development policies. Linear goal programming at the University of Tennessee resulted in a successful distribution of funds among different subjects (Wise and Perushek, 1996). Centralized selection was used at Indianapolis-Marion County Public Library (Gibson, 1995) and this has led to a more varied distribution of subjects to branches without increasing the purchase of multiple copies.

Two recent books on collection development are by Evans (1995) and Futas (1995). A further book (Fales, 1996) describes the training of collection development staff.

Time can be a constraint on efficient selection but there are ways in which selection can be speeded up, although the results may not be ideal (Quinn, 1995).

Types of library and material, and subjects

If we consider collection development in particular types of library, university and other academic libraries have received considerable attention. In the case of a brand new library the opportunity exists to devise a collection development policy from scratch (Hurt *et al.*, 1995). The involvement of the potential users, and the need to keep the collection up to date once it is established, are important. In such a library there is a need for retrospective collecting; this is also the case for university libraries in the former East Germany whose collections need modernizing (Griebel, 1996). Kennedy (1996) examines some isolated university libraries in Australia and the South Pacific and highlights the particular difficulties that such libraries face in building up their collections. Zappen (1995) describes the effect of rising subscription costs at the Rensselaer Polytechnic Institute Libraries in Troy, NY, and recommends various strategies to deal with financial stringency. These include protection of book money, educating and involving the faculties, and exploiting journal use studies. The problem with the last of these is that use patterns in one organization may not be the same as in another; faculty participation is a more useful approach. Selection in the University of Georgia library is described by Bequet (1995).

Collection development in academic libraries in developing countries is the subject of a number of papers (Boakye, 1994a; 1994b; Bablarabe, 1995; Kanjilal and Tripathi, 1995; Sowole, 1995; Andrade and Vergueiro, 1996). A field trip by the National Library of Australia to Polynesia to obtain material from the area is described by Cunningham (1996).

The Canada Institute for Scientific and Technical Information (CISTI) has established collection development policies for its libraries based on a single model. Topics covered include selection, collection management and policy revision (Belzile and Venne, 1994). In the Netherlands, collection development policies in public libraries were investigated in a recent report commissioned by the Ministry of Education, Culture and Science and the Dutch Centre for Libraries and Reading (De Jong, 1996); this concluded that not enough was known about such policies and that a national programme for cooperative acquisition was required. Public library acquisitions in Slovakia are covered by Gonda (1996). Nassimbeni (1995) discusses collection development in public libraries in South Africa in the light of the new language policy.

Schools in Baton Rouge, Louisiana, benefited from a grant for the Library Power school library reform project (Doiron and May, 1995). The resulting collection development was carried out in collaboration with teachers to ensure that the collections meet the needs of the pupils. Kachel (1995) looks at cooperative collection development in connection with media centres in school libraries. A conspectus approach is recommended for analysing individual collections. The problems in providing an adequate resource in school libraries are best dealt with by consultation with teachers who use them (Dubber, 1995). Knotts *et al.* (1996) describe procedures for the selection and acquisition of juvenile books with reference to the St. Louis (Missouri) Public Library.

Turning to collection development of particular types of literature, a recent report funded by the British Library Research and Development Department deals with book selection in public libraries (Book, 1996). Approvals schemes and possible alternatives for book selection, such as supplier selection, prepublication information and using CD-ROMs as sources of information, are reviewed by Aitchison (1995). Collection development policies for free newspapers in the British Library are necessary on account of the Library's archival responsibilities (Smith, 1995). Archives themselves are the subject of a paper by Heald (1995), which highlights the differences between archives and libraries and the implication of this for collection development. In a similar area, the Royal Commission on Historical Manuscripts has published a standard for record repositories which recommends that governing bodies should approve a clearly defined statement of collecting policy (Kitching and Hart, 1995). Digital maps are the subject of two papers presented at the ninth conference of the Groupe des Cartothécaires de LIBER at Zurich in 1994 (McGlamery, 1995; Parry, 1995). These present both the problems inherent in digital map collections but also the opportunities which they provide to use maps in a greater variety of ways than hitherto. The selection of audiovisual materials is covered by Harrison (1995), who draws attention to their particular characteristics and how these affect collection development. Selection of spoken-word cassettes is discussed by Hudson (1996).

Germany presents an interesting example of a country where collection development policies depend to some extent on regional divisions and also on the former separation into two states. Financial constraints have however meant that cooperation between libraries over acquisitions is becoming greater (Ratcliffe, 1995). A country with different problems is Pakistan, where most acquisitions are imported and dependent on limited budgets, inflation and the scarcity of trained personnel (Haider, 1996). The return of Hong Kong to Chinese sovereignty in 1997 has prompted the Library of the City University of Hong Kong to develop a collection on the adjacent Pearl River Delta area, but problems arose from the lack of a similar collection on which to model it and the difficulty of obtaining suitable material. These problems were dealt with by cooperation with academic staff and other institutions both in Hong Kong and in China (Poon, 1995). Another geographical collection formed recently is the South Asian collection at the University of North London which will serve its new course on South Asian Studies (Wiewiorka, 1995). Collection development for Spanish-speaking people has particular problems and remedies (Developing, 1996). Sullivan (1995) describes the challenges involved in collection development of traditional Maori knowledge which involves both oral and written information.

The proliferation and high cost of scientific literature, notably serials, can distort the collection activities of libraries with the result that other subject areas such as the social sciences and humanities are disadvantaged. As a result the Subcommittee for Library Resources of the Royal Dutch Academy of Sciences produced a report (Upset, 1994) whose recommendations include the setting up of a national library plan and the introduction of mandatory legal deposit, which the Netherlands at present lacks. The report is described in detail by Richards (1995) who also makes the valuable point that the increasing specialization of scientific subjects (and their literature) is counterproductive to scientific innovation, which often results from cross-fertilization between different disciplines – a good argument for having a comprehensive reference collection of scientific material in an easily accessible location. Voorbij (1996) analyses collections of foreign academic publications in Dutch libraries and concludes that coverage is inadequate and shrinking. Cooperation, interlibrary loans and increased availability of electronic publications are not likely to solve this problem in the short to medium term, and additional funding is essential.

Collection development in particular subject areas has been well covered in the period under review. Fiction selection in public libraries is described by MacLennan (1996b), while Carter (1994) deals with the selection of books for young adults. Selection of Jewish books for children is described by March (1996). Books on European languages for children and their provision in libraries were the subject of a national study which found that low priority is given to such material (Lonsdale and Everitt, 1996). Acquisitions problems in building a multicultural collection, for example, inadequate knowledge of what is available, are dealt with by Raker (1996). Interdisciplinary collection development is discussed by Wilson and Edelman (1996).

The special collection development needs of law libraries are dealt with by Bluh (1996) and in three chapters (Kearley, 1995; Lyman and Geldmacher, 1995; Strzynski, 1995) of a book devoted to law librarianship. Science, technology and medical collection development are covered in a number of papers, for example, science and mathematics (Chudy, 1995), physical sciences and engineering (Franklin, 1994), GIS (Longstreth, 1995), HIV/AIDS (Luckenbill, 1995), engineering (Miller and Stringer-Hye, 1995), science in Romania (Naicu and Popescu,1995), medicine (Oshida, 1995) and health issues for coloured people (Prendergast and Gray, 1995). Articles on collection development policies in arts, humanities and social science topics include political science (Lowe, 1995), genealogy (Thoroddsen and Petursdottir, 1995), local history (Koppel, 1995), career development (Intner, 1995), music (Hogh, 1995) and alternative literature (Frost, 1995).

The problem of serials

Serials are a particular headache for librarians because of the ongoing commitment and the effects of inflation on library budgets. Cancellation of titles has a negative impact on the services that a library can provide, and has led to increased use of document delivery services (Martin, 1996). There are dangers inherent in such an approach:

> The rise of global communications via the Internet, improvements in transmission, such as Ariel, and the emergence of commercial and not for profit document delivery services seems to have given librarians a false sense of security. In the rush to replace interlibrary loan with document delivery, it generally has been forgotten that such services are, themselves, dependent on library collections for the recovery of needed materials. Now it would appear that it is not possible to presume that what is wanted will be available somewhere, certainly not within the US (Martin, 1996).

Coordinated selection and deselection are suggested as a solution to this problem. Martin then makes another important point which is often overlooked in the access versus ownership debate:

> In the electronic world there won't be the same alternative available as in the print world, where the user who doesn't want to pay for using a database can read the printed version and take notes or make copies as needed.

The ability to browse, to reject irrelevant material without paying for delivery from a remote source and to conduct multidisciplinary research in a well-stocked library are all under threat. Electronic serials are unlikely to relieve this situation because they will still have to be paid for and the ability to browse without needing first to obtain articles from a remote source is limited. Stankus (1995) addresses the problem of inflation among physical sciences serials and asks why publishers do not lower rather than raise costs to enable libraries to continue to subscribe. Publishers have not abandoned print because they obtain more money (and obtain it up front) from print sales to libraries than from electronic serials aimed at faculties. There is also some faculty resistance to contributing important manuscripts to serials that are not reliably archived in print in libraries. The importance of the 'just in case' versus 'just in time' debate is discussed by Naylor (1994) who concludes that university libraries need to adapt to electronic developments in academic serials.

Serial price escalation is particularly acute: projections for 1995 (Brooke and Powell, 1994) suggest an average increase of 6% for US libraries; however, some periodical publishers have been known to increase the price of their serials by over 20% in one year, putting exceptional strain on library funds. Evidently the losses from serial cancellations have so far been more than compensated for by the extra revenue. The situation in Canada is reviewed by Garlock (1995) with suggestions for how to cope with serial price rises. Canada is particularly dependent on foreign serials (unlike the USA or even the UK) and like most 'smaller' countries it is vulnerable to exchange rate fluctuations. The measures suggested (improved cancellation techniques, cooperation, improvement in access, etc.) while helping the short-term problems do not deal with the long term crisis in serials. Garlock draws attention to the fact that some publishers increase prices annually to anticipate further cancellations and makes an important point:

> Every once in a while publishers either wishfully suggest or aggressively assert that the real solution to the serials crisis is better funding. Greeted with incredulity on the librarian's part, the idea is quickly dismissed in the light of the harsh economic realities of funding for libraries. Also implicit in the dismissal is the recognition that even if funding were available, the current economic situation (where research libraries constitute a captive market for commercial STM publishers) needs to be changed (Garlock, 1995).

Academic periodical price statistics for 1996 are given in the *Library Association Record* (Annual, 1996).

The access versus ownership issue is discussed by Line (1995) who proposes that local libraries should concentrate on provision of current material with a centralized stock of older literature. Users like direct exposure to documents and by browsing they can make crucial links between disciplines. Access rather than ownership is no good for this sort of crucial browsing activity. There is also the possibility that material not in public hands might eventually become unavailable unless some agreement is reached on archiving electronic material. Line suggests that the British Library's Document Supply Centre could become the centralized store in the UK for older material, for which browsing might be less important. This may not be an ideal solution: older material does still need to be browsed and compared to some extent, which would suggest that a central store should be somewhere more accessible (e.g. London for the UK), even if storage costs are greater there.

The economics of access versus ownership was the subject of a survey in four libraries of the State University of New York and occupies an entire issue of the *Journal of Interlibrary Loan, Document Delivery & Information Supply*. Costs of interlibrary loans are compared with costs of serial subscriptions and a set of decision rules on whether to provide access via loans or to subscribe to serials are presented (Kingma and Irving, 1996). One important aspect of this research is that it includes an assessment of the opportunity cost to users who will have to wait for interlibrary loans. The study focused on high-priced low use serials in science and mathematics. The authors point out that the widespread adoption of such decision rules could result in many serial cancellations that might cause publishers to raise serial prices. They suggest that other libraries need to assess how closely their own costs of serial subscriptions and interlibrary loan match those presented in the study.

A depressingly high number of articles is concerned with serial deselection. The involvement of users is obviously important, to try to limit the damage as much as possible, and the methodology used at the Louisiana State University Medical

Centre is described by Tucker (1995). Other methodologies, based on institutional cost ratio or cost per use, were used in a deselection exercise at the Chalmers University of Technology in Sweden (Hasslow and Sverring, 1995). Wessels (1995) has developed a model to indicate the optimum size of a serial collection in a given library, but warns that it will work only when the quality of remote document supply is guaranteed.

Chrzastowski and Schmidt (1996) report on cancellations of serials in academic libraries, which are also the subject of an article by Jenkins (1996). Science titles are most likely to be cancelled and least likely to be ordered. Other articles on serial selection and deselection are by Germain (1996) and Green (1996). A more positive note is struck by Kenreich and Stewart (1995) who describe an adopt-a-journal scheme at the Portland State University Library in Oregon to counteract serial cancellations. Serial literature is perhaps unnecessarily swollen by the pressure on many researchers to publish in order to qualify for research grants. The implications of this for libraries are reviewed by Anderson (1996). Bensman (1996), in a study of chemistry serials, concluded that there is little relationship between the value of a serial and its price. Serials in electronic form are considered later in the section on **Electronic serials**.

User interaction

Libraries need to be aware of the needs of their users, and some of them are. User comment and feedback are of great importance in developing and evaluating the library's holdings, and also in formulating its collection development policy. Nevertheless, a library should also provide a lead and inspiration to its users in the development of its holdings and not be merely a passive channel through which users' views on stock development pass. For example, a library can introduce its users to new forms of material in its subject areas such as CD-ROMs and identify key works in its area. Libraries may even have to resist the demands of users if the material requested does not come within the collection development policy or if there is pressure to censor certain subjects.

Surveys and questionnaires are of course a popular way of finding out what the users want. Francis (1996) describes three surveys carried out in 1993 in Northern Ireland among users of public libraries. These suggested that limiting stock to popular subjects would not in itself be popular and that minority interests need to be considered. Another study, however, suggests the opposite (Ito, 1995). Measurement of student satisfaction with academic libraries by means of questionnaires is described by Doyle (1995) and Harvey (1995).

Stewart (1996) describes feedback from chemists at Cornell University on the provision of full-text electronic serials. Other articles on user–library interaction in university libraries are by Angulo (1995) and Chu (1995). Benchmarking can also be used in surveys to establish the success or otherwise of library services as compared with other libraries (Coult and Jackson, 1996).

Although in future many users may come to the library having already consulted an electronic catalogue, many others will pick up useful references on arrival at the library by browsing the shelves. The importance of browsing in revealing useful if unexpected material cannot be overemphasized: no amount of electronic wizardry can replace it. The advantages of browsing in pharmaceutical libraries are described in two Japanese articles (Endo, 1996; Taketomi, 1996).

Studies of user needs, including those of particular user groups, are not necessarily confined to collection development. One study, on women library users, argues however that concentration on collection development has led to a relative neglect of information needs (King, 1995). An article on the needs of Native Americans (Patterson, 1995) identifies relevant areas such as employment, tribal history, civil rights and health. E.L. Yang (1995) discusses library provision for Asian Americans in Colorado. Papers on user interaction in the arts include ones on theatre (Kolganova, 1995) and music (Casey and Taylor, 1995). Finally, an entire issue of *Reference Librarian* is devoted to library users and reference services (Whitlach, 1995).

The issue of censorship is also related, if less positively, to user interaction: this can sometimes be the work of librarians themselves, either consciously or not. In some cases the censorship can arise simply as a result of financial constraints which can preclude the building up of extensive collections (Rodney, 1995). There may also be pressure not to select controversial material. Corporate libraries may be more influenced by the importance of an item in meeting company objectives rather than its intrinsic value and thus build up an unbalanced collection (Scroggs and Leonard, 1995). Nationwide surveys on censorship in public and academic libraries in the USA are described by Wirth (1996) and Bukoff (1995). Harmeyer (1995) has used a quantitative method to investigate holdings of books on abortion in California libraries and concludes that there is a rather greater bias towards so-called pro-choice books in academic and public libraries than there is towards so-called pro-life books in religious affiliated academic libraries. This article has been criticized by Pankake *et al.* (1995) on account of the methodology and assumptions that it makes. The particular problems connected with Holocaust denial literature in libraries are covered by Wolkoff (1996). Other censorship issues in collection development and maintenance include sex (Carmichael, 1995), homosexuality (Foerstel, 1994) and hunting (Wiese, 1996).

Automation

Selection is essentially an activity that needs to go through a brain and so the scope for automation is restricted. Acquisition functions are rather more amenable to information technology. Electronic Data Interchange (EDI) enables acquisitions librarians to perform their work more efficiently (Lamborn, 1995). Brown (1994) describes the application of EDI to serials acquisition and in particular discusses the linking of an integrated library system and an online subscription service.

Problems can arise when staff in an acquisition department move from one online acquisitions system to another; ideally the people who develop the procedures should be those who are to use the new records (Heath, 1994). Kraft (1996) raises concerns about the usefulness of online integrated library systems in acquisitions. Particular acquisitions systems described in the review period include ERWIN (Kemminer and Summann, 1994), KeyNOTIS (Zheng and Huang, 1994) and MSUS/PALS (Hudson, 1994). Automation of standing order card files is described by Hogan (1994).

Expert systems have considerable potential in collection development, but although applications have so far been limited they have considerable potential in integrated library systems (Jeng, 1995). Another review on expert systems highlights existing research projects related to acquisitions and various other aspects of collection management. (Hawkes, 1994).

CD-ROM sources can be used in collection development, for example in a survey to discover whether the proportion of out-of-print books is higher in some broad subject areas than in others (Nisonger, 1995). A review of Bookscape, a Windows based CD-ROM of current books, suggests that it mainly covers North American material (MacLennan, 1996a).

Collection management, evaluation and retention/ disposal

Open access collections are more convenient for users and can cut down the work of library staff. The Auraria library, which serves three academic institutions in Colorado, has moved from closed to open access for its current periodicals. The result has been that use of the collection has doubled and library staff have found that they can spend more quality time with users (Jurries, 1995). A similar move at the University of Toronto is described by McCaskill *et al.* (1995). Inevitably not all material can be stored on site, whether on open or closed access, and Silverstein and Shieber (1996) discuss various methods to predict book use to determine which books should be stored at a remote site. Usage studies were undertaken on 300 review periodicals in the physical sciences at Pennsylvania State University with a view to reorganizing their shelving: as a result, periodical titles were merged into the main periodicals collection, while series were incorporated with monographs (Butkovich, 1996).

Shortage of space is a serious problem for many libraries. Sapp and Suttle (1994) present a method of quantifying annual expansion of stock and shelf capacities using a spreadsheet in order to make the best use of the space available. Cutting down on acquisitions or converting to electronic forms are dismissed as options by Johnson (1996c), who highlights aspects of collection management policy that will help make decisions on withdrawals and transfers to storage. Tilevitz (1996) looks at space problems in law libraries of small firms by assessing the advantages and disadvantages of printed, online and CD-ROM products, as well as reconciling a reduction in overcrowding with the need to maintain access to information. Larger and academic law libraries are the subject of an article by Puckett (1996) which emphasizes that space is needed for their collections: conversion to electronic form is expensive so that not all necessary stock will be converted.

Collections in the Federal Reserve Bank of Cleveland, Ohio, have been evaluated both by looking at loan and acquisitions records to identify weaknesses in the collection, and also by comparing bibliographies of research papers from other Federal Reserve Banks with the Cleveland collection (Green, 1995). Day and Revill (1995) used circulation data to evaluate the collection at the Learning Services Library of Liverpool John Moores University. Collection evaluation at Seoul National University Library is described by Coe (1995). Ephraim (1994) has reviewed measures for collection analysis and concludes that a combination is most effective so that weaknesses in one approach are covered by another. Methods of measuring the use of serials to decide which ones to cancel are described by Ozbudak(1994). Evaluation in particular subject areas includes studies on economics (Carpenter and Getz, 1995), health (Fenske, 1994), local documents (Kelly, 1995) and psychology using the Conspectus (Dorner, 1994).

Disposal of library stock, in particular of serials, can become necessary because of space or other considerations. Various alternatives, such as reformatting or storage off-site are possible (Intner, 1994). Alcock (1996) takes a vigorous attitude to stock weeding and suggests that departmental academic libraries should be charged for storage of their collections. A survey of the practice of 300 libraries in the UK with suggestions for greater coordination of disposal policies is described in a BNB Research Fund Report (Capital Planning Information, 1995).

Preservation and disaster management

According to Foot (1996), management of library collections should be determined both by the aims of the library and by the collections themselves. Many factors must be considered in the storage and maintenance of collections, for example, climate, nature of the buildings, fire risk and security. An IFLA satellite meeting held in Budapest in August 1995 was devoted to conservation and preservation in libraries, and a report of the meeting is available (Hanus and Hanusova, 1996). The involvement of the IFLA Core Programme for Preservation and Conservation in the Unesco 'Memory of the World' initiative, designed to safeguard the world's documentary heritage, is described by Varlamoff (1995). Loughborough University has surveyed preservation policies in UK libraries, archives and record offices with the aim of developing a national preservation and retention policy, and also of preparing a manual of good practice in this area (Feather, 1996a); there is a book on policies and practices in British libraries from the same author (Feather, 1996b).

Rowley and Hanthorn (1996) describe a conservation treatment unit at Iowa State University.

Disasters fortunately do not strike libraries very often but it is nevertheless wise to take precautions against their occurrence. Emergency planning can include the identification of risks, assembling a disaster kit, and preparing a disaster plan, team and manual (George, 1995). A research project, again from Loughborough University, reviews disaster management practice in the UK with recommended guidelines on disaster management (Matthews and Eden, 1996). Higginbotham (1995) sets out an eight-step strategy for dealing with disaster, including the emergency planning process. There is also a recent book on disaster preparation in special libraries (Kahn, 1995). The potential of libraries to help with an actual disaster, namely the destruction of libraries in Bosnia, is suggested by Reidlmayer (1996).

Digital preservation of illustrated texts is a difficult problem, and a combined solution using scanning of microform is described by Gertz (1996). Preservation in particular localities includes work in Krakow (Rhys-Lewis, 1995) and New York State (Gertz, 1995).

Security

Libraries, particularly those with open access collections, are especially prone to theft and mutilation of their stock. Security can be costly, but such costs need to be balanced against those likely to be incurred through loss. Some items may of course be irreplaceable. Many factors can contribute to poor security, for example, lack of security policies, reductions in the number of library employees, lack of penalty notices, lack of electronic security devices, poor space arrangement, and even negative attitudes to security by some library staff. These and other factors were highlighted in a study of security problems in public libraries in Taipei (Chiu, 1996) but are generally applicable. Thefts can go undetected; it can then be difficult to determine the extent of loss and hence the cost of replacing the stolen items. Foster (1996) describes four sampling methods and assesses their relative effectiveness. Security at Las Vegas Library in Nevada University has been provided through the unusual step of using student security patrols (Nicewarner and Heaton, 1995). Shockowitz (1995) describes security with special reference to archives and rare books.

Security devices and their costs are discussed by Holt (1995). The Black River Technical College Library in Arkansas, faced with the need to install a security system, sent a questionnaire to all other academic college libraries in Arkansas and based its choice of system on the replies (Ulmer, 1996). Compact discs can be a tempting target for thieves and Werbelow and Kalk (1996) compare the security systems that can be used. The use of safety strips for both printed and audiovisual material proved effective in cutting down theft in the Berlin-Marzahn central library (Wuthe, 1996). Map security in the University of Hawaii's Hamilton Library Map Collection is described by Togashi (1995).

The digital library

General

The noise made by advocates of extreme positions 'shred the books' versus, 'nostalgic for cuneiform' can unfortunately drown out the more moderate views of most librarians and information officers, who see electronic products as a further but not exclusive weapon in their armoury of resources. It is unlikely that electronic serials and the Internet will replace more traditional sources of information, but nevertheless there will be occasions when they will be the best tools to use. Pitman (1995) presents the two opposing points of view and urges a sensible middle course.

The debate over the electronic library has perhaps tended to push the most important person, the user, into the background. The need is, however, for information suppliers to ensure that the user has trouble-free access to information that is of value (Sylge, 1996). Issues for libraries in development of electronic usage include awareness of technology trends, collaboration with suppliers in the development of new products and appropriate staffing (Cox, 1996). Use of electronic media, including the Internet, in a wide range of libraries is described by Slavens (1996). Policy issues in digital library development are discussed by Kahin (1995), with particular reference to costs of electronic serials. There are of course copyright problems associated with the provision of serials in electronic format: Dijkstra (1994) describes how Tilburg University came to an agreement with Elsevier as part of its development of digital facilities. The impact of electronic media on change in electronic libraries is described by Young and Peters (1996).

The implications of electronic publishing for collection development and management are examined by Hitchingham (1996) with reference to the Virginia Polytechnic Institute and State University. Collection development, copyright and royalty payments for electronic documents with particular regard to the Library of Congress are described by Peters (1995). The impact of electronic publishing on libraries is the subject of a recent book (Brown, 1996) and the effect on the British Library reading rooms is described in a report (Mark Fresco Consultancy, 1996).

Collection policies for electronic media, and the effect of such media on collection development generally, are addressed by a number of papers. Johnson (1995) describes various collection development and management issues raised by electronic media, while a recent book (Dickinson, 1994) also addresses this issue.

There are various decisions that need to be made when selecting electronic resources (Johnson, 1996b); for example, which particular medium to select depends on the type of information delivery that is needed. The issues influencing acquisitions policy for electronic media are also discussed by Arnold (1996) with particular reference to the ELINOR electronic library project at De Montfort University. Greenstein (1995) describes a new collection development policy for digital research data for the services contributing to the new UK Arts and Humanities Data Service.

Electronic serials

Stanley (1995) argues that libraries should provide access to electronic serials and points out some of their advantages, for example, cost benefits, storage advantages and environmental benefits. Cancer and AIDS are areas where Stanley believes electronic communication can bring advantages by providing timely access to the latest developments for researchers. Another article on the effect of electronic serials on libraries presents some possible collection development options (Ungern-Sternberg and Lindquist, 1995); the development of such formats will lead to changes in the role of information professionals (Hatvany, 1996).

Issues involved in collecting and providing access to electronic serials are discussed by Weston *et al.* (1995). While they undoubtedly have their advantages, a note of caution is sounded by Crawford and Gorman (1995) on moving too far in this direction, or indeed in the direction of electronic media generally. Printed sources still have a very powerful role, and also have some advantages over new media which can be ignored in the rapidly changing environment that libraries now find themselves in.

The selection of CD-ROMs presents particular challenges, not least because of their increasing numbers. The increasing availability of full text serials in electronic form may lead to less dependence on secondary sources. Networking of CD-ROMs should become easier with developments in technology (Jacsó, 1995). Bentley *et al.* (1995) discuss selection and weeding of CD-ROMs as well as giving a list of reference CD-ROMs. The switch from paper to CD-ROM collections at the USA Documentation Center in Copenhagen has been helped by the search system used, and has also led to increased stock and more space becoming available for other purposes (Sorensen,1996).

The Internet

The Internet represents a valuable source of information that can be used to supplement, but not necessarily replace, a library's existing resources. Its size and the lengthy response times can make it difficult to use. However, there is a need to incorporate identification of relevant Internet resources within a library's overall collection development policy. Demas *et al.* (1995) present methods for developing the systematic identification, evaluation and selection of Internet resources. These include training of selectors, selection strategy, specification for workstations and the establishment of communication channels between selectors. Pratt *et al.* (1996)

describe guidelines for selecting Internet resources in a medical library; these form an addition to the main collection development policy. A similar approach is described by Cassel (1995) for a public library considering offering the public access to the Internet. The usefulness of the Internet in academic libraries is described by Bakker (1996). Many libraries and information centres now have their own Web pages and some include their collection development policies.

Particular collections

Space does not permit mention of more than a small number of articles that have appeared on particular collections during the reporting period. Several articles describe national libraries and their collections, for example, Australia (National, 1996), China (Weiming and Ning, 1996), France (Revelli, 1996), Kenya (Brief, 1995) and Macedonia (Jankoska and Kostavska, 1996). Other specific libraries include the Clothworkers Hall in London (Wickham, 1995), the National Library of Education in Washington (Floyd, 1995) and the Science, Industry and Business Library of the New York Public Library (Harriott, 1996). Other libraries or collections on specific subjects or types of material include the City Business Library in London (Humphreys and Smith, 1996), the Gerald Tucker Memorial Medical Library (Dudden, 1995), the Siriraj Medical Library in Thailand (Pruess, 1996), history of science (Miniati and Berni, 1995), toy libraries (Jackson, 1996), German collections (Kelly, 1996) and reports (Pilling, 1996).

Acknowledgements

The author would like to thank Adrian Shindler and Helen Robbins of the British Library Information Science Service for their invaluable help in identifying the references for this article. Alan Gomersall, Director of the British Library Science Reference and Information Service, read the original manuscript and made a number of helpful suggestions.

References

Adams, V. (1994) Cooperative selection. *Cape Librarian*, **38**(6), 14–15.
Aitchison, C. (1995) Hands-off selection. *Bookseller*, (4665), 19 May, 22, 24.
Alcock, D. (1996) Is iconoclasm a virtue? Or the importance of stock editing. *Library Review*, **45**(6), 54–57.

140   *Collections*

Anderson, P. (1996) Excessive publication in scholarly journals: what information managers need to know. *Managing Information*, **3**(5), 24, 27–28.

Andrade, D. and Vergueiro, W. (1996) Collection development in academic libraries: a Brazilian library's experience. *New Library World*, **97**(1128), 15–24.

Angiletta, A.M. (1995) Collection development in the large American research library: at an end or at a beginning? In: *Information Superhighway: the role of librarians, information scientists and intermediaries. 17th International Essen Symposium, 24–27 October 1994*, eds. A.H. Helal and J.W. Weiss. Essen: Universitätsbibliothek Essen, pp. 337–348.

Angulo, S.C. (1995) The users of the university library. *Boletin de la Asociacion Andaluza de Bibliotecarios*, **11**(41), 9–28.

Annual (1996) periodical prices for 1996. *Library Association Record*, **98**(5), May, 264.

APT (1995) *review, The: a review of library and information cooperation in the UK and the Republic of Ireland for the Library and Information Cooperation Council (LINC)*. Sheffield: LINC. (British Library R&D Report 6212).

Arnold, K. (1996) Acquisitions policy in an electronic world. In: *Electronic documents and information: from preservation to access. 18th International Essen Symposium, 23–26 October 1995*, eds. A.H. Helal and J.W. Weiss. Essen: Universitätsbibliothek Essen, pp. 68–77.

Bablarabe, A.A. (1995) Contemporary issues in collection development programmes of Nigerian university libraries. *International Information and Library Review*, **27**(4), 333–343.

Bakker, T. (1996) Collection building in the digital age: Internet – a useful tool for academic libraries. *Open*, **28**(6), 142–144.

Beech, P. (1996) Reduced budgeting – an exercise in prioritization. *Taking Stock*, **5**(1), 25–27.

Belzile, S. and Venne, L. (1994) Collection development policies in CISTI branch libraries. *Documentation et Bibliothéques*, **40**(1), 21–24.

Bensman, S.J. (1996) The structure of the library market for scientific journals: the case for chemistry. *Library Resources and Technical Services*, **40**(2), 145–151, 154–170.

Bentley, S. *et al.* (1995) Reference resources for the digital age. *Library Journal*, **120**(13), 45–48.

Bequet, G. (1995) The selection of traditional materials and databases: the University of Georgia Library in the United States. *Bulletin des Bibliothéques de France*, **40**(3), 40–47.

Bluh, P. (1996) The winds of change: acquisitions for a new century. *Law Library Journal*, **88**(1), 90–95.

Blunden-Ellis, J. (1996) LAMDA: a new venture in document delivery. *Law Librarian*, **27**(2), 97–98.

Boakye, G. (1994a) The academic libraries of developing countries: towards effective book provision in the face of austerity. *New Library World*, **95**(1116), 12–17.

Boakye, G. (1994b) Challenges and frustrations of an acquisitions librarian in a developing country: the case of Balme Library. *Taking Stock*, **3**(1), 26–31.

Boissé, J.A. (1995) Library cooperation: a remedy but not a panacea. *IFLA Journal*, **21**(2), 89–93.

Book (1996) selection in public libraries. (Chambers and Stoll – British Library Research and Development Department. British National Bibliography Research Fund Report 80). Boston Spa: British Library.

Borm, J.V. (1995) Regional library cooperation in Belgium. *European Research Libraries Cooperation*, **5**(4), 373–382.

Brief (1995) on Kenya's National Library Service, A. *FID News Bulletin*, **45**(9), 267–270.

Brin, B. and Cochran, E. (1994) Access and ownership in the academic environment; one library's progress report. *Journal of Academic Librarianship*, **20**(4), 207–212.

Brooke, F.D. and Powell, A. (1994) EBSCO 1995 serial price projections. *Serials Review*, **20**(3), 85–94.

Brown, D.J. (1996) (comp.) *Electronic publishing and libraries: planning for the impact and growth to 2003*. East Grinstead: Bowker-Saur.

Brown, L.C.B. (1994) Electronic data transfer: what's in it for the serials department? *Acquisitions Librarian*, (11), 149–160.

Buckland, M.K. (1995) What will collection developers do? *Information Technology and Libraries*, **14**(3), 155–159.

Bukoff, R.N. (1995) Censorship and the American College Library. *College and Research Libraries*, **56**(5), 395–407.

Burch, B. (1996) Library and information cooperation: a personal reflection. *LASER Link*, (Spring/Summer), 6–7.

Butkovich, N.J. (1996) Reshelving study of review literature in the physical sciences. *Library Resources and Technical Services*, **40**(2), 139–144.

Capital Planning Information (1995) *Disposal of printed material from libraries*. London: British Library. (BNB Fund Report, 72.)

Cargille, D. and Cargille, K. (1996) Sleeping with the enemy: the love/hate relationship between acquisitions and collection development. *Library Acquisitions: Practice and Theory*, **20**(1), 41–47.

Carmichael, J.V. (1995) Sex in public (libraries): an historical sampler of what every librarian should know. *North Carolina Libraries*, **53**(2), 59–64.

Carpenter, D. and Getz, M. (1995) Evaluation of library resources in the field of economics: a case study. *Collection Management*, **20**(1/2), 49–89.

Carpenter, K.E. (1995) A librarians challenge. *Harvard Library Bulletin*, **6**(2), 30–1.

Carrigan, D.P. (1995) Toward a theory of collection development. *Library Acquisitions: Practice and Theory*, **19**(1), 97–106.

Carrigan, D.P. (1996) Collection development – evaluation. *Journal of Academic Librarianship*, **22**(4), 273–278.

Carter, B. (1994) *Best books for young adults: the selection, the history, the romance*. Chicago: American Library Association.

Casey, J. and Taylor, K. (1995) Music library users: who are these people and what do they want from us? *Music Reference Services Quarterly*, **3**(3), 3–14.

Cassel, R. (1995) Selection criteria for Internet resources. *College and Research Libraries News*, **56**(2), 92–93.

Chiu, S.-P. (1996) A study of theft and mutilation in public libraries in Taipei Metropolitan. *Journal of Educational Media and Library Sciences*, **33**(4), 454–477.

Chrzastowski, T.E. and Schmidt, K.A. (1996) Collections at risk: revisiting serial cancellations in academic libraries. *College and Research Libraries*, **57**(4), 351–364.

Chu, F.T. (1995) Collaboration in a loosely coupled system: librarian–faculty relations in collection development. *Library and Information Science Research*, **17**(2), 135–150.

Chudy, S. (1995) Developing a collection in the 1990s. *Arkansas Libraries*, **52**(2), 17–19.

Coe, D.W. (1995) Global perspectives: evaluating collections at Seoul National University Library, part 1. *Technicalities*, **15**(4), 13–14.

Coult, G. and Jackson, L. (1996) Measuring up to the competition. *Library Association Record*, **98**(9), 471.

Cox, J. (1996) Towards the electronic library: meeting the challenge. *Serials*, **9**(2), 163–169.

Crawford, W. and Gorman, M. (1995) *Future libraries: dreams, madness and reality.* Chicago: American Library Association.

Cunningham, A. (1996) Polynesian pathways: the National Library of Australia Pacific Acquisition Trip, 1995. *Australian Academic and Research Libraries*, **27**(2), 124–131.

Day, M. and Revill, D. (1995) Towards the active collection: the use of circulation analyses in collection evaluation. *Journal of Librarianship and Information Science*, **27**(3), 149–157.

De Jong, J. (1996) Reducing or improving services? A review of collection development in public libraries. *Open*, **28**(5), 123–125.

Demas, S. *et al.* (1995) The Internet and collection development: mainstreaming selection of Internet resources. *Library Resources and Technical Services*, **39**(3), 275–290.

Deschamps, C. (1996) *Networking and cooperation in France.* Boston Spa: British Library Research and Development Department, 91–93. (BLRD Report 6249).

Developing (1996) collections for the Spanish speaking. *RQ*, **35**(3), 330–342.

Dickinson, G.K. (1994) *Selection and evaluation of electronic resources.* Englewood, CO: Libraries Unlimited.

Dierickx, H. and Evans, J. (1996) EUROLIB and SPARDIN: a tale of two continents. *International Information and Library Review*, **28**(1), 59–78.

Dijkstra, J. (1994) A digital library in the mid-nineties, ahead or on schedule? *Information Services and Use*, **14**(4), 267–277.

Doiron, C. and May, C. (1995) Book power: the role of collection development in library power. *LLA Bulletin*, **57**(3), 173–175.

Dorner, D.E. (1994) A study of the collection inventory assessments for psychology in the Canadian Conspectus database and an analysis of Conspectus methodology. *Library and Information Science Research*, **16**(4), 279–297.

Doyle, C. (1995) The perceptions of library service questionnaire (PLSQ): the development of a reliable instrument to measure student perceptions of and satisfaction with quality of service in an academic library. *New Review of Academic Librarianship*, **1**, 139–160.

Dubber, G. (1995) To buy or not to buy: resourcing the curriculum in the primary school library. *School Librarian*, **43**(1), 14–15.

Dudden, R.F. (1995) Gerald Tucker Memorial Medical Library. *Colorado Libraries*, **21**(4), 45–47.

Endo, H. (1996) The usefulness of browsing: from the viewpoint of the difference between materials and information. *Pharmaceutical Library Bulletin* [*Yakugaku Toshokan*], **41**(1), 28–29.

Ephraim, P.E. (1994) A review of qualitative and quantitative measures in collection analysis. *Electronic Library*, **12**(4), 237–242.

Evans, G.E. (1995) *Developing library and information center collections.* 3rd ed. Englewood, CO: Libraries Unlimited. (Library Science Text Series).

Fales, S. (1996) (ed.) *Guide for training collection development librarians.* American Library Association. (Collection Management and Development Guides, 8).

Feather, J.P. (1996a) *National preservation policy: a manual for libraries, archives and record offices.* London: British Library.

Feather, J.P. *et al.* (1996b) *Preservation management: policies and practices in British libraries.* Aldershot: Gower.

Fenske, R.E. (1994) Evaluation of monograph selection in a health sciences library. *Bulletin of the Medical Library Association*, **82**(3), 265–270.

Flowers, K.A. *et al.* (1995) Special selection: library reorganization for the 21st century: collection development and acquisitions in a changing university environment. *Library Acquisitions: Practice and Theory*, **19**(4), 463–469.

Floyd, N.L. (1995) A new national library fuels the engine of education. *American Libraries*, **26**(10), 1032–1034.

Foerstel, H. (1994) Conflict and compromise over homosexual literature. *Emergency Librarian*, **22**(2), 28–30.

Foot, M.M. (1996) Housing our collections: environment and storage for libraries and archives. *IFLA Journal*, **22**(2), 110–114.

Foster, C. (1996) Determining losses in academic libraries and the benefits of theft detection systems. *Journal of Librarianship and Information Science*, **28**(2), 93–104.

Francis, J.P.E. (1996) The complete library. *Public Library Journal*, **11**(4), 111–115.

Franklin, H.L. (1994) Sci/Tech book approval plans can be effective. *Collection Management*, **19**(1/2), 135–145.

Frost, S. (1995) Beyond the mainstream: examining alternative sources for stock selection. *Assistant Librarian*, **88**(4), 62.

Futas, E. (1995) *Collection development policies and procedures*. Phoenix: Oryx Press.

Garlock, G.N. (1995) The crisis of rising serial prices in a Canadian context revisited. *Serials Librarian*, **26**(3/4), 33–41.

George, S.C. (1995) Library disasters: are you prepared? *College and Research Libraries News*, **56**(2), 80, 82–84.

Germain, J.C. (1996) Serial selection and deselection decisions: the view from America. *Learned Publishing*, **9**(2), 87–93.

Gertz, J. (1995) Ten years of preservation in New York State: the comprehensive research libraries. *Library Resources and Technical Services*, **39**(2), 198–208.

Gertz, J. (1996) Selection for preservation: a digital solution for illustrated texts. *Library Resources and Technical Services*, **40**(1), 78–83.

Gibson, C. (1995) How we spent 2.7 million dollars, with the help of centralized selection. *Library Journal*, **120**(14), 128–130.

Gonda, M. (1996) Doplňovanie fondov vo verejných knižniciach. [Public library stock acquisition]. *Knižnice a Informácie*, **28**(8–9), 352–355.

Green, L. (1995) Evaluating a corporate library collection. *Journal of Interlibrary Loan, Document Delivery and Information Supply*, **6**(1), 49–61.

Green, M. (1996) Serial selection and deselection. *Serials*, **9**(1), 69–72.

Greenstein, D. (1995) *Collection policies*. Boston Spa: British Library Research and Development Department. (BLRD Report 6238), pp. 7–27.

Griebel, R. (1996) Bajor költségvetési modell és állományfejlesztés Németország új szövetségi tartományainak egyetemi könyvtáraiban. [Bavarian budget model and collection development in the universities of the new German Federal States.] *Tudományos és Műszaki Tájékoztatás*, **43**(6), 215–222.

Haider, S.J. (1996) Acquisition and collection development in Pakistan. *Library Acquisitions: Practice and Theory*, **20**(2), 147–156.

Hanus, J. and Hanusová, E. (1996) Library preservation and conservation in the 90s. *Knižnice a Informácie*, **28**(2), 84–87.

Harmeyer, D. (1995) Potential collection development bias: some evidence on a controversial topic in California. *College and Research Libraries*, **56**(2), 101–111.

Harriott, E. (1996) New York's door to the information age. *American Libraries*, **27**(6), 58–59.

Harrison, H.P. (1995) Selection and audiovisual collections. *IFLA Journal*, **21**(3), 185–190.

Harvey, L. (1995) Student satisfaction. *New Review of Academic Librarianship*, **1**, 161–173.

Hasslow, R. and Sverring, A. (1995) Deselection of serials: the Chalmers University of Technology Library method. *Collection Management*, **19**(3/4), 151–170.

Hatvany, B. (1996) Towards a worldwide library. *IFLA Journal*, **22**(3), 246–247.

Hawkes, C.P. (1994) Expert systems in technical services and collection management. *Information Technology and Libraries*, **13**(3), 203–212.

Hazen, D.C. (1995) Collection development policies in the information age. *College and Research Libraries*, **56**(1), 29–31.

Heald, C. (1995) Are we collecting the right stuff? *Archivaria*, **40**, 182–188.

Heath, B. (1994) Migrating between online acquisitions systems: organizing information and staff. *Acquisitions Librarian*, (12), 15–26.

Higginbotham, B.B. (1995) Before disaster strikes; be prepared. *Technicalities*, **15**(7), 4–5.

Hitchingham, E. (1996) Collection management in the light of electronic publishing. *Information Technology and Libraries*, **15**(1), 38–41.

Hogan, W.P. (1994) Standing order matrices; or, only a mother could love a non-periodical continuation. *Acquisitions Librarian*, (12), 95–101.

Hogh, B. (1995) Listen to Denmark. *Fontes Artis Musicae*, **42**(1), 51–53.

Holt, G.E. (1995) Vigilant eyes, bugs and firewalls: the costs of library security. *Bottom Line*, **8**(4), 35–36.

Horseman, J. (1995) Endangered species: evolving strategies for library collection management. *Serials*, **8**(2), 112–116.

Hudson, A. (1996) Spoken word: the book of the future? *Assistant Librarian*, **89**(3), 44–46.

Hudson, G.A. (1994) The MSUS/PALS Acquisitions Subsystem Vendor File. *Acquisitions Librarian*, (11), 161–186.

Humphreys, G. and Smith, L. (1996) The City Business Library. *Law Librarian*, **27**(2), 70–71.

Hurt, C.S. *et al.* (1995) Collection development strategies for a university center library. *College and Research Libraries*, **56**(6), 487–495.

Intner, S.S. (1994) Options for collection review. *Technicalities*, **14**(5), 3–6.

Intner, S.S. (1995) Collection cosmology, or is it only a big bang after all? *Technicalities*, **15**(1), 2–5.

Ito, S. (1995) Changing users and public library services. *Toshokan-Kai* [Library World], **47**(3), 163–170.

Jackson, V. (1996) Toy libraries down under. *Play Matters*, (10), 7.

Jacsó, P. (1995) CD-ROM collection development dilemmas. *Information Today*, **12**(1), 22.

Jankoska, S. and Kostavska, V. (1996) The St Clement of Ohrid National and University Library: Macedonia's national library. *Alexandria*, **8**(2), 117–131.

Jeng, J. (1995) Expert system applications in cataloging, acquisitions, and collection development: a status review. *Technical Services Quarterly*, **12**(3), 17–28.

Jenkins, C. (1996) Serial selection and deselection: policies and decision-making. *Learned Publishing*, **9**(3), 157–162.

Jensen, N. (1995) Library cooperation in Denmark – new model. *Scandinavian Public Library Quarterly*, **28**(1), 25–26.

Johnson, P. (1995) Collection development in the electronic library: still a puzzlement! *Technicalities*, **15**(6), 4–6.

Johnson, P. (1996a) Collection development librarians and restructuring: preparing for change. *Technicalities*, **16**(1), 9–11.

Johnson, P. (1996b) Selecting electronic resources: developing a local decision-making matrix. *Cataloging and Classification Quarterly*, **22**(3/4), 9–24.

Johnson, P. (1996c) Space: the final frontier. *Technicalities*, **16**(4), 1, 6–8.

Jurries, E.F. (1995) Moving from closed to open current periodicals access: factors to consider. *Technical Services Quarterly*, **13**(1), 17–29.

Kachel, D.E. (1995) Looking inward before outward: preparing the school library media center for cooperative collection development. *School Library Media Quarterly*, **23**(2), 101–113.

Kahin, B. (1995) Institutional and policy issues in the development of the digital library. In: *Proceedings of the Second Conference on scholarship and technology in the humanities, Elvetham Hall, Hampshire, UK, 13–16 April 1994*, eds S. Kenna and S. Ross. East Grinstead: Bowker-Saur, pp. 127–140.

Kahn, M. (1995) *Disaster prevention and response for special libraries: an information kit.* Washington D.C.: Special Libraries Association.

Kanjilal, U. and Tripathi, S.M. (1995) Collection development: planning for IGNOU library system. *Library Acquisitions: Practice and Theory*, **19**(1), 83–95.

Kearley, T. (1995) Foreign and international collections. Part 1: Foreign. In: Kehoe, P.E. *et al.* (1995) pp. 257–312.

Kehoe, P.E. *et al.* (1995) (eds) *Law librarianship: a handbook for the electronic age.* Littleton, CO: Rothman.

Kelly, M.C. (1995). Redefining local documents collections. *Illinois Libraries*, **77**(1), 17–19.

Kelly, W.A. (1996) The German collections in the National Library of Scotland. *German Studies Library Group Newsletter*, (20), 2–11.

Kemminer, R. and Summann, F. (1994) ERWIN: the acquisition system of Bielefeld university library. *Bibliotheksdienst*, **28**(5), 675–684.

Kennedy, J. (1996) Collection development: is the isolated university library a special case? *Australian Academic and Research Libraries*, **27**(2), 132–138.

Kenreich, M.E. and Stewart, W. (1995) Adopt-a-journal: reducing the effect of journal cancellations. *Serials Librarian*, **27**(4), 61–70.

King, G.B. (1995) Women library users and library users of traditional womens subjects. *Reference Librarian*, (49/50), 179–193.

Kingma, B. R. and Irving, S. (1996) The economics of access versus ownership: the costs and benefits of access to scholarly articles via interlibrary loan and journal subscriptions. *Journal of Interlibrary Loan, Document Delivery and Information Supply*, **6**(3), 1–76. [Also published as a monograph, New York: Haworth Press.]

Kitching, C. and Hart, I. (1995) Collection policy statements. *Journal of the Society of Archivists*, **16**(1), 7–14.

Knotts, B. *et al.* (1996) Making collection development work: the successful collaboration of St. Louis Public Library's Youth Services and Acquisitions staff. *Journal of Youth Services in Libraries*, **9**(4), 366–377.

Kolganova, I. (1995) Creative cooperation between librarian [sic] and artists in the Russian State Arts Library. *Art Libraries Journal*, **20**(2), 25–27.

Koppel, J. (1995) Local history collections in Hungary: problems and solutions of the current collection development. *Focus on International and Comparative Librarianship*, **26**(3), 153–156.

Kraft, N.O. (1996) The acquisitions model: stepchild of the IOLS. *Electronic Library*, **14**(3), 211–215.

Kytömäki, P. (1996) Korkeakoulukirjaston arvot ristipaineissa: Kirjastotoimen ja tiedonvälityksen eettisiä kysymyksiä. [The values of a university library under pressure: ethical questions of library services and information delivery]. *Signum*, **29**(5), 98–102.

Lamborn, J.G. (1995) Library acquisitions without paper: dream or reality? *Colorado Libraries*, **21**(4), 48–51.

Line, M.B. (1995) Access as a substitute for holdings: false ideal, costly reality? *Interlending and Document Supply*, **23**(2), 29–31. Also published in *OCLC Systems and Services*, **11**(4), 11–13.

Line, M.B. (1996) National self-sufficiency in an electronic age. In: *Electronic documents and information: from preservation to access. 18th International Essen Symposium, 23–26 October 1995*, eds. A.H. Helal and J.W. Weiss. Essen: Universitätsbibliothek Essen, pp. 170–193.

Liu, E.F. (1994) Regional coordination of collection development: a feasible step for academic libraries in resources sharing. *Journal of Information, Communication, and Library Science*, **1**(2), 19–23.

Longstreth, K. (1995) GIS collection development, staffing and training. *Journal of Academic Librarianship*, **21**(4), 267–275.

Lonsdale, R. and Everitt, J. (1996) Breaking down the barriers: the provision of European literature to children by British public libraries. *Journal of Librarianship and Information Science*, **28**(2), 71–81.

Lowe, D. (1995) Collecting political science materials. *German Studies Library Group Newsletter*, (17), 17–19.

Luckenbill, W.B. (1995) Providing HIV-AIDS information for youth in libraries: a community psychology and social learning approach. *Journal of Youth Services in Libraries*, **9**(1), 55–67.

Lyman, L. and Geldmacher, B. (1995) Collection development and acquisitions. In: Kehoe, P.E. *et al.* (1995), pp. 97–150.

McCaskill, D. *et al.* (1995) The undergraduate research collection: an open approach. *College and Undergraduate Libraries*, **2**(2), 45–55.

McGlamery, P. (1995) Maps and spatial information: changes in the map library. *European Research Libraries Cooperation*, **5**(3), 229–234.

MacLennan, A. (1996a) Bookscape on CD-ROM. *Managing Information*, **3**(7/8), 52.

MacLennan, A. (1996b) Fiction selection – an AI at work? *New Library World*, **97**(1126), 24–32.

March, S.F. (1996) Selecting Jewish books for children in general library collections. *Journal of Youth Services in Libraries*, **9**(2), 143–154.

Mark Fresco Consultancy (1996) *Impact of digital resources on British Library reading rooms.* (British Library Research and Innovation Report, 3.) Boston Spa: British Library.

Martin, M.S. (1995) *Collection development and finance: a guide to strategic library-materials budgeting.* Chicago: American Library Association.

Martin, M.S. (1996) The vanishing serial. *Technicalities*, **16**(3), 1, 4–6.

Matthews, G. and Eden, P. (1996) *Disaster management in British libraries. Project report with guidelines for library managers.* London: British Library. (Library and Information Research Reports, 109).

Merrifield, M. (1995) The funding of rural libraries. *Library Trends*, **44**(1), 49–62.

Miller, J.P. and Stringer-Hye, R. (1995) Improved access to engineering society technical papers. *Reference Services Review*, **23**(3), 63–68.

Mills, C. (1994) Aid for libraries: should one look the proverbial gift horse in the mouth? *Australian Academic and Research Libraries*, 25(4), 240–246.

Miniati, M. and Berni, M. (1995) The Florence Institute and Museum of the History of Science. *Archivi & Computer*, (4), 360–363.

Naicu, O. and Popescu, S. (1995) Spre o politică națională in domeniul achizițiilor de literatură științifică și tehnică din străinătate. [Towards a national policy in the field of science and technology. Foreign literature acquisition.] *Probleme de Informare și Documentare*, 29(4), 198–205.

Nassimbeni, M. (1995) Collection development in public libraries in South Africa; new library and language policies. *Library Acquisitions: Practice and Theory*, 19(3), 289–297.

National (1996) libraries of the Commonwealth Part 1: Oceania. National Library of Australia: recent developments and activities. *COMLA Newsletter*, (89), 3–5.

Naylor, B. (1994) Just in case vs just in time: a librarian ruminates about journals, technology and money. *Logos*, 5(2), 101–104.

Nicewarner, M. and Heaton, S. (1995) Providing security in an urban academic library. *Library and Archival Security*, 13(1), 9–19.

Nisonger, T.E. (1995) The use of CD-ROM to investigate the in-print/out-of-print subject patterns for books. *Library Resources and Technical Services*, 39(2), 117–132.

Nyffenegger, I. (1996) British libraries: some thoughts on British cooperation organizations in general and the London region in particular. *LASER Link*, (Spring/Summer), 4–5.

O'Brien, D.R. (1995) The politics of funding. *New Jersey Libraries*, 28(4), 3,5.

Odini, C. (1994) Collection development: the experience of Kenya Polytechnic library. *Library Management*, 15(4), 12–16.

Oshida, I. (1995) Collection development of academic library [sic]: a case report of a medical library. *Pharmaceutical Library Bulletin* [*Yakugaku Toshokan*], 40(3), 223–228.

Ozbudak, E. (1994) Sureli yayinlar icin kullanimin olculmesi. [Measuring the use of periodicals]. *Turk Kutuphaneciligi/Turkish Librarianship*, 8(4), 272–288.

Pankake, M. (1996). Állományfejlesztési modell a Minnesotai Egyetem Központi Könyvtárában. [The collection development model at the University of Minnesota Central Library]. *Tudományos és Műszaki Tájékoztatás*, 43(7–8), 262–266.

Pankake, M. et al. (1995) Commentaries on collection bias. *College and Research Libraries*, 56(2), 113–118.

Parry, R.B. (1995) The electronic map library: new maps, new uses, new users. *European Research Libraries Cooperation*, 5(3), 262–273.

Patterson, L. (1995) Information needs and services of Native Americans. *Rural Libraries*, 15(2), 37–44.

Peters, M. (1995) Custodianship of digital collections. *European Research Libraries Cooperation*, 5(2), 135–136.

Pilling, S. (1996) The National Reports Collection at the Document Supply Centre. *LASER Link*, (Spring/Summer), 9.

Pitman, R. (1995) Welcome to Jurassic Library. *American Libraries*, 26(4), 352–354.

Plaister, J.M. (1996) The APT partnership. *Journal of Librarianship and Information Science*, 28(1), 63–64.

Poon, P.W.T. (1995) Developing a special collection on the Pearl River Delta of China: process and strategies. *Asian Libraries*, 4(3), 31–36.

Pratt, G.F. et al. (1996) Guidelines for Internet resource selection. *College and Research Libraries News*, 57(3), 134–135.

Prendergast, N. and Gray, S.A. (1995) A core collection on minority health: resources about people of color. *Medical Reference Services Quarterly,* **14**(4), 23–43.

Pruess, J. (1996) Library profile. Siriraj Medical Library. *Asian Libraries,* 5(1), 5–9.

Puckett, A. (1996) Space and cyberspace in large law libraries. *Trends in Law Library Management and Technology,* 7(7), 1–5.

Quinn, B. (1995) Guerrilla collection development: time-saving tactics for busy librarians. *College and Undergraduate Libraries,* **2**(1), 107–119.

Raker, J.W. (1996) Multicultural acquisitions: one librarians perspective. *Against the Grain,* 8(2), 28–29.

Ratcliffe, F.W. (1995) German acquisitions policies: library problems before and after reunification. *Focus on International and Comparative Librarianship,* **26**(3), 135–146.

Read, M. (1995) New Zealand libraries funding hit. *New Zealand Libraries,* **48**(2) 34–35.

Reid, M.T. (1996) Acquisitions and collection development. In: *Technical services management, 1965–1990. A quarter of a century of change and a look into the future,* eds. L.C. Smith and R.C. Carter. New York: Haworth Press, pp. 57–75.

Reidlmayer, A. (1996) Libraries are not for burning: international librarianship and the recovery of the destroyed heritage of Bosnia and Herzegovina. *Inspel,* **30**(1), 82–94.

Revelli, C. (1996) The National Library of France. *Biblioteche Oggi,* **14**(2), 30–37.

Rhys-Lewis, J. (1995) Conservation facilities in the city of Krakow. *Paper Conservation News,* (73), 9.

Richards, P.S. (1995) The upset balance: the Dutch Academy report on the distortions in national library resources caused by the prioritization. *Alexandria,* 7(3), 171–179.

Robinson, W.C. (1995) Price of materials and collection development in larger public libraries. *Library Acquisitions: Practice and Theory,* **19**(3), 299–312.

Rodney, M. (1995) Subtle censors: collection development in academic libraries. *North Carolina Libraries,* **53**(2), 74–77.

Rowley, G. and Hanthorn, I. (1996) Designing a conservation treatment facility: charting a course into a less familiar region of planning for libraries. *Journal of Academic Librarianship,* **22**(2), 97–104.

Sapp, G. and Suttle, G. (1994) A method for measuring collection expansion rates and shelf space capacities. *Journal of Academic Librarianship,* **20**(3), 156–161.

Schmidt, K.A. (1995) The vision thing: developing a vision for acquisitions. *Library Acquisitions: Practice and Theory,* **19**(1), 5–7.

Scroggs, J. and Leonard, T. (1995) Mission position: censorship in the corporate library. *North Carolina Libraries,* **53**(2), 65–67.

Shockowitz, T. (1995) Security issues for archives, rare books and special collections: a bibliographic essay. *Current Studies in Librarianship,* **19**(1/2), 4–12.

Silverstein, C. and Shieber, S.M. (1996) Predicting individual book use for off site storage using decision trees. *Library Quarterly,* **66**(3), 266–293.

Slavens,T. P. (1996) Electronic media in libraries. *Reference Librarian,* (53), 97–103.

Smith, G. (1995) Free newspapers: a national policy for their collection and preservation. *Local Studies Librarian,* **14**(1), 13–14.

Snow, R. (1996) Wasted words: the written collection development policy and the academic library. *Journal of Academic Librarianship,* **22**(3), 191–194.

Sorensen, K.K. (1996) Periodicals on paper? We dont have it! About the transition from traditional to electronic printed stock. *DF-Revy,* **19**(3), 73–75.

Sowole, I.A. (1995) Collection development at the University of Agriculture Library, Abeokuta, (UNAAB) Nigeria. *International Information and Library Review,* **27**(4), 383–391.

Stankus, T. (1995) Could long term shifts of publishing sector dominance among the top 100 physical science journals slow rates of invoice inflation? *Science and Technology Libraries*, **15**(3), 77–89.

Stanley, N.M. (1995) The case for acquiring and accessing electronic journals in libraries. *Collection Management*, **19**(3/4), 29–34.

Stewart, L. (1996) User acceptance of electronic journals: interviews with chemists. *College and Research Libraries*, **57**(4), 339–349.

Strzynski, J. (1995) Foreign and international collections. Part 2: International. In: Kehoe, P.E. *et al.* (1995), pp. 313–347.

Sullivan, R. (1995) Nga taonga tuku iho kei roto i nga whare matauranga o Aotearoa: collection management in the field of traditional Maori knowledge. *New Zealand Libraries*, **48**(1), 5–10.

Sumsion, J. (1995) Public library funding; preparing for the gloom. *Bookseller*, (4659) 7 April, 22–24.

Sykes, J. (1996) M25 information flows in two directions. *Library Technology*, **1**(4), 75,78.

Sylge, C. (1996) Back to the future: the case of the electronic library. *Managing Information*, **3**(7/8), 25–26, 28, 30.

Taketomi, S. (1996) The pleasure and necessity of browsing: morning trips to the library. *Pharmaceutical Library Bulletin* [*Yakugaku Toshokan*], **41**(1), 30–31.

Thoroddsen, D. and Petursdottir, K.H. (1995) Aettfraedi og almenningsbokasofn. [Genealogy and public libraries]. *Bokasafnid*, (19), 18–21.

Tilevitz, S.L. (1996) Reconciling space and access needs in a small law firm library: a modest proposal. *Law Library Journal*, **88**(1), 96–120.

Togashi, R. (1995) Photo essay: relief map storage and map case security device. *Western Association of Map Libraries Information Bulletin*, **27**(1), 12–15.

Topp, B. (1996) Forging a new library network in Indiana. *Illinois Libraries*, **78**(1), 43–46.

Truesdell, C.B. (1994) Is access a viable alternative to ownership? A review of access performance. *Journal of Academic Librarianship*, **20**(4), 200–206.

Tucker, B.E. (1995) The journal deselection project: the LSUMC-S experience. *Library Acquisitions: Practice and Theory*, **19**(3), 313–320.

Tzeng, S.S. (1995) Exploration on the international cooperation among national libraries. *Journal of Library and Information Science* (USA/Taiwan), **21**(1), 71–92.

Ulmer, E.D. (1996) Electronic security systems in Arkansas academic libraries. *Arkansas Libraries*, **53**(3), 3–8.

Ungern-Sternberg, S. van and Lindquist, M.G. (1995) The impact of electronic journals on library functions. *Journal of Information Science*, **21**(5), 396–401.

Upset (1994) balance, The: scholarly literature and library resources in the Netherlands. Den Haag: Koninklijke Nederlandse Akademie van Wetenschapen.

Varlamoff, M.T. (1995) The involvement of the IFLA Core Programme for Preservation and Conservation (PAC) in Unesco's Memory of the World Programme. *IFLA Journal*, **21**(3), 183–184.

Vasilchenko, N.P. (1996) Formirovanie bibliotechnykh fondov. [Building up of library stock]. *Nauchnye-Technicheskie Biblioteki*, (5), 22–28.

Voorbij, H.J. (1996) Are Dutch academic libraries keeping up with research material? The coverage of foreign academic publications in Dutch libraries. *Alexandria*, **8**(3), 189–204.

Wang, B. (1996) A study on status and problems of library resources sharing in mainland China. *Journal of Library and Information Science* (USA/Taiwan), **22**(1), 93–103.

Weiming, J. and Ning, A. (1996) The National Library of China. *Alexandria*, **8**(2), 143–147.

Werbelow, C. and Kalk, T. (1996) Choice of security systems for the open-access presentation of compact discs. *Forum Musikbibliothek*, (1), 13–20.

Wessels, R.H.A. (1995) Optimizing the size of journal collections in libraries. *Interlending and Document Supply*, **23**(3), 18–21.

Weston, B. *et al.* (1995) Methods for collecting, processing, and providing access to electronic serials. *Serials Librarian*, **25**(3/4), 327–331.

Whitlach, J.B. (1995) Library users and reference services. *Reference Librarian*, (49/50), 1–346.

Wickham, D.E. (1995) The Library at Clothworkers Hall in the City of London. *Private Library*, **8**(3), 100–124.

Wiese, W.H. (1996) Is hunting ethical? A core collection of books. *Reference Services Review*, **24**(2), 35–44.

Wiewiorka, A. (1995) Developing a South Asian collection at UNL: joys and constraints. *SALG Newsletter*, (42), 53–56.

Wilén, R. (1995) Kokoelmayhteistyö Suomen tieteellisissä kirjastoissa. [Cooperative collection development in Finnish research libraries]. *Signum*, **28**(8), 178–182.

Wilson, M.C. and Edelman, H. (1996) Collection development in an interdisciplinary context. *Journal of Academic Librarianship*, **22**(3), 195–200.

Wirth, E. (1996) The state of censorship. *American Libraries*, **27**(8), 44, 46–48.

Wise, K. and Perushek, D.E. (1996) Linear goal programming for academic library acquisitions allocations. *Library Acquisitions: Practice and Theory*, **20**(3), 311–327.

Wolkoff, K.N. (1996) The problem of holocaust denial literature in libraries. *Library Trends*, **45**(1), 87–96.

Wuthe, C. (1996) A year's media security in the Berlin-Marzahn central library. *Forum Musikbibliothek*, (1), 45–53.

Yang, E.L. (1995) Library services to ethnic populations: an Asian-American's perspective. *Colorado Libraries*, **21**(2), 27–29.

Yang, M.H. (1995) Library cooperation and resource sharing in Taiwan. *Journal of Information, Communication and Library Science*, **1**(3), 31–46.

Young, A.P. and Peters, T.A. (1996) Reinventing Alexandria: managing change in the electronic library. *Journal of Library Administration*, **22**(2/3), 21–41.

Zappen, S.H. (1995) Are the methods working? Where do we go from here? *Collection Management*, **19**(3/4), 171–183.

Zheng, T. and Huang, J. (1994) Book acquisitions: a purchasing system. *Computers in Libraries*, **14**(5), 15–16.

Zhu, Q. (1996) Establishing an academic library and information network of China. *International Information and Library Review*, **28**(1), 31–38.

Zipp, L.S. (1995) Identifying core geologic research journals: a model for interlibrary cooperative collection development. In: *Proceedings of the 29th meeting of the Geoscience Information Society, Seattle, Washington, 24–27 October 1994*, eds B.E. Haner and J. O'Donnell. Alexandria, VI: Geoscience Information Society, pp. 59–65.

Rare books and special collections   **7**

B.C. Bloomfield

Introduction

There are two questions about rare books and special collections commonly asked both by library administrators and those who know little about libraries. The first is 'What is a rare book?' Without wasting too much time, a book is rare because:

- it is unique, very scarce, difficult to find;
- it embodies knowledge that is significant;
- it is worth a lot of money;
- it represents and embodies significant national, local or tribal values.

Any book that scores high marks in more than one of these categories is a 'rare' book, and curators may like to amuse themselves by devising a matrix game to assess their collections using these criteria. But there are more extensive discussions of the question and guides for the perplexed such as Van Wingen (1989a, 1989b), Gauvin (1989), and more recently Bernard *et al.* (1994) and Lieberman (1995). The following survey of developments in the area of rare books and special collections inevitably presents an idiosyncratic and very selective view of developments and publications over the past ten to fifteen years.

The second question, asked mainly by library administrators, trustees, and accountants is 'What use is this special collection?': the unspoken, but often implied, corollary is that the collection is of no use for the holding institution's mission, and only of value if sold. In these hard financial times the question is commonly posed and Lee (1993) edited a symposium of British and American delegates to attempt some answers, while Auchstatter (1990), Chodorow and Claasen (1995), Frakes (1992) and Freshwater (1987) present the view that rare book collections need to be integrated into the institution's curriculum and research programme, and that they bring it distinction. Case and Xu (1994) raise the interesting question of the validity of restrictions on access to rare collections in the light of Freedom of information policies, citing the restricted access to the

Dead Sea scrolls photographs and the consequent impediment to researchers until they were unilaterally released by the Huntington Library.

The general administration of rare books and special collections has generated some interesting publications, but the basic sources remain Schreyer (1984), an issue of *Library Trends* (Cloonan, 1987) and Cave (1982). In the UK most rare books and special collections are held in university libraries and the Follett report (Joint, 1993) allocated some £12 million to accelerate automated cataloguing and access to such collections through networked work stations. In the UK Wilson (1983) surveyed the crisis in managing such collections, and this was followed by the report commissioned by the British Library (BL) (Enright, 1989), discussed at length in Jenkins and Morley (1991). All of these relate to questions of selection and retention for the national printed archive – a problem that faces almost every national library.

Anglin (1994) sets out some policies, procedures and guidelines for special legal collections, while Ng (1990) does the same for rare books in a college library, Garvey (1993) for religious collections, and Feather *et al.* (1995) and Gancs (1994) for local studies collections, in an English regional context and in Hungary respectively. Dowler (1995) deals with a question of some importance: how far should the research library go in resource sharing when institutions are nowadays in competition for funding, the best students, or researchers?

Collections

Most of the literature on rare books and special collections is specific and descriptive and often illuminates national custom as much as good bibliographic practice. Most rare book collections are nowadays always looking for financial support to continue to acquire important material in a steadily rising market; manuscript prices particularly have shown spectacular increases over the past 20 years. But collections have continued to grow by purchase, gift and bequest. In the UK the cash generated by the National Lottery and distributed through the National Heritage Memorial Fund has filled the funding gap in many cases, especially for the national libraries. Bloomfield (1994) examines some of these problems in a paper from a one-day seminar. The directory of UK collections edited by Williams (1985) was a signal achievement for the Rare Books Group of the Library Association (LA) and the 1997 revision is described by Bloomfield (1995). Selecting interesting and significant examples from the UK literature is a lottery, but *Treasures of the British Library* (Barker *et al.*, 1989) was a significant example of an increasingly popular genre, as collections strive to justify their existence and role in the eyes of the tax-paying public.

The BL restructured its administration in 1994 and formed an Early Collections Service to embrace rare books, special collections, and the various bibliographic activities such as the *Eighteenth century short-title catalogue* (ESTC) and the *Incunabula short-title catalogue* (ISTC), together with its own Centre for the Book, copying the American model which has proved so successful. But the main focus of attention has been on the new building that began to be occupied in December 1996, although it will not be fully operational until 1999. Day (1994) deals with this in detail and how it affects all departments and special collections. Harris (1991) examines the past history of the BL's printed book departments, and *The Book Collector* (1995) devotes a whole issue to the reconstruction of one particularly important library – that of John Evelyn, the diarist – much of which has now been reunited there.

Of special importance for Oxford is Morgan (1980) with his survey of libraries and collections outside the Bodleian, and Latham's (1978-94) catalogue of the Pepys library at Magdalene College fittingly displays a major Cambridge collection. The National Library of Scotland (1989) celebrated its tercentenary with a descriptive history, and McCann (1990) describes the scene in Northern Ireland, while Fox (1986) edits another 'Treasures' volume for the library of Trinity College, Dublin, and Kissane (1995) does much the same for the National Library of Ireland.

Sheehan (1991) surveys the collections in the Vatican Library which is adopting a more open policy for researchers. But in France the main focus of attention has been the new building for the Bibliothèque nationale de France (BnF), which, like the BL's new building, has attracted a quite extensive literature. Coron (1996) sets out the plans for moving the rare books and other collections from the rue de Richelieu to the Tolbiac building, beginning in autumn 1997. Kessler (1994) discusses the project from a perhaps less sympathetic view. Guy (1991) gives an overview of French rare book collections based on a survey incorporated in a library school dissertation, while two contributions by Morien (1994) and Macouin (1993) deal with music libraries and foreign art collections respectively in Paris.

But it is in Germany that the most interesting developments have taken place in the field of rare books. Fabian (1986b) sets out the background, and this is later supplemented by Eckelmann (1993) and Jefcoate (1991) more specifically on Wolfenbüttel, all leading up to the magnificent scheme of the *Handbuch der historischen Buchbestände in Deutschland*, planned to be in nineteen volumes and beginning publication in 1992, with seven volumes published so far. In the absence of a true central national library the intention is to create comprehensive historical descriptions of the collections in all major libraries, originally simply in the federal republic, but after 1989 extended to include all the German *Länder*. Supported by the Deutsche Forschungsgemeinschaft, the series is well advanced. This descriptive project is complemented by the programme funded by the Volkswagen Foundation designed to create a national printed archive in German language materials – the *Sammlung Deutsche Drücke 1450–1912* (later extended to 1945). Responsibility for retrospective acquisition is allocated by period to five libraries in Munich (1450-1600), Göttingen (18th century), Wolfenbüttel (17th century), Frankfurt (1801–1870) and Berlin (1871–1945), with adequate funding provided.

Kaltwasser (1990) and Vogt (1993) review the Bavarian success story, while Botte (1993) provides an interim overview of the whole scheme. These two projects alone are of major importance for rare books and special collections in Europe and provide models for others to follow. Feldmann (1993) shows that other rare collections survive in older school libraries and need to be recorded and exploited.

Descriptive articles dealing with other countries have been selected to display unusual collections or particular aspects of rare books. In Japan a survey (Outline, 1994) of Korean language materials revealed unsuspected strengths; and Ozaki (1992) describes a newly established library of privately printed books, a category which represents half the output of Japanese language books but is sparsely recorded and collected in national collections. In the USA the output of descriptive articles is considerable. Melville (1980) describes the special collections in the Library of Congress (LC), and Matheson (1989) sets out the results of a survey showing the results of institutional collecting of 20th-century literature, supplemented by Staley (1990) on the effects of literary studies and reputations on library collections in this field. Covington (1994) deals with a science fiction collection in Texas A&M University, and Mayo-Jefferies (1994) with special collections in law school libraries, based on yet another questionnaire, while Neu (1994) deals with the magnificent collections in the history of science at the University of Wisconsin, Madison. Two 'unexpected' collections are dealt with by Olson (1993), who sets out for German scholars the strengths of the German language collections in American universities, and Okuizumi (1989) and Murakami (1995), who both describe the extensive Gordon Prange collection at the University of Maryland library, which contains Japanese language material (70,7812 books; 689,690 issues of newspapers; 82,287 periodical parts; etc.) from the period 1945-52 arising from American censorship activities in Japan after World War II.

Mills (1985) provides an annotated bibliography of references for Australian rare book collections; Thaiveegan (1993) describes a Tamil language collection in multilingual Malaysia; Blake (1992) examines the collections of Colin MacKenzie divided between Madras and London; the Alexander Turnbull Library (1995) provides a finding list of pre-1801 titles in the libraries around Wellington, New Zealand (the first of three similar regional lists); and Graham (1992) describes Sir George Grey's influence on the collections of Auckland Public Library.

After the fall of the communist governments in eastern Europe more published descriptive material on rare and special collections appeared. For example, Stuart (1995) deals with the Rossica collection of the Imperial Public Library, Wojnowska (1995) with music libraries in Poland, Balik (1995) with the Bohemica collection in Prague, and Mazulis (1995) with the collections in the Latvian Academic library; while Häkli (1992) examines the excellent Slavonic collection held in Helsinki University Library, mostly arising from when Finland was a province of Imperial Russia and received all books published under Russian legal deposit legislation. Two more articles raise significant questions: Kiraly (1994) considers the history and raison d'être of the closed, or forbidden, collections held in the libraries of eastern Europe, and Sabov (1995) examines the difficulties caused by new laws requiring the restitution of religious library collections confiscated under former communist regimes. The rejuvenated activities of IFLA's Rare and Precious Books and Manuscripts Section at annual IFLA conferences nearly always produce papers describing important rare book collections in the cities where the conferences are held. One such example is Ulker (1995), which describes manuscript and rare book libraries in Turkey.

One significant category of rare books which has enjoyed an unparalleled revival of interest over the past ten years or so is that of incunabula. The old *Gesamtkatalog der Wiegendrücke* began publication in 1925 but was virtually stopped by World War II, and when restarted in the DDR was hampered by lack of adequate finance and motivated staff. Publication of the revised edition of the catalogue began again with vols 1–7 (1968), 8–9 (1972–91), 10, parts 1–2 (1992–4), parts 3–4 (1996), but still lags alarmingly behind any schedule. This led Hellinga and colleagues in the BL to begin the *Incunabula short-title catalogue* (ISTC) on the basis of an automated version of Goff's Census. ISTC is available on the BL's BLAISE-line and on RLIN, while *The illustrated ISTC on CD-ROM* (1997) makes the 28,000 records available with 10,000 selected images. The best survey of the whole scholarly field is in Hellinga and Goldfinch (1987), supplemented by an interim report by Hellinga *et al.* (1993); Van Wingen (1989b) deals with incunabula in LC; Rhodes (1981) those in Greece; Frimmová (1994) those in Bratislava; Singh (1986) lists those in India, and the catalogue of those in the BnF continues its stately progress, while the BL's catalogue still lacks the British volume. Serrai (1993) deals with statistical inference in considering questions relating to incunables, and Wellisch (1994) examines printed and manuscript indexes found in a census of nearly 1,000 incunables.

Many other contributions examine and describe various special collections and categories of rare material. French (1993) describes African collections in the UK and Europe, and Diekamp (1995) deals with auction catalogues in museum collections and outlines the programme funded by the Getty Trust to microfilm catalogues up to 1880, supplementing the lists in Lugt (1938–53, 3 vols) *Répertoire des catalogues de ventes publiques intéressant l'art où la curiosité*. An entire issue of the *Papers of the Bibliographical Society of America* (1995) is devoted to book catalogues generally and should be noted. Hesselager (1994) considers national collections of ephemera, Schoeman (1994) picture collections, and O'Neill, 1994) the legally deposited collections of Canadian photographs in the BL, and the programme for digitizing, indexing and storing them. A similar private commercial library with enormous and important architectural resources for the UK is described by Hall (1994) in considering the photographic archive of the magazine *Country Life*. Finally two authors consider the problems of that hardy perennial 'grey literature': Gelfand (1994) on the place of this material in academic libraries, in the *Proceedings of the First international conference* on the subject, and Ebozoje (1988) in relation to Nigerian publications.

Access

It is in access to collections that the most striking advances have been made in the past ten or so years. The advent of electronic mail and automated networks – local, national and international with their bulletin boards – have made it relatively easy for rare book librarians and curators of collections to keep in touch with each other and to be aware of professional developments in their field. Scholars and library users with access to these networks can also consult automated library catalogues at a distance to discover what collections hold what titles. Through the Internet collections are universally known, and their resources are advertised through institutional World Wide Web sites, permanently displayed and regularly updated. There are also many national academic networks, like JANET and SuperJANET in the UK, centrally funded and available free to institutional users. However, to be included in these automated facilities the catalogues of rare book and special collections have to be converted to machine-readable formats. These collections are often at the end of the queue for resources to achieve this desirable end, added to which their records have special requirements. Law (1988) reviews this problem in the UK, and, to some extent, this difficulty has later been met in the USA by special grants from the National Endowment for the Humanities and Title II-C grants from the Department of Health, Education and Welfare, but both programmes are now reduced or eliminated by budgetary cuts. In the UK the National Heritage Memorial Fund has made numerous grants for cataloguing rare material, with money provided by the National Lottery, and the Joint Higher Education Funding Councils provided some £12 million to academic libraries following the recommendations of the Follett report (Joint, 1993). In Germany the Volkswagen Foundation has funded projects of retrospective cataloguing in addition to its support for the Sammlung Deutsche Drücke. Turner (1991) attempts to survey developments in retrospective bibliography.

To address the special problems involved with rare books, IFLA (1991) issued its *International standard bibliographic description (antiquarian)* in a second edition and the same year saw the LC (1991) issue the second edition of its *Descriptive cataloging of rare books*, discussed by Hillyard (1993) in the light of UKMARC – with suggested amendments. (The coming together of USMARC and UKMARC will eliminate many of these problems. Hillyard and Pearson (1996) offer a British view supplementary to the LC's guide.) This was followed by a survey of UK practices by Lennon and Pearson (1991), and a similar view from the USA by Stalker and Dooley (1992). Pasternack (1990) deals with retro-conversion, and Shaw (1993) with cataloguing rare material online. A special issue of *Rare Books and Manuscripts Librarianship* (1992) deals specifically with the problems posed by 19th-century material, while Caswell (1991) and Saunders (1994) assess the difficulties general cataloguers face dealing with copy-specific and provenance issues. An article that put the cat among the pigeons in regard to cataloguing records and provenance was by Baker (1994), which elicited a librarian's response from Douglas (1994).

In Germany Rutz (1992) describes the cataloguing of material in older collections, and Fabian (1994) covers the programme for name authority work in Germany. Guy describes name authority work in the BnF (1996), and Tsioli and Corsini (1994) outline an indexing system for books printed before 1800 based on Brunet's original classification and further developed recently. Hayashi (1993) deals with the creation of a catalogue of pre-Meiji books in Europe, devised by the author and P. Kornicki, in a sense complementing Gardner's (1993) catalogue of the BL's pre-1700 Japanese books.

But the main developments in retrospective cataloguing of rare books and special collections have been in Europe. They are outlined in Kaltwasser and Smethurst (1992) which contains the proceedings of the first Munich conference in 1990 on retrospective cataloguing in Europe for 15th- to 19th-century materials sponsored by the Bayerische Staatsbibliothek and the BL. Papers mostly describe developments in individual European countries, and there are final conclusions and recommendations. The second Munich conference in 1991 considered the final report of the European Working Party (1992) on retrospective cataloguing established by the first conference, and approved the setting up of a European Union catalogue of catalogue data for the period of the hand-printed book using UNIMARC and ISBD(A). The database is now hosted by RLIN. Hellinga (1994) describes later progress.

The traditional printed catalogue is by no means dead. The publication of the BL's printed catalogue (1967–) in various formats has stimulated rare book cataloguing and made access to its collections more readily available than any other national library. In particular, the Readex reduced facsimile (or 'eyestrain' edition) found ready acceptance in smaller libraries and the book trade, while the CD-ROM version covering the period to 1975, published by Chadwyck-Healey, was networked in most academic libraries. Similarly the Bodleian Library (1993) published *The Bodleian Library pre-1920 catalogue on compact disc* and made many rare and special collections more easily accessible to scholars. The second edition of *A short-title catalogue (1986–92) of books printed in England, Scotland and Ireland and of English books printed abroad 1475-1640* (STC) was published by the Bibliographical Society. The Modern Language Association of America completed the revision of Donald Wing's volumes covering the period from 1641 to 1700 in 1994, with a version on CD-ROM published by Chadwyck-Healey in 1996. Meanwhile the *Eighteenth century short-title catalogue* (ESTC) was going from strength to strength; its progress can best be studied in the pages of its house journal *Factotum* (1978–); a CD-ROM version was published by the BL in 1992, and another expanded version is promised for 1997. Snyder (1988) proposed that ESTC should be expanded to include both Wing and the second edition of STC. This proposal was approved by its International Advisory Committee, the BL and ESTC/North America and is being implemented, with completion provisionally set for 2006. The database is available through RLIN and now contains more than 406,400 fully catalogued bibliographic entries for titles between 1475 and 1800. The *Nineteenth-century short-title catalogue*, announced in May 1983, is a compilation of entries from the catalogues of the BL, Cambridge University Library, Trinity College Dublin, the National Library of Scotland and Newcastle University. (Other major libraries' holdings have subsequently been added.) Compiled in several segments (1801–15, 1816–70, 1871–1918), publication in hard copy has been speedy, and an edition of the first two segments on CD-ROM was published in 1997, containing more than 650,000 records.

In the UK the Care of Cathedrals Act (1990) stimulated progress on the *Cathedral libraries catalogue* (1984–) with volume 2 promised for 1998, although the project was founded as long ago as 1943 with a grant from the Pilgrim Trustees. Rees (1987) produced an authoritative catalogue of Welsh language books, and Shaw (1982) the first part of a similar record, using ESTC software, covering the period 1556–1800 for publications from the sub-continent of South Asia.

Preservation

There is no space to deal adequately with the extensive literature on preservation, rare books and special collections. But mention must be made of the disastrous fires at the Academy of Science Library in St Petersburg (described by Matthews, 1988), the Public Libraries in Los Angeles and Norwich, and the destruction of the National and University Library in Sarajevo during the civil war in what was Yugoslavia. All of these emphasize the continuing importance of preservation, disaster plans, and the diffusion of rare materials in surrogate copies. Feather and Vitiello (1991) discuss the *European register of microfilm masters*, which is one tool to lessen the impact of losses caused by such disasters. There are similar registers for the UK and USA available through RLIN, that for the UK funded by grants from the Mellon Foundation.

One major advance has been the formulation of standards and the campaign for the adoption of permanent paper for printed books. Led by the Americans, whose revised National Standard (ANSI/NISO Z39.48:1992) provides the basis for ISO 9706:1944 (E) *Paper for documents – requirements for permanence*, this campaign still needs vigorous support.

Another technique of utility for rare book and special collections has been digitization. Hillyard (1996) reports a conference on this subject, and the Research Libraries Group's Digital Image Access Project in 1994 united eight major libraries in the USA in a consortium to digitize selected photographs of the urban landscape. Meanwhile the BL had digitized the unique fire-damaged Thorkelin transcript of *Beowulf* and revealed additional parts of the text not previously deciphered (to be published as the *Electronic Beowulf*.) The BL's Dunhuang project, in cooperation with the Academy of Social Sciences in Beijing, may also use this technique in dealing with the *Diamond sutra*, the earliest dated printed work.

Other libraries are using different surrogate means to make texts more widely available. The University of Texas is mounting the *Ramayana* on the Internet, and a project is well advanced in Cambridge to convert the text of the *Mahabharata* – probably the longest single poem in the world with some 110,000 couplets – into machine-readable form in UNIX. Moir (1992) describes the use of optical disc technology to improve access to historic photographs. But rare book librarians and scholars will be well advised to remember that the CD-ROM is expected to become obsolete within about ten years, together with much of the machinery used to read it. Modern technology always seems to bring with it associated preservation problems.

The remaining topics, usually subsumed under preservation and conservation, that generate a deal of interest are those of security and theft. Matheson (1995) usefully describes security for rare books in the National Library of Scotland. Allen (1995) recommends using the Internet to report thefts, and Ogden (1996) deals with general problems, provides recommendations and suggested further reading. The Guidelines (1994) prepared by the Association of College and Research Libraries (ACRL) build on earlier drafts. The 'Bookwatch' (1989) scheme originally sponsored by the Antiquarian Booksellers Association (ABA), the Provincial Booksellers' Fairs Association (PBFA) and the Rare Books Group of the LA developed into the ABA's 'Stolen book chain' scheme for speedy notification of thefts. This was reviewed by librarians and bookdealers at two one-day conferences in London in 1995 and 1996, and, as a result of these meetings, a draft code of conduct for booksellers and librarians in cases of dispute relating to stolen books and manuscripts was promulgated.

Dispersals, standards, ethics

Within the UK there has been controversy about dispersals and sales from rare book and special collections. The sale in 1988 of some 100 items from the John Rylands University Library of Manchester to provide money to found a bibliographical research institute was castigated by Barker (1988) and others, and the University of Edinburgh sold its copy of Audubon's *Birds of America* and other bird books by Gould in 1992. West (1991) had already noted with concern the often unplanned and wholesale dispersals from public libraries, and Barker (1994) again noted similar dispersals from academic libraries. The Royal Society of Literature, concerned at libraries' lack of financial support which caused these dispersals, sponsored a seminar 'The chaining of the libraries' (1994) to discuss the problem. As a consequence, the British Library sponsored a study by Capital Planning Information Ltd (1995) to establish guidelines for dispersals from libraries. (Some of the background to all this was examined at an international conference held at Newnham College, Cambridge, in September 1989 and sponsored by the Rare Books and Manuscripts Section of ACRL, the Rare Books Group of the LA and the Manuscripts Committee of the Standing Conference of National and University Libraries (SCONUL) with the assistance of the ABA.) The LA had previously approved a policy statement on sales from libraries (Sales, 1989). But the problem is universal, as is witnessed by the Doheny sale and by Bradbury's (1994) description of happenings at Kansas City Public Library.

With the collapse of former governments in eastern Europe after 1989 many libraries there found themselves without funds for purchases or staff salaries, and rumour and legend abound of rare books and other items being illegally removed and sent westwards for sale. It is of considerable professional importance for librarians that they conduct themselves ethically in such situations and the draft second edition of *Standards* (1991) *for ethical conduct for rare book, manuscript and special collections libraries and librarians* is essential reading. Provenance has almost become a forensic branch of librarianship. On the other side of the fence Rota (1995) considers how antiquarian bookselling has changed over the past 50 years in response to this situation.

Libraries often establish close links with collectors who may subsequently prove benefactors. Basbanes (1993) deals only with American experience but is illuminating, while Brower (1991) warns of dangers in unwritten agreements for gifts. Three articles display interesting potential problems for manuscript curators. Crews (1990) examines copyright, fair use and management difficulties in unpublished manuscripts; Hodson (1991) deals with confidentiality, copyright and possible libellous statements in collections of modern manuscript material; and Godan (1994) examines the distinction between the protection of manuscripts and the diffusion of their intellectual content.

Staffing and training

One perennial problem affecting rare book and special collections has been the training and education of staff. Posts in these collections bring their own rewards, but these are usually intellectual rather than financial. New entrants perceive that success in their future careers depends more on training and experience in financial and personnel management, computer skills and publication, rather than the close examination of, and familiarity with, old books. The School of Library Service at Columbia University closed and the short summer schools previously offered there moved in 1993 to the University of Virginia, under the direction of Professor T. Belanger. Joyce (1995) and Cox (1995) both review the situation and needs in the USA, the latter in the light of the problem of continuing education after graduation.

In the UK hardly any library school provides more than exiguous training in bibliography and book history, and the system of 'apprenticeship' offered by the national libraries and leading antiquarian booksellers has atrophied as a result of financial and staffing cuts. Joyce (1995) discusses the problem, and so do Crump *et al.* (1996), while Feather and Lusher (1989) summarize the situation with regard to conservation training in British library schools. (It might be described as desperate. The sudden need for cataloguers to assist in retro-conversion projects for older material has highlighted this acute shortage of experienced staff.) Smyth and Martin (1994) describe how volunteer help may be found from Friends organizations; and Morgan (1986) describes the needs of cathedral librarians.

Bibliography and scholarship

The trend in scholarly research has been away from the previous emphasis on descriptive and analytical bibliography, with its special applications to textual criticism, towards a more all-embracing *'histoire du livre'* pioneered by French scholars like H.J. Martin and Roger Chartier. Bowers (1975) first attempted to set out the relationship between bibliography and librarians, and this was developed by Tanselle (1979); Feather (1982) and Willison (1983) consider the relationship from a European viewpoint, as does Fabian (1986a). The best summary and description of this tradition, with extensive bibliographies, is to be found in Greetham (1994), which should be on the desk of every rare book curator. The antics of modern theoretical critics (deconstructionist, modernist, or post-modernist) will affect rare books and special collections; the possible effects are discussed by Oram (1993).

The example of Martin and Chartier (1983–6) in their *L'histoire de l'édition française* and the parallel *Histoire des bibliothèques françaises* (1988–92) has been copied in the UK by the 'History of the book in Britain' project sponsored by the Book Trade History Group and the British Academy, funded by the Leverhulme Trust, to be published by Cambridge University Press (CUP), and *A history of libraries in Britain and Ireland*, edited by Peter Hoare and also to be published by CUP. P.H. Jones and E. Rees project a similar history for Wales. The Book Trade History Group's *Newsletter* contains useful information, and Weedon and Bott (1996) contains locations for all publishers' records and book trade archives between 1830 and 1939 in British and foreign depositories. The British Book Trade Index, maintained at Newcastle University library under its general editor, Peter Isaac, continues to grow and aims to include the names of all recorded members of the British book trade up to 1851.

Some examples of unusual but significant work that may influence research and the use of rare books in the future are by Leedham-Green (1986), who analyses book use and personal libraries from Tudor and Stuart probate records, together with the series of *Libri pertinentes* she has originated; Todd and Bowden's (1988) huge bibliography and analysis of the Tauchnitz publishing record and its significance; Pearson's (1994) trail-blazing book on provenance; and Tsien Tsuen-Hsien's (1985) work on paper and printing in China.

The various series of bibliographic lectures have progressed and many of the Sandars and Lyell lectures have been published. Bond's (1990) lectures on Thomas Hollis and his influence are a singular example. The Panizzi Lecture series was launched in 1985 by the BL with the aid of an anonymous benefactor, and the first by McKenzie (1986) started the series with a bang.

An innovation which has spread from the USA is the creation of numerous short-term fellowships to encourage the study of bibliography and the use of special collections. The Bibliographical Society of America has an extensive annual fellowship programme and, in emulation, as does the Bibliographical Society in the UK. Many large libraries also award fellowships to encourage scholars to visit and use the collections, notably the Beinecke Library at Yale University, the Library Company of Philadelphia, the John Carter Brown Library, the American Antiquarian Society, and the Centre for the Book in the BL (although this is non-stipendiary). These awards are advertised annually in the bibliographical press.

Institutions, apart from libraries, have continued to contribute much to the rare books field. The distinguished Grolier Club (1984) celebrated its centenary with an appropriate publication (more than 600 exhibitions, more than 150 publications), and Breslauer and Folter (1984) provide a bibliography of its achievement. Burkett and Hench (1992) edit a second edition of a work describing the American Antiquarian Society, and Davison (1992) edits the centenary publication of the Bibliographical Society, surveying developments in bibliography over the past 50 years, and the Society's contribution to bibliographical scholarship. However, the award of prizes for published works of bibliographical scholarship seems to be in decline. The Premio Felice Feliciano has been suspended for lack of financial backing, but the occasional prize awarded by the International League of Antiquarian Booksellers has continued, and the Bibliographical Society in the UK has continued to award its own medal.

Finally, lest one should think working in such circumstances is unduly rarefied, some personal reminiscences provide a useful corrective. Snelling (1982) describes buyers and the book trade from an auctioneer's point of view; Weinreb (1994) recounts how a dealer looks at rare books; Gordan (1994) writes about life in a famous rare book collection: and Liebaers (1980) explains how a national librarian decides whether or not to buy rare books.

Bibliographical note

The best way to keep up to date with developments in the field of rare books and special collections is to read assiduously the various periodicals and journals that specialize in such matters. It is worth noting how many of them are fairly recently founded. The most significant are as follows:

Rare Books and Manuscripts Librarianship, vol. 1–, April 1986–. From the Rare Books and Manuscripts Section of the ACRL. Also issues *RBMS Newsletter* to members.

Rare Books Newsletter, no. 1– March 1974–. From the Rare Books Group of the Library Association, previously titled *Rare Books Group Newsletter*.

Nouvelles du Livre Ancien, 1–, 1974–. From the Réserve des imprimés of the BnF.

Bibliography Newsletter [BiN], no. 1–, 1973–.

For bibliographic references:

ABHB. Annual Bibliography of the History of the Book, vol. 1–, (publications of 1970), 1973–. The Hague: Nijhoff.

Bibliographie der Buch- und Bibliotheksgeschichte (BBB), Bd. 1– 1980/1–, 1982–. Bad Ilburg: Bibliographischer Verlag Horst Meyer. Concentrates almost exclusively on Germany and German language areas.

For scholarly bibliographical matters:

The Library. vol. 1–, 1892–. Published by OUP for the Bibliographical Society. Contains regular analytical lists of bibliographical books and articles in other journals.

Papers of the Bibliographical Society of America. vol. 1–, 1906–. Usually cited as *PBSA*.

Book Collector, vol. 1–, 1952–.

Studies in Bibliography. vol. 1–, 1948/49–.

In addition many of the major libraries with rare book and special collections publish their own house journals with news of acquisitions, exhibitions, collections and publications.

References

Alexander Turnbull Library (1995) *Early imprints in New Zealand libraries: a finding list of books printed before 1801 . . . in the Wellington region*. Wellington: Alexander Turnbull Library.

Allen, S.M. (1995) Using the Internet to report rare book and manuscript thefts. *Rare Books and Manuscripts Librarianship*, **10**(1), 22–37.

Anglin, C. (1994) Special collections policies, proceedings and guidelines (a model plan for the management of special legal collections). *Library Resources and Technical Services*, **38**(2), 202–203.

Auchstatter, R.M. (1990) The role of the rare book library in higher education: an outsider surveys the issue. *College and Research Libraries*, **51**(3), 221–230.

Baker, N. (1994) Discards. *New Yorker*, **70**(7), 4 April, 64–86. [Reprinted in *The size of thoughts*. London: Chatto & Windus, 1996, pp. 125–181.]

Balik, V. (1995) The Czech National Library and its special collections. *Inspel*, **29**(2), 84–88.

Barker, N.J. (1988) The rape of the Rylands. *Book Collector*, **37**(2), 169–184.

Barker, N.J. (1994) The shrinking of the university libraries. *Times Literary Supplement*, 4 March, 13.

Barker, N.J. *et al.* (1989) *Treasures of the British Library.* London: British Library.

Basbanes, N.A. (1993) Collectors and libraries: some studies in symbiosis. *Rare Books and Manuscripts Librarianship,* 8(1), 37–48.

Bernard, P. *et al.* (1994) *Antiquarian books: a companion for booksellers, librarians and collectors.* Aldershot: Scolar.

Blake, D.M. (1992) The antiquarian and economic consequences of Colin Mackenzie. *SALG [South Asia Library Group] Newsletter,* 39, 12–18.

Bloomfield, B.C. (1994) A special case? Preserving and funding heritage collections in research libraries: the British example. *Alexandria,* 6(3), 205–214. [The seminar is reported in *Rare Books Newsletter,* 48(1994), 36–47, with the speech by Lord Egremont on the work of the Friends of the National Libraries.]

Bloomfield, B.C. (1995) The revision of the *Directory of rare books and special collections in the UK and Republic of Ireland. Library Review,* 44(6), 23–27.

Bodleian library (1993) *Bodleian Library pre-1920 catalogue on compact disc.* Oxford: Oxford University Press.

Bond, W.H. (1991) *Thomas Hollis of Lincoln's Inn. a Whig and his books.* Cambridge: Cambridge UP.

Book Collector (1995), 44(2) [issue solely devoted to John Evelyn's library in the British Library].

Book watch (1989) *Library Association Rare Books Group Newsletter,* 33, 18.

Botte, G.-J. (1993) Die Sammlung deutscher Drücke 1450–1912: eine Zwischenbalanz. *Bibliotheks Forschung und Praxis,* 17(3), 301–321.

Bowers, F. (1966) Bibliography and modern librarianship. In: *Essays in bibliography, text and editing.* Charlottesville, VA: University Press of Virginia, pp. 75–93.

Bowers, F. (1975) Bibliography and modern librarianship. In: *Essays in bibliography, text and editing.* Charlottesville: University Press of Virginia, pp. 75–93.

Bradbury, D.J. (1994) Barbarians within the gates: pillage of rare book collection. *Rare Books and Manuscripts Librarianship,* 9(1), 8–16.

Breslauer, B.H. and Folter, R. (1984) (comps) *Bibliography: its history and development.* New York: Grolier Club.

British Library (1967–) *Catalogue.* New York: Readex Corporation. To 1955 in 27 vols (1967); 1956–65 in 5 vols (1969); 1966–70 in 3 vols (1974); 1971–75 in 2 vols (1980). [The revised compilation published in London and Munich by K.G. Saur: to 1965 in 360 vols; 1979–87 in 6 vols plus supp. (1987–88); 1976–82 in 50 vols (1983); 1982–85 in 26 vols (1986); 1986–87 in 22 vols (1988). Also published in microfiche by the BL, on CD-ROM (to 1975) by Chadwyck-Healey, and mounted on BLAISE-LINE.]

Brower, L. (1991) An oral contract isn't worth the paper it's printed on. *Rare Books and Manuscripts Librarianship,* 6(2), 100–107.

Burkett, N.H. and Hench, J.B. (1992) (eds.) *Under its generous dome: the collections and programs of the American Antiquarian Society.* 2nd ed. Worcester, MA: AAS.

Capital Planning Information Ltd (1995) *Disposal of printed material from libraries.* London: British Library. (BNB Research Fund Report 72). [A four-page summary, with the same title, by the Libraries and Information Council (1995) is issued free in its series *Issues in Focus,* no. 11.]

Case, B. and Xu, Y. (1994) Access to special collections in the humanities: who's guarding the gates and why? *Reference Librarian,* 47, 129–146.

Caswell, S.C. (1991) Item level access to special collections: a prototype for an integrated automated index. *Journal of Library Administration,* 15(3/4), 101–120.

Cave, R. (1982) *Rare book librarianship.* 2nd ed. London: Bingley.

Chodorow, S.A. and Claasen, L.C. (1995) Academic partnership: a future for special collections. *Journal of Library Administration*, **20**(3/4), 141–148.

Cloonan, M.V. (1987) ed. Recent trends in rare book librarianship. *Library Trends*, **36**(1) [entire issue].

Coron, A. (1996) La réserve des livres rares à la Bibliothèque de la France. *Bibliothèques de France*, **41**(3), 20–25.

Covington, V. (1994) The science fiction research collection at Texas A&M. *Popular Culture in Libraries*, **2**(1), 81–87.

Cox, R.J. (1995) Continuing education and special collections professionals. *Rare Books and Manuscripts Librarianship*, **10**(2), 78–96.

Crews, K.D. (1990) Unpublished manuscript and the right of fair use: copyright law and the strategic management of information resources. *Rare Books and Manuscripts Librarianship*, **5**(2), 61–70.

Crump, M.J. *et al.* (1996) *Rare book librarians for the future: issues in training and education.* Brussels: CBBB-BCBB.

Davison, P. (1992) (ed.) *The book encompassed: studies in twentieth century bibliography.* Cambridge: Cambridge University Press.

Day, A. (1994) *The new British Library.* London: Library Association.

Diamond Sutra. *New Scientist* (1990), **127**(1729), 11 August, 22.

Diekamp, B. (1995) Auktionskatalog in Museum-bibliotheken: Verfilmung alter Auktionskataloge aus dem Stadelschen Kunstinstitut. *Bibliotheksdienst*, **29**(1), 29–38.

Douglas, N.E. (1994) Debating 'discards': a response to Nicholson Baker. *Rare Books and Manuscripts Librarianship*, **9**(1), 41–47.

Dowler, L. (1995) The research university's dilemma: resource sharing research in a transinstitutional environment. *Journal of Library Administration*, **21**(1/2), 5–26.

Ebozoje, F. (1988) The need for the collection and bibliographic control of grey literature in Nigeria. *African Journal of Academic Librarianship*, **6**(1/2), 51–56.

Eckelmann, J.S. (1993) Erschliessung buch- und bibliotheksgeschichtlicher Quellenbestande. *Bibliotheksdienst*, **27**(6), 884–891.

Enright, B. *et al.* (1989) *Selection for survival: review of acquisition and retention policies [in the BL].* London: British Library.

European Working Party (1992) on Retrospective Cataloguing: final report. *European Research Libraries Co-operation*, **2**(1), 47–60. [Summarizes the first and second Munich conference proceedings and subsequent work; includes a report by C. Fabian, The Eurodatabase and European co-operation in early book cataloguing, pp. 63–79.)

Fabian, B. (1986a) Libraries and humanistic scholarship. *Journal of Librarianship*, **18**(2), 79–82.

Fabian, B. (1986b) Rare books in the Federal Republic of Germany: some comments. *Rare Books Group Newsletter*, **28**, 7–22.

Fabian, B. *et al.* (1992–) *Handbuch der historischen Buchbestände in Deutschland*, Bd. 1–. Hildesheim: Olms.

Fabian, C. (1994) Personnamen der Antike (PAN): eine neue Normdatei für alte Namen. *Bibliotheksdienst*, **28**(9), 1426–1441.

Feather, J.P. (1982) The rare book librarian and bibliographical scholarship. *Journal of Librarianship*, **14**(1), 30–44.

Feather, J.P. and Lusher, A. (1989) Education for conservation in British library schools: current practices and future prospects. *Journal of Librarianship*, **21**(1), 129–38.

166   *Rare books and special collections*

Feather, J.P. and Vitiello, G. (1991) The European register of microfilm masters: a new bibliographical tool. *Journal of Librarianship and Information Science*, **23**(4), 177–182.

Feather, J.P. *et al.* (1995) The management and use of reserve and special collections in public libraries: a study of the East Midlands. *Journal of Librarianship and Information Science*, **27**(2), 89–97.

Feldmann, R. (1993) Historische Sammlungen der Schulbibliotheken im Rheinland und in Westphalen. *Schulbibliothek Aktuell*, **2**, 150–156.

Fox, P. (1986) (ed.) *Treasures of the library, Trinity College Dublin*. Dublin: Royal Irish Academy.

Frakes, S.M. (1992) A closed book is a mute witness: rare book collections in the academic library. *Current Studies in Librarianship*, **16**(1), 8–20.

French, T. (1993) (ed.) *The SCOLMA directory of libraries and special collections on Africa in the United Kingdom and Europe*. 5th ed. London: Zell.

Freshwater, P.B. (1987) Rare book collections as centres of excellence. *Rare Books Group Newsletter*, **29**, 16–38.

Frimmová, E. (1994) I. Výskum inkunábalía na Slovensku. II.Tlače 16 storočia v Univerzitnej knižnici v Bratislave. *Knižnice a Informácie*, **29**(8/9), 376–378.

Gancs, E. (1994) Local studies in Hungary: a case study. *Local Studies Librarian*, **13**(1), 25–27.

Gardner, K.B. (1993) (comp.) *Descriptive catalogue of Japanese books in the British Library printed before 1700*. London: British Library.

Garvey, T. (1993) Managing special collections in the field of religion in university libraries. *Bulletin of the Association of Theological and Philosophical Libraries*, **2**(18), 16–26.

Gauvin, D. (1989) (ed.) *Canadian guide to rare books*. Montreal: The Author.

Gelfand, J.M. (1994) Academic libraries and collection development implications for grey literature. In: *Proceedings of the 1st International Conference on grey literature Amsterdam, December 1993*, comp. D.J. Farace. Amsterdam: Transatlantic, pp. 123–140.

Godan, J.C. (1994) Zur rechtlichen Zulassigkeit besonder Bedingungen von Handschriftbibliotheken. *Bibliotheksdienst*, **28**(10), 1638–1650.

Gordan, L.L. (1994). Life in the Berg collection. *Wilson Library Bulletin*, **68**(8), 26–31.

Graham, T. (1992) To (pre)serve them all our days. *Archifacts*, (October), 1–10.

Greetham, D.C. (1994) *Textual scholarship: an introduction*. New York: Garland.

Grolier Club (1984) *1884–1984: its library, exhibitions and publications*. New York: Grolier Club.

Guidelines (1994) regarding theft in libraries. *College and Research Libraries News*, **55**,(10) 641–646.

Guy, F. (1991) Les réserves dans les bibliothèques françaises. *Bulletin des Bibliothèques de France*, **36**(1), 14, 16–20, 22–24.

Guy, M. (1996) The Bibliothèque nationale de France and authority files. *International Cataloguing and Bibliographical Control*, **25**(3), 59–62.

Häkli, E. (1992) The Slavonic library at the Helsinki University library. *European Research Libraries Co-operation*, **2**(1), 91–96.

Hall, M. (1994) Treasures of the Country Life library. *Country Life*, **187**(46), 17 November, 82–85.

Harris, P.R. (1991) (ed.) *The library of the British Museum: retrospective essays on the Department of Printed Books*. London: British Library.

Hayashi, N. (1993) [On the creation of the catalogue of pre-Meiji books in Europe.] *Toshokan Zasshi*, **87**(1), 34–37. (in Japanese).

Hellinga, L. (1994) Konsortium europäischer wissenschaftlicher Bibliotheken. *Bibliotheksdienst*, **28**(8), 1901–1903.

Hellinga, L. *et al.* (1993) News from ISTC. *Rare Books Newsletter*, (45), 32–37.

Hellinga, L. and Goldfinch, J. (1987) *Bibliography and the study of 15th century civilization.* London: British Library. (Occasional Papers, no. 5).

Hesselager, L. (1994) National collections of printed ephemera: those papers of the day. *Alexandria*, 6(3), 193–204.

Hillyard, B. (1993) Descriptive cataloguing of rare books. *Rare Books Newsletter*, (43), 33–49.

Hillyard, B. (1996) Preservation and digitization: principles, practice and policies. *Rare Books Newsletter*, (54), 49–53.

Hillyard, B. and Pearson, D. (1996) *Guidelines for the cataloguing of rare books.* London: LA Rare Books Group. (draft).

Histoire des bibliothèques françaises (1988–92) Paris: Promodis. (4 vols).

Hodson, S.S. (1991) Private lives: confidentiality in manuscripts collections. *Rare Books and Manuscripts Librarianship*, 6(2), 108–118.

IFLA (1991) *International standard bibliographic description (Antiquarian).* 2nd ed. London: Saur.

Jefcoate, G. (1991) The rare book scene in Germany: news of Wolfenbüttel. *Rare Books Newsletter*, (39), 27–30.

Jenkins, C. and Morley, M (1991) (eds) *Collection management implications of the British Library review of acquisition and retention policies.* London: National Acquisitions Group.

Joint (1993) Funding Councils Libraries Review Group. [Chair: Sir Brian Follett]. *Report.* Bristol: HEFCE.

Joyce, W.L. (1995) Education and training special collections librarians. *Rare Books and Manuscripts Librarianship*, 10(2), 73–76.

Kaltwasser, F.G. (1990) Sammlung deutsche Drücke, 1450–1945. *Zeitschrift für Bibliothekwesen und Bibliographie*, 37(2), 115–128.

Kaltwasser, F.G. and Smethurst, J.M. (1992 eds) *Retrospective cataloguing in Europe: 15th to 19th century materials. Proceedings of the International Conference, Munich 28–30 November, 1990.* München: K.G. Saur. (Bibliothekspraxis, Bd 31).

Kessler, J. (1994) The Bibliothèque nationale de France project: access or expediency. *Journal of Librarianship and Information Science*, 26(3), 121–133.

Kiraly, I. (1994) Fonds secrets où fonds interdits? *Bulletin des Bibliothèques de France*, 39(6), 77–85.

Kissane, N. (1995) (ed.) *Treasures from the National Library of Ireland.* London: Alpine Fine Arts Collection.

Latham, R. (1978–94) (ed.) *Catalogue of the Pepys library at Magdalene College, Cambridge.* 11 vols. Cambridge: D.S. Brewer.

Law, D. (1988) The state of retrospective cataloguing in the United Kingdom: a review. *Journal of Librarianship*, 20(2), 81–93.

Lee, S.H. (1993) (ed.) The role and future of special collections in research libraries: British and American perspectives. Binghampton, NY: Haworth Press. [Also published as *Journal of Library Administration*, 19(1).]

Leedham-Green, E.S. (1986) *Books in Cambridge inventories.* Cambridge: Cambridge University Press. (2 vols).

Lennon, A. and Pearson, D. (1991) *Rare book cataloguing in the British Isles.* London: British Library. (BL R&DD Research Paper, 94). [See also *Rare Books Newsletter*, (40), 21–29.]

Library of Congress (1991) *Descriptive cataloguing of rare books.* 2nd ed. Washington, DC: LC. [See also *Rare Books Newsletter*, (43), 33–40 by B. Hillyard, with suggested amendments, 41–49.]

Liebaers, H. (1980) *Mostly in the line of duty*. The Hague: Nijhoff. (Especially chapters 6 and 7).

Lieberman, R. (1995) What makes a book rare? A primer for the enthusiastic but hesitant librarian. *College and Undergraduate Libraries*, 2(2), 139–145.

McCann, W. (1990) The rare book scene in Northern Ireland. *Rare Books Newsletter*, (37/ 38), 21–23.

Maccouin, F. (1993) De l'Indochine à l'Afghanistan: des arts étrangers dans les bibliothèques parisiennes. *Inspel*, 27(4), 288–295.

McKenzie, D.F. (1986). *Bibliography and the sociology of texts*. London: British Library. [Panizzi Lectures, 1985.]

McLeod, M.S.G. *et al.* (1984–) (eds) *Cathedral libraries catalogue*, vol. 1. London: British Library & Bibliographical Society.

Martin, H.-J. and Chartier, R. (1983–86) (eds) *L'histoire de l'édition française*. 4 vols. Paris: Promodis.

Matheson, A. (1995) Rare book security in the National Library of Scotland. *Rare Books Newsletter*, (51), 42–51.

Matheson, W. (1989) Institutional collecting of twentieth century literature. *Rare Books and Manuscripts Librarianship*, 4(1), 7–41.

Matthews, G. (1988) Fire at Academy of Sciences library at Leningrad, 14 February. *Library Association Record*, 90(5), 279–281.

Mayo-Jefferies, D. (1994) Special collections in law school libraries. *Law Library Journal*, 86(3), 503–528.

Mazulis, V. (1995) The collections of rare books and manuscripts in the Latvian Academy library. *Rare Books Newsletter*, (49), 37–39.

Melville, A. (1980) *Special collections in the Library of Congress: a selective guide*. Washington, DC: Library of Congress.

Mills, T. (1985) *Rare books collections in Australian libraries: an annotated bibliography*. Melbourne: Bibliographical Society of Australia and New Zealand. (Occasional Publication, no. 3).

Moir, M.B. (1992) The use of optical disc technology to improve access to historical photographs. *Archives and Museum Informatics*, 6(1), 5–12.

Morgan, C. (1986) Cathedral librarianship. *Journal of Librarianship*, 18(3), 153–164.

Morgan, P. (1980) *Oxford libraries outside the Bodleian*. 2nd ed. Oxford: Bodleian Library.

Morien, C. (1994) Musikbibliotheken in Paris. Teil 1. *Forum Musikbibliothek*, (3), 226–242.

Murakami, H. (1995) [The Prange collection]. *Toshokan Zasshi*, 89(8), 611–614. (in Japanese).

National Library of Scotland (1989) *For the encouragement of learning: Scotland's national library, 1689–1989*. Eds P. Cadell and A. Matheson. Edinburgh: HMSO.

Neu, J. (1994) History of science collections in the University of Wisconsin, Madison. *Science and Technology Libraries*, 14(4), 17–24.

Ng, E. (1990) The establishment and management of a special collection in a college library. *Journal of the Hong Kong Library Association*, (14), 75–80.

Ogden, S. (1996) Security from loss, water and fire damage, biological agents, thefts and vandalism. *Rare Books and Manuscripts Librarianship*, 11(1), 43–47.

Okuizumi, E. (1989) [The Gordon W. Prange collection at the University of Maryland: American censorship activities in Japan]. *Toshokan Zasshi*, 83(8), 438–441. (in Japanese).

Olson, M.P. (1993) Die Bedeutung amerikanischer Universitätsbibliotheken für die Pflege und Erforschung der deutschen Literatur. Das Beispiel der deutschen Sammlung der University of California, Los Angeles. *Bibliotheksforum Bayern*, 21(3), 293–303.

O'Neill, P.B. (1994) Canadian photographs in the British Library. *Archivaria*, (38), 240–241.

Oram, R.W. (1993) The new literary scholarship: the contextual point of view, and the use of special collections. *Rare Books and Manuscripts Librarianship*, 8(1), 9–16.

Outline (1994) of results of a survey into the collection, processing and provision of Hangul materials. *Toshokan Zasshi, [Library Journal]*, 88(3), 176. (in Japanese).

Ozaki, K. (1992) [The Japanese library of privately printed books]. *Toshokan Zasshi*, 86(8), 542–433. (in Japanese).

Papers of the Bibliographical Society of America (1995), 89(4) [whole issue devoted to book catalogues].

Pasternack, H. (1990) Online catalogs and the retrospective conversion of special collections. *Rare Books and Manuscript Librarianship*, 5(2), 71–76.

Pearson, D. (1994) *Provenance research in book history: a handbook.* London: British Library.

Rare Books and Manuscripts Librarianship (1992), 7(2) [whole issue devoted to descriptive cataloguing of 19th century imprints].

Rees, E. (1987) (ed.) *Libri Walliae. A catalogue of Welsh books and books printed in Wales, 1546–1820.* 2 vols. Aberystwyth: National Library of Wales.

Rhodes, D.E. (1981) *Incunabula in Greece: a first census.* Munich: Kraus International Publications.

Rota, A. (1995) *The changing face of antiquarian bookselling 1950–2000 AD.* Charlottesville, VA: Book Arts Press. [The 1994 Sol. M. Malkin Lecture in Bibliography.]

Rutz, R. (1992) Die Erschliessung alterer Bestände in Programmen der Deutscher Forschungsgemeinschaft. *Bibliotheksdienst*, 26(8), 1157–1170.

Sabov, P. (1995). Historičke knižnice fondy Slovenskej narodnej knižnice a restitučny proces po roku 1989. *Knižnice a Informácie*, 27(5), 241–243.

Sales (1989) of rare books and manuscripts: a Library Association policy statement. (1989). *Library Association Rare Books Group Newsletter*, (33), 8–10.

Saunders, R. (1994) Collection- or archival-level description for monograph collections. *Library Resources and Technical Services*, 38(2), 139–147.

Schoeman, K. (1994) Picture collections and picture research: some general thoughts. *Quarterly Bulletin of the South African Library*, 48(4), 139–148.

Schreyer, A.D. (1984) (ed.) *Rare books 1983–84.* New York: Bowker.

Serrai, A. (1993). Le inferenze statistiche in bibliografie. *Bibliotecario*, (38), 19–25.

Shaw, D.J. (1993) Cataloguing rare books on-line. *Law Librarian*, 24(4), 187–191.

Shaw, G.W. (1987) *South Asia and Burma retrospective bibliography (SABREB): first stage, 1556–1800.* London: British Library.

Sheehan, W.J. (1991) Special collections in the Vatican library. *European Research Libraries Co-operation*, 1(1), 99–103.

Short-title catalogue (1986–92) of books printed in England, Scotland and Ireland and of English books printed abroad 1475–1640. 2nd ed. rev. by W.A. Jackson and F.S. Ferguson and completed by K.A. Pantzer (1986–92). 3 vols. London: Bibliographical Society.

Singh, R.D. (1986) (ed.) *The National union catalogue of incunabula and early printed books.* Calcutta: National Library.

Smyth, E.B. and Martin, R.S. (1994) Working with friends of the library to augment staff resources: a case history. *Rare Books and Manuscripts Librarianship*, 9(1), 19–28.

Snelling, O.F. (1982) *Rare books and rarer people: some personal reminiscences of the trade.* London: Werner Shaw.

Snyder, H. (1988) Proposals for the English STC. *Library*, 10, 191–193. [Also published in *PBSA* (1988), (82), 333–336.]

Staley, T.F. (1990) Literary canons, literary studies and library collections. *Rare Books and Manuscripts Librarianship*, 5(1), 9–21.

Stalker, L. and Dooley, J.M. (1992) Descriptive cataloguing and rare books. *Rare Books and Manuscripts Librarianship*, 7(1), 7–23.

Standards (1991) for ethical conduct for rare book, manuscript and special collections librarians. A draft. 2nd ed. *College and Research Libraries News*, 52(11), 721–729.

Stuart, M. (1995) Creating culture: the Rossica collection of the Imperial Public Library and the construction of national identity. *Libraries and Culture*, 30(1), 1–25.

Tanselle, G.T. (1979) Descriptive bibliography and library cataloguing. In: *Selected studies in bibliography*. Charlottesville, VA: University Press of Virginia, pp. 37–92.

Thaiveegan, K. (1993) Pembinan koleksi Tamil di Perpustakaan Universiti Malaya. *Kekal Abadi*, 12(3), 7–9.

Todd, W.B. and Bowden, A. (1988) *Tauchnitz international editions in English, 1841–1955.* New York: Bibliographical Society of America.

Traister, D. (1992) What good is an old book? *Rare Books and Manuscripts Librarianship*, 7(1), 26–42.

Tsien Tsuen-Hsuin (1985) Paper and printing. In: J. Needham (ed.) *Science and civilization in China*, vol. 5, pt 1. Cambridge: Cambridge University Press.

Tsioli, M. and Corsini, S. (1994) Indexation livres anciens Brunet/Parguez. *ARBIDO-Bulletin*, 9(4), 17–18.

Turner, J.R. (1991) Developments in retrospective bibliography since 1975. *Journal of Librarianship and Information Science*, 23(3), 147–152.

Ulker, M. (1995) Manuscripts and rare book libraries in Turkey. *Turk Kutuphane-ciligi*, 9(3), 270–280.

Van Wingen, P. (1989a) *Your old books.* Chicago: American Library Association.

Van Wingen, P. (1989b). The incunabula collection at the Library of Congress. *Rare Books and Manuscripts Librarianship*, 4(2), 85–100.

Vogt, W. (1993) Munificentia Locupletata. Die Sammlung deutscher Drücke 1450–1600 in der Bayerischen Staatsbibliothek. *Bibliotheksforum Bayern*, 21(3), 250–265.

Weedon, A. and Bott, M. (1996) *British book trade archives 1830–1939: a location register.* Oxford and Bristol: History of the Book on Demand (HOBODS).

Weinreb, B. (1994) Antiquarian books and bookselling. *Logos*, 5(1), 31–36.

Wellisch, H.H. (1994) Incunabula indexes. *Indexer*, 19(1), 3–12.

West, W.J. (1991) *The strange rise of semi-literate England: the dissolution of the libraries.* London: Duckworth.

Williams, M. (1985) (ed.) *Directory of rare books and special collections in the United Kingdom and the Republic of Ireland.* London: Library Association.

Willison, I. (1983) Current developments in international rare book librarianship. *Journal of Librarianship*, 15(3), 170–182.

Wilson, A. (1983) The crisis in rare book management: a United Kingdom perspective. *BiN*, 11(3/4), 23–26.

Wojnowska, E. (1995) Musikbibliographien und Quellensammlungen in Polen. *Forum Musikbibliothek*, (1), 24–34.

Health services information

8

Jennifer MacDougall
and J. Michael Brittain

Introduction

The aim of this chapter is to provide an overview of the scope of health (or health-care) information, outlining recent developments and trends, with illustrations from the literature worldwide. The main focus is on the management of health information and the application of information technology (IT) to support the provision of efficient and cost-effective health services. This aspect of health information, termed health informatics, is defined as the systematic use of data and application of IT to manage and provide health services (Stroh and Wall, 1995). Medical informatics, which has a longer history, has a more specific definition and involves the use of IT for medical scientific research, clinical diagnosis and treatment, including such applications as imaging techniques, magnetic scanning and receptor site modelling. There is continuing confusion and disagreement over the use of terminology, particularly whether it be medical or health informatics. This is in part due to a difference of meaning between Europe and the USA, where 'medical' tends to refer to physicians only. Health or healthcare informatics has recently become the preferred term to include information systems in clinical practice and in healthcare management (MacDougall *et al.*, 1996). However, this current tendency to prefer health informatics as the wider, more embracing, term may be short-lived, as argued by Haux (1995), who concludes that medical informatics and health informatics constitute one discipline. This chapter will concentrate on the broader area of health information, including informatics in relation to healthcare practitioners, patients, scientists, managers, and carers.

The last two decades have been a time of fundamental review and change in the structure and financial organization of national health services worldwide. Increasingly competitive global markets for healthcare management and delivery, vast technological advances in computing and telecommunications, more sophisticated customer and patient requirements, economic and legislative restructuring, and an enormous increase in the amount of information needed to provide modern healthcare services, have all led to reforms in many countries in Europe, the USA, Canada, and Australasia (Pfaff, 1990; Lee, 1991; Buchan, 1993;

Von Stillfried and Arnold, 1993). While governments seek to improve the efficiency and cost-effectiveness of their services, the emphasis on healthcare outcomes and evidence-based practice requires a much wider knowledge base and extensive information support for all areas of healthcare delivery.

The healthcare reforms in Europe have been led by legislative changes such as budgetary controls, national health targets, integrated care and the separation of purchases from the provision of services. In contrast, the changes in the USA resulted largely from private institutions attempting to reduce costs and manage risks. These contrasts are well described in a recent report which also provides an excellent summary of the development of information management to support managed healthcare in Europe (Coopers and Lybrand, 1997).

Health information types and applications

Health information encompasses an enormous range of formats and applications. This is illustrated here by reference to the diverse and complex nature of the field with examples of developments from various countries. For convenience the many types of information are divided here into four categories as: scientific, clinical and health services information; patient-generated clinical data; corporate activity management information; and information for patients, carers and the public. These categories are not mutually exclusive and incorporate all types of data – textual, graphical and numerical.

Scientific, clinical and health services information

This is mainly in the form of text and graphics, and includes information in textbooks, research reports, journal articles, computer-based knowledge systems, databases, reference books, and 'grey' literature, or documents circulated within organizations. The huge investment in healthcare information systems is clinically led, as stated, for example, in the national information management and technology strategy document of the UK National Health Service (Great Britain, 1992).

The need for improved access to clinical, scientific and biomedical information was recognized in the 1960s by the US National Library of Medicine which has since developed many information management initiatives now used worldwide. These include the MEDLARS system of databases which have led to the widespread development of specialized databases in a variety of formats, searching and document request software (Grateful Med and Lonesome Doc), the Unified Medical Language System and the Visible Human Project which is currently developing a complete, anatomically detailed, three-dimensional representation of the body which can be accessed on CD-ROM and the Internet (Visible Human Project, 1997). The Integrated Advanced Information Management

Systems (IAIMS) programme encourages the integration of all clinical and academic information systems (Carmel, 1995).

The increasing importance of quality assurance programmes, accountability and accreditation of healthcare services has led directly to a steady improvement in clinical information systems (CIS) although much work still remains to be done in this area. There are numerous examples of CIS covering all areas of medicine developed in many countries worldwide. A variety of these is described in the proceedings of the Current Perspectives in Healthcare Computing Conference held in England in March 1996 (Richards, 1996), one session of an annual conference which is the largest event in Europe devoted to healthcare computing. The 1996 conference was notable for the increased attention given to the impact of clinical, as opposed to purely administrative, computing developments. These included departmental computer systems, expert systems, image information and decision support systems. The range of subjects covered included the evaluation of a digital speech processor system for use by radiologists in Germany (Kahle *et al.*, 1996), the computer-assisted diagnosis of metabolic emergencies in Romania (Alecu *et al.*, 1996), and the computer-aided analysis of medical interferometric images in Poland (Podbielska, 1996).

A CIS developed for community health services in Australia shows how the apparent success of IT application can, however, provide relatively little overall benefit and incur high organizational costs. Little use was made of the PC-based system by clinicians and few important decisions were made on the basis of information provided. The study shows that the fact that a system is used does not prove it is therefore beneficial, that the main users of the system must be able to realize the benefits, and that the use of a CIS must be carefully defined before implementation (Southon and Yetton, 1996).

Patient-generated clinical data

Information generated directly from the patient's own medical record or clinical information documentation may be textual and numerical in format. This category includes details on symptoms, medical history, diseases, diagnostic and preventive procedures, operative and therapeutic procedures, treatment regimes or drugs usage. This information can be used in epidemiological surveys to assess trends and spread of disease, and in morbidity statistics to provide both local and/or national pictures of disease patterns. Patient-generated clinical data is also vital for research and teaching purposes, and is essential for successful medical audit and the development of outcome and performance indicators. In the UK the NHS Information Management and Technology Strategy *Getting better with information* places the emphasis on person-based information integrated systems which can be shared across the whole National Health Service (Great Britain, 1992).

Much attention and many human and financial resources have been devoted to the research and development of the electronic medical record (EMR): 'The electronic health record is a pivotal focus for advancement in health informatics' (Stroh and Wall, 1995). In a few years the electronic record will include graphics, video, colour, moving images and sound as well as the textual and statistical information which the record now comprises. Electronic access will expand to allow multi-location access to provide a database of up-to-date, accurate and secure information which can be used at every healthcare service outlet, home and office. Several major research programmes into the electronic patient record are in progress, including the European Advanced Informatics in Medicine (AIM) which aims to integrate decision support systems with hospital information systems (MacDougall, 1995, p. 39).

Decision support systems (DSS) were developed as diagnostic expert systems over 20 years ago. However, over-ambitious early models led to a cautious level of acceptance by the medical profession. In spite of this there are numerous examples of local and specific DSS developments worldwide, as well as remote decision support through telemedicine technology (De Glanville, 1994). A DSS on the health of the foetus *in utero* was described at the third National Health Informatics Conference in Australia in 1995. The system comprises an expert system to support the clinician; software which processes data from the ultrasound scan to the DSS; and a database which stores current results plus historical data on the foetus and its parents. The main aim is to provide rule based decisions on the well-being of a foetus and predictions on its future health to be used by both clinicians and educators (Falconer and Villanueva, 1995).

The shortage of time available for medical documentation in a surgical setting is a critical factor behind the development in Romania of a computer-based patient record system in neurosurgery. The value of this electronic patient record will not be fully realized until a critical mass of medical data is reached and the networking potentiality is explored with possible extensions into drug and disease interactions (Popescu *et al.*, 1996).

The improvements in electronic information systems for patient records should directly improve patient care, in spite of earlier problems with inadequate medical record information. The direct booking of outpatients by clinicians through computerized patient information systems means that relevant information is available at the consultation, which reduces clerical time, and generates standard discharge summaries and outpatient letters. Computer linkage with laboratories and wards and resource management data are easily added to such a system. A fuzzy logic control method for simulating human judgement and decision-making to interpret the results of pathology tests is explained by Naghdy *et al.* (1995). The work focuses on quantitative biochemistry data and aims to provide advice on a patient to the treating practitioner based on test results and medical history; the results and progress achieved so far are also reported.

Recently an increasingly considered and realistic attitude has emerged towards the development of the EMR, based more on the patient/clinician interaction than on the technological issues. Ten points towards achieving the effective EMR are outlined by Lamberts and Hofmans-Okkes (1996), including the importance of defining the episode of care, structured data entry, and decision-making shared between patient and clinician. A model of the medical record developed in Canada incorporates the context, structure, process and use of the medical record within a single narrational framework. It aims to show how the patient's narration of their medical state can be used within the context of the EMR to provide a more representative record (Kay and Purves, 1996).

An example of the National Integrated Clinical Workstation (ICWS) Project run by the NHS Executive in England is described by Jones *et al.* (1996). This pilot site of community and day hospitals is a trial for a multidisciplinary noting tool covering admission assessment, inpatient progress, treatment, and discharge summary. In this way electronic record keeping for nursing and the professions allied to medicine is included, the documentation is easily retrievable and transmittable, and auditing of large amounts of data is faster. This hospital information support system (HISS) facilitates the incorporation at any stage of document image processing, workflow and text retrieval/Intranet systems, as well as information for providers.

An application on a smaller scale to develop a model information system for patient records in a small hospital in Botswana is described by Harding (1996). Here the overriding problem was one of organization and collating of the records, which were incomplete, inaccurate, time-consuming to write up and difficult to interrogate for statistical analysis and research. The available software, four IBM-compatible PCs and one Apple Mac machine were used to create a management system for inpatients, and a full-time hospital computer programmer and a data inputter have been employed. Linkup to the Healthnet e-mail telecommunications network of health organizations in Africa and South Asia was another expected benefit.

The main single barrier to the widespread use of electronic medical record (EMR) systems has been the poor human–computer interface. A project in South Australia is developing a system to improve the usability of EMRs by clinicians and other health professionals. The aim is to reduce costs and non-productive time of clinicians, thus improving the quality of patient care through more timely, accurate and readable information to support clinical decision making (Brittain *et al.*, 1996). The work continues through to 1999 with a major grant from the Australian Research Council Collaborative Grants Scheme in conjunction with Medical Communications Associates Pty Ltd, a company specializing in supplying software to the health industry.

Management information

Information for the management of healthcare services is made up largely of internally generated throughput data, often numerical in format, plus externally produced statistics (e.g. by local and central government). Examples include Patient

Administration Systems (PAS) which provide the vital records of hospital admissions and procedures; contract and service specifications; statistical information on service utilization and costs, waiting lists, bed occupancy rates, theatre schedules, etc.; numbers, costs and usage of drugs; financial and personnel information; demographic and epidemiological reports; and other survey data and reports produced by a variety of organizations.

As the global healthcare environment becomes more competitive, subject to increasing pressures of accountability, and required to incorporate numerous organizational changes and technological innovations, high quality management information systems assume greater significance (Smith, 1995). The information needs of commissioning authorities in a purchaser/provider healthcare system are examined by Mason (1996), using the example of Northern Ireland. Commissioners have to assess the health needs of their population, purchase the appropriate services and monitor and evaluate their effectiveness. This process involves purchaser specification, contract negotiation and monitoring and measuring health outcomes. A central contradiction is explored between the purpose of information management and technology (IM&T) strategies, which encourage communication and cooperation, and that of the healthcare market which encourages competition and diversity. In order to achieve a mutually satisfactory cooperative relationship information management systems should:

- promote understanding of patterns of healthcare delivery;
- facilitate links between purchasers/commissioners and providers;
- deal with information from a variety of provider systems;
- be able to integrate all information for use by others;
- provide adequate security and confidentiality.

The need for information to support the new purchasing role, reinforced by the needs of the evidence-based movement, resulted in the establishment of the Developing Information Systems for Purchasers initiative in England and Wales (Great Britain, Department of Health, 1993). In Scotland the Scottish Office decided that a similar initiative was required to support purchasing primarily, but also to provide information useful to the whole Scottish health service and to patients. The Scottish Health Purchasing Information Centre was set up in January 1995 and a study was conducted by independent researchers to establish what information was being used by senior purchasing managers. The main types of information required were outcomes indicators, especially those important to patients, effectiveness information, and performance information, including benchmarking, comparative strategies and good practice. Overall, the study showed that senior managers would like more assistance with filtering the range of information available and need a clearer idea of the roles of the various organizations providing effectiveness information in Scotland and the UK generally (Farmer and Chesson, 1996).

The development of a Community Health Information System in New South Wales is described by Bargenquast and Williams (1996); this has been designed to overcome the particular information problems of this sector. Community health is difficult to define in terms of service boundaries, and the variety of services provided means that widely differing types of information are needed. An important outcome of the work was to identify users' needs for an information system that was clinically useful. The development of data and function models was followed by an information management strategy which raised a number of issues such as systems integration and standards for information provision. Three pilot sites are implementing the office automation programme which will be complete by late 1997; the Community Health Information System will be developed in 1998, followed by a review and evaluation process.

The World Health Organization (WHO) Management Information System was developed to support the monitoring and evaluation processes of WHO activities worldwide. The main components comprise:

- information on planning, programming, implementation, monitoring and evaluation of WHO activities;
- easy and rapid access to WHO policy documents and records of management and policy decisions;
- summary information on global health trends allows member states and WHO management staff quickly to assess the world health situation (World Health Organization, 1997).

Consumer health information

Consumer health information (CHI) is the fastest growing area of health information provision. There is an increasingly sophisticated demand for knowledge on all matters related to health, as consumer expectations generally are much higher than a decade ago. The individual is assuming much greater responsibility for maintaining a healthy lifestyle and demands more information with which to make decisions about healthcare generally. The development of CHI is charted by Gann (1991) in a paper covering its history and the development of a wide variety of services in the USA and UK. As he explains in a more recent editorial even the term consumer is not strictly accurate as we produce as much healthcare (self-care and mutual support) as we consume from professional services (Gann, 1994).

The sources of consumer healthcare information are many and diverse: medical dictionaries and encyclopaedias, articles in nursing and medical journals, health authorities' information on local services, leaflets such as those produced by health promotion agencies, booklets from self-help groups and charities, even women's magazines. One study examined the content of the health information provided in weekly magazines which represent an important source for millions of women and men who read them (Elliott, 1994).

Consumer health information services have been developing and increasing worldwide in the 1990s, particularly in the UK and USA. These services have sprung from a variety of backgrounds including public, university and medical libraries, high street information shops and drop-in centres, hospital information desks, advice and community centres, mobile libraries and centres for people with disabilities. The benefits of providing information to health service consumers are detailed by Sweetland (1996) in a paper which describes the results of a survey of users of a health drop-in information centre at a hospital in Bristol, England. Information provided increased patients' understanding of their condition, enabled them to cope better with the situation, and to make informed choices. There was a noted reduction in anxiety and stress as a result of increased knowledge, and a tendency to take positive action to improve health and lifestyle, such as giving up smoking and taking more exercise.

It has been shown that increased access to specific healthcare information leads to real improvements in patients' understanding, better compliance with treatment regimes, and a decrease in stress, which in turn often lead to improved recovery rates. The effect of information provision on patient anxiety levels is examined in a paper by Bolton and Brittain (1994). The role of libraries and information services in providing information for patients in general practice, hospital and community settings is discussed. All primary healthcare practitioners should be aware of the importance of information as central to the successful communication between doctor and patient. Patient libraries in surgeries and good local information centres are recommended. In the hospital setting the authors suggest that every hospital should have a medical library or information service to cater for patients as well as staff. At a local level each main public library should have a health information service to advise on and coordinate other information services and medical libraries available in the area.

The development of consumer health informatics, and the application of computer and telecommunication systems for use directly by the public, have made healthcare information available and accessible to millions of people. Ferguson (1995) reviews these new applications and identifies examples including:

- home health workstations for people with chronic illnesses such as AIDS, diabetes and depression;
- interactive decision-making support systems
- voice-mail based self-help systems;
- consumer-initiated searches of the medical literature;
- health forums and self-help groups on the Internet and other computer networks.

Some of the hazards surrounding consumer health informatics from an Australian viewpoint are discussed by O'Connor (1996). While the obvious benefits are acknowledged, problems to be addressed include those of privacy, patient access to medical records, confidentiality, ownership and coding of data.

An issue of great concern to patients and physicians alike is the effectiveness of the communication exchange, the provision of information that is not necessarily sought and/or understood by the patient. A fascinating project to devise an intelligent interactive system for delivering information specifically targeted at individual patients is explained by Buchanan *et al.* (1995). This is a long-term project which, if carried through successfully, will represent a major breakthrough in information systems because it is based on the provision of individualized information and treatment regimes for patients based upon available evidence. State-of-the-art artificial intelligence techniques are used to build an interactive explanation system based on empirical data on what the the patient actually needs. The two main components of the system are (a) an interactive history-taking module that collects information from patients prior to each visit, builds a patient model and summarizes the patients' status for their physicians; (b) an intelligent explanation module that produces an interactive information sheet which contains explanations in everyday language, tailored to individual patients, and responds intelligently to follow-up questions about topics covered in the information sheet. The importance of improving the information exchange between practitioners and patients, and increasing the amount and quality of information available, is reflected in this major research project.

Issues of current concern

Evidence-based medicine

The evidence-based healthcare movement is one of the most exciting current issues in healthcare. Increasingly the movement involves information professionals and this is likely to grow substantially over the next decade. Evidence-based medicine has been defined as 'the process of systematically finding, appraising, and using con-temporaneous research findings as the basis for clinical decisions' (Rosenberg and Donald, 1995). This requires efficient literature searching and the systematic review and evaluation of clinical research literature to link research results to improved outcomes. Previously reviews had not been carried out systematically and exhaustively, so the use of some effective medical treatments has been delayed for many years, and other forms of healthcare have continued to be used long after research has shown them to be ineffective or even harmful (Antman *et al.*, 1992; Coulter *et al.*, 1993).

In 1972 Cochrane argued that only findings derived from blind randomized control trials would provide valid evidence for the effectiveness of healthcare procedures. It is this argument that has formed the foundation of the Cochrane Collaboration (Long and Harrison, 1996b). This is an international network of individuals and institutions that prepare, maintain and disseminate systematic reviews of the effects of healthcare. There are six guiding principles on which the aims of the organization are based:

- collaboration;
- building on people's existing enthusiasm and interests;
- minimizing duplication of effort;
- avoidance of bias;
- keeping up to date;
- ensuring access.

The Collaboration is still at an early stage of development but the structure and methods of working have been established. An overview of its work and a strategic plan, published in 1996, are available on the Web site (Cochrane, 1997). Cochrane Centres are located in many countries including Australia, Canada, Italy, Denmark, USA, Netherlands, and England. Other initiatives include the *Effective health care* bulletins from the UK universities of York and Leeds, *Effectiveness matters* from the NHS Centre for Reviews and Dissemination, University of York, and *The Cochrane Library* which comprises four databases of sources of evidence in CD-ROM format. Journals which aim to provide practitioners with the evidence needed include *Evidence-based Medicine* and the *American College of Physicians (ACP) Journal Club* (Davidoff *et al.*, 1995; Long and Harrison, 1996a).

Another aspect of the Cochrane Collaboration is the work on effective professional practice (CCEPP), which undertakes reviews of interventions designed to improve health professionals' practice and the delivery of health services. Systematic reviews completed include patient adherence to medications and the effectiveness of printed educational materials on outcomes. An annual colloquium is held (1996 in Australia, 1997 in Amsterdam) and the newsletter reports on developments worldwide: for example a project to make available information on effectiveness of medical interventions in Italy is described by Liberati and Grilli (1997).

The role of information professionals is central to the development and effectiveness of evidence-based medicine. The evidence-based movement has grown out of a general acceptance that healthcare professionals do not have the time (or sometimes the skills or motivation) to retrieve all the reliable information from reports of original research on diagnosis and treatment and on the effects of treatment. There is a new and crucial role for information specialists in advising reviewers on ways of exploiting the information services available, and on appropriate search and retrieval techniques. In the next few years information professionals with navigational skills on the Internet will be at a premium. Various studies have shown that information professionals can effectively provide a quality filtering process for the clinician, which can also be extended to other areas of healthcare (Kuller, 1993; Haines, 1994).

The importance of evidence-based practice for patients and their carers is paramount, as they suffer or benefit most directly as a result of treatment outcomes. Consumers need to have access to information based on evidence in order to make informed choices and participate in decision making with medical staff. The dissemination of this information is now of concern to many information professionals (Hope, 1995). Since April 1996 the Health Information Service, a freephone helpline linking the public to a network of consumer health information services (CHI) in England and Wales, has been required to provide information on clinical effectiveness. There is a need for CHI services to make more use of the effectiveness-based information sources such as those mentioned above, rather than of literature produced by self-help groups or other organizations, which may not necessarily be based on the best current evidence of effectiveness (Gann and Buckland, 1994). Improved awareness of evidence-based information for patients and the public in general, and more training in the use and accessing of the resources available, are needed for health information staff. These issues are currently being addressed in a pilot study under the Kings Fund Promoting Patient Choice initiative (MacDougall *et al.*, 1996, p. 435).

A major demand on information providers in evidence-based healthcare is the ability quickly and systematically to construct a case history and assess the current status of professional consensus within specific areas of medicine. A novel approach has been taken by Brittain (1997) using bibliometrics and citation analyses as a contribution to the process of identifying relevant research, its systematic organization, and evaluation. The work provides a prototype information retrieval facility based on the analysis of citation indexes, which can complement existing methods of identifying evidence and also shorten the time-consuming process. This work is of particular interest to librarians and information scientists because it demonstrates that methods and tools which have been developed almost entirely within the library and information science professions have a major role to play in evidence-based healthcare.

The introduction of problem-based learning in medical schools, following the example of McMaster University in Ontario, has been a subject of interest during 1996. Medical libraries have had to adapt new methods to support the self-directed learning component of the new curriculum and the related emphasis on evidence-based medicine (Fitzgerald, 1996). Taylor and Lande (1996) describe the progress of a traditional medical library in meeting the needs of a problem-based learning curriculum in Norway. The process of change is described, including the development of facilities and services, upgrading librarians' skills and greatly increased use by students.

Telecommunications and integration

The multimedia nature of modern clinical information requires a sophisticated range of telematics technologies which will enable clinicians to communicate and access interactively, provide remote consultation, and offer diagnosis and treatment.

Telemedicine involves the ability to transmit voice, video and data between distant sites using advanced networking technology. It includes digitized X-ray, computer radiology, nuclear medicine, ultrasound, magnetic resonance, imaging electron microscopy, and endoscopy, all of which rely on audiovisual and computer technologies. The eventual application of telemedicine will facilitate the development of more innovative clinical practice and contribute to seamless healthcare.

The European Union has a long-standing commitment to the development of telemedicine technologies and integration of information systems. The emphasis has been on improving overall standards of healthcare, increasing access and awareness of services, establishing standards in hardware and terminology, and improving communication through integrated health systems. The main tasks of the Advanced Informatics in Medicine (AIM) programme were to integrate decision support systems with hospital information systems; to integrate medical informatics generally with communication concepts and systems; and to develop the telemedicine concept. The enormous range of services now available from healthcare units demands more sophisticated communications networks, and it is essential to increase the levels of data exchange and integration. The integrated broadband communication (IBC) service introduced in 1996 is a new multimedia communications network intended to facilitate improved integration of European healthcare services and a greater exchange of healthcare data. IBC is integrated with hospital information systems to allow these new developments in Europe. The overall shift of emphasis towards primary care increases the role of effective communication between patients, medical practitioners and healthcare units. Tele-communications also have a major role in the continuing education of, and updating of information for, healthcare professionals through such means as distance learning and remote consultation and conferencing, as well as in supporting collaborative treatment programmes. It is hoped that, through telemedicine, multimedia information for patients and the public on health promotion and the latest advances in the diagnosis and treatment of such diseases as AIDS may be transmitted easily and effectively to a widely-spaced and disparate population (Mantas, 1992).

Kwok (1996) provides an overview of applications and current developments in telemedicine worldwide, with examples of standards for its implementation. He paints a useful picture of the main challenges ahead, particularly those which involve the availability of suitable communications infrastructure and coherent implementation strategies for the integration and exchange of multimedia clinical data.

It is essential that the role of information professionals in relation to telemedicine be defined as soon as possible to facilitate the exploitation and dissemination of information. For example, they play an important part in the continuing education of healthcare professionals by distance learning, supporting collaborative treatment programmes, and providing patients and the public with up-to-date information on the latest treatments more effectively.

Healthcare managers and clinicians need access to many different types of information, including biomedical and scientific information and patient-generated data as well as hospital activity data and management information. Clinicians are gradually becoming more involved in the management of their units, while managers require more information on outputs and health gain. The emphasis is now on quality of outcome at the lowest cost. The aim is, therefore, to integrate the systems dealing with medical and scientific knowledge with those concentrating on the management of healthcare and internal throughput data. In the USA the NLM has developed a major initiative in the integration of healthcare information systems, called Integrated Advanced Information Management Systems (IAIMS). The programme is designed to encourage health sciences institutions to plan and implement an integrated organizational approach to information management for clinical practice, medical education and biomedical research. This demands the collaboration of libraries with computing and telecommunications providers in bringing disparate institutional databases and systems into a single network (Lindberg *et al.*, 1992; Weise, 1993). Originally IAIMS was based on the concept of the library supporting the development of information network systems, the integration of IT into the health professions and education, and encouraging the development of information staff in academic health sciences institutions. The IAIMS grant programme has spread to include 40 institutions; in some of these it is the computing or medical informatics departments which have taken the lead, although the role of the library in accessing reference material always remains a core feature. Most health science centres are beginning to study the role of information in their organizations and to commit resources to its development and systems networking: 'The term IAIMS is becoming a generic acronym for the carefully planned information system' (Lindberg *et al.*, 1992).

A period of transition in the health services of Hong Kong and its effects on the demand for health and medical information are investigated by Cheng (1996). The new Hong Kong Hospital Authority has taken over 39 hospitals with a widely disparate and uneven development of libraries and information provision. The emphasis of the Library Network System is on access to information rather than ownership of resources. Library service networks have been developed with centre libraries serving other hospitals and the Hospital Authority Library Information Systems provides a backbone 'library without walls' integrated information system accessible to all in the authority.

Outcomes and health information for consumers

With the fast developing consumer health information (CHI) sector the issue of outcomes for the patient and carer has demanded more attention from healthcare practitioners, managers, and information professionals alike. As we have already discussed here, more information has become available through new CHI services and initiatives like the freephone Health Information Service in England and Wales. But until recently the involvement of the patient or carer in the assessment of outcomes has been notable by its absence (Neuberger, 1993).

A review of the progress made on outcomes measurement from the consumer's or user's perspective is provided by Long and Brettle (1996) from the UK Clearing House on Health Outcomes. One interesting point made is that the evidence-based medicine initiative has led in some cases to a narrow interpretation of evidence gained from randomized control trials and a focusing on short-term clinical outcomes. Other issues considered include the need to clearly identify the consumers' desired outcomes and the value placed on them; developing measures that reflect consumer priorities; and the use of outcomes information to inform decision-making, service evaluation, audit and planning.

The second 'But will it work, Doctor?' conference was held in England in 1996 to review progress made on outcomes information for consumers (Needham, 1996). The decision-making process and the complex information needs of patients offered a choice of treatments were discussed, as well as the doctor–patient relationship and the importance of developing a partnership approach. The role of information professionals in helping consumers to assess the information and research available, its value and relevance, was emphasized. Making information on evidence more accessible is potentially a major role for the CHI services available on a freephone number. The increasing availability of information on the Internet and through CD-ROM technology raised questions about the quality of information available and inequality of access (since those without the technology are denied access to this information). The development of high quality information packs incorporating evidence on treatments and questions patients need answered is another initiative providing information for healthcare users based on the latest research and outcomes measures.

Criteria to establish the quality of information provided for consumers of healthcare are set out by Gann (1996), based on a variety of research carried out in this area (Arthur, 1995). Readability and legibility are vital in public information; but much is still produced which requires a high level of reading skills. More symbols and illustrations could be used to help those with learning difficulties and people with lower reading levels such as children and those who are reading in a second language. Improving recall, compliance with treatment and patient satisfaction are also important criteria. Information designed to empower patients, however, must also respect their autonomy and improve their choices. Evidence-based healthcare is beginning to meet this need, together with the recognition of the importance of shared decision-making between patient and doctor (Hope, 1995). The evaluation of patient information materials should include whether it is:

- of interest to the patient;
- based on good evidence;
- free from bias;
- accessible;
- able to be used/understood;
- enhancing choice (Gann, 1996).

A European perspective is provided by Ovretveit (1996), who reviews the need for outcomes information, and looks at experience in Europe and the USA in a cogent and well-structured paper. The dissemination and quality of outcome information are now a public health and policy issue in Europe. This is the result of several developments including research into evaluating outcomes generally and the influence of patient characteristics on outcomes. New information technology which reduces the cost of data collection makes it easier to collect and analyse outcomes measures. The emphasis on quality in auditing and customer satisfaction is another trend which has highlighted this area. The concerns of purchasers for ensuring value for money means that providers must show outcomes benefits and quality performance. The importance of primary care referrers who need to know about outcomes and costs and often pass this information on to their patients, also contributes to this trend. The rise in consumerism and patient power is a major reason for the concern with quality of healthcare information for the public. People expect to have more information about their treatments, outcomes and alternative courses of action.

Networking and the Internet

During 1995 the growth of information on the Internet was explosive. An enormous amount of healthcare information of all kinds is now accessible by anyone with a computer connected to an Internet provider. As a rapidly expanding worldwide source of healthcare information, the Internet is fast becoming an indispensable resource for both professionals and consumers. As a result a number of guides have been published pointing out the benefits and advantages of accessing information from the Internet. For professionals it would seem to be yet another information source requiring time and effort to use. However, there are several reasons why healthcare professionals can benefit from its use:

- Information is current and up to date, facilitating instant publishing and retrieval.
- Access is possible to both traditional and electronic sources of information through database systems such as MEDLINE.
- The facility to access worldwide information sources through one connection to an Internet provider and one piece of software (a World Wide Web browser) on a local telephone number means simple, fast, convenient and cheap access.

- The opportunity is available to discuss problems, and question colleagues and experts worldwide, through e-mail, discussion lists, and newsgroups.
- Personal research interests and continuing education may be conducted at any convenient time (Kiley, 1996).

Internet training sites are also available for healthcare professionals and are cited by Kiley (1996), who also provides a bibliography for those not yet connected. Information for those health professionals wanting to set up their own services on the Internet is included in another work on health information on the Internet by Anthony (1996). This includes sections on electronic publishing, Telnet, setting up online services and creating newsgroups.

A conference dedicated to this area is held annually in October in Brighton, England – the World Congress on the Internet in Medicine. A Virtual Conference is held in parallel on the Internet with delegates able to participate in discussions with speakers at the main event. The conference covers all applications of the Internet in medicine including telemedicine, primary care, medical libraries, hospital management, access to healthcare information, research using the Internet, security, and the developing world (Virtual, 1997).

For the healthcare consumer the Internet provides a huge information resource for those who may never have direct access to consumer health information services, medical libraries or information specialists. Many of the benefits listed above apply equally to lay people and healthcare professionals, but often with additional advantages for the former. Web pages produced by healthcare organizations may give details of services offered, the latest facilities, treatment regimes, research studies and care policies. Voluntary organizations, self-help groups, charities and interested individuals set up pages providing invaluable information on areas of specific interest. For example, for those suffering from, treating or caring for those with epilepsy, the National Society for Epilepsy UK Web Page is a useful source of information of all types (Epilepsy, 1997), while newsgroups or USENET groups such as *alt.support.epilepsy* provide an open forum for discussion. Many Web pages are designed either for professionals or for users of healthcare, but some manage to aim at both. CancerHelp UK is a free information service on cancer for the general public and healthcare professionals, and is developed by CRC Institute of Cancer Studies, University of Birmingham, and the British Association for Cancer United Patients (BACUP) (Cancer, 1997).

A report published on the Internet details the results of a study into the demand for health and medical information on the Internet by American consumers; it includes an analysis of the provision of healthcare information and the barriers to meeting the needs of sophisticated users (Brown, 1996). The report concludes that many sites aimed at consumers are owned by organizations or individuals who may be providing inaccurate or biased information. While there is an abundance of health information available it is a daunting challenge to locate sources of timely, accurate, relevant and unbiased material. There is no guarantee that the content is of good quality. The fact that anyone can set up a Web page anonymously means that it is an ideal medium for personal ideas or propaganda. Some of these are easily identified but others are very difficult to see (Lindsay, 1996).

The benefits and pitfalls of medical information on the Internet are highlighted in an illuminating article by Payne (1996), who describes its impact on general practitioners. Consultation by Internet is a growing trend worldwide, especially where patient anonymity is a factor. Research conducted in the USA is referred to and the implications for UK physicians are examined in the light of possible litigation threats.

The role for information professionals is one of filtering and assessing the quality of information accessed from the Internet. This is of particular relevance to consumer information where knowledge of information quality and origin may not be obvious. There is a need for some form of peer review, as is used in conventional scientific publishing.

Other forms of networking using the Internet are also developing worldwide. For example, the New Zealand Centre for Health Informatics (1997) was set up to provide electronic information services and a responsive Internet service for health professionals, pharmacists and their organizations. One recent landmark accomplishment at Columbia University, New York, involves the use of the World Wide Web (WWW) as a clinical information system. Whereas the Internet already provides access to many healthcare and biomedical information sources and applications, most of these have been based on the concept of the electronic library and education (Kassirer, 1996). This development will enable healthcare professionals to access secure information on their patients, integrated with other medical information sources from anywhere on the Internet. Some authors expect these applications to enable healthcare professionals and patients to access medical information and carry out consultations (Rizzolo and Dubois, 1994; Cross, 1995).

In Vietnam, in spite of huge economic and political problems, the medical library community has made remarkable progress. The Ministry of Health runs the Central Institute for Medical Science Information, which acts as a national coordinating body for a network of medical libraries serving all areas of the country. It also promotes cooperation in networking and collection development in medical libraries, carries out research in information management and technology, and acts as a focal point for health services information in the western Pacific region (Brennen, 1992).

In the UK networking is playing a crucial part in managing information to improve the quality, quantity and range of services in the NHS. The NHS Information Management and Technology Strategy has launched several initiatives to ensure a single infrastructure and an integrated approach to information management and the sharing of information. These include a common set of standards such as a thesaurus of coded clinical terms for communication, and NHS-wide networking to link hospitals, GPs, libraries and other organizations by

1996. There are many problems to be overcome and the process may be rather more incremental than originally envisaged, but the NHS is nevertheless committed to the implementation of the network (King, 1996). The benefits of a fully integrated communications network will include, for example, pathology systems in one hospital interconnecting with a GP's computer in a remote location, direct access to medical libraries and full-text transmission of journal articles, X-ray images transferred across the country, or the transfer of data from one district nurse's laptop computer to a colleague in another region (Ruck, 1993).

British Telecom (BT) has launched the HealthNet service offering connection to the NHS-wide network and the Internet for hospital trusts, access to the NHS message handling service, and interactive systems which, for example, will allow GPs to browse hospital information systems and book outpatient appointments. The BT message handling service is now linked to its rival Healthlink from Racal Network Services. NHS users can communicate with users on both services while subscribing to either. There are widespread concerns about the need for a firewall between the NHS-wide network and the Internet. Guidance to NHS Trusts and Health Authorities is that one-way access should be allowed from the NHS network to the Internet but not via the Internet to the NHS network (Dunham, 1996; Fowler, 1996).

The mission statement of the New Zealand Health Sciences Network is to strengthen and maximize access to information resources through a dynamic and user-friendly computer network in order to improve the health status of New Zealanders. This network, set up in 1990, comprises a set of databases, both textual and bibliographic, available nationally from the Department of Health in Wellington. The system can be used for electronic mail and the transmission of interlibrary loan requests and as a gateway to other systems and databases. An important service offered by the network is the US National Library of Medicine's online catalogue, CATLINE. Other services include computerized cataloguing, training and consultancy, end-user searching and selective dissemination of information (Jamieson, 1990). The New Zealand *Health information strategy for the year 2000* (Shipley, 1996) deals with the wider issues of health information systems development and management.

In Texas a demonstration project was designed specifically to help doctors in isolated areas maintain contact with their peers by providing access to information, consultative and diagnostic services and continuing education. This was done through interactive video, telecommunication services and fax. Isolated practitioners are able to consult face to face with specialists, and fax machines are used to transmit clinical tracings, foetal monitoring strips and other documents. The librarian works as an information specialist in conjunction with a subject specialist for each continuing education programme, identifying relevant information, combining the various multimedia resources into individual study packages and delivering them to the doctors. The librarian acts as curriculum developer and evaluation specialist for the continuing education programmes, locating resources and directing the programmes for doctors (Moore and Hartmen, 1992).

A survey of the information needs of rural healthcare practitioners in Hawaii found that the main barriers to information access included lack of adequate hardware, infrastructure problems and insufficient knowledge of information sources and how to access them. Recommendations included the development of a centralized rural health clearing house or library with a health information specialist, avoiding over-duplication of resources, maximizing access through increased use of fax, online searching and subsidizing the costs of information delivery to equalize the availability of information to all (Lundeen *et al.*, 1994).

Access and quality assurance in healthcare information services

A recent study in the Republic of Ireland has highlighted the lack of access to and awareness of healthcare information services by both professionals and the public, in spite of modern technological advances as discussed elsewhere in this chapter. A national survey of a range of healthcare practitioners revealed that:

- There are serious deficiencies in access, awareness and availability of information for both healthcare staff and patients in Ireland.
- Many health service staff and patients, particularly in rural areas, have been severely disadvantaged in their access to up-to-date specialized information.
- There has been a lack of recognition in the past from central government of the importance of library and information services and of the potential use of information technology in accessing healthcare information.
- The lack of any central lead on information strategy and future planning has meant that the development, cooperation and coordination of healthcare information services have been restricted.
- The sophisticated access necessary to the worldwide knowledge base of healthcare (for example on the Internet) is not available to many staff and is under-utilized.

Since the publication of this report several important steps have been taken by both the government and the health boards in Ireland, including further funding to investigate the provision of consumer health information and increased resources for library and information services (MacDougall, 1995).

In the Netherlands the focal point for biomedical information is the Library of the Royal Netherlands Academy of Sciences, with 10,000 current journals in this area alone. The library has developed a strategic approach to quality service delivery by involving the users in the improvement and development of the service. By means of a questionnaire survey of users the library identified the satisfaction rate of requested articles and speed of delivery as key areas for improvement. Document delivery processes must be strengthened and revived by libraries if they are not to be at risk of being taken over by commercial document delivery services. The strength of libraries is their expertise in the relationship between services, collections and user needs, which forms the strategic triangle at the core of the Library of the Royal Netherlands Academy of Sciences (Brandsma, 1994).

A comparison of the acquisition of relevant, up-to-date information by medical staff in Brazil and the UK reveals information requirements and library use to be similar. However, the process of acquiring information is affected by the differing environments. The more restricted information provision in Brazil in terms of availability and currency means that user expectations are much lower. Healthcare practitioners in Brazil have adapted to the restrictions by purchasing their own materials, using books where their British counterparts would consult a journal, and making use of more interlibrary loans. Problems of using out of date information and language difficulties are the main issues recognized by staff. Limited resources affect many developing countries and while many of these problems could be solved with increased automation this would need to be affordable (Mendes and Meadows, 1996).

Quality healthcare relies on quality information services and provision. Research in Mexico was conducted to identify the value and impact of, and barriers to, information access and use as related to quality of healthcare. A soft systems methodology approach was used to build a consensus model from which feasible and desirable changes were proposed to improve access and use of information (Macias-Chapula, 1995). In contrast, access to drug information in the Czech Republic is the subject of a study by Müllerová and Vleek (1996). The authors evaluated the activities of a regional drug information centre in terms of access, enquiries, sources of information and costs. The project highlighted problem areas which can now be addressed, such as the need to advertise the service more, the poor quality of telephone lines, and difficulties obtaining databases on CD-ROM.

The value of information to clinicians is the subject of a research project carried out at the University of Wales. The findings led to the development of a toolkit to assist healthcare information services to deliver more effective support for clinical decision making (Urquhart and Hepworth, 1995a). The information skills of both staff and users must be assessed and improved where necessary. An audit approach is used to enable information staff to help staff identify their own training needs and continuing education. The research had examined the processes by which information contributed to clinical decisions and those factors which affected the delivery and uptake of information (Urquhart and Hepworth, 1995b).

Information strategy

The significance of strategies for health information management and technology (IM&T) is outlined by Brittain (1996), who highlights the importance of education and training for IM&T. The main reasons for developing and implementing an information strategy are given as:

- enabling a detailed plan of activity to be agreed, facilitating financial planning, and allowing progress to be assessed against objectives;
- assisting in justifying expenditure of large sums;
- providing a vehicle for publicity;
- helping to develop local ownership and motivation;
- reducing the chance of duplicated effort and wasted resources;
- providing coherence to a national, state, or international activity;
- helping to plan for the future.

A case study of the training programme developed by the UK NHS is provided. This addresses the IM&T training needs of clinicians, professionals allied to medicine, administrative, clerical, technical and auxiliary staff at all levels.

The importance of integrating information services of all types is a major concern. In the UK the Information Management Group of the NHS has developed an information strategy to implement the government reforms in information terms. However, this has concentrated mainly on statistical information and other management information and pays less attention to textual knowledge and information. The necessity of redressing this imbalance has been stressed (MacDougall and Brittain, 1992), and the Cumberlege initiative is actively seeking to achieve this. The main strategic objectives of the initiative are

- to improve the quality of the knowledge base of healthcare and its coordination;
- to ensure that the knowledge base is disseminated widely using the technology that is becoming available;
- to identify, promote and disseminate good local practice;
- to improve local organization and transmission of the knowledge base (New, 1995).

A key development arising from the Cumberlege initiative was the appointment of the NHS Library Advisor in January 1995. The remit includes advising on the coordination of library and information services within the NHS and, in particular, on standards and good practice. The encouragement of cooperative initiatives and local support for library and information networks is a priority, as well as the development of a library and information strategy (Haines, 1996).

The success of the new health reforms in New Zealand will depend to a large extent on appropriate information systems, according to the Associate Minister for Health (Williamson, 1992). He describes how the Health Information Strategy for New Zealand identified several problems with current information systems, which have developed on an ad hoc basis and generally do not meet the needs of individuals or the public or private sectors. A national New Zealand Health Information Service has been set up to establish the core elements of:

- a national minimum dataset;
- a national health index;
- a national household health survey;
- access to documentary databases;
- a national health information service network;
- standards and guidelines for technology, data and quality.

This strategy included provision for the integration of textual information as well as statistical data. A clearing house was set up to provide a 'one stop shop' for access to all information, whether it be statistical and quantitative, research and analytical or textual and qualitative: this would be available to all. In 1996 a new *Health information strategy for the year 2000* updated the 1991 strategy, building on the improvements achieved with an emphasis on a new patient-focused approach, evidence-based medicine, and seamless healthcare. The strategy was one of eight key result areas addressed as part of the Ministry of Health's 1995–96 work programme. It aims to achieve a consensus on the future coordinated management of health information (Shipley, 1996).

In Australia a National Health Information Development Plan has been developed to set out priorities for health information at national level (Australian Institute of Health and Welfare and Australian Health Ministers' Advisory Council, 1995). The plan outlines 59 priority areas or 'development directions' for information over the next five to ten years. Eight directions are given highest priority and include:

- a plan to improve information on health for Aboriginal and Torres Strait Island peoples;
- developing a national health and welfare information model;
- a plan to improve information on health outcomes;
- developing and collecting standardized information on mental illness outcomes and on primary care encounter data;
- systematically reviewing current major health data collections.

As Fett (1996) reports, it is essential to have accurate and timely healthcare information to facilitate policy development, planning and management of a national health service. This plan is an important contribution to the development of future coordinated healthcare in Australia.

Another initiative to support health information development in Australia is described by Mercer and Moss (1995). The National Health Information Model aims to provide a framework for information systems development and management. This is achieved through:

- a common vocabulary and framework for health information in Australia;
- a means to identify gaps and deficiencies in current information holdings, systems and strategies;

- a vehicle for coordinating investment in information management and systems strategies.

The authors describe the development of the model, its use and its role in conjunction with the *National Health Data Dictionary*, which is the source of all health data definitions. Other national projects are working with and contributing to the National Health Information Model and the *National Health Data Dictionary* including palliative care, outpatient and emergency information, community health and mental health.

Conclusion – opportunities and obstacles for the future

Health informatics is a growing and thriving activity in North America, Europe, and Australasia. It now has most of the characteristics of a self-contained profession. There are a number of professional journals and professional societies; conferences, meetings, and educational and training programmes are offered by universities and other sectors of higher education. There are textbooks on health informatics and a growing body of research. Progress has been made quickly during the last ten years. The present status of health informatics is very different from the beginnings in the 1970s.

Throughout the 1970s and most of the 1980s many attempts were made to apply IT to existing healthcare administration and delivery, often without success. During this period the application of IT to the solution of healthcare management and practice came to have a bad name: many people referred to IT in health services as 'a black hole'. Governments invested heavily in IT and computerization of healthcare, but the results were patchy. There were many cases of failed, inadequate information systems, and indeed in some countries IT investment in healthcare by governments has been the subject of public enquiries and reports.

There were exceptions to the dismal record of IT in this area. There have been pockets of activity, and genuine success by healthcare professionals pursuing their own goals and strategies, and by medical scientists and others continuing to work in the productive area of medical informatics – mainly in the application of computing and communication technologies to the diagnosis and direct treatment of diseases and other medical conditions.

In the 1990s there has been a dramatic change in emphasis and driving forces. The emphasis is no longer on IT applications and computing in healthcare. Instead, it is on cost containment, improvements in clinical effectiveness and patient management, streamlining of health administration, outsourcing, the internal market (in which one part of the health service purchases healthcare for another part), the evidence-based medicine movement, patient information services and the involvement of patients in healthcare decision making. These are all aspects of health administration and health delivery that involve complex information systems if they are to operate successfully.

The single most important fact in determining the direction of healthcare in the 1990s, in all developed countries, has been the reforms initiated by central governments, although these differ considerably from one country to another. Containment of costs and the reallocation of resources continue to dominate the application of IT in health. Those countries that have instigated the so-called internal market have given much attention to information systems for the purchasing of healthcare. Health authorities, health departments, community health services, and general practitioners, as well as hospitals, stand to lose considerable amounts of money if they do not have accurate and timely information systems in place when contracts are being negotiated.

The evidence-based medicine movement has taken considerable time to gain momentum, but there is now a general recognition that the delivery of healthcare can be improved greatly (and also, by implication, litigation can be reduced) by healthcare professionals acting only upon treatments and procedures that are supported by consensus agreement derived from large databases, which in turn draw upon worldwide practice. In the 1990s the consumer health information movement has reached maturity and looks set for continued growth, and more patients, their relatives and carers will all become more closely involved in the process.

During the 1970s and 1980s the library and information science (LIS) professions were largely ignored by government health departments, healthcare professionals, and healthcare administrators. During this period the number of information and information management positions in health services increased exponentially, but few LIS personnel were recruited. However, towards the end of the 1980s the operation of the internal market, purchasing of healthcare considerations, the assessment of the healthcare needs of defined populations, and more recently the evidence-based medicine movement, have demonstrated beyond doubt that the LIS professions have much to offer, particularly in the way of identifying information resources, producing state-of-the-art reviews, and making sense of the vast amount of material now available on the Internet. LIS professionals have for the most part been slow to realize and capitalize upon their strengths, particularly those that complement (rather than duplicate) existing strengths in the health services. There are a few exceptions, and in some countries the professional library associations have active special interest groups in health informatics. A review of health information in ten years' time would almost certainly demonstrate that health informatics in the late 1990s and early 21st century will be a growth area, and also an area of increasing employment for LIS professionals.

This review has demonstrated that many current concerns, activities, and strategies for improved healthcare delivery within the context of cost containment are dependent upon timely, relevant and appropriate information, delivered (usually in a value-added way) to healthcare professionals and healthcare administrators.

References

Alecu, S. *et al.* (1996) Computer-assisted diagnosis of metabolic emergencies. In: Richards, B. (1996) (ed.), pp. 173–178.

Anthony, D. (1996) *Health on the Internet.* Oxford: Blackwell Science.

Antman, E.M. *et al.* (1992) A comparison of results of meta-analyses of randomized control trials and recommendations of clinical experts. *Journal of the American Medical Association*, **268**, 240–248.

Arthur, V.A.M. (1995) Written patient information: a review of the literature. *Journal of Advanced Nursing*, **21**, 1081–1086.

Australian Institute of Health and Welfare and Australian Health Ministers' Advisory Council. (1995) *National health information development plan.* Canberra: AGPS.

Bargenquast J. and Williams, P. (1996) Development of an information solution for public sector community health services in New South Wales. *Informatics in Healthcare – Australia*, **5**(2), 57–61.

Bolton, V. and Brittain, J.M. (1994) Patient information provision: its effects on patient anxiety and the role of health information services and libraries. *Health Libraries Review*, **11**(2), 117–132.

Brandsma, R. (1994) User needs, services and collection. In: *Health information – new possibilities. Proceedings of the 4th European conference of medical and health libraries*, Oslo, Norway, 28 June–2 July, 1994, ed. T. McSean. Dordrecht: Kluwer Academic.

Brennen, P.W. (1992) The medical libraries of Vietnam. *Bulletin of the Medical Library Association*, **80**(3), 294–299.

Brittain, J.M. (1996) National strategy for information management. In: E.J.S. Hovenga *et al.* (eds) *Health Informatics: an overview.* London: Churchill Livingstone and Health Informatics Society of Australia, pp. 271–280.

Brittain, J.M. (1997) Consensus issues in evidence-based medicine: the role of citation analysis. Unpublished paper, Health Informatics Research Group, University of South Australia, Adelaide.

Brittain, J.M. *et al.* (1996) Electronic medical records: design of the human-computer interface. In: Richards, B. (1996) (ed.), pp. 367–372.

Brown, M.S. (1996) *Consumer health and medical information on the Internet: supply and demand.* http://etrg.findsvp.com/health/mktginfo.html

Buchan, H. (1993) New Zealand's health care reforms. *British Medical Journal*, **307**, 635–636.

Buchanan, B.G. *et al.* (1995) An intelligent interactive system for delivering individualized information to patients. *Artificial Intelligence in Medicine*, **7**, 117–154.

Cancer (1997) http://med714.bham.ac.uk/cancerhelp/

Carmel, M. (1995) Health care services in the USA. In: M. Carmel (ed.) *Health care librarianship and information work.* 2nd ed. London: Library Association Publishing, pp. 259–269.

Cheng, G. (1996) The market for medical and health information in transition: the case of the Hong Kong Hospital Authority libraries. *Health Libraries Review*, **13**(2), 69–80.

Cochrane (1997) http://hiru.mcmaster.ca/cochrane/stratp96.htm

Coopers and Lybrand (1997) *Informatics management – the key to managed healthcare in Europe*. London: Coopers and Lybrand Europe Ltd.

Coulter, A. *et al.* (1993) Diagnostic dilatation and curettage: is it used appropriately? *British Medical Journal*, **306**(4), 236–239.

Cross, M. (1995) The future has finally arrived. *Health Service Journal*, (19 October, IT update), 1–2.

Davidoff, F. *et al.* (1995) Evidence-based medicine. *British Medical Journal*, **310**, 1085–1086.

De Glanville, H. (1994) And specialist shall speak unto superspecialist. *British Journal of Healthcare Computing and Information Management*, **11**(10), 12–13.

Dunham, C. (1996) Building a firewall between your network and the outside world. *British Journal of Healthcare Computing and Information Management*, **13**(1), 30–31.

Elliott, J. (1994) A content analysis of the health information provided in women's weekly magazines. *Health Libraries Review*, **11**(2), 96–103.

Epilepsy (1997) http://bay.erg.ion.bpmf.ac.uk/NSEhome

Falconer, J. and Villanueva, H.E. (1995) Fetal health decision support system using real time physiological data derived from an ultrasound scan. In: W. Swinkels *et al.* (eds) *IT's time for healthcare: proceedings of the Third National Health Informatics Conference, Adelaide, Australia, 16–17 October 1995*. Melbourne: Health Informatics Society of Australia, pp. 27–30.

Farmer, J. and Chesson R. (1996) The informers. *Health Service Journal*, **106**(5488), 28–29.

Ferguson, T. (1995) Consumer health informatics. *Healthcare Forum Journal*, **38**(1), 28–33.

Fett, M.J. (1996) Information for all by the year 2000. *Medical Journal of Australia*, **164**, 264–265.

Fitzgerald, D. (1996) Problem based learning and libraries: the Canadian experience. *Health Libraries Review*, **13**, 13–32.

Fowler, J. (1996) The road to the NHSnet: practical problems ahead. *British Journal of Healthcare Computing and Information Management*, **13**(8), 18–20.

Gann, R. (1991) Consumer health information: the growth of an information specialism. *Journal of Documentation*, **47**(3), 284–308.

Gann, R. (1994) Editorial. *Health Libraries Review*, **11**(2), 79–81 [whole issue devoted to CHI].

Gann, R. (1996) Information for patients and carers on effectiveness of treatments. In: A. Long and A. Brettle (eds). *Outcomes Briefing*, **8**, 38–41.

Gann, R. and Buckland, S. (1994) *Dissemination of information on treatment outcomes by consumer health information services*. Report to the King's Fund, Winchester: Help for Health Trust.

Great Britain. (1992) National Health Service Management Executive Information Management Group. *Getting better with information: IM&T strategy overview*. London: National Health Service Management Executive.

Great Britain. Department of Health. (1993) NHS management executive information management group. *Information for effective purchasing*. Leeds: Department of Health.

Haines, M. (1994) Editorial – evidence-based practice: new opportunities for librarians. *Health Libraries Review*, **11**(4), 221–225.

Haines, M. (1996) The role of the library adviser in developing NHS library and information services. *IFMH Inform*, **7**(3), 11–13.

Harding, F.O. (1996) A model information system for a small hospital. In: Richards, B. (1996) (ed.), pp. 345–352.

Haux, R. (1995) Medical informatics: a key to the future of medicine and health care? *Methods of Information in Medicine*, **34**(5), 454–457.

Hope, T. (1995) *Evidence-based patient choice*. Oxford: Oxford Practice Skills Project.

Jamieson, D.G. (1990) A band of committed visionaries: the New Zealand health sciences network. *New Zealand Libraries*, **46**(7/8), 28–31.

Jones, A. *et al.* (1996) Mutidisciplinary working towards seamless care and the electronic patient record. *British Journal of Healthcare Computing and Information Management*, **13**(5), 24–27.

Kahle, B. *et al.* (1996) Evaluation of a digital speech processor system in clinical practice. In: Richards, B. (1996) (ed.), pp. 79–84.

Kassirer, P. (1996) The next transformation in the delivery of healthcare. *New England Journal of Medicine*, **332**(1), 52–54.

Kay, S. and Purves, I.N. (1996) Medical records and other stories. *Methods of Information in Medicine*, **35**(2), 72–87.

Kiley, R. (1996) *Medical information on the Internet*. Edinburgh: Churchill Livingstone.

King, T. (1996) Networking the NHS – making it happen. *British Journal of Healthcare Computing and Information Management*, **13**(8), 16–18.

Kuller, A.B. (1993) Quality filtering of the clinical literature by librarians and physicians. *Bulletin of the Medical Library Association*, **81**(1), 38–43.

Kwok, J. (1996) Multimedia telematics for telemedicine. In: Richards, B. (1996) (ed.), pp. 699–707.

Lamberts. H. and Hofmans-Okkes, I. (1996) The generic patient record. *Methods of Information in Medicine*, **35**(1), 5–7.

Lee, K. (1991) Competition versus planning in health care. *Australian Health Review*, **14**(1), 9–34.

Liberati, A. and Grilli, R. (1997) Effectiveness in Italy. *Cochrane Collaboration on Effective Professional Practice (CCEPP) Newsletter*, (3), 10.

Lindberg, D.A.B. *et al.* (1992) IAIMS – an overview from the National Library of Medicine. *Bulletin of the Medical Library Association*, **80**(3), 244–246.

Lindsay, B. (1996) Information on the Internet: consumer guides to healthcare. *British Journal of Health Care Management*, **2**(8), 445–447.

Long, A. and Brettle, A. (1996) eds. Outcomes for patients and carers. *Outcomes Briefing*, (8). (whole issue).

Long, A. and Harrison, S. (1996a) An ABC of EBM. *Health Service Journal: Health Management Guide*, (January), 3–5.

Long, A. and Harrison, S. (1996b) The balance of evidence. *Health Service Journal: Health Management Guide*, (January), 1–2.

Lundeen, G.W. *et al.* (1994) Information needs of rural healthcare practitioners in Hawaii. *Bulletin of the Medical Library Association*, **82**(2), 197–205.

MacDougall, J. (1995) *Information for health*. Dublin: Library Association of Ireland.

MacDougall, J. and Brittain, J.M. (1992) *Use of information in the NHS*. London: British Library. (British Library and Information Report, 92.)

MacDougall, J, *et al.* (1996) Health informatics: an overview. *Journal of Documentation*, **52**(4), 421–448.

Macias-Chapula, C. (1995) Development of a soft systems model to identify information values, impact and barriers in a health care information system. *Journal of Information Science*, **21**(4), 283–288.

Mantas, J. (1992) The application of advanced information technology in medicine and healthcare: a European approach. *International Journal of Technology Management*, **7**(6/ 8), 560–571.

Mason, C. (1996) Making IT happen for purchasers and providers. *Informatics in Healthcare – Australia*, **5** (3), 92–96.

Mendes, H.M. de C. and Meadows, A.J. (1996) Information acquisition by users of hospital libraries: a comparison of Brazil and the UK. *Journal of Librarianship and Information Science*, **28**(1), 7–13.

Mercer, N.E. and Moss, E. (1995) The National Health Information Model. In: W. Swinkels *et al.* (eds) *IT's time for healthcare: proceedings of the Third National Health Informatics Conference, Adelaide, Australia, 16–17 October 1995*. Melbourne: Health Informatics Society of Australia, pp. 59–62.

Moore, M. and Hartmen, J.T. (1992) Information technology for rural outreach in west Texas. *Bulletin of the Medical Library Association*, **80**(1), 44–45.

Müllerová, H. and Vleek, J. (1996) Drug information centre – establishment and evaluation of a regional centre. In: Richards, B. (1996) (ed.), pp. 60–63.

Naghdy, F. *et al.* (1995) Fuzzy logic based diagnosis in pathology. In: W. Swinkels *et al.* (eds) *IT's time for healthcare: proceedings of the Third National Health Informatics Conference, Adelaide, Australia, 16–17 October 1995*. Melbourne: Health Informatics Society of Australia, pp. 21–25.

Needham, G. (1996) But will it work, Doctor? Conference 23rd and 24th May 1996, Northampton. In: A. Long and A. Brettle (eds). *Outcomes Briefing*, 8, pp. 35–38.

Neuberger, J. (1993) The public face of outcomes. *Health Services Journal*, **25**, (February), 19.

New (1995) body to speak out on health information. *Library Association Record*, **97**(3), 139.

New Zealand Centre for Health Informatics (1997). http://www.irl.cri.n/-nzchi/

O'Connor, D. (1996). Health consumer issues. In: E.J.S. Hovenga *et al.* (eds) *Health Informatics: an overview*. London: Churchill Livingstone, pp. 251–259.

Ovretveit, J. (1996) Informed choice? Health service quality and outcome information for patients. *Health Policy*, **37**, 75–90.

Payne, W. (1996) Medical consultations on the Internet. *British Journal of Healthcare Computing and Information Management*, **13**(10), 30–32.

Pfaff, M. (1990) Differences in health care spending across countries: statistical evidence. *Journal of Health Politics, Policy and Law*, **15**(1), 1–23.

Podbielska, H. (1996) Computer-aided analysis of medical interferometric images. In: Richards, B. (1996), pp. 292–304.

Popescu, A. *et al.* (1996) A computer-based patient record in neurosurgery. In: Richards, B. (1996) (ed.), pp. 107–112.

Richards, B. (1996) (ed.) Current perspectives in healthcare computing. *Conference Proceedings, Harrogate, 18–20 March 1996*. Weybridge: British Computer Society.

Rizzolo, M.A. and Dubois, K. (1994) Developing AJN Network. In: J.G. Ozbolt (ed.) *Proceedings of the 18th annual symposium of compute applications in medical care. Journal of the American Informatics Association* [supplement 27–31].

Rosenberg, W. and Donald, A. (1995) Evidence-based medicine: an approach to clinical problem solving. *British Medical Journal*, **310**, 1122–26.

Ruck, A. (1993) Only connect. *British Journal of Healthcare Computing and Information Management*, **10**(7), 23–26.

Shipley, J. (1996) *Health information strategy for the year 2000*. Wellington, New Zealand: Ministry of Health.

Smith, J. (1995) The scope and functions of management information systems in health care. In: W. Swinkels *et al.* (eds) *IT's time for healthcare: proceedings of the Third National Health Informatics Conference, Adelaide, Australia, 16–17 October 1995*. Melbourne: Health Informatics Society of Australia, pp. 81–85.

Southon, G. and Yetton, P. (1996) A study of information technology in community health services. *Informatics in Healthcare – Australia*, **5**(2), 43–47.

Stroh, J. and Wall, L. (1995) Trends in health informatics. *Informatics in Healthcare Australia*, **4**(2), 49–54.

Sweetland, J. (1996) Information as therapy. *Health Matters*, (26), 16–17.

Taylor, S.I. and Lande, R.E. (1996) A library for problem based learning. *Health Libraries Review*, **13**, 9–12.

Urquhart, C.J. and Hepworth, J.B. (1995a) *The value of information to clinicians: a toolkit for measurement*. Aberystwyth: University of Wales Aberystwyth, Open Learning Unit (DILS).

Urquhart, C.J. and Hepworth, J.B. (1995b) *The value to clinical decision making of information supplied by NHS library and information services*. Boston Spa: British Library Document Supply Centre. (British Library R&D Report no. 6205).

Virtual (1997) Conference. http://www.mednet.org.uk/mednet/mednet.htm

Visible Human Project (1997) http://www.nlm.nih.gov/research/visible/visible_human.html

Von Stillfried, D. and Arnold, M. (1993) What's happening to health care in Germany? *British Medical Journal*, **306**, 1017–1018.

Weise, F. (1993) Developments in health sciences libraries since 1974. *Library Trends*, **42**(1), 5–24.

Williamson, M. (1992) New health reforms need support of appropriate information systems. *New Zealand Health and Hospital*, (December), 9–14.

World Health Organisation (1997) http://www.who.ch/

Research and consultancy 9

Alan Gilchrist

Scope and definitions

The juxtaposition of the two words 'research' and 'consultancy' in the title of this chapter, further combined with the phrases 'library work' and 'information work' poses severe problems in defining the scope, focus and slant to be adopted.

One could take the easy way out and adopt the combined scope of *Current Research in Library and Information Science* and *Library and Information Science Abstracts*: but while these were heavily used in writing this chapter they do not penetrate deeply into the wider reaches of information work; not surprisingly, since this term is so diffuse and difficult to define. Furthermore, the results of consultancy projects are rarely reported, though consultants may often undertake or contribute to research projects.

Nicholas (1996) discusses the differences between research and consultancy, arguing that consultancy is essentially practical and focused on the problems of a specific organization. However, Hannabuss (1995) notes that while there has been an increasing emphasis on research in library and information studies, applied research, as opposed to pure research, appears to be more popular: 'Applied research is pragmatic and stresses the importance of gathering and analysing information which can be used in resolving real-life problems'. Similarly, McKee, quoted by Pluse (1996), says: 'I do not want a piece of research that is academically rigorous, analytically comprehensive, methodologically impeccable, unreadable, 200 pages too long and two years too late. What I want is an OK investigation which is analytically and methodologically maybe 80% satisfactory, brief, of practical utility, and timely'. There is clearly a similarity here between research and consultancy, further strengthened by the economic imperative for results; but the effective consultant should apprise himself of the results of research projects, in the same spirit as many researchers undertake consultancy or field work in order to experience operational systems outside the laboratory.

Another variable, affecting both researchers and consultants, is the size and duration of the project, which can range from a brief investigation to a five-year programme of work involving teams at different sites and requiring disciplined project management. In some cases the latter may include elements of research on the way to a more or less foregone conclusion, such as the establishment of a cooperative library scheme; while the former may (though perhaps rarely) produce some innovation with far-reaching consequences.

However, not all research is applied: indeed some workers are concerned with the study of the research process itself within library and information services (LIS). Vakkari (1996) presents the results of a comparative study of library and information research in Scandinavia, looking at its development, internationalization, and social and cognitive institutionalization. In Portugal, Targino (1995) discusses the interdisciplinary nature of information as a field of research.

It is true that multi-disciplinary team work is becoming more common in library and information work (LIW), again largely because of the diffuse nature of such work in the nascent creation of the information society. Consequently, new skills are being imported into LIW research and LIW consultants are increasingly engaged on projects outside the more traditional areas of library and information services (LIS). However, researchers must publish, whereas consultants are usually bound by confidentiality and copyright clauses in their contracts. The report on work which follows makes no distinction between research and consultancy, but inevitably will be biased towards the former. There may well be omissions in coverage, which spans the years 1995, 1996 and the early part of 1997, for which the author apologizes, particularly to the slighted researchers. Readers may also detect what they may see as a personal focus for which a more muted apology is made, in the belief that most authors asked to write this piece would be similarly constrained.

The sections which follow are grouped very broadly and for convenience, rather than academic correctness. There is today, with regard to the big issues, a high degree of convergence and overlapping. The headings chosen are:

- electronic libraries;
- the Internet;
- electronic publishing;
- information retrieval;
- the user domain;
- management issues;
- value for money.

Before embarking on a review of research in progress and/or reported, there follows a brief overview of research funding and a report on developments within the funding agencies.

A perspective on funding

Johanson (1997) reports that the USA currently spends about $US500 billion[1] a year on information technology research (about £310 billion). In the European Union, the Commission (1996) marked the information revolution with a 1996 budget of:

- Ecu 1,991 million for information technologies (about £1,412 million);
- Ecu 843 million for telematics (about £598 million);
- Ecu 630 million for communication technologies (about £447 million).

According to a report issued by the UK Department of Trade and Industry (1996) the biggest spender in the world on research (in all subjects) is General Motors; while the biggest in the UK is Glaxo with £1,200 million in 1996. British Telecom spends £271 million, while the biggest in the information provider sector is Reuters with £191 million (ranked ninth in the UK and 149th in the world). Against this, Microsoft spends £390 million and Sun Microsystems £290 million.

In contrast with the colossal figures above, Meadows *et al.* (1995) report that funding by the British Library through its Research and Development Department (now renamed the Research and Innovation Centre) has been falling steadily if adjusted by the retail price index. In short, starting with £810,000 in 1974–75 it has 'risen' to £1,467,000 – or £356,000 in real terms.

Within the European Union, Mahon (1996) reports that the Commission's Framework Programme is projected to spend some 14 billion ECU for the period 1994–98 (about £10 billion); and offers his opinion that the amounts provided for the Libraries Programme (50 million ECU, about £35.5 million) and for Information Engineering (30 million ECU, about £21.3 million) is correspondingly unrealistic.

Mendes (1996) reports that NORDINFO (the Nordic Council for Scientific and Technical Information) has an annual budget of some FM4 million (about £0.5 million) of which about a half is expended on salaries, administration, travel, publication activities, conferences, etc.

It is impossible to judge what scale of revenue is attracted by consultancy in the LIS sector, for the obvious reason that figures are not available and for the equally obvious reason that the activity is so diffuse, being practised by the large management consultancy firms as a part of larger projects; by software suppliers; by a handful of professional LIS consultants (probably fewer than ten in the UK belong to the accreditation body, the Institute of Management Consultants); by freelance consultants; and by academics.

However, revenue figures for the large management consultancy firms are published periodically, often with a number of analyses. Abbott (1995) produces figures for the year 1994 in a paper designed to show how UK business was picking up in Europe.

The league table leader, by a long way, was Andersen Consulting taking £465.2 million in Europe outside the UK and posting £3.2 billion world-wide in 1996 as announced in March 1997. By far the biggest slice of consultancy work goes to information technology projects, estimated at 68.5% in 1994. Much of this is earned in the lucrative area of facilities management. For example, as has been reported in the trade press, the giant firm EDS secured the biggest IT outsourcing contract ever won in the UK: a staggering £1 billion over ten years to run the IT facilities for the Inland Revenue. This was increased at the beginning of 1997 by a further 60% in order to cope with the extra demands created by the introduction of self assessment.

National LIS research and the funding agencies

The old British Library Research and Development Department was reorganized in 1996 to become the British Library Research and Innovation Centre (RIC) (URL)[2] With this reorganization and change of title comes a new staff structure and the objective to be more proactive. The programmes of research to be supported in 1996–97 are:

- the Digital Library;
- information retrieval;
- management of libraries and information services;
- value and impact of libraries and information services;
- cooperation and libraries;
- preservation of library and archive materials;
- providers and users of information.

Small-scale projects in the book and information worlds are also funded by the British National Bibliography Research Fund, and information on this can also be found through RIC's URL.

Founded in 1995 by the Department of National Heritage, the independent Library and Information Commission is establishing a working relationship with RIC and is housed in the same building. The Commission has now established a Research Sub-Committee (1996) which has further set up a number of working groups to look at the following key topics:

- lifelong learning;
- digital content;
- competitiveness and impact of library and information science;
- national information policy.

The Sub-Committee also provides a professional focal point for cooperation with the Department of Trade and Industry's response to the European Commission's Fifth Framework Programme.

Accounts of national research programmes are to be found in a British Library

R&D Report (Haynes and Cotton, 1996): for Italy by Paci (1996); for Hungary by Kovács and Bátonyi (1996); for Ireland by Casey (1996); for Spain by De la Viesca (1996); and for Greece by Tzekakis (1996). The situation in the Nordic countries is covered by Mendes (1996); and the scope of the European Commission's LIS research is illustrated by Iljon (1996). (The Commission's INFO 2000 Programme (URL) can be consulted on its website; and Thackray (1997) has produced a useful summary of EC initiatives, programmes, documents and websites). In addition to the specific country reports noted above, Haynes (1996) examines the results of a questionnaire survey covering nineteen countries. Not surprisingly, he reports that, despite some encouraging cooperation, further advances are hampered by different definitions of what constitutes LIS research, by the disparate amounts of funding available, and in most cases by the lack of a single national focal point.

Alemna (1996) discusses research in librarianship in Ghana and bemoans the lack of finance, time and good journal collections; but points out that librarians have a role to play in the overall development of a research culture. OCLC maintain a busy research programme in the LIS sector; their grants are announced each year in the *OCLC Newsletter* (1996).

Electronic libraries

Collier (1995) defines the electronic library at the beginning of the ELINOR project (discussed below) as 'a teaching and learning environment for higher education in which information is held primarily in electronic form;' but quickly found that 'definition is too limited, extending it to a managed environment of multimedia materials in digital form, designed for the benefit of its user population, structured to facilitate access to its contents and equipped with aids to navigation of the global network.' The change in scope and emphasis is significant and properly implies the range of considerations to be addressed in the radical process of re-engineering libraries and information services. Therefore, it is not surprising that this topic supports collaborative programmes, phased projects and spin-off studies pervading the whole field of LIS.

A useful website is maintained by D-Lib (URL), giving pointers to some of the major cooperative projects, funding and coordinating agencies in the area of digital library research. In the USA the Digital Library Initiative, jointly funded by NSF, DARPA and NASA, is supporting six projects at the University of California, Berkeley; University of California, Santa Barbara (the Alexandria Project, concentrating on images and spatially referenced information); Carnegie Mellon University (the Information Project concerned with integrated speech, image and language understanding for creation and exploration of digital video libraries); University of Illinois at Urbana-Champaign; University of Michigan; and Stanford University.

In the UK the major programme is the Electronic Libraries Programme (eLib) (URL). This programme operates under the aegis of FIGIT (Follett Implementation Group on Information Technology) which was set up after the Follett Report, Joint (1993) Funding Councils' Libraries Funding Review; it is financed by the Joint Information Systems Committee (JISC). The programme works with UKOLN (UK Office for Library and Information Networking – URL), which grew out of the earlier Centre for Catalogue Research and later Centre for Bibliographic Management. Ongoing eLib/UKOLN projects include:

- MODELS: an applications framework to enable the effective management of distributed collections of autonomous, heterogeneous information resources and services;
- NewsAgent: led by the Library and Information Technology Centre (LITC), and comprising a consortium of publishers, academic institutions and suppliers, investigating a user-configurable news and current awareness service for the LIS community, incorporating metadata;
- ROADS: a project to design and implement a user-oriented resource discovery system piloted on the existing UK Social Science Information Gateway (SOSIG) and on the Organizing Medical Networked Information (OMNI) service.

De Montfort University has set up the International Institute for Electronic Library Research (URL), having initiated one of the first UK electronic library projects called ELINOR (Electronic Library and Information Online Retrieval). Zhao and Ramsden (1995) report on the system architecture, management of copyright, and the user aspect of ELINOR. One of the early conclusions from this project, taken from Wu *et al.* (1995), was that it seemed to indicate that it is quicker to search and find a known book from the Electronic Library than the conventional library but it is slower to find an answer from the electronic book than the printed book once the books are retrieved . Not only must the technology develop, but the human factor needs to be taken into account in this radical cultural change, as indicated by Montasser-Kohsari *et al.* (1994), who say of the users, 'they are more comfortable in reading papers they really want on paper; we have not yet installed convenient printing facilities, but they are vital'.

Whereas these remarks are spin-offs from development projects, one eLib project, IMPACT 2 (URL), is looking specifically at the impact on people of electronic libraries, complementing other eLib projects in taking a more holistic view. Project EARL (URL) is an ambitious initiative, in conjunction with UKOLN, whose business plan (prepared by a consultant) can be found on the Internet. EARL currently has 78 partners, aims to have 100 by the end of this year, and is concerned with the whole range of issues of networking public libraries. The consortium was established with the help of funding from BL RIC, but will seek finance for research from Europe and the Library and Information Commission, and also from agents outside the LIS community, such as the Department of Trade and Industry, the Department for Education and Employment and the British Tourist Authority.

All the industrial countries are pursuing the goals of the electronic library with D-Lib (URL) specifically noting a NORDINFO initiative and major programmes in Australia, New Zealand and Japan.

The Scandinavian countries seem to be particularly active: for example Finland is creating a virtual library as part of the Ministry of Education's programme 'Finland as Information Society – a national strategy.' This will actually be a range of specialist virtual libraries connected to the home pages of university libraries (currently thirteen virtual libraries and five universities). Finland is also a key player in the EU project CHILIAS (Current, 1997), which will build a virtual library for schoolchildren between the ages of nine and twelve in the UK, Spain, Greece, Portugal, Germany and Finland.

Document delivery

Projects on and around electronic libraries tend to be very diffuse, but some focus on specific issues such as document delivery. Price *et al.* (1996) present an overview of electronic document request and delivery research, while Tuck and Moulton (1995) discuss technical aspects and future developments in this area; Blunden-Ellis (1996) reports on the progress of LAMDA (URL) in setting up a cooperative structure for document delivery between academic libraries in London and Manchester. A number of projects started in 1995–96 include:

- Focused (URL) investigation of document delivery options (FIDDO), aimed at providing decision-makers with evaluative information on document delivery systems;
- EDDIS, an eLib project, aiming to produce an integrated end-user driven identification and ordering system;
- SEREN, sharing educational resources;
- JEDDS (URL) an Australian project with an IT bias;
- BIBDEL, a cooperative project between the UK, Ireland and Greece.

Multimedia delivery

Trant (1995) has reported on the Getty AHIP Imaging Initiative, launched in 1994 to act as a catalyst in the development of the guidelines and standards which would enable the development and network communication of digital image archives. Another particular area of concern is the handling of maps. A JISC-funded project started in 1996 to look at the problems involved in providing national online access to Ordnance Survey digital map data: DIGIMAP involves collaboration between five map libraries. The journal *Information Services & Use* has a strong interest in multimedia, often reporting on progress in this area. A special issue included papers by Pfaff (1994) and Notman (1994) on the EmbARK programme designed to handle collections management for museums; by Cisneros and Delclaux (1994) on RAMA, a project sponsored by the European Commission under the RACE programme with the objective of offering a tool for any professional user to retrieve multimedia information from museum archives through public telecommunication networks, regardless of the database type; and by Redfern (1994) and Bunn (1994) on LACE, another European Commission RACE project, which Kurtz (1994) compares to RAMA.

The Z39.50 standard

One of the more important standards to emerge in this area is Z39.50 which allows queries to be networked to databases supporting different retrieval systems. The CATRIONA project looked at the development of application programs to support cataloguing, classification and retrieval across networks. Nicolson *et al.* (1995) describe a demonstrator project, while Fletcher (1996) discusses the wider outcomes of the project. In Ireland, Murray (1995) describes two projects, IRIS and DALI, which use the Z39.50 standard in linking Irish university libraries; while Holm (URL) is working in Norway on a project funded by the European Commission.

A caveat

Finally, in this section, a paper by Burke (1996) is well worth reading for all those involved in such major projects. He analyses causes of the failure of project INTREX, led in the 1960s by the Massachusetts Institute of Technology and jointly funded by the Council on Library Resources, the National Science Foundation, the Department of Defense, and the Carnegie Corporation to the tune of $20 million. The objective was to redefine the library and its technology, but Burke claims that INTREX produced little and did not establish the basis for the hoped for fundamental changes. In summary, the reasons were:

- the technology was not ready to meet the demands of the project;
- the pursuit of an MIT only policy in terms of people, ideas, technology and software;
- confusion concerning goals.

The Internet

Much of the research and development in the previous section is associated with the facilities and protocols provided by the Internet; but the Internet is itself a rich source of problems. A report on the information infrastructure issued by the

US National Research Council (1996) has this to say on the significance of the Internet: 'understanding the Internet may be a key to understanding many of the opportunities in the national information infrastructure (NII). Is the Internet a model for a commercially dominated interoperable infrastructure, or is it a remarkable but transitory development from the world of research and education? Whatever it is, the wired world is here to stay and will increasingly pervade our work and home environments. A small industry has grown up with the objective of making sense of the apparent anarchy; and involving website cataloguing, evaluation and information broking. Woodward (1996) reviews the efforts to catalogue and classify the resources on the Internet and concludes by saying: 'In considering such a diverse assortment of traditionally based projects, one finds reasons for hope, but the larger picture is also somewhat depressing. No one solution appears to be sweeping the Internet. In fact, most Internet users are probably unaware of the existence of these experimental efforts'.

The CATRIONA, EARL and OMNI projects have already been mentioned in the section on *Electronic libraries*. In the USA, OCLC (Online Computer Library Center) is working on a number of projects, including NetFirst, a comprehensive database of Internet-accessible resources, and the use of the Dewey Decimal Classification to organize the Web; this latter project is described by Shafer (1996). In Europe, and claiming to be one of the largest projects funded in the Telematics for Research Sector of the EU Fourth Framework Programme, the project Development of a European Service for Information on Research and Education (URL) [DESIRE] started in 1996 to extend the technology of the World Wide Web and implement information services on behalf of European researchers. Certain deliverables can be downloaded from the DESIRE Website in either HTML or RTF format. Again, Finland is active in this area and is building a nationwide system of Internet access in public libraries. This initiative, called The House of Knowledge project, is described by Svedberg (1996).

Electronic publishing

The third section in this chapter is also closely related to the preceding discussion, particularly if one accepts the definition of electronic publishing proposed by Hawkins *et al.* (1992) as 'the use of electronic media, computers or tele-communications systems to deliver information to users in electronic form or from electronic sources'.

In one sense, publishing can be taken to mean one-to-many distribution, and armed with word processing and possibly desktop publishing software anybody can become a publisher over a network. However, most research is concentrating on the more traditional areas of the publishing and distribution of books and journals in electronic format. Brown (1996) with a grant from the BLR&DD

undertook a study to provide information which would help in the British Library's assessment of the acquisition policy for digital information within a national legal deposit mandate. While highly specific in its purpose (nearer to consultancy than research?) his comparison of demand-side and supply-side economics will be of interest to many.

Loughborough University has had a long association with all aspects of electronic journal delivery, with periodic funding from BLR&DD. McKnight (1996) reviews this work in a BLR&DD Report, covering the BLEND, QUARTET, ADONIS and ELVYN projects.

Rowland *et al.* (1995) report extensively on Project ELVYN, covering the technical, economic and human issues in a dual publishing experiment run collaboratively by publishers and libraries. One major concern that emerged from the study was for the need to standardize the handling of electronic journals: 'for libraries to try to establish different handling systems for different titles would be both expensive and an organizational nightmare. Correspondingly, publishers who insisted on tackling things in their own individualistic way would soon encounter resistance'.

Two of the concerns of electronic publishing of scholarly journals lie in the availability of such material and in its quality if it bypasses the refereeing process. Harter (1996) started a citation analysis project in 1995 at Indiana University with the title 'The impact of electronic journals on scholarly communication' to throw light on these and other problems. Another impact study also started in 1995 is conducted by Tenopir (1996) at Tennessee University, but directed at special libraries, with the hypothesis that they may no longer need to maintain collections.

At the University of Central Lancashire, a team has been designing an electronic journal from first principles and the use of electronic network services as a substitute. A demonstrator project is being developed in the field of librarianship and information science. The first phase is described by Brophy (1995) and Brophy and Senior (1995).

A major concern in the area of electronic libraries and electronic publishing is the use of mark-up languages for formatting and handling text and graphics. François *et al.* (1995) report on a study, conducted jointly between Aerospatiale and Electricité de France, on the use of SGML (Standard Generalized Mark-up Language) and HyTime (Hypermedia and Time-based Mark-up Language), in the context of industrial documentation.

Information retrieval

The area of information retrieval, in common with the preceding topics and, indeed, affected by them, is undergoing radical transformation. There are several interconnected reasons for this:

- The increasing power of hardware is making it possible to implement concepts from the years of research and development by such people as Salton (1989).
- Information retrieval (which originally signified, in practice, bibliographic reference retrieval) is a phrase which can now more closely approximate the claim implicit in the phrase.
- With the saturation of the traditional markets of LIS, information retrieval is now being sold to end-users; this is further spurred by the availability of a range of search engines on the Internet.

These factors have generated a fresh surge of research into the design and evaluation of retrieval systems; and perhaps a rather closer cooperation between software houses and the research community, with consultancy fairly active in the middle ground.

The perceived wisdom is that the Boolean model is on the way out and giving way to newer methods involving statistical and linguistic processing techniques. Evans (1994) outlines this development in terms of what is becoming available. Weiner and Liddy (1995) give a foretaste of what is to come in a paper which discusses the creation of software to emulate the way in which humans process text at six known levels; and creates a vector space model from a range of analytical techniques based on these processes.

- morphological: forms of words;
- lexical: the word forms themselves;
- semantic: the meanings associated with words and phrases;
- syntactic: word order – which can also affect meaning;
- discourse: material derived, above the word and sentence level, from surrounding text;
- pragmatic: that which we know above the text.

The authors go on to describe the software package which emanated from research funded by the US government, but admit that the package still requires very significant computing power. Much research, therefore, is pitched at a somewhat less ambitious and pragmatic level, though much of it is attempting to tackle similar problems.

One of the leading world centres (funded by the National Science Foundation) is the US based Center for Intelligent Information Retrieval (URL), which has as its main goal the development of software which will support accurate and efficient access to, and analysis of, the enormous and growing amount of information that is stored in text databases throughout business and government (note the word 'analysis' in this quotation). The Center has an ambitious research programme, which relates to a list compiled by its Director, Croft (1996), in a paper entitled 'What do people want from information retrieval?' Croft lists ten wants in approximate reverse order of importance:

- relevance feedback;
- information extraction;
- multimedia retrieval;
- effective retrieval;
- routing and filtering;
- interfaces and browsing;
- magic (e.g. automatic query expansion and other devices invisible to the searcher);
- efficient, flexible indexing and retrieval;
- distributed information retrieval;
- integrated solutions.

The advance from the Boolean to the vector space model has moved information retrieval firmly into the area of full-text natural language and away from the artificial language of the controlled vocabulary to support indexing and searching. Keen (1994, 1995) reports on research into interactive ranked retrieval, which compared various retrieval devices operating within both Boolean and ranking systems, and seemed to show that the latter had a more marked beneficial effect on recall, with precision actually lower in two sets of tests. One conclusion seems to this author to be particularly significant. The role of searcher learning and searcher psychology must be incorporated into future evaluation testing, not as a replacement for effectiveness measurement, but as an additional dimension, to incorporate the qualitative element in as reproducible and controlled a manner as can be achieved. These two human factors should also be carried as far as possible into the retrieval products themselves.

Most reported research into full-text processing (not surprisingly) concerns the English language. However, other languages present similar problems in quite different settings. One such is the agglutinative language of Finnish: the University of Tampere is much involved in such work, and some reports have appeared by, for example, Pirkola and Järvelin (1996).

An area of information retrieval research that continues to attract attention is that of natural language processing (NLP). Lewis and Sparck Jones (1996) review the current state of the art of NLP research for information retrieval and the particular problems to be tackled.

As a measure of how far fundamental information retrieval research has advanced, it is salutary to read of the progress made in the two application areas of text summarizing and of information extraction. In the former, Sparck Jones and Endres-Niggemeyer (1995) introduce a special issue of the journal *Information Processing & Management*, with a discussion of disciplinary resources and forward directions. In the latter area, Cowie and Lehnert (1996) discuss the application of NLP to the task of isolating relevant text fragments, extracting relevant information from the fragments, and piecing together the targeted information into a coherent framework. The authors maintain that a number of practical applications can be expected within five years. The research area is supported by US government funding through the Message Understanding Conferences (MUC) and ARPA's Tipster Text Program, which coordinates multiple research groups and government agencies, seeking to improve information retrieval and information extraction technologies (Sparck Jones, 1995).

Some practical applications are beginning to emerge in the notoriously tricky area of image retrieval. Enser (1995) extensively reviews the subject. One problem is that a picture may be of something and perhaps amenable to retrieval by pattern matching, but also about something, thereby involving the interplay of visual and verbal data. Turner (1994), undertaking research in Canada, makes the point that, though detailed indexing of film and video images is costly, if it is not effected a considerable cost is passed to the end-user. Development and evaluation of a retrieval system for trade marks was due to be completed in 1996. Funded at Northumbria University by BLR&DD, project SAFARI is described by Shields *et al.* (1995). Image retrieval requires powerful computing capability, such as the use of neural networks; Rickman and Stonham (1994) report on research in this area.

The growing importance of direct access by the end user has prompted much research and the use of iterative prototyping. In the UK the Centre for Interactive Systems Research (URL) at City University is conducting an experiment on end-user searching in a highly interactive retrieval environment using specially developed graphical user interfaces. Pollitt *et al.* (1994) describe a series of applications of their HIBROWSE system. HIBROWSE has been developed to present the user with views based on complex pick lists generated from the database and any associated thesauri or classifications.

Despite the growing use of full-text search systems, there is still a large number that continue to use the older techniques of indexing and abstracting. Milstead (1994) observes that though research in this area has declined over the previous ten years, there is little evidence that many of the problems in either the making or the use of indexes have been resolved, and attributes this to the shifting of attention and funding to the output end of the retrieval process. Certainly there is much work on automatic indexing and abstracting, the design and application of summarizers, and automatic thesaurus generation: see, for example, Sparck Jones and Endres-Niggemeyer (1995), work at the Center for Intelligent Information Retrieval (URL), and Bertrand-Gastaldy and Pagola (1994).

Input issues

However, there is some research into manual methods. For example. Bertrand and Cellier (1995) look at the human factors in the indexing process and the effect of several of these on indexing behaviour. The number of bibliographic systems around the world surely lends weight to Milstead's claim, and there have been, in fact, several projects aimed at improving the quality of abstracts. McIntosh (1994) shows that structured abstracts contain more information than unstructured abstracts; while Hartley and Sydes (1996) and Hartley *et al.* (1996) investigate the efficiency of structured abstracts and the efficacy of designed layouts.

The Centre for Interactive Systems Research (URL) is one of the leading proponents of information retrieval research and has based a series of experiments on its own retrieval engine known as OKAPI, which uses a best-match algorithm based on term weighting rather than Boolean searching. Jones *et al.* (1995) describe some work attempting to enrich the OKAPI performance by building in thesaurus navigation and query enhancement. An old concept which has returned again with new and enormous potential, particularly if it can be applied to the problems of searching the Internet, is that of metadata. Metadata is data about data, and work is now ongoing to create metadata standards for the vast array of records appearing on the Internet. Some of this work is arising out of the work of UKOLN, and Miller (1996) presents a useful account of the technique, while Heery (1996) reviews the existing metadata formats.

Approaching the problem from a historical perspective, Fattahi (1996) seeks to investigate the validity and adequacy of current cataloguing principles to the online environment.

Evaluation

There are many relatively small-scale evaluation projects and quality assessment exercises which help to build up an understanding of the efficacy of particular software packages or specific retrieval devices. This is particularly true of evaluation within the fast moving Internet scene. Thus, Watson *et al.* (1996) look at the way in which four software suppliers have adapted their products for the Internet; while Zorn *et al.* (1996) evaluate four of the leading Web search engines.

At a somewhat deeper level than the snapshot evaluations described above, Lancaster *et al.* (1994) conducted a study into the effectiveness of searching a specific CD-ROM, comparing the results achieved by end users and skilled intermediaries. The authors claim that the search results were not really inspiring, and show that the end users were more capable of achieving higher precision than the intermediaries, while the latter achieved higher recall. They conclude that library patrons are frequently misled into thinking that CD-ROM databases are easy to use and that the 'technology' guarantees satisfactory results.

Soergel (1994) in a paper entitled 'Indexing and retrieval performance: the logical evidence maintains that: Information is about meaning. While we can in many cases get at meaning through statistical and syntactic/semantic processing, in many other cases – perhaps the more important ones – we cannot, and human judgement – no matter how often it is maligned as subjective – must step in.'

OKAPI, the OPAC test bed used by the Centre for Interactive Systems Research has promulgated many interesting research reports and papers. Hancock-Beaulieu *et al.* (1995) describe an experiment to compare interactive query expansion with automatic query expansion. Perhaps surprisingly, the take-up of the former option was found to be lower and its retrieval performance less effective. OKAPI has been one of the more successful participants in the TREC (Text Retrieval Conferences) discussed below. Accounts of the OKAPI involvement are given by Robertson *et al.* (1995a, 1995b).

TREC

The first Text Retrieval Conference was launched in 1992, and followed up by four more conferences, with TREC-6 being planned at the time of writing. TREC is the largest and most ambitious programme of information retrieval evaluation since the Cranfield experiments over 30 years ago. The goals of TREC as listed by Smeaton and Harman (1997) are:

- to increase research in IR on large scale text collections;
- to increase communications among academia, industry and government through an open forum;
- to increase technology transfer between research and products;
- to provide a state of the art showcase of retrieval methods for TREC sponsors;
- to improve evaluation techniques.

The TREC mechanism consists of the distribution of a large collection of heterogeneous documents to participants for them to install locally. This is followed by a set of user queries which each runs against the collection, returning the 100 document identifiers for each query which are pooled, reduplicated and presented to experts for relevance assessment. To date, over one million documents have been used and over 50 companies, universities and research centres have taken part. It is not the intention that the participants compete to find the best package, rather that the range of possible approaches and techniques is tested, covering probabilistic indexing, natural language processing, query expansion, Boolean search and many more. Consequently, though the details are complex and far-ranging, the overall impression is that there is no single system or approach to information retrieval which is the 'best' or most effective, but certain techniques are proving useful and, most importantly, the effectiveness of modern information retrieval techniques is not at all bad . Full reports have been produced by Harman (1993, 1994, 1995, 1996). Sparck Jones (1995) reviews the findings of TREC-1 and TREC-2 and concludes *inter alia* that 'statistical techniques currently seem to be the most effective, supported by relevance ranking, and that sets of techniques have to be carefully combined and require tailoring to generic collection properties and . . . specific collection characteristics'.

Evaluation techniques

One of the objectives of TREC is to improve evaluation techniques, and BLRIC is funding work in this area at the UK Centre for Interactive Systems Research (URL).

There has been heated debate over the years from Cranfield onwards concerning the validity of information retrieval evaluation. Ellis (1996) concludes that:

> The original vision of information retrieval research as a discipline founded on quantification proved restricting for its theoretical and methodological development and that increasing recognition of this is reflected on growing interest in qualitative methods ... in relation to cognitive, behavioural and affective aspects of the information retrieval interaction.

The user domain

Many of the projects described above are devoted to electronic libraries or information retrieval and incorporate user studies if only at the level of prototype testing. Mention was previously made of the IMPEL project, a range of studies looking at the impact on people of electronic libraries, and Edwards *et al.* (1995) discuss some of the findings. As an indication that IT is now really infiltrating the workplace he reports that 80% of information librarians consider that job satisfaction is increased by the use of electronic information, while 60% feel frustrated by a lack of technical expertise.

Erens (1996), in a similar study on the effect on the research process in university libraries, confirms the growing strength of IT, noting that respondents agreed that access to information is now easier and research has improved as a result of easier access to external databases; however, the same respondents were alarmed at the corresponding cuts in library collections.

Pivec *et al.* (1996) have embarked on a five-year longitudinal study of the users of the Slovenian COBISS system (Cooperative Online Bibliographic System and Services); while Wijngaert (1996) investigates the users' perspective of audiotext, teletext, CD-I and CD-ROM, videotex and the Internet in the Netherlands.

East *et al.* (1995) further corroborate the growing dependency on electronic services, showing that the mean annual expenditure by British universities on database access as a whole nearly doubled in the period 1992 to 1994; and that expenditure on end-user online services more than doubled. The authors also report on usage patterns.

The Department of Information Studies at the University of Sheffield (URL) continues to feature user studies as a specialism within its strong research programme. One current project, NetLinks, aims to increase understanding of the practice of networked learner support, described by Fowell and Levy (1995).

Considering that one weakness of the cognitive viewpoint in user studies is that it pays little attention to the social aspects of information processes, Talja (1995) describes an alternative approach, based on discourse analysis. There are many studies in the healthcare sector, for example, Lee and Pow (1996) and Farmer and Williams (1997). Not unnaturally, some of these studies involve public access, as does that of Stevens *et al.* (1997); while Furner and Willett (1995) conducted a survey on public access systems in UK libraries. This is an area likely to attract more research as the principle of open government extends. The alternative to public access systems is the home information system, but preliminary findings from Davenport *et al.* (1996) suggest that take-up is slow, partly because people prefer to keep their technological devices separate, and that disposable time is a major constraint.

Management issues

One of the effects of the so-called information revolution has been to draw the attention of senior management to the problems and opportunities of information. There is now much talk of information as an asset and of information management. A committee has been set up in the UK under the chairmanship of Robert Hawley, the Chief Executive of British Energy and containing equally senior managers: the aims of the Hawley Committee are described by Houlder (1997). However, it would appear from a survey conducted by management consultants Touche Ross (1995) that there is some way to go in turning brave concepts into good practice. Some of the findings are:

- Of organizations, 40% admitted to repeating work, due to difficulties in locating information.
- Of large companies, 90% have too much paper, and much of this is generated internally
- While organizations spend up to 10% of turnover on administrative procedures, the handling of information does not receive as much attention as other functions, such as information technology.

Information management, of course, means different things to different people; and in the business field is more akin to document management. This is one of the growth areas in the software industry, and DMS (Document Management Systems) are beginning to add facilities such as text retrieval and work flow to their core modules of electronic document generation and publishing.

These activities may be closely related and systems are beginning to appear which retrieve relevant text as context-sensitive help screens embedded in a work flow process. One of the leading players in these developments is Xerox, which maintains large research laboratories at Palo Alto and Grenoble. Blomberg *et al.* (1996) of Xerox reflect on the problems of work-orientated design in an American law firm, an area which is beginning to generate interesting results from this sort of cross-fertilization.

Quality management

Gilchrist and Brockman (1996) argue that information management and quality management are closely linked, and that their interaction could be examined with reference to the Business Excellence Model promoted by the British Quality Foundation for the British Quality Award and for self-assessment.

In fact, interest in application of quality management within the LIS sector appears to be limited and yet, with its focus on the measurement of user satisfaction, it would appear to be highly relevant.

Some research has been conducted into quality management issues. Two projects which started from the basis of the international standard on quality management appear to have set foundations for further work. Brophy and Coulling (1996) have surveyed the area with particular reference to research conducted at the University of Central Lancashire; and Brophy (1996) describes project EQLIPSE, arising from the previous work. This ambitious project led by the university involves libraries from seven European countries. In Denmark, Johanssen (1996a, 1996b) carried out in-depth surveys of the application of quality management within the LIS function of the Danish Jutland Telephone Company and the Norwegian firm Norsk Hydro.

Surveys have shown that take-up of quality management techniques by the LIS sector has been scattered and tentative. Garrod and Kinnell (1996, 1997a, 1997b) confirm this in their particular study of best practice benchmarking, even finding a degree of hostility towards what some LIS managers see as yet another management fad. Building on this work in the UK, Kinnell and Oda (1996) compare the application of quality management in public libraries in the UK and Japan, showing the former country to be significantly further advanced – a small irony in the context of Japan's supremacy in the application of quality management in the manufacturing sector. Philip and Hazlett (1996), starting from the SERVQUAL model developed in the USA in the marketing sector, have developed an alternative approach, which they call the P-C-P Model (Pivotal-Core-Peripheral). Both models attempt to evaluate user perceptions of quality with reference to prior expectations and subsequent experience.

Other workers have attempted to tackle the problem of evaluating satisfaction from the angle of performance indicators. Ward *et al.* (1995) describe a European project; while Pickering *et al.* (1996) put forward the interesting 'stakeholder approach' to the construction of performance measures. This recognizes one of the fundamental features of the Business Excellence Model, which views customers, fund holders and service personnel as joint stakeholders.

Ward *et al.* (1995) could be speaking for all these research workers when they point to:

- the need for further education of librarians in relevant techniques;
- identification of time and resources to implement evaluation techniques;
- improved access to datasets and tools.

It is true that one factor which appears to deter managers from applying quality management techniques is the inherent cost. Herget (1995) conducted some useful research in Germany into the 'cost of non-quality', producing some convincing figures. As always, though, it is the human factor which is all-important and needs to be understood. Klobas (1995) conducted some revealing research in Australia into how users viewed quality (or 'fitness for purpose' as it is often defined). She demonstrates clearly that the users' perceptions were formed by convenience and, most significantly, by the extent to which potential users believe that using the resource will benefit them.

Decision Support Systems

The old adage says that if you can't measure, you can't manage, and attempts at objective measurement in the LIS sector must be pursued for that reason. Adams (1996) presents an overview of Decision Support Systems (DSS) within the library area; these are, of course, based on performance indicators. Mention was made above of the EQLIPSE project. Other DSS projects include DECIMAL, described by Oulton *et al.* (1996); MINSTREL by Burton *et al.* (1996) and DECIDE by Davies *et al.* (1996), all of which involve partners in several countries.

Information politics and organizational culture

Reuters (1994) commissioned a survey from Taylor and Nelson AGB of issues surrounding the use, flow and politics of information in British business; they produced some alarming conclusions, including:

- Over 60% of Britain's businesses have no formal information policy to handle the flow and management of business information.
- Nearly two-thirds of Britain's business managers waste time searching for the right information.
- Only four out of 515 people named their company libraries as a source of internal information.

Again, these are human and social issues which continually need to be addressed. Brown and Starkey (1994) managed a case study on the premise that it is necessary to understand an organization's culture in order to make sense of the way in which it manages its communication processes, while Adam and Murphy (1995) investigated information flows among executives. Another phrase found in current literature is 'knowledge management', a concept related to intellectual capital and the learning organization. Sligo (1996) examines barriers to information access in New Zealand companies, found to be caused mainly by the different levels of status of employees.

Legal issues

One of the major legal issues facing the advancement of networking is that of copyright. The Information Highway Advisory Council (1995) of Canada is just one of the official bodies looking at this problem; while electronic library projects such as CATRIONA and ELINOR are also addressing the issue. The latter is developing a system called ERCOMS (URL), building on its copyright and usage tracking experience, to allow libraries to provide required feedback to publishers.

In another complex legal area, Davies (1996, 1997) surveys practice and attitudes concerning the Data Protection Act.

Value for money

The new-found interest in information as an asset prompted Reuters (1995) to undertake a study to explore the current and future value of information in business. Though the report, based on research conducted by the Industrial Research Bureau, was mainly concerned with data it produced some interesting ideas of insuring information stores and capitalizing information on the company balance sheet.

Owens *et al.* (1996, 1997) produced some important insights into the problem they describe as the 'recent mass introduction of information technology [which] has confused the issues of information management and information provision'. They conclude that the traditional information specialist is playing a diminishing role and that the IT personnel are taking over, putting the emphasis on effective storage and retrieval rather than the quality of the information itself. Based on case studies of twelve high-performing companies, the project produced and proved the legitimacy of a research model which, the authors suggest, could provide the basis for further research into less successful companies.

Many would still argue that the only way to attach a value to information is to charge for it, a practice which is increasing. Wormell (1996) reports on an Anglo-Nordic survey jointly funded by NORDINFO and BLR&DD to identify success factors for fee-based information services.

On a wider front, Menou (1995a, 1995b) reports on work at the International Development Research Centre in Canada into the impact of information on development.

Postscript on consultancy

This chapter has been unable to throw much direct light on to the practice of LIS consultancy, for the reasons enunciated in the first section. This is regrettable, as there are still some people in the LIS community who appear to think that the practice of consultancy is somewhat akin to that of the mercenary soldier – taking money from anybody without loyalty to organization or profession. Even Nicholas (1996), comparing research and consultancy, adopts a slightly disparaging tone concerning the latter.

However, it is arguable that a profession which is healthy, and wants to remain so, should be able to support a cadre of consultants. This was always the case and may become increasingly significant. The tendency in all organizations, irrespective of their function, is to buy in or outsource certain specialist facilities, from canteens to information technology support; and the LIS sector is not immune to this tendency. There is often a short-term need for the injection of some particular skills which may not warrant the establishment of a full-time post, and a short-term contract or a consultancy are obvious alternatives.

The skills bought in may be purely technical (in the broad sense), purely managerial, or very often a mix of the two. The focus might be libraries or information services, document management, records management, archives or indeed any process to which LIS skills can be applied; and the techniques brought to bear will very largely be drawn from the applied science of management. It is important that the LIS consultant has the ability to straddle these two areas of LIS and management in some depth, even though he or she may specialize in some aspect or other. Width of experience becomes increasingly valuable, which is why many elder statesmen in the LIS sector are able to offer such good consultancy. The only problem with this type of arrangement can be that such consultants are unable to commit the required amount of time to a project, though many academic institutions have established workable mechanisms for combining research and consultancy.

The full-time professional consultant, that is to say one who forges his or her career in such work, would be well advised to become a member of a professional consultants organization, which would normally oblige its members to adhere to a code of conduct and to a programme of continuous professional development. The code of conduct, which will contain features often required by clients anyway, will cover such aspects as impartiality and confidentiality. Given that most consultancy work is now very practically focused and may be commercially sensitive, it is this confidentiality which most clearly distinguishes research from consultancy.

Conclusion

The word 'information' has become debased and lost in a plethora of clichés concerning the very real changes afoot. An information evolution may develop, but the information revolution is, at the moment, more particularly a revolution in the ability to store and transmit terabytes of binary digits at low cost and great speed. The consequent promise of huge markets is now the driver behind the construction of new *modi operandi*, and the desktop and the sitting room are the battlegrounds for the big commercial players. The leading applications are likely to be home entertainment, banking and shopping, and EDI, email, video-conferencing and telecommuting. An Ovum report by Moroney and Matthews (1995) suggests that in the year 2005, for superhighway applications in the USA, an annual revenue of $57.76 billion will come from domestic, and $28.32 billion from commercial applications. (The corresponding figures for the UK are $5.21 billion and $4.21, representing on average £6 per week from each domestic site). With such prizes in view, investment is high, competition fierce and intellectual property jealously guarded. Cawkell (1997) reports that BSkyB, as a member of a digital TV consortium, 'has commissioned a study at the Centre for Communications Interface Research at Edinburgh University. BSkyB will provide no details and nothing has been or will be published by the University'.

It was not always so, and Laddie (1996), complaining about the changing nature of copyright, says:

> The whole of human development is derivative. We stand on the shoulders of the scientists, artists and craftsmen who preceded us. We borrow and develop what they have done; not necessarily as parasites, but simply as the next generation. It is at the heart of what we know as progress . . . borrowing and developing have always been acceptable.

Librarians and information workers are caught up in this maelstrom. Readers are now end users and directly targeted by manufacturers of hardware and software and by information providers. These merchants have even coined the hideous word 'disintermediation' to denote the strategic side-stepping of the traditional information intermediary. And so librarians are re-engineering their libraries (or as Creth (1996) puts it in the title of her Follett Lecture: 'Slouching toward the future' while information work *per se* becomes increasingly diffused throughout the various information supply chains. Yet a digital library is still a library; cataloguing and SGML have some striking similarities; and the catalogue card is seen as an early and pervasive manifestation of metadata. The role of librarians and information workers is very largely that of intermediaries, and if the nature of the channel changes then so does the job of organizing information for optimal access. In a paper which is otherwise devoted to the latest techniques of information retrieval, Weiner and Liddy (1995) have this to say: 'We also see short-sighted efforts to eliminate the experienced search intermediary from some organizations, a loss whose long term implications can be severe, but difficult to measure.'

The job of the intermediary has never been so complex, as has been shown in this chapter: it includes helping to build the electronic library and electronic publishing infrastructures, charting the Internet, integrating libraries and information services more closely in organizational work and culture, and, underpinning all these activities, carrying out performance measurement and quality assurance.

In all this, development and the consultancy approach outstrip research in the competition for funding, a fact which is regretted by Galliers (1995) in a paper calling for major rethinking in information management research. This chapter closes with the paradox as he enunciates it:

'At a time when there is considerable interest in the topic [of information management] and a burgeoning of academic departments and journals in the field; at a time when we are promised the "information society" – an information revolution, brought about by the power of IT in much the same way that the Industrial Revolution occurred as a result, *inter alia*, of the invention of the steam engine, at a time when we hear talk of the "information superhighway" and of IT-enabled business, business innovation, and at a time when IT-related projects account for over half of the revenue earned by major management consultancies, we still see a waning of interest and relevance of the discipline'.

It is hard to resist ending with an unfair and mischievous poke at the Internet. One of the search engines was asked to search on the phrase 'information management'. The result was as follows:

Word count = management: 6249474
Ignored = information: 22588290
Documents 1–10 of about 10000000 matching the query, best matches first

Note

1. Here and elsewhere in this chapter billion means the US billion, i.e. 10^9, rather than the English 10^{12}.
2. (URL) rather than a date denotes an entry in the end references, giving the Universal Resource Locator.

References

Abbott, P. (1995) UK firms step up performance in European arena. *Management Consultancy*, (September), 18, 21, 23.

Adam, F. and Murphy, C. (1995) Information flows amongst executives and their implications for systems development. *Journal of Strategic Information Systems*, 4(4), 341–355.

Adams, R. (1996) Decision support systems: an overview. *Vine*, (103), 3–7.

Alemna, A. (1996) Research in librarianship in Ghana: status constraints and controls. *Education Libraries Journal*, **39**(2), 5–8.

Bertrand, A. and Cellier, J.M. (1995) Psychological approach to indexing: effects of the operator's expertise upon indexing behaviour. *Journal of Information Science*, **21**(6), 459–472.

Bertrand-Gastaldy, S. and Pagola, G. (1994) *Le controle du vocabulaire et l'indexation assistée par ordinateur; un approche methodologique pour l'utilisation de SATO*. Montreal: University of Montreal.

Blomberg, J. *et al.* (1996) Reflections on a work-oriented design project. *Human-Computer Interaction*, **11**(3), 237–265.

Blunden-Ellis, J. (1996) LAMDA – a project investigating new opportunities in document delivery. *Program*, **30**(4), 385–390.

British Library Research and Innovation Centre (URL)
http://portico.bl.uk.ric

Brophy, P. (1995) JAVELIN: an approach to the development of a new kind of electronic journal. *Library Technology News*, (17), 6–9.

Brophy, P. (1996) EQLIPSE: Evaluation and quality in library performance: system for Europe. *Vine*, (103), 20–24.

Brophy, P. and Coulling, K. (1996) *Quality management for information and library managers*. London: Aslib Gower.

Brophy, P. and Senior, C.M. (1995) *JAVELIN (Journal and Virtual Electronic Library Investigation) Project. First phase: JAVELIN – O*. London: British Library (BL R&D Report 6192).

Brown, A.D. and Starkey, K. (1994) The effect of organizational culture on communication and information. *Journal of Management Studies*, **31**(6), November, 807–828.

Brown, D.J. (1996) *Electronic publishing and libraries: planning for the impact and growth to 2003*. London: Bowker-Saur. (British Library Research Series).

Bunn, B. (1994) The LACE multimedia programme in Oxford. ATM technology. *Information Services and Use*, **14**(3), 189–190.

Burke, C. (1996) A rough road to the information highway. Project INTREX: a view from the CLR archives. *Information Processing & Management*, **32**(1), 19–32.

Burton, J. *et al.* (1996) MINSTREL – management made simple? *Vine*, (103), 25–31.

Casey, M. (1996) Library and information research in the Republic of Ireland: an outline position paper. In: Haynes, D. and Cotton, R. (1996) (eds), pp. 22–28.

Cawkell, T. (1997) The information superhighway: a review of some determining factors. *Journal of Information Science*, **23**(3), 187–208.

Center for Intelligent Information Retrieval (URL)
http://ciir.cs.umass.edu/

Centre for Interactive Systems Research (URL)
http://web.soi.city.ac.uk/research/cisr/aca

Cisneros, G. and Delclaux, A.L. (1994) RAMA – Remote Access to Museum Archives. *Information Services & Use*, **14**(3), 171–181.

Collier, M. (1995) Defining the electronic library. In: Collier, M. and Arnold, K. (1995a) (eds), pp. 1–5.

Collier, M. and Arnold, K. (1995a) (eds) Electronic library and visual information research. ELVIRA 1. *Proceedings of the first ELVIRA Conference, May 1994, De Montfort University*. London: Aslib.

Collier, M. and Arnold, K. (1995b) (eds) Electronic library and visual information research ELVIRA 2. *Proceedings of the second ELVIRA Conference. May 1995.* De Montfort University. London: Aslib.

Cowie, J. and Lehnert, W. (1996) Information extraction. *Communications of the ACM,* **39**(1), 80–91.

Creth, S.D. (1996) The electronic library: slouching toward the future or creating a new information environment. (Follett Lecture Series). http://www.ukoln.ac.uk/follett/creth/paper.html

Croft, W.B. (1996) What do people want from information retrieval? *D-Lib Magazine,* (6 pages). http://www.dlib.org/dlib/november95/11croft.html

Current (1997) Research in Library and Information Science, (28, March).

Davenport, E. *et al.* (1996) Designing a probe to explore home information systems in the United Kingdom. *Online & CD-ROM Review,* **20**(2), 75–80.

Davies, J.E. (1996) *Data protection and LIS management in academic libraries* London: BLR&DD. (British Library Research and Development Report no. 6248).

Davies, J.E. (1997) Data protection management in university libraries. *Journal of Information Science,* **23**(1), 39–58.

Davies, R. *et al.* (1996) DECIDE: decision support models and a DSS for European academic and public libraries. *Vine,* (103), 8–12.

De la Viesca, R. (1996) Spain – the national R&D plan. In: Haynes, D. and Cotton, R. (1996) (eds), pp. 30–31.

Department of Information Studies, University of Sheffield (URL) http://www.shef.ac.uk/uni/academic/I-M/is/home.html

Department of Trade and Industry (1996) *The 1996 U.K. R&D scoreboard.* Edinburgh: Company Reporting Ltd.

Development of a European Service for Information on Research and Education (URL) [DESIRE]. www.nic.surfnet/projects/desire

D-Lib (URL) ukoln.bath.ac.uk/dlib/projects.html

East, H. *et al.* (1995) *A huge leap forward. A quantitative and qualitative examination of the development of access to database services by British Universities, 1988–1994.* London: University of Westminster. (BLR&DD Report 6202).

Edwards, C. *et al.* (1995) IMPEL project: the impact on people of electronic libraries. In: Collier, M. and Arnold, K. (1995b) (eds), pp. 18–29.

Electronic Libraries Programme [eLib] (URL) ukoln.bath.ac.uk/elib/intro.html

Ellis, D. (1996) The dilemma of measurement in information retrieval research. *Journal of the American Society for Information Science,* **47**(1), 23–36.

Enser, P.G. (1995) Pictorial information retrieval. *Journal of Documentation,* **51**(2), 126–170.

ERCOMS (URL) http://www.ford.mk.dmu.ac.uk/Projects/ERCOMS

Erens, B. (1996) *Modernizing research libraries: the effect of recent developments in university libraries on the research process.* London: Bowker-Saur. (British Library Research Series).

European Commission (1996) *Research and technological development activities of the European Union. Annual Report. 1995.* Brussels: European Commission, DGXII.

European Commission (URL) The INFO2000 Programme. www2.echo.lu/libraries.html

Evans, R. (1994) Beyond Boolean: relevance ranking, natural language and the new search paradigm. In: *Proceedings of the 15th National Online Meeting, 1994*, ed. M.E. Williams. New York: Learned Information.

Farmer, J. and Williams, D. (1997) Decision-making by health purchasing organizations in Scotland: the role and influence of evidence from the research literature. *Journal of Information Science*, **23**(1), 59–72.

Fattahi, R. (1996) Super records: an approach towards the description of works appearing in various manifestations. *Library Review*, **45**(4), 19–29.

Fletcher, M. (1996) The CATRIONA project: feasibility study and outcomes. *Program*, 30(2), April, 99–109.

Focused Investigation of Document delivery options (URL) [FIDDO]. A report. http://www.lboro.ac.uk/departments/dils/reseach/fiddo/fiddo.html

Fowell, S.P. and Levy, P. (1995) Developing a new professional practice: a model for networked learner support in higher education. *Journal of Documentation*, **51**(3), 271–280.

François, P. *et al.* (1995) SGML/HyTime repositories and object paradigms. *Electronic Publishing*, **8**(2/3), 63–79.

Furner, J. and Willett, P. (1995) A survey of hypertext-based public-access point-of-information systems in UK libraries. *Journal of Information Science*, **21**(4), 243–255.

Galliers, R.D. (1995) A manifesto for information management research. *British Journal of Management*, **6**, December, 545–552, [special issue].

Garrod, P. and Kinnell, M. (1996) Performance measurement, benchmarking and the UK library and information services sector. *Libri*, **46**(3), September, 141–148.

Garrod, P. and Kinnell, M. (1997a) Benchmarking development needs in the LIS sector. *Journal of Information Science*, **23**(2), 111–118.

Garrod, P. and Kinnell, M. (1997b) Towards library excellence: best practice benchmarking in the library and information sector. In: J. Brockman (ed). *Quality Management and Benchmarking in the Information Sector*. London: Bowker-Saur, (British Library Research and Innovation Report No. 47) pp. 305–398.

Gilchrist, A. and Brockman, J. (1996) Where is the Xerox Corporation of the LIS sector? *Library Trends*, **44**(3), 595–604.

Hancock-Beaulieu, M. *et al.* (1995) An evaluation of interactive query expansion in an online library catalogue with a graphical user interface. *Journal of Documentation* 51(3), 225–243.

Hannabuss, S. (1995) Approaches to research. *Aslib Proceedings*, **47**(1) 3–11.

Harman, D. (1993) *The first Text REtrieval Conference (TREC-1)*. Gaithersburg: NIST. (NIST special publication 500–207).

Harman, D. (1994) *The second Text REtrieval Conference (TREC-2)*. Gaithersburg: NIST. (NIST special publication 500–215).

Harman, D. (1995) *The third Text REtrieval Conference (TREC-3)*. Gaithersburg: NIST. (NIST special publication 500–225). [Also available at http://potomac.ncsl.nist.gov:80/TREC/]

Harman, D. (1996) *The fourth Text REtrieval Conference (TREC-4)*. Gaithersburg: NIST. (NIST special publication 500–236). [Also available as http://potomac.ncsl.nist.gov:80/TREC/]

Harter, S.P. (1996) The impact of electronic journals on scholarly communication: a citation study. *Current Research in Library & Information Science* (September/December), 207.

Hartley, J. and Sydes, M. (1996) Which layout do you prefer? An analysis of reader s preferences for different typographic layouts of structured abstracts. *Journal of Information Science*, **22**(1), 27–37.

Hartley, J. *et al.* (1996) Obtaining information accurately and quickly: are structure abstracts more efficient? *Journal of Information Science*, **22**(5), 349–356.

Hawkins, D.T. *et al.* (1992) Forces shaping the electronic publishing industry of the 1990s. *Electronic Networking*, **2**(4), 38–60.

Haynes, D. (1996) A summary of research activities in Europe. In: Haynes, D. and Cotton, R. (1996) (eds), pp. 74–80.

Haynes, D. and Cotton, R. (1996) (eds) *European library and information research policy. Proceedings of a seminar held at the Hotel Russell, London, 7–9 December 1994.* London: BLR&DD. (British Library R&D Report 6249).

Heery, R. (1996) Review of metadata formats. *Program*, **30**(4), 345–373.

Herget, J. (1995) The cost of (non-) quality – why it matters for information providers. *FID News Bulletin*, **45**(5), 156–159.

Holm, L.A. (URL) http://www.bibsys.no/one.pr.html

Houlder, V. (1997) Management: information overload. *Financial Times*, 16 January, 23.

Iljon, A. (1996) European Commission library and information research policy. In: Haynes, D. and Cotton, R. (1996) (eds), pp. 42–49.

Impact2. (Impact on People of Electronic Libraries) (URL) http://www.unn.ac.uk/~liw5/impact2.html

Information Highway Advisory Council (1995) *Copyright and the information highway: preliminary report of the Copyright SubCommittee.* Ottawa. The Council.

International Institute for Electronic Library Research www.iielr.dmu.ac.uk

Johanson, G. (1997) Information, knowledge and research. *Journal of Information Science*, **23**(2), 103–110

Johanssen, C.G. (1996a) Strategic issues in quality management. 1 Theoretical considerations. *Journal of Information Science*, **22**(3), 155–164.

Johanssen, C.G. (1996a) Strategic issues in quality management. 2 Survey analysis. *Journal of Information Science*, **22**(4), 231–245.

Joint Electronic Document Delivery Software project (URL). http://www.gu.edu.au/alib/iii/docdel/jointdev.html

Joint (1993) Funding Council's Libraries Review Group Report. [Chairman: Sir Brian Follett]. Bristol: Higher Education Funding Council for England (URL) http://www.bubl.bath.ac.uk/follett/follett report.html

Joint Information Systems Committee (URL) http://ukoln.bath.ac.uk/figit

Jones, S. *et al.* (1995) Interactive thesaurus navigation: intelligence rules, OK? *Journal of the American Society for the American Society for Information Science*, **46**(1), 52–59.

Keen, E.M. (1994) Designing and testing an interactive ranked retrieval system for professional searchers. *Journal of Information Science*, **20**(6), 389–398.

Keen, E.M. (1995) *Interactive ranked retrieval.* London: BLR&DD. (BLR&DD Report 6200).

Kinnell, M. and Oda, M. (1996) Coals to Tokyo: quality management in UK and Japanese public libraries. *Public Library Journal*, **11**(5), 131–133.

Klobas, J.E. (1995) Beyond information quality: fitness for purpose and electronic information resource use. *Journal of Information Science*, **21**(2), 95–114.

Kovács, E. and Batonyi, V. (1996) State of the art of research and development in library and information science in Hungary. In: Haynes, D. and Cotton, R. (1996) (eds), pp. 16–21.

Kurtz, D.C. (1994) The LACE multimedia programme in Oxford Academic background. *Information Services and Use*, **14**(3), 183–186.

Laddie, J. (1996) Copyright: over-strength, over-regulated, over-rated? *European Intellectual Property Review*, **19**(5), 253–261.

LAMDA (URL) http://www.ucl.ac.uk/Library/lamda.html

Lancaster, F.W. *et al.* (1994) Searching databases on CD-ROM: comparison of the results of end-user searching with results from two modes of searching by skilled intermediaries. *RQ*, **33**(3), 370–386.

Lee, M.K.O. and Pow, J. (1996) Information access behaviour and expectation of quality: two factors affecting the satisfaction of users of clinical hospital information systems. *Journal of Information Science*, **22**(3), 171–180.

Lewis, D.B. and Sparck Jones, K. (1996) Natural language processing for information retrieval. *Communications of the ACM*, **39**(1), 92–101.

Library and Information Commission: Research Sub-Committee (1996) *Research and Innovation Centre Research Bulletin*, (15), 2.

Library & Information Science Abstracts published monthly with annual indexes by Bowker-Saur (and available on CD-ROM combined with *Current Research in Library & Information Science*).

McIntosh, N. (1994) *Structured abstracts and information transfer*. London: BLR&DD. (British Library R&D Report 6142).

McKnight, C. (1996) *Digital libraries '95*. London: BLR&DD. (British Library Research and Development Report 6239).

Mahon, B. (1996) The future of LIS research in Europe. *Information UK Outlooks*, (16).

Meadows, J. *et al.* (1995) The future of library and information science research in the UK. *Information UK Outlooks*, (13)[entire issue].

Mendes, H.R. (1996) NORDINFO – cooperation in the Nordic countries. In: Haynes, D. and Cotton, R. (1996) (eds), pp. 39–41.

Menou, M.J. (1995a) The impact of information – I. Toward a research agenda for its definition and measurement. *Information Processing & Management*, **31**(4), 455–477.

Menou, M.J. (1995b) The impact of information – 2. Concepts of information and its value. *Information Processing & Management*, **31**(4), July, 479–490.

Miller, P. (1996) Metadata for the masses. *Ariadne*, (5). www.ukoln.ac.uk/ariadne/issue5/metadata.mass

Milstead, L. (1994) Needs for research in indexing. *Journal of the American Society for Information Science*, **45**(8), 577–582.

Montasser-Kohsari, G. *et al.* (1994) *Online access to multimedia documents*. London: BLR&DD. (BLR&DD Report 6139).

Moroney, J. and Matthews, J. (1995) *Applications for the superhighway*. London: Ovum.

Murray, R. (1995) IRIS and DALI: the dawn of a new era in distributed library systems. *Library Technology News*, (19), 1–3.

National Research Council, Computer Science and Telecommunications Board (1996) *The unpredictable certainty. Information infrastructure through 2000*. Washington, DC: National Academy Press.

Nicholas, D. (1996) But is it research? *Assignation*, **13**(1), 1–3.

Nicolson, D. *et al.* (1995) CATRIONA: towards a Z39.50 and MARC-based distributed catalogue of Internet resources. *Library Technology News*, (17), 1–3.

Notman, A.T. (1994) The EmbARK programme. Project update: DCI, the Harvard University Art Museums and EmbARK. *Information Services & Use*, **14**(3), 153–160.

OCLC (1996) *Newsletter*. OCLC awards 1996 research grants. (222), 22.

Oulton, T. *et al.* (1996) The DECIMAL Project: decision-making and decision support in small to medium sized libraries. *Vine*, (103), 13–19.

Owens, I. *et al.* (1996) *Information and business performance.* London: Bowker-Saur.

Owens, I. *et al.* (1997) Information and business performance: a study of information systems and services in high-performing companies. *Journal of Librarianship and Information Science*, **29**(1), 19–28.

Paci, A.M. (1996) Library and information research in Italy. In: Haynes, D. and Cotton, R. (1996) (eds), pp. 8–15.

Pfaff, K.M. (1994) The EmbARK programme: The development of EmbARK. *Information Services & Use*, **14**(3), 141–145.

Philip, G. and Hazlett, S-A. (1996) *Service quality of industrial information services.* London: BLRIC. (British Library Research and Innovation Report 32).

Pickering, H. *et al.* (1996) *The stakeholder approach to the construction of performance measures: a report to the British Library Research and Development Department.* Glasgow: Caledonian University.

Pirkola, A. and Jarvelin, K. (1996) The effect of anaphora and ellipsis resolution on proximity searching in a text database. *Information Processing & Management*, **32**(2), 199–216.

Pivec, F. *et al.* (1996) Pristop k longitudinalnemu studiju uporabnikov COBISS. *Knjinica*, **40**(3/4), 65–78.

Pluse, J. (1996) Research in public libraries: a project to find a way forward. *Public Library Journal*, **11**(1), 20–21.

Pollitt, A.S. *et al.* (1994) HIBROWSE for bibliographic databases. *Journal of Information Science*, **20**(6), 413–426.

Price, S.P. *et al.* (1996) An overview of electronic document request and delivery research. *Electronic Library*, **14**(5), 435–48.

Project Earl (URL) *Business plan for 1996–1999.* http://www.earl.org.uk/plan.html

Redfern, J. (1994) The LACE multimedia programme in Oxford. Computer graphics. *Information Services & Use*, **14**(3), 187–188.

Reuters (1994) *To know or not to know: the politics of information. A report exploring the issues surrounding the use, flow and politics of information in British business. Based on research conducted by Taylor Nelson AGB.* London: Reuters.

Reuters (1995) Business Information. *Information as an asset: the invisible goldmine. A report exploring the current and future value of information in business. Based on research conducted by the Industrial Research Bureau.* London: Reuters.

Rickman, R.M. and Stonham, T.J. (1994) *Image database retrieval using neural networks.* London: BLR&DD. (British Library R&D Report 6165).

Robertson, S.E. *et al.* (1995a) Large test collection experiments of an operational, interactive system: OKAPI at TREC. *Information Processing & Management*, **31**(3), 345–360.

Robertson, S.E. *et al.* (1995b) *OKAPI at TREC-3.* London: BLR&DD. (BLRD Report 6209).

Rowland, F. *et al.* (1995) (eds). *Project ELVYN: an experiment in electronic journal delivery.* London: Bowker-Saur.

Salton, G. (1989) *Automatic text processing. The transformation, analysis and retrieval of information by computer.* Reading, Mass: Addison-Wesley.

Shafer, K. (1996) Scorpion Project explores using Dewey to organize the Web. *OCLC Newsletter*, (222), 20–21.

Shields, K. *et al.* (1995) Automatic image retrieval using shape features. *New Review of Document and Text Management*, **1**, 183–198.

Sligo, F. (1996) Disseminating knowledge to build a learning organization. *International Journal of Human Resource Management*, **7**(2), 508–520.

Smeaton, A.F. and Harman, D. (1997) The TREC experiments and their impact on Europe. *Journal of Information Science*, **23**(2), 169–174.

Soergel, D. (1994) Indexing and retrieval performance: the logical evidence. *Journal of the American Society for Information Science*, **45**(8), 589–599.

Sparck Jones, K. (1995) Reflections on TREC. *Information Processing & Management*, **31**(3), 291–314.

Sparck Jones, K. and Endres-Niggemeyer, B. (1995) Introduction: automatic summarizing. *Information Processing & Management*, **31**(5), 625–630.

Stevens, C.A. *et al.* (1997) Health information: a role for public access systems? *Journal of Information Science*, **23**(2), 1997.

Svedberg, S.E. (1996) *Electronic media in public libraries – from experiment to concept.* http://www.lib.hel.fi/julkaisut/media.html

Talja, S. (1995) Constituting information and information user as objects of research: a theory of knowledge formations as an alternative to information man-theory. *Kirjastotiede ja Informatiika*, **14**(2), 48–60.

Targino, M.d.G. (1995) A interdisciplinaridade da ciência da informação como area de pesquisa. *Informacao & Sociedade: Estudos*, **5**(1), 11–19.

Tenopir, S.P. (1996) The impact of electronic publishing on special libraries in the future. *Current Research in Library & Information Science*, (September/December), 17.

Thackray, B. (1997) Developing the information society. *Managing Information*, **4**(3), 15–17.

Touche Ross (1995) *Information management. A survey of current practices and trends.* London: Touche Ross.

Trant, J. (1995) The Getty AHIP Imaging Initiative. *Information Services & Use*, **15**(4), 353–364.

Tuck, B. and Moulton, R. (1995) Electronic document delivery: technical aspects and future developments. In: Collier, M. and Arnold, K. (1995a) (eds), pp. 66–75.

Turner, J. (1994) Indexing film and video images for storage and retrieval. *Information Services & Use*, **14**(3), 225–236.

Tzekakis, M. (1996) Library and information research policy in Greece. *In*: Haynes, D. and Cotton, R. (1996) (eds), pp. 32–38.

United Kingdom Office for Library and Information Networking [UKOLN] (URL) http://ukoln.bath.ac.uk/ukoln/about/mission.html

Vakkari, P. (1996) Social and cognitive institutionalization of library and information science research in Scandinavia. *International Forum on Information and Documentation*, **21**(3), 25–36.

Ward, S. *et al.* (1995) *Library performance indicators and library management tools.* Luxembourg: European Commission DG XIII-E3. (Libraries in the Information Society Series EUR 16483 EN).

Watson, J. *et al.* (1996) Evaluating Internet text retrieval products. *Document World*, (May/June), 26–27, 29, 31–33, 35–36.

Weiner, M.L. and Liddy, E.D. (1995) Intelligent text processing, and intelligence tradecraft. *Journal of AGSI*, (July) (unpaginated reprint).

Wijngaert, L.v.d. (1996) A user s perspective on information services. *Information Services & Use*, **16**(2), 103–21.

Woodward, J. (1996) Cataloging and classifying information resources on the Internet. In: M.E. Williams *Annual Review of Information Science and Technology, 1996*. New Jersey: Information Today Inc. for ASIS, pp. 189–220.

Wormell, I. (1996) *Success factors for fee-based information services*. Helsinki: NORDINFO. (NORDINFO Publication 36).

Wu, Z. *et al.* (1995) The user perspective of the ELINOR electronic library. *Aslib Proceedings*, **47**(1), January, 13–22.

Zhao, D.G. and Ramsden, A. (1995) Report on the ELINOR electronic library pilot. *Information Services & Use*, **15**(3), 199–212.

Zorn, P. *et al.* (1996) Searching: tricks of the trade. *Online*, (May/June), 15–28.

Staff management **10**

Beryl Morris

The 1990s have seen unprecedented changes in library and information work in all sectors. There is constant pressure to make optimum use of static or diminishing resources, to provide services which are increasingly responsive and to exploit IT for the benefit of staff and customers. In terms of staff management, in many libraries, these influences have meant a reduction in the numbers of staff employed, a demand for greater flexibility in the way people work, pressure on time and deadlines, an emphasis on performance and an increased need to manage a diverse range of staff as effectively as possible. There is also a need to ensure that all staff respond well to rapid change and keep their skills and expertise honed and up to date. Of course, the world of library and information work is not unique. All sectors of employment have seen similar changes, and in some areas of employment the changes have been far more radical.

In 1996, the literature of staff management has been varied. Within general management literature, there is an increasing emphasis on leadership, teamwork and the management of change, together with employability and managing staff performance. There is also an apparently insatiable supply of books on quality, process re-engineering and the like. There is also a trend towards short, easily understood management texts such as those published by the Industrial Society, the Institute of Management and Kogan Page in the UK. Within the field of library and information literature there has been a similar emphasis. A particular trend seems to be articles which seek to predict the future for the profession and the consequent interest in the skills needed by information specialists and, as a result, staff development and training.

Staff management, of course, includes a number of aspects. This chapter tries to follow a logical approach, commencing with works on organizational development, followed by the recruitment and selection of staff, issues of employment and employability, training and development, performance management, including appraisal, and a miscellaneous section which includes reference to works on safety among other topics. Although the emphasis is on literature from within library and information work, reference is made to more general works where they are thought to be particularly relevant or interesting. Similarly, reference is made to a small number of works published before and after 1996, where these are thought to be especially relevant.

Introductory texts

Staff management seems simple when you are an observer or on the receiving end of other people's management. It is when you start to manage others that you realize that what seems logical to you does not always seem to make sense to others. A particularly useful introduction to the whole field of staff management is Jordan (1995). Now in its third edition, this is a comprehensive book which covers recruitment and selection, staff motivation, training and development, and discipline and dismissal. A useful starting point, it is also very readable with many practical examples.

For newly appointed or promoted managers, 1996 has seen a number of works that aim to provide practical help and reassurance. For example, Wilson (1996) aims to convince those new to management that it is largely a matter of commonsense. Similarly, my own book *First steps in management* (1996) is also intended to help those who have become managers for the first time. Chapters on staff management and teamwork aim to provide practical advice and help managers to feel more confident. Finally, Piccininni (1996) provides concise, sensible advice on topics such as motivation, delegation, keeping clear goals and learning from others.

Organizational development

Many library and information services are undergoing restructuring as part of their attempt to become more customer-focused and cost-effective. In the UK, local government reorganization has created a number of new unitary authorities, many of which have elected to establish their own library services. Although restructuring does not always result in a better service, a new structure does create a different emphasis and also allows new priorities to be promoted.

A useful start for any library service contemplating a restructuring could be 'The universal library report' (Line, 1996a). This would assist staff in any library to review the services they offer and to evaluate their way of working. Similarly Boissé and Bentley (1996) on 'Reorganizing libraries' could assist in identifying the key elements in a successful reorganization. Having addressed the need for change, Shaughnessy (1996) could also be a useful read. This article describes the issues, expected and unexpected, which arise when a large academic library undergoes a major restructuring. Although problems are acknowledged, the author suggests that the new structure has produced a more nimble, team-directed and responsive service. Another library which has undergone major restructuring in the 1990s is Harvard University Library. A useful review of the process, together with lessons to be learned and recommendations for other libraries, is provided by Lee and Clark (1996).

Library Administration and Management is an interesting and useful journal that in 1996, contained several articles which looked at the principles and practice of organizational development. For example, Haka (1996) suggests that there is no one best way to organize a library and that organizational development (OD) is not as simple as might be supposed. Successful OD is always a matter of compromise and trade-off, the most important aspect being a clear understanding of what the organization wishes to accomplish. The need to clarify the library's mission is also discussed by Smith (1996), and an overview of how to develop a strategic approach is given by Corrall (1996).

The move towards flatter organizations has been popular in the USA and is being adopted elsewhere. Boissé (1996) looks at the different pressures which lead to restructuring and, in particular, the implications for career progression, appraisal, accountability and communication. Outsourcing is another approach which is gaining credibility in some libraries, although there can be negative consequences for staff. Bigus (1996) describes the implications of outsourcing for paraprofessional staff, while Glenn (1996) sounds a note of caution and questions whether a quasi-commercial culture is really appropriate for public sector organizations. The need to motivate staff during rapid change is well known; Rowley (1996) provides a useful reminder of the key elements.

Employment and employability

The changing nature of libraries and information units is having a major impact on the employment and employability of staff. In the run up to the millennium, a number of writers are attempting to predict the future and, in particular, the skills that will be useful to library and information staff into the next century. For example, Abell (1996), Moore (1996) and Schement (1996) all analyse the skills which will be needed by the 'new' information professional, while Mendelsohn (1996a) also addresses this question and ponders whether a different kind of person will be required to staff information services in the future.

The skill needs of different sectors of the profession are also debated in a number of references. Allinson (1996), for example, considers the changing role of acquisitions and collection development librarians, while Beasley (1996) and Kesslor (1996) suggest skills for survival for school media coordinators and media specialists. These include public speaking, writing clear goals and objectives, curriculum development including the ability to exploit the contribution of media, negotiation skills, and stress and time management. Longenecker (1996) also identifies a number of survival skills including the need for business acumen and understanding and the ability to match services with customer expectations. The future challenges for education for librarianship in New Zealand and the Pacific Islands are explored in Ronnie (1994), while Luther and Grace (1996) are very dismissive of librarianship and information work courses which train students to work in industry, but ignore the needs of business.

The future for American public libraries is also addressed in a special issue of *Library Trends* entitled 'Focusing on quality for the 21st century'. Topics include the need for clearly defined core values, user-friendly IT, seeing and developing libraries as a visitor destination and encouraging a customer focus through staff development and training.

Academic libraries are also considering their futures and in a contentious article Stoffle *et al.* (1996) suggest that there will be no future for academic libraries unless they become more customer-focused and proactive within their own organizations. Jurow (1996) also advocates the need to think strategically about work in academic libraries and identifies some of the core competencies which will be needed in the future. Koenig *et al.* (1996) discuss a continuing concern, namely the need for faculty status for library professionals, while Crowley (1996), suggests that academic library staff should redefine their status to meet core academic standards and be ready to fight on behalf of the library against the emerging electronic competition. Morgan (1996) also discusses ways to develop academic library skills for the future. Finally, rare book librarians are not forgotten; Crump (1996) looks at their changing education and training needs.

Medical libraries are also in the business of identifying factors which will effect their future. Bradley (1996) writes about the changing face of health information and health information work; in two articles Palmer (1996a, 1996b) discusses new roles and new skills for health libraries and identifies practical ways in which medical librarians might improve their skills and competence for the future.

Among the skills which are likely to be in demand are negotiation (Lyons, 1996b), time management (Mendelsohn, 1996b), managing an increasingly diverse workforce (Whitewell, 1996) and managing people for whom one is not directly responsible (Lawes, 1996). Library managers will also need to consider and resolve the changing role and responsibilities of paraprofessional staff, according to Rider (1996) and Johnson (1996). The increased use of volunteers in libraries is likely to be an issue, thanks to the UK's recently published *Public library review* (Department of National Heritage, 1997). The *Review* advocates the use of volunteers to assist libraries to be open when the public want them and is likely to provoke a heated debate within the UK. McCarthy (1996) is likely to be relevant to this debate. Finally, those who wish to explore new opportunities for themselves might find Lyons (1996a) on becoming self-employed of interest.

The career patterns and prospects of library and information staff are also analysed and debated in the literature. Hunter (1996) looks at the career patterns of librarians in government departments, while the career barriers facing women in library work have been investigated by Poland *et al.* (1996). This research study, funded by the Library Association, reports that in the UK 74% of the LA's membership is women, yet women make up less than 5% of those earning more than £20,000. The report includes a survey of library staff and identifies the barriers that exist in women's career progression. Related to this research, Amos-Wilson (1996) questions whether there are gender related differences in accomplishing career development tasks, while Ford and Miller (1996) suggest that one of the reasons women may do less well is their reluctance to embrace IT. Their article 'Gender differences in Internet perceptions and use' describes a survey of undergraduate and postgraduate students in the UK. They found that women reported greater levels of disorientation and disenchantment with the WWW and concluded that this might have the effect of limiting career prospects for women.

These concerns aside, most writers suggest that the future is bright for those in information work. Hyams (1996) suggests that the prospects are rosy for information professionals, while other writers examine the skills which impress employers. Avery and Ketcher (1996), for example, suggest that instructional skills make a difference in academic institutions, while Zhou (1996) analyses the trends in demand for computer-related skills for academic librarians. Davies (1996) looks at prospects for the information professional in Europe and identifies the training support which will help staff to take advantage of the expanded opportunities available.

Flexible working is an increasingly topical issue. Although some libraries have adopted flexible working patterns, they have perhaps been slow to accept teleworking or other more radical approaches. Goulding and Kerslake (1996) report on a survey of libraries and include a series of case studies on the use of flexible working. Reasons cited for its use include weekend opening, to retain valuable staff and as a result of staff demand. On a more sombre note, Brill (1996) discusses the increasing unemployment which is affecting some parts of the library workforce.

Leadership and management

The changes in the nature and demands of organizsations are creating different needs for leadership. Line (1996b), in a challenging piece entitled 'But what can be done about our bosses?', suggests that leadership is sadly neglected in many organizations. Two writers, Bucher (1996) and Goulding (1996) stress the importance of staff in delivering library and information services, as does Euster (1996). Mech (1996) emphasizes the importance of leadership in the evolution of academic librarianship, while Auret (1996) considers the changing role of directors of academic libraries and identifies four distinct roles – liaison, leadership, entrepreneur and resources. Anderson (1996) examines techniques which can help to ascertain management competencies. He describes the use of management exercises, such as the Myers-Biggs Index, in recruiting senior library staff and identifies the advantages and disadvantages of this approach.

Leadership training is seen as increasingly important as the manager's job becomes more complex. Horton *et al.* (1996) describe the work of the Aurora Leadership Institute in Australia which trains senior staff to feel more confident. The use of formal and informal approaches to leadership is described by Reynolds (1996). Kinnell (1996) also writes about management development for information professionals and describes the first MBA designed for library and information staff.

Recruitment and selection

The literature in 1996 appears to have less emphasis on recruitment and selection. This may have something to do with the reductions in staffing and the tendency, in many organizations, to recruit from within. However, for those involved in the recruitment and selection of staff, or who are in the process of restructuring their services or reviewing jobs within their department, the following could be useful. *Job descriptions for the information professional*, an Aslib know-how guide by Castelyn (1996), provides sample job descriptions from a range of libraries. Advice on interviewing techniques might also be useful and is provided by Heery (1996).

Staff training and development

The large number of writings on training and development is testimony to the growing importance of this activity across all the sectors. Training is seen as an essential element in helping staff to feel confident and competent and respond positively to changing circumstances. It is also seen as a key component in helping staff to improve their employability.

The year saw a plethora of articles and books on the role of staff development and training. Two general introductions are Trotta (1996) and Oldroyd (1996). A number of writers stress the importance of staff development in supporting change. For example, Campbell (1996) suggests that encouraging staff to understand the purpose of the change, together with help in acquiring the relevant skills and expertise, are crucial to its success. 'How much staff training?' is the question posed by Holt (1996) who argues that changing situations demand that staff should feel skilled and confident and suggests that all library budgets should include a substantial element for staff training and development.

Working papers from different libraries always make interesting and useful reading and the University of Newcastle's Staff development policy (Morrow, 1996) is a good example. This is a comprehensive document, covering entitlement to training including specific hours, attendance at courses, visits, professional qualifications and other ways to develop skills and confidence. The University of Newcastle pledges that at least 1% of its staff budget will be dedicated to staff development and therefore provides a useful benchmark for other libraries. 'The training programme at Barr Smith Library', (Beaumont, 1996) is another example from an academic library. The author advocates that a specific person should take on the training role and suggests that a proportion of staff development costs should be supported by the institution.

Induction training is a vital aspect of helping staff to 'settle in' to a new position and understand the basic elements of their job and the organization. Berry (1996) looks at the components of a good induction programme. Staff who work on their own may find such training difficult to obtain, as may those who are temporary, part-time or on contract. Bryant (1996) looks at training and development for the solo librarian, while Kerslake and Goulding (1996), describe a British Library funded project which looks at induction training for flexible staff. The methodology for the research is explained as well as the interim findings. The report concludes that temporary and contract staff may not receive any induction training at all, as it is not considered cost-effective and part-time staff may have to wait a considerable time for their induction training to be provided.

Training and development issues for the new millennium are also well covered in the literature. Harrison (1996) laments the rise and fall of the bookish librarian, while Harris (1996) considers practical ways to retrain librarians to meet the needs of the virtual library patron. Training for specific aspects of service is also included. Quinn (1996) for example, looks at methods for training library staff members in the use of CD-ROMs in federal depository libraries in Texas, while Sipos (1996) describes a programme to assist trainers in teenage services to improve library services to young people. Quality remains an issue for libraries and information units, and although Brophy and Couling (1996) is about the broader aspects of delivering a quality service, it stresses the need for staff training in the development of responsive services. Similarly, Barter (1995) examines the management writings of Tom Peters and their implications for library and information services, including the need for competent and confident staff. Finally, in order to develop and deliver quality services, a systematic approach is necessary. Wehmeyer (1996) describes the importance of training in implementing a customer service plan at Wright State University.

The 1990s have seen much discussion on the changing role of reference services and in 1996 several articles have continued the debate. Low (1996), for example, writes about 'The role of reference librarians: today and tomorrow', while Stalker and Murfin (1996) analyse practical ways to develop a quality reference service. Training for reference services is well represented, with Etkin (1996) considering the need for core knowledge for electronic reference services, and Heaton (1996) looking at different levels of provision and how to make optimum use of staff for the benefit of the service.

Different methods of staff training and development are also well covered in the literature and there is an increasing number of articles about alternative approaches to help staff develop skills and confidence. Raddon (1996), for example, contains a useful overview of approaches, while Guidelines (1996) examines the design and operation of post-masters residencies. These are American techniques which allow recently qualified (or possibly mid-career) staff to work within a library to gain or update their skills. The article includes useful advice for those contemplating this arrangement and discusses the possible legal risks involved.

Staff exchanges are a common approach to staff development in many countries. Abareh (1996), in his survey of academic library staff in Nigeria, concludes that while exchanges are not yet employed there, there is considerable interest in the idea and suggests that this approach should be adopted as a matter of urgency. Another interesting approach, this time in Hawaii, is by Harada (1996), who describes the collegial assistance network which provides contacts and a professional network to assist with updating.

Two approaches that have particular significance in the UK are the Continuing Professional Development Framework which was introduced by the Library Association in 1993 and the development of National Vocational Qualifications (NVQs). The CPD framework encourages individuals to take responsibility for their own personal and professional development. Farmer (1996) describes the need for transferable skills for information professionals, while Evans (1996) and Norby (1996) describe the use of the framework in supporting career development. Arundale (1996) is a useful introduction for those who seek to gain NVQ qualifications, while Herzog (1996) is aimed at managers and employers. Finally, the potential of a competence framework for other countries is discussed by Jackson (1996). Self-teaching texts and those aimed at training in a particular aspect of library and information work are beginning to appear. For example, Biddiscombe (1996) is aimed at those who wish to develop these essential skills in themselves or colleagues.

Teams and teamwork

Team management and the move towards self-managed teams have become a much more generally accepted approach, especially in academic libraries, often as a result of convergence of the library with other services such as computing and media. Bluck (1996), aimed at those involved in training management teams, is a useful introduction to the principles of effective teamwork and contains chapters on training for teamwork including a number of sample training programmes.

An article by Kearns (1996) looks at the application of semi-autonomous teams to small college libraries in Australia, while a more quirky approach is to be found in Lubans' article 'I ain't no cowboy, I just found this hat' (1996) which looks at self-managing teams and their use in Duke University. This useful article covers different leadership styles, together with practical ways to address the need for continuous improvement. It includes different examples of coaching, encouraging and empowering leadership and incorporates useful information about the library service as appendices – the vision statement and expectations of team leaders.

Communication

Libraries are increasingly concerned with the motivation and morale of their staff. While training and development are seen as important aspects, there is also an increasing awareness of the importance of communication in all its forms. Forrest (1996) talks about the need for different channels of communication for library staff, while Bryce (1996) describes the use of newsletters as part of the library's communication strategy and provides a helpful reminder of some of the important elements. The use of staff conferences to encourage involvement and help them respond to change is described in McConnell (1996). However, the prize for conciseness must go to Smallen's 'The standing meeting' (1996). In two pages he covers how he runs daily meetings with staff. They always take place at the same time, cover relevant information and allow staff birthdays and other occasions to be celebrated. The trick, according to Smallen, is to hold them regardless of who can or cannot attend and the real benefit is that they remain quick.

Safety and security

One aspect of library work that is of increasing concern is the threat to workplace and personal safety. The year 1996 has seen a number of references on this and related topics. For example, Pantry (1996) has produced a useful book, providing an introduction to dealing with aggression and violence in the workplace. Duitman (1996) also looks at the potential dangers of library work for staff. Crime is on the increase and Arterburn (1996) considers practical ways to tackle it in libraries. Chadley (1996) also looks at ways to address and discourage crime, this time in universities. Finally, another growing problem area for library staff is the potential for stress or burnout. Lacey (1996) discusses the potential for burnout among bibliographic instruction librarians. Perhaps Mendelsohn

(1996b) on managing one's time would be useful here, as would the article 'Towards a stress free library' (Dubber, 1996).

Managing performance

Another growth area is the increasing emphasis on managing performance, both at service and individual level. A particularly useful review of the literature on performance appraisal is by Osif and Harwood (1996). This includes information about what appraisal is and why it is increasingly important in libraries. It also introduces new approaches such as 360° appraisal, team appraisal and peer review. The literature of performance appraisal in libraries is also reviewed.

Keeping up to date with the literature

We all have our own favourite methods of keeping ourselves up to date with recent publications. However, one source which is particularly interesting to academic librarianship is the *Journal of Academic Librarianship*. Each issue includes the *JAL* 'Guide to professional literature', which consists of short but useful reviews of book and journal articles, mainly American and British.

The other useful source is of course electronic and, in the last two years, the Web has become an excellent way to find working papers from libraries and other organizations. E-mail is also becoming invaluable and services such as LISLINK allow people to ask for information and advice on specific subjects. The tendency, in the UK at least, is for the enquirer to prepare a short summary of responses which can assist others in their information gathering. One useful Web page is that of the American Special Libraries Association which, as well as publications and general information, is developing a core skills list for special librarians (the site is http://www.sla.org).

I will leave the last word on references to management literature to Charles Handy, a British management guru. In a short review (1996) of the *International encyclopaedia of business and management*, he questions the assumption that knowledge is really a source of effectiveness. In every profession, he says, there is a need for a minimum understanding of the body of knowledge; however, to assume that you are a good manager because you have read a certain text is a misapprehension – it is how you apply the knowledge that really matters.

Handy's warning aside, in putting together this chapter, I have had regard for works that will be useful, that will reassure those who are embarking on something new, that are practical and helpful for those who have a problem to tackle and that will challenge us when, perhaps, we are in danger of becoming complacent.

References

Abareh, H.M. (1996) Shared human resources in academic libraries in Nigeria. *Aslib Proceedings*, **48**(3), 81–84

Abell, A. (1996) The information professional in 1996. *Information Management Report*, (January), 1–6.

Allinson, T. (1996) I love me, I love me not: schizophrenic behaviour among acquisitions/collection development librarians. *Library Acquisitions: Practice and Theory*, **20**(1), 103–116.

Amos-Wilson, P. (1996) Accomplishing career development tasks: are there gender related differences? *Librarian Career Development*, **4**(1), 25–32.

Anderson, A. (1996) How do you manage? *Library Journal*, **121**(8), 53–54.

Arterburn, R. (1996) Librarians: caretakers or crimefighters? *American Libraries*, **27**(7), 32–34.

Arundale, J. (1996) *Getting your S/NVQ: a guide for candidates in the information and library sector*. London: Library Association Publishing.

Auret, H.E. (1996) Nature of academic library management. *South African Journal of Library and Information Science*, **64**(1), 22–38.

Avery, C and Ketcher, K. (1996) Do instructional skills impress employers? *College and Research Libraries*, **57**(4), 249–258.

Barter, R.F. (1995) In search of excellence in libraries: the management writings of Tom Peters and their implications for library and information services. *Asian Libraries*, **4**(3), 47–63.

Beasley, A.E. (1996) Leadership 101: Survival skills for school media co-ordinators. *North Carolina Libraries*, **54**(2), 54–57.

Beaumont, S. (1996) Training programme at Barr Smith Library. *Australian Academic and Research Libraries*, **7**(3), 186–196.

Berry, C.E. (1996) Library induction programmes: how do we do that? *Law Librarian*, **27**(1), 41–43.

Biddiscombe, R. (1996) *Training for IT*. London: Library Association Publishing.

Bigus, P. (1996) Outsourcing: one para professional experience. *Associates*, **2**(13), 6.

Bluck, R. (1996) *Team management*. London: Library Association Publishing.

Boissé, J.A. (1996) Adjusting the horizontal hold: flattening the organization. *Library Administration and Management*, **10**(2), 77–81.

Boissé, J.A. and Bentley, S. (1996) Reorganizing libraries. *Advances in Librarianship*, **20**, 27–46.

Bradley, J. (1996) The changing face of health information and health information work. *Bulletin of the Medical Library Association*, **84**(1), 1–10.

Brill, A. (1996) Unemployment issues hit the library workforce. *Library Personnel News*, **10**(1), 1–3.

Brophy, P and Couling, K. (1996) *Quality in libraries and information units*. Aldershot: Gower.

Bryant, S. (1996) *Personal professional development and the solo librarian*. London: Library Association Publishing.

Bryce, B. (1996) Using newsletters in the library's communication strategy. *Library Administration and Management*, **10**(4), 246–251.

Bucher, V. (1996) Staff: a critical part of today's libraries. *DF Revy*, **18** (January), 315–318.

Campbell, J.D. (1996) Building an effectiveness pyramid for leading successful organisational transformation. *Library Administration and Management*, **10**(2), 82–86.

Castelyn, M. (1996) *Job descriptions for the information professional*. London: Aslib.

Chadley, O.A. (1996) Campus crime and personal safety in libraries. *College and Research Libraries*, **57**(4), 385–390.

Corrall, S. (1996) Balancing the business. *Library Manager*, (15), 14.

Crowley, B. (1996) Redefining the status of the librarian in higher education. *College and Research Libraries*, **57**(2), 113–121.

Crump, M. (1996) *Rare book librarians for the future: issues in training and education*. Brussels: CBBB-BCBB.

Davies, R. (1996) The information professional in Europe: perceptions and realities. *Aslib Proceedings*, **48**(9), 215–220.

Department of National Heritage (1997) *Public library review*. London: HMSO.

Dubber, G. (1996) Towards a stress free library. *School Librarian*, **44**(1), 5.

Duitman, P. (1996) Perils, pits and pitfalls in libraries. *PNLA Quarterly*, **60**(2), 11–12.

Etkin, C. (1996) Creating a core knowledge for electronic reference services. *Tennessee Librarian*, **48**(1), 16–28.

Euster, J.R. (1996) Maturity, leadership and generational change in libraries. *Library Management*, **17**(1), 5–10.

Evans, J. (1996) CPD framework. *Education for Library and Information Services*, **13**(1), 37–42.

Farmer, J. (1996) A framework of transferable skills of information professionals. *Library and Information Research News*, **20**(64), 17–22.

Ford, N. and Miller, D. (1996) Gender differences in Internet perception and use. *Aslib Proceedings*, **48**(7/8), 183–192.

Forest, C. (1996) Talking the library: channels of communication for library staff. *Georgia Librarian*, **32**(2/4), 95.

Glenn, J. (1996) A few thoughts of effectiveness. *An Leabharlann*, **12**(2/3), 67–72.

Goulding, A. (1996) *Managing change for library support staff*. Aldershot: Avebury.

Goulding, A. and Kerslake, E. (1996) Flexible working in libraries: profit and potential pitfalls. *Library Management*, **17**(2), 8–16.

Guidelines (1996) for the practicalities and principles in the design, operation and evaluation of post masters residence programmes. *Library Personnel News*, **10**(3), 1–5.

Haka, C.H. Organizational design: is there an answer? *Library Administration and Management*, **10**(2), 74–76.

Handy, C. (1996) Education isn't an open book. *Management Today*, (8), 5.

Harada, V.H. (1996). Alternative for professional renewal: a critical analysis of a collegial assistance network in Hawaii. *School Library Media Quarterly*, **24**(2), 77–83.

Harris, H. (1996) Retraining librarians to meet the needs of the virtual library patron. *Information Technology and Libraries*, **15**(1), 48–52.

Harrison, K. (1996) The rise and fall of the bookish librarian. *Library Review*, **45**(3), 21–24.

Heaton, G. (1996) Rethinking problems of reference services in academic medical school libraries. *Bulletin of the Medical Library Association*, **84**(1), 17–24.

Heery, M. (1996) Getting the questions right. *Library Manager*, 15, 10–11.

Herzog, J. (1996) *Implementing S/NVQs in the information and library sector: a guide for employers*. London: Library Association Publishing.

Holt, G.E. (1996) Staff training: How much is enough? *Bottom Line*, **9**(1), 43–44.

Horton, W. *et al.* (1996) The Aurora Leadership Institute. *Australian Library Journal*, **45**(1), 10–32.

Hunter, C. (1996) Career patterns of librarians in government departments. *Librarian Career Development*, **4**(1), 5–12.

Hyams, E. (1996) Professional futures: why are the prospects so rosy? *Aslib Proceedings*, **48**(9), 204–208.

Jackston, T. (1996) Setting a standard: library industry competence standards. *Education for Library and Information Science*, **13**(1), 3–11.

Johnson, C.P. (1996) The changing nature of jobs: a paraprofessional time series. *College and Research Libraries*, **57**(1), 59–67.

Jordon, P. (1995) *Staff management in library and information work*. 3rd ed. Aldershot: Gower.

Jurow, S. (1996) Core competencies: strategic thinking about the work we do. *Journal of Academic Librarianship*, **22**(4), July, 300–302.

Kearns, S.D. (1996) Considerations in the applications of semi autonomous teams to small college libraries. *Australian Academic and Research Libraries*, **27**(1), 58–66.

Kerslake, E. and Goulding, A. (1996) Developing a flexible library and information workforce: a new research project. *Personnel, Training and Education*, **12**(3), 4–7.

Kesslor, D. (1996) Media specialists in the millennium: accepting the challenge. *North Carolina Libraries*, **54**(1), 6–8.

Kinnell, M. (1996) Management development for information professionals. *Aslib Proceedings*, **48**(9), 209–214.

Koenig, M. *et al.* (1996) Faculty status for library professionals: effect on job turnover and job satisfaction among university research library directors. *College and Research Libraries*, **57**(3), 295–300.

Lacey, M.A. (1996) Burnout among bibliographic instruction librarians. *Library and Information Science Research*, **18**(2), 165–183.

Lawes, A. (1996) Managing people for whom one is not directly responsible. *Records Management Bulletin*, **73**, 15–16, 20.

Lee, S. and Clark, M.E. (1996) Continued organizational transformation: the Harvard College experience. *Library Administration and Management*, **10**(2), 98–104.

Line, M.B. (1996a) The universal library report. *Library Management*, **17**(1), 33–36.

Line, M.B. (1996b) 'But what can be done about our bosses?' *Library Management*, **17**(3), 32–37.

Longenecker, C.O. (1996) Survival skills for the information science professional. *Information System Management*, **13**(2), 26–31.

Loughbridge, B. *et al.* (1996) Career development: follow up studies on Sheffield MA graduates 1885/6 to 1992/3. *Journal of Librarianship and Information Science*, **28**(2), 105–117.

Low, K. (1996) *The role of reference librarians: today and tomorrow*. New York: Haworth Press.

Lubans, J. (1996) I ain't no cowboy, I just found this hat! *Library Administration and Management*, **10**(1), 5–15.

Luther, D. and Grace, J. (1996) A not so modest proposal. *Against the Grain*, 8(2), 25–26.

Lyons, J. (1996a) Whatever turns you on. *Library Manager*, (14), 16–18.

Lyons, J. (1996b) Gentle art of negotiation. *Library Manager*, (15), 8–9.

McCarthy, C.A. (1996) Volunteers and technology. *American Libraries*, **27**(1), 56–59.

McConnell, F. (1996) It ain't broke . . . the fixings gone. *Library Management*, **17**(7), 37–44.

Mech, T. (1996) Leadership and the evolution of academic librarianship. *Journals of Academic Librarianship*, **22**(5), 345–354.

Mendelsohn, S. (1996a) Will a different kind of person be needed to staff the information service of the future? *Information World Review*, (112), 28–29.

Mendelsohn, S. (1996b) How to have time for everything. *Library Manager*, (17), 6–8.

Moore, N. (1996) Creators, communicators and consolidators : the new information professional. *Managing Information*, 3(6), 24–25.

Morgan, S. (1996) Developing academic library skills for the future. *Library Review*, 45(5), 41–53.

Morris, B.A. (1996) *First steps in management*. London: Library Association Publishing.

Morrow, J. (1996) The University of Newcastle upon Tyne Library staff development policy. *Personnel Training and Education*, 13(3), 6–8.

Norby, K.A. (1996) Steps for a professional workout. *Library Association Record*, 98(4), 211.

Oldroyd, M. (1996) *Staff development in academic libraries: present practice and future challenges*. London: Library Association Publishing.

Osif, B.A. and Harwood, R.L. (1996) Performance appraisal. *Library Administration and Management*, 10(3), 176–181.

Palmer, J. (1996a) Skills for the millennium: the librarian of the 21st century. *Librarian: Career Development*, 4(1), 13–17.

Palmer, J. (1996b) Effectiveness and efficiency: new roles, new skills for health libraries. *Aslib Proceedings*, 48(10), 247–252.

Pantry, S. (1996) *Dealing with aggression and violence in your workplace*. London: Library Association Publishing.

Piccininni, J. (1996) Advice for first time library directors. *Library Administration and Management*, 10(1), 41–43.

Poland, F. *et al.* (1996) *Women and senior management*. London: Library Association Publishing.

Quality (1996) for public libraries in the 21st century. *Library Trends*, [Special issue].

Quinn, A.B. (1996) Methods for training library staff members in the use of CD-ROMs in federal depository libraries in Texas: a survey. *Journal of Government Information*, 23(2), 151–159.

Raddon, R. (1996) Career development. *Librarian Career Development*, 4(2), 28–30.

Reynolds, J. (1996) There must be 50 ways to be a leader. *College and Research Libraries News*, 57(3), 208–210.

Rider, M.M. (1996) Developing new roles for paraprofessionals in cataloguing. *Journal of Academic Libraries*, 22(1), 26–32.

Rochester, M.K. (1996) Professional communication through journal articles. *Australian Academic and Research Libraries*, 27(3), 191–199.

Ronnie, M.A. (1996) *Education for librarianship in New Zealand and the Pacific Islands*. London: Mansell.

Rosenqvist, K. (1996) Librarian's conscience. *Scandinavian Public Library Journal*, 29(1), 18–23.

Rowley, J. (1996) Motivation of staff in libraries. *Library Management*, 17(5), 31–35.

Schement, J.R. (1996) A 21st century strategy for librarians. *Library Journal*, 121(8), 34–36.

Shaughnessy, T. (1996) Lessons from restructuring the library. *Journal of Academic Librarianship*, 22(4), 251–256.

Sipos, C. (1996) Training trainers in teenage services. *American Libraries* 27(9), 54–55.

Smallen, D. (1996) The standing meeting. *Cause/Effect*, 19(1), 49–50.

Smith, V.T. (1996) Library mission: embracing change in the year 2000. *Journal of Educational Media and Library Science*, 33(3), 281–288.

Special Libraries Association (URL) http://www.sla.org

Stalker, J.C. and Murfin, M.E. (1996) Quality reference service: a preliminary case study. *Journal of Academic Librarianship*, **22**(6), 423–429.

Stoffle, C. *et al.* (1996) Choosing our futures. *College and Research Libraries*, **57**(3), 213–226.

Stott, H. (1996) A quick guide to achieving information and library services NVQs. *Managing Information*, **3**(3), 36–38.

Trotta, M. (1996) *Successful staff development: a how-to-do-it.* New York, London: Neal-Schuman.

Wainwright, E. (1996) The big picture: reflections on the future of libraries and librarians. *Australian Academic and Research Libraries*, **27**(1), 1–14.

Wehmeyer, S. (1996) Saying what we will do . . . implementing a customer service plan. *Journal of Academic Libraries*, **27**(3), 173–180.

Whitewell, S. (1996) Intimate world, intimate workplace. *American Libraries*, **27**(2), 56–59.

Wilson, L. (1996) *People skills for library managers: a common sense guide for beginners.* Littleton, CO: Libraries Unlimited.

Zhou, Y. (1996) Analysis of trends in demand for computer related skills for academic librarians. *College and Research Libraries*, **57**(3), 259–272.

Librarianship and information work in South Asia

Jagtar Singh

Introduction

South Asia is characterized by asymmetry, in size, population, economic and military power. India is larger than all other countries in the region put together. South Asia is a split spectrum of a once monolithic political entity consolidated and welded into the Indian subcontinent by the British, mainly in the 19th and early 20th centuries. Despite the linguistic and religious diversities and differences in milieu in different parts of the south Asian region, there exists a unique cultural unity in the subcontinent. Unfortunately the nations of South Asia have not had good relations with each other. The entire region is economically backward. The continued existence of problems such as unemployment, poverty, inflation, balance of payment difficulties, regional inequality, and continued demographic pressures have forced these countries to resort to massive foreign aid, leading to a heavy foreign debt burden. At the same time the South Asian nations have had to be on guard against any attempt to undermine their sovereign status, whether in the name of human rights, environment, intellectual property rights or security.

The countries of this region can be put into two categories. The first group consists of India, Pakistan, Bangladesh and Sri Lanka, and covers the major part of the region, in terms of area, population and economic development. Much of the development in librarianship has also been in the countries of this category, particularly in India. The other group consists of the three smaller states of Nepal, Bhutan and the Maldives. Except for the Maldives, which have the highest literacy rate (93%) and the highest per capita income ($726) in the region, Nepal and Bhutan are among the least developed countries in the world, with per capita incomes of $180 and $190 and literacy rates of 27% and 40% respectively. As far as development of librarianship and information work is concerned, these nations have not much to speak of. Nepal has made some progress in the field, but the Maldives, in spite of being the most literate of the seven countries, have not made progress parallel to their economic achievements (Manorama, 1997).

Relevant literature from the various countries is hard to obtain, largely for political reasons. Another reason is the language diversity of these countries. The professional literature in English was used as the basis of this chapter.

In the long run, regional cooperation must lead to removal of artificial barriers. The South Asian Association for Regional Cooperation (SAARC) has made some noticeable, if not spectacular, progress in this field. The idea of establishing a SAARC Documentation Centre (SDC) at New Delhi was approved in principle at the second SAARC meeting held in Bangalore in November 1986. It was decided unanimously that for the SDC the Indian National Scientific Documentation Centre (INSDOC) should be a focal point in India to look after the documentation activities. The work of the SDC will be based on published materials available with focal points, information about which would be compiled into a SAARC Bibliography. SDS conducts human resource programmes on information management in the SAARC region. It includes short-term courses, seminars and workshops every year. Participants are drawn from all SAARC nations and the target groups include professionals engaged in library and information activities (SAARC, 1996). Strengthening (1997) emphasizes that the SDC should facilitate access to all information about the Integrated Programme of Action (IPA) for interested scholars and other users. The possibility may be explored for disseminating such information through cyberspace, including the Internet. Establishment of the SAARC Net – the Online Computerized Data Information System, headquartered in FICCI BISNET – makes a good beginning (Ramaiah, B.B. 1997).

Publishing and libraries

Shaw (1995) throws out a challenge to librarians and historical bibliographers to locate the missing bits of information to complete the map of the history of printing and publishing in South Asia. He suggests that the national libraries of the region should cooperate closely – to their mutual benefit – in improving retrospective bibliographic control for South Asia. Boost (1996) reveals that the rising cost of printing and growing demand for high quality and cheaper books in the neighbouring countries have given an edge to the Indian book industry. Traders and publishers in Pakistan, Bangladesh, Nepal or Bhutan say that a large percentage of books sold and bought are Indian. They are preferred for their reasonable price tag and richness of content. Compared with the books of England, the USA and even Pakistan, Indian books seem cheap. Girija Kumar (1996) is of the view that Indian publishing has lost its moorings. He gives statistical data and specifies the reasons for this decline: general institutional decline; overbearing official sectors; lack of reading culture; narrow market base; inadequate public library system; rising index of book prices; lack of editorial expertise; low level intellectual input; unethical practices; and low societal status.

Govil (1996) highlights the fact that with liberalization of the economy and an improving literacy rate, book publishing in India is experiencing unprecedented growth. He points out that India has two assets which should strengthen its domestic publishing scene: a huge middle class (150 million people of whom 18 million read and write in English) and a maturing indigenous industry. He notes that textbooks for primary and secondary schools are produced by the public sector school bureau and textbooks for English-medium public schools and colleges and universities are still being published by private publishers. Publication of low-priced, mass market paperbacks to meet the growing demand of Indian readers is a significant development. Experiments have been successfully launched in English and regional languages. He further notes that India, because of its rich literary cultural heritage, variety of religions, diversity of tradition and multiplicity of communities and languages, publishes books on a very large number of subjects catering for the various interests and aptitudes of buyers in foreign countries. Ghai (1995) highlights the role of the Institute of Book Publishing in specialized training in various aspects of publishing. He reports that the Institute has already trained over 270 participants from all over South Asia and South East Asia. He also (Ghai, 1994) indicates that scholarly publishing is no longer the preserve of the university presses and research institutions. The commercial publishers are taking over under special financial arrangements, varying from part sponsorship, full sponsorship, buy-back arrangements and substituting an honorarium for royalties. Commercial publishers are exploring regional and international markets, regional cooperation in marketing, sharing research and publishing data, and co-publishing. National (1994a) provides useful information on the National Book Trust and its activities. India (1994) includes basic information relating to the publication division of the Ministry of Information and Broadcasting, Government of India.

Singh (1997) discusses the growing use and the advantages offered by CD-ROM in meeting user requirements. He concludes that CD-ROM is a feasible and durable publishing media. Suchak (1994) is a landmark in the history of CD-ROM publishing in India. It is a bibliographic database developed by SNDT Women's University Library and covers the fields of sociology, women's studies, nutrition, community health, human development, library and information science, and special education. It includes 90,000 references to articles in journals, theses, chapters in books, and reports. The CD-ROM has been developed using leading edge technology and is among the first bibliographic CD-ROM products published in India. Lahiri (1996) points out that in order to facilitate access to science and technology information in India, the principal concern is to increase the market share of modern information products and services in relation to the traditional ones. At present, this share is very small. All the database publishers have good hard copy business and they are not aggressive in marketing their CD-ROM products. He emphasizes that the concept of marketing would have to be adopted if India is to come out of the library-based information culture and adopt modern information products and services. Mehla and Singh (1995) predict that CD-ROM technology will remain as a medium of choice for the publishing industry. Different types of libraries in general, and health science libraries in particular, will be able to procure CD-ROM products.

Beena (1996) analyses the trends in publishing of books in Malayalam and concludes that there is an unbalanced growth in different disciplines. Humanities rank first, while social sciences and sciences rank second and third respectively. She also notes the lack of translations. She suggests that more publications should be brought out by private publishers and the universities. In spite of having the highest state literacy rate, book publishing is not a flourishing industry in Kerala. Ganesan (1992) has helped to ameliorate the state of the Indian publishing industry by conducting a survey with special reference to regional language publishing. He has identified four weaknesses in the Tamil publishing industry: insufficient market orientation; exploitation of authors by publishers; booksellers' indifference to stocking and selling general books; and the large share of public spending on magazines, mainly due to the lack of promotional activities. The Tamil Nadu Textbook Society (TTS) is found guilty of favouritism in the selection of authors, reviewers and printers. The quality of school books published by TTS is poor while their prices are high. At university level publishing, availability of subsidized low-cost books from abroad has ruined the Indian publishing and printing industry. The indifference of Indian universities to the adoption of regional languages as the medium of instruction is also a contributing factor for this miserable condition.

Suresh Chand (1996) ponders over the problem of children's book publishing in India, discusses the role of the few institutions involved and suggests an increase in book publishing for children in the context of a total literacy mission. Varma (1996) highlights the problems of publishing in Indian languages, such as the lack of distribution mechanism, absence of ISBNs in most cases, and non-availability of information about new books. He also suggests certain measures such as improvement of the distribution systems and use of credit cards.

Malhotra (1994) talks about the publishers' awareness of copyright issues in developing countries, particularly India. He also discusses enforcement of copyright law in India and suggests how it might be achieved. Chawla (1996) examines the book distribution system in India and suggests ways to make it successful. Ahuja (1995) points out that in spite of ISBNs being free in India, not many publishers bother with them. Indian (1995b) includes a list of useful publications on Indian standards of documentation information and graphic technology. Publishers, printing presses, authors, binders, educational institutions and all concerned with publication and information, printing and graphic technology can derive assistance from these publications. Amarasuriya (1991) discusses the position occupied by scientific journals in the dissemination of scientific information and provides a succinct description of the historical background of scientific and technical journal publishing and the problems involved. He illustrates the problems and constraints of scientific journal publishing in Sri Lanka.

Library services

National libraries

Sugunavathi (1989) feels that the availability of and access to information generated in any country of South Asia will be more appropriate and adoptable by other countries in the region than the sophisticated information from technologically advanced countries. In view of the resources crunch, she thinks that there is greater scope for resource sharing. She discusses the national information and documentation services emanating from the region. She points out the drawbacks in the system and discusses the economic viability and feasibility of extending the scope of mission/commodity-oriented national information centres, particularly in India, to other countries backed up by an effective document delivery system. For the Ninth Five Year Plan of India, a working group of the Planning Commission has proposed Rs 2,442 crores for the libraries and information sector, giving maximum privileges to academic libraries (Libraries, 1997).

Suseela Kumar (1995) gives a bird's-eye view of the current library and information scene in India. It is a very useful first-hand account of Indian librarianship. Report (1996a) underlines the availability of adequate numbers of users and adequate reading material in local languages, along with the willingness of the government to provide necessary funds as the prerequisites for public library development in India. Report (1996b) makes useful recommendations for the development of public, academic, special and national library systems in India. It further emphasizes the need for strengthening different types of library networks in India. Jagtar Singh and Kalra (1996) emphasize the need to adopt a national information policy and develop an information infrastructure. They further stress the need for involving the private sector in national efforts to enhance global access to information. Navalani (1995) traces the history of efforts made to formulate a national policy on library and information systems in India. She highlights the salient features of the proposed policy submitted to the Department of Culture, Government of India, by the Raja Rammohun Roy Library Foundation. The final report was submitted to the Government of India in 1986, but no action has been taken.

The National Library of India reports on its present functioning and future plans under these headings: collection building and collection organizing programmes; reader services (including bibliographic) programmes; conservation of library materials programme; and modernization and development programmes (National, 1996, unpublished data). It also includes facts and figures relating to the National Library as at 31 March 1996. Shahid Pervez (1994) portrays the National Library, Calcutta. He consolidates the users' views and reports on the work of the three-member committee set up by the Department of Culture, Ministry of Human Resource Development, Government of India, to suggest ways to improve the National Library. Majumdar (1996) points out that the automation programme of the National Library, is essentially concerned with information gathering and storing, both from within the organization and from external sources. The automation programmes have been implemented in phases: acquisition and serial control (first phase); computerized cataloguing (second phase); and circulation control and computer-aided reference service (third phase). Dasgupta (1995) tries to focus on issues that require special consideration in dealing with multilingual publications. She gives examples from the National Library, where the creation of a machine-readable bibliographic database is now in progress.

Delhi occupies a special position in India's economic, social and political order. A review of library and information services in Delhi gives a fair outline of what is happening in India in this field. Bhatt (1995) presents a good overview of important libraries and information centres in Delhi. It covers the British Council Division Library; the American Centre Library; Delhi Public Library; Delhi University Library system; Jawaharlal Nehru University Library; Indian Institute of Public Administration Library; Indian Council of World Affairs Library; ICSSR; ICHR; NCERT; IIIS; National Archives Library; the Parliament Library; IARI Library; National Science Library; National Medical Library; AIIMS Library; IIT Library; INSDOC; Defence Scientific Information and Documentation Centre (DESIDOC); National Information System for Science and Technology (NISSAT); NASSDOC; NDCMC. NIEPA and Centre for Women's Studies (CWDS) are the important libraries and information centres among others discussed in the fifth chapter. Malhotra (1995) gives a detailed account of collections and services of the Indian Parliament library. Ramesh and Sahu (1996a) stress the need for setting up library and information centres in government departments and LAN facilities along with mobile library services to ensure information at village level.

Corea (1991b) comments on the wide range of activities currently being undertaken to promote library and information development in Sri Lanka. She presents a bird's-eye view of the growth and development of library services and concludes that a modern technological information system has yet to be realized. She describes the duties of the Sri Lanka National Library Services Board, which is responsible for the coordination and formation of an effective library and information system for the country. Amarasiri (1991) describes current proposals for the expansion and coordination of the library and information system in the country, with an overview of the entire library and information network in Sri Lanka. Lankage (1987) highlights the common problems faced by the developing countries, particularly in the Asian region. Lack of funds, shortage of trained manpower, lack of hands-on experience, bureaucratic apathy and absence of computer facilities to handle local scripts are the main problems. Developing an indigenous information technology industry and training a core of professionals with the help of national and international support are the suggestions put forward to ameliorate the situation.

Riazuddin (1991) traces the development of librarianship and information work in Pakistan. He notes the expansion of libraries from cities to villages along with growth in their resources and services. Librarianship in Pakistan is faced with numerous problems pertaining to staff, money, materials and management. Anis Khurshid (1987) highlights the state of the art in Pakistan. He assigns the inadequate development of library and information services to the absence of a coordinated library infrastructure; lack of resource sharing; inadequate bibliographic control; absence of physical access to library resources; imbalance in manpower, money and materials; lack of dynamic leadership from PLA. Besides these, the other reasons are the brain drain; absence of systematic and realistic planning; and organizational culture/congenial environment. Khalid (1996) presents a statistical and subjective review of the journal articles on various aspects of library and information services in Pakistan.

Provision of library services in Nepal, Bhutan and the Maldives is not adequate. The National Library of Nepal was founded in 1952 at Kathmandu and consists of 70,000 volumes in eleven languages. It is more like a museum than a library. It is the Tribhuvan University Central Library in Kathmandu which publishes the Nepalese *National Bibliography* and brings out other occasional bibliographies on various subjects of interest. It also promotes the importance of improving library services for national development. It serves as a depository library of the UN for Nepal and cooperates in other international activities. The National Archives, Kathmandu, founded in 1967, consist of 35,000 manuscripts, 60,000 microfilm copies of manuscripts in private collections, 16,000 historical documents and 10,000 volumes. The Archives facilitate access to researchers and publish *Abhilekh* (Nepal, 1995).

The National Library of Bhutan was founded in 1967 at Thimphu. It consists of 1,600 volumes of Tibetan manuscripts and block-print books, 90,000 Tibetan books in other forms; and 15,000 foreign (mainly English) books (Bhutan, 1995). The main libraries of the Maldives are located in its capital Male. The National Library, Male, was founded in 1945 and provides public library facilities. It consists of 14,000 volumes, with special collections in Dhivehi, English, Arabic, Urdu, and of FAO, and UNESCO publications. It publishes the *Bibliography of Dhivehi publications* (Maldives, 1995).

Reading and user education

Gupta (1994) (ed.) has prepared a critical bibliography on different aspects of south Asia including library and information services.

Shah (1996) reports that India and other developing countries of the Asian and African regions now have an effective solution to the problem of keeping up to date with all types of information, provided by NICTAS (National Information Centre for Textile and Allied Subjects). NACID (NISSAT Access Centre for International Databases) at NICTAS can satisfy the information needs of industrialists, businessmen, manufacturers, exporters, importers, technologists, researchers, educationists, students, consumers, small-scale or large-scale industries; and centralized or decentralized sectors of any industry.

Sen (1996) gives economic indicators for a few Asian countries and suggests that a country's self-reliance is directly related to its experts. He underlines the need to make use of Internet-based resources and services for national development. Report (1994) recommends the improvement of collections, procedures, personnel and users' services in college libraries in India to create and maintain a reading habit and love for books among students.

Satyanarayana (1996) states that the objective of constituting the National Book Trust in India was to promote and assist balanced growth of book development in the country. NBT's main activities include publishing, organizing book fairs at regional, national and international level, along with writers' conferences/seminars, symposia and workshops. Through these book fairs NBT has been able to spread the book-reading culture throughout the country. The tremendous response from book lovers to these book fairs has encouraged book trade organizations in various states of the country to organize book fairs in their own states.

Sasikala *et al.* (1994) examine the need for and use of audiovisual collections in different types of libraries in India. They also highlight the problems of bibliographic control of audiovisual materials. Agrawal and Sharma (1992) bring out a union catalogue of about 3,550 non-serial library and information publications available in about 33 libraries in Delhi. It is a valuable aid to researchers and helps in promoting interlibrary loan transactions and use. Subba Rao (1997) discusses the efforts being made by the IIT Bombay to provide current bibliographic and full-text services to end users, the objective being to facilitate literature search and respond to the information needs of users.

Preeti (1996) notes the lack of awareness of electronic information sources among providers (libraries), users, and generators (publishers). The users and the generators have not shown much interest in electronic information sources. However, the providers are ready to adapt to the changing environment. There is a strong need for educating the library staff at the initial stage and then to train them on their jobs. Dutta and Mitra (1996) present the information scenario as well as the information needs of business houses in Calcutta. The survey reveals that large firms have good libraries, but most organizations are not aware of information services. The attitude of authorities towards information services is apathetic and there is a strong need to create an awareness among them.

Gulati and Manjunath (1996) report the findings of the Hyper-Catalogue Experiment at IIT, Kharagpur. They highlight the lack of awareness and training of Internet-based services, especially the hyper-catalogue. Scarcity of Internet providers and the cost of connection are the problems. Jagtar Singh (1997b) emphasizes the need to follow technology-based teaching and learning (TLT).

The networks must be used to strengthen the learning and teaching process. The professional associations should provide the necessary leadership in helping users to adapt to the changing information environment. Corea (1991a) reports the experiences of three projects in Sri Lanka in the provision of library services to the doorsteps of children living in shanties and slums.

Public libraries

Verma and Aggarwal (1994) have done a good job in presenting a comprehensive overview of public library services in India. The introductory chapter traces the history of public libraries in India and highlights the landmarks in this field. The remaining chapters present the state-of-the-art reports on different states and union territories. A few states with or without library legislation have good library infrastructures and facilities, but others do not. The common problems of public libraries relate to lack of adequate funds, trained manpower, buildings, equipment and reading materials. Sastry (1994) elaborates the concept of modernization and describes the public library scene in India. He also gives an agenda for the libraries of tomorrow.

Raja (1996) Rammohun Roy Library Foundation highlights the variation of size, population, literacy rates, production of literature in regional languages, and library infrastructures. L.S. Ramaiah (1997) discusses the case for adopting library legislation in all the states of India and emphasizes the needs of various minority groups. Delhi Public Library (DPL) is termed the busiest public library in Asia, according to a survey conducted by UNESCO. While the ongoing programmes are being strengthened, the library activities are to be modernized. Paucity of funds has always hampered the development of DPL, but the linking of the book purchase policy with the receipt of books under the Delivery of Books and Newspapers (Public Libraries) Act, 1954 (amended 1956) has enabled the library to receive a large number of books free of cost (Khanna, 1996).

In order to improve the image of the state libraries, much needs to be done in terms of input, status, functions and scope of services (Janak Raj, 1996b; Mohamed Taher, 1996; Ohdedar, 1996). State libraries are coming up to the expectations of people in Orissa and Madras (Padhi and Panda, 1996; Venkatappaiah, 1996). The need for establishing and maintaining public libraries under the clear mandate of library legislation is widely echoed in the professional literature (Chandel, 1996; Janek Raj, 1996a; Karisiddappa and Kumbar, 1996; Sukhdev Singh, 1996; Venkatappaiah, 1996). The dismal state of public libraries in Punjab, Haryana and Himachal Pradesh is an eye-opener. This shows the apathetic attitude of the authorities. Private organizations are doing good work in many places, but they do not have a regular flow of funds. Noise pollution, inadequate and untrained staff, lack of sufficient funds and up-to-date collections, inconvenient working hours, insufficient buildings, furniture and equipment, lack of preservation and conservation of rare documents, declining reading habits, lack of professional leadership, bureaucratic apathy, mismanagement of libraries, lack of publicity and public relations, subordination of library services under different departments of the state governments, and finally the absence of library legislation or ineffective implementation of library acts are the main constraints in the establishment, development and maintenance of a comprehensive public library service in rural and urban areas of this region (High, 1996; Noise, 1996; Rare, 1996; Sole, 1996; Staff, 1996; Upkeep, 1996; Where, 1996; Oldest, 1997; Rare, 1997; Sorry, 1997; Where, 1997). Shah (1995) traces the history of public libraries in Gujarat and gives a detailed account of the efforts being made for public library legislation. He presents statistical data and emphasizes the need for further development of public libraries in Gujarat without waiting for library legislation.

Nepal is believed to have been a repository of untold treasures of manuscripts on Tantrism, philosophy, Sanskrit grammar, astrology, medicine and vedic literature. Nepal can be called a country with ancient library traditions, yet education and libraries could not develop in Nepal under the autocratic rule from 1846 to 1951. Books, magazines, newspapers, the radio and other media of communication and academic study were banned for the majority. Even expressing the need for a library was forbidden and could lead to punishment. In 1929 a great Nepali poet, Laxmi Prasad Dev Kota, and some of his friends were punished for their decision to establish a public library in Nepal. After 1951, public library services were introduced in the hope of giving people free access to knowledge (Mishra, 1986). It is said that Nepal has 400 public libraries, but they can hardly be called true public libraries, judged by professional standards, because of deficiencies in objectives, space, subject books and newspaper collection. They have only randomly donated collections and often have difficulty in keeping open a few hours a day or a week at a time.

The Pukhara Public library currently has about 2,500 books in Nepali, English and Hindi on different disciplines and about 50 daily and weekly newspapers, bulletins and magazines. The Nepal–India Cultural Centre and Library, Kathmandu, was founded in 1952 and contains 73,000 volumes. The British Council Library, Kathmandu, was founded in 1959 and contains 19,000 volumes and 100 periodicals. No information about the Secretariat Library, Kathmandu, is available. Bir Library was founded in the 14th century at Kathmandu and consists of 15,000 manuscripts. Madan Puraskar Pustakalaya is located at Lalitpur and consists of 13,000 books, periodicals and posters in the Nepalese language besides 2,800 periodical titles. It publishes *Nepali* (a quarterly) in the Nepali language. (Nepal, 1995).

The government of Nepal and UNESCO have recently reached an agreement on the opening of public libraries in five development regions within five years and initiating a mobile library service through them. As part of the programme,

Pokhara Public Library has been entrusted with the responsibility of running a mobile library in the Kaski district of Nepal. The mobile library service has been launched for the first time in five rural resource centres of the Primary Education Project at Henya, Lamachaur, Baidam, Bhandrakali and Barpatan. The National Library in Kathmandu is to make all necessary arrangements for providing training, technical advice and facilitating materials collection for the smooth functioning of the library service. It will also provide orientation to library users and undertake supervision and monitoring (Mobile, 1996).

Saiful Islam (1990) delineates the current status and structure of public library systems and services in Bangladesh and Great Britain. He highlights the major difference between the countries in regard to provision of public library services and makes a few recommendations to develop public libraries services in Bangladesh. In Bhutan, the Thimphu Public Library was founded in 1980 and consists of 6,000 volumes. Information about public libraries in Pakistan, Sri Lanka, Bhutan and the Maldives was not available.

Academic libraries

Ravichandra Rao (1997) discusses status, problems, and future of automation in academic libraries in India. Automation activities have picked up, but the challenges remain the same over the last two or three decades, namely, manpower requirements, preparation of machine-readable catalogues, free flow of funds, etc. Vyas (1997) underlines the problems faced by academic libraries and emphasizes their vital role in higher education and research. Cholin and Prakash (1997) discuss the status of financial support by INFLIBNET (Information and Library Network) to academic libraries for modernization and computerization of housekeeping activities. They describe the efforts of INFLIBNET in formulating guidelines and formats for library automation work, including data capture, software for data creation and training of personnel.

D.K. Gupta (1997) discusses the open university library system and the services available to distance learners. He pleads for library automation and networking to implement successfully the concept of distance learning. Upadhaya (1997) enlists the benefits and problems in integrating information technologies in academic libraries. Salgar and Doctor (1994) stress the need for automation of library operations and networking of libraries and databases to share optimally the available resources. They describe the INFLIBNET programme and discuss the issues relating to the computerization of university libraries, training library staff in library automation, the establishment of suitable networks and the creation of databases.

Isaac (1995) describes university libraries in India and gives suggestions for their improvement. Sherikar (1996) reports that both the professionals of the library and the Gulbarga University authorities are deeply concerned with development of the university library as an Information Database and Retrieval Centre to enable one-stop shopping for its users. Mohamed Taher (1997) suggests that NCERT, ICSSR, UGC, and AIU in India should sponsor a project for rewriting the intellectual history of libraries.

Haider (1989) surveys the existing library resources in science and technology in the university libraries of Pakistan. He describes the financial aspects, procurement of books, import restrictions, book order work and procurement of periodicals, and gifts and exchanges, and presents proposals for further action.

The state of academic libraries is not encouraging in Nepal. Tribhuvan University Central Library, which was founded in 1959, contains 200,000 volumes – almost three times as much as the holdings of the National Library of Nepal. It also serves as a depository library for the UN. It publishes *Nepali National Bibliography; Education Quarterly; Journal of Tribhuvan University;* and a quarterly *Bulletin* (Mishra, 1986). The National Institute of Education in Bhutan, founded in 1992, has a library which contains 11,000 volumes and 200 periodicals. The Royal Bhutan Polytechnic Library, Deothang, was founded in 1974 and has only 1,992 volumes. The Royal Institute of Management Library, Thimphu, was founded in 1986 but has only 3,000 volumes and subscribes to 50 periodicals. The Sherubtse Degree College Tashigang, founded in 1983, supports a library with 21,000 volumes (Bhutan, 1995). It is obvious from the preceding paragraph that library and information infrastructure is not adequate in Bhutan.

School libraries

As far as school libraries in Nepal, Bhutan, the Maldives and even India are concerned, they are a shambles. Only the public (i.e. privately funded) schools have good library collections, but so far as government schools are concerned, the position of libraries is pitiable wherever they exist. In many cases the school librarians are required to teach the school students, instead of providing library services.

Mangla (1993) reports that many of the secondary and senior secondary schools in India have fairly good libraries and most of them are manned by professionally qualified staff, though much remains to be achieved in this sector. Textbooks are generally available, but lack of literature for general reading, particularly in local languages, greatly hampers the development of these libraries. Sunil Kumar (1993) discusses the present position of school libraries in India and enumerates the objectives of the school library in the light of changing trends in school education. He describes the role of the school library in the teaching and learning process, as well as personality development of the pupils, and pleads that schools should be provided with suitable libraries containing useful books to promote lifelong learning among children after their schooling has finished. Schools (1992) reports the plight of schools as far as the provision of library facilities is concerned to support the learning and teaching programmes in schools.

Kulkarni (1994) prepares an inventory of school libraries in Bombay and underlines that the Campian School Library, and Smt JGMS Trust Children's Library have good collections and are models, as far as architectural design, furniture and services are concerned. Most of the schools in Nepal lack adequate library facilities (Mishra, 1986).

Special libraries

DEVINSA, a unique South Asian database service on socio-economic development for researchers, policy-makers and development agencies, is not free from problems. It is a cooperative venture of leading social science institutions in Bangladesh, India, the Maldives, Nepal, Pakistan and Sri Lanka. Declining input and the time lag are the main problems (Seetharama, 1996). Siddique (1989) summarizes the development of science and technology, and scientific and technological libraries and documentation centres in Bangladesh. He describes the problems of acquiring scientific literature through purchase, gift and exchange and highlights the lack of foreign exchange, and postal delays. He makes proposals for future action and suggests cooperative acquisition programmes.

Raman Nair and Francis (1996) emphasize that the agricultural information system in India is not well organized or developed. Information is collected by research institutions under state and central governments, but the pooling and sharing of information is not well coordinated or effective. Raman Nair (1997) discusses the need for standardizing library and information systems in universities with special reference to agricultural university libraries. He suggests delegation of powers and linkages between information networks of the UGC, ICAR, and AICTE for optimum use of resources. Rauf Meah (1994) notes that the agricultural library system in Gazipur, the heart of agricultural research in Bangladesh, is in its infancy. He underlines the need for improvements in the library administration, organization and personnel. Majid (1993) reports that inadequate collections, lack of information technology, and trained manpower have always prevented agricultural libraries in Pakistan from catering to the information needs of the Pakistani scientific community. A library strengthening project has been designed with the financial assistance of the US Agency for International Development (USAID) to develop multimedia collections and procure core journals on microforms. He stresses the need for more funding and promotional activities.

Gupta (1994) traces the genesis, growth and development of government of India libraries. Barman (1994) underlines the need for networking of research libraries in the North-Eastern region, because of geographical isolation, non-availability of information and books locally, poor budget, etc. He highlights the difficulties in networking, namely, lack of computer facilities, coordinating agency, apathy of parent institutions, dearth of qualified manpower, poor tele-communications and postal infrastructure.

Deb and Bhagwan Das (1994) describes the organization of information in the petroleum industry. They underline the need for networking of petroleum information for its optimum use by geoscientists and planners in the industry. Srivastava and Tyagi (1994) produce a model for petroleum libraries and information networks. They emphasize that a national petroleum information policy is a prerequisite for planning and developing effective and efficient petroleum information systems and services in India. They discuss the policy framework, highlight the problems and give solutions for networking of petroleum libraries and information units. Lack of standardized practices and procedures in information processing, inadequate infrastructure, nature of petroleum information, heterogeneity of hardware and software are a few of the problems identified.

Special libraries are inadequate in number in Nepal, Bhutan and the Maldives. There are about 70 libraries in various government departments, research organizations and other institutions in Nepal. Notable among them are the Madan Puraskar Pustakalaya, the Library of APROSC (Agricultural Projects Services Centre), the Department of Botany Library, the Rastra Bank Library, and the Library of the Trade Promotion Centre. Madan Puraskar Pustakalaya is well known for its good collection of Nepali language and literature. APROSC Library serves as the National Agricultural Documentation Centre (Mishra, 1986). In the Maldives, the Islamic library, Male, was founded in 1985 and specializes in Islamic studies and literature. It contains 4,500 volumes. The Institute of Islamic Studies in the Maldives has a library which consists of only 5,000 volumes. In spite of a 93% literacy rate and $726 per capita income, the library and information infrastructure seems inadequate (Maldives, 1995).

Library automation and networking

Murthy (1994) takes stock of IT developments in libraries and predicts that library networks in India will be operational by the year 2000. Certain developments may alter the present scenario of library and information activities in India for the better. Murthy (1996) gives an overview of the development of library networks in India. The main problems in the early operation of library networks are identified as retro-conversion of holdings data, non-availability of suitable software for operating large databases and online searching in a WAN mode at affordable prices, lack of adequate standardization, and non-availability of adequate training facilities to cover all the library staff participating in the network programmes. He puts forward a few solutions to ameliorate the situation. Ramesh and Sahu (1996b) give a brief account of national and international computer and library networks. They make special reference to INFLIBNET, NICNET, INDONET, I-NET, SIRNET, ERNET, DELNET, CALIBNET, MALIBNET, BSN, RABMN, and BTISNET. They also discuss the library and information services available via these networks and the Internet. Malviya and Rajan (1996) specify the gateways of online services available to Indian libraries and list the hardware needed to use such services. Some of the developing Indian networks are also briefly discussed by the authors. Powar (1996) reports on the role of different networks and programmes in the field of higher education in India. He advocates the use of these networks for the successful implementation of distance learning programmes. Prakash and Cholin (1997) briefly discuss the information technology scenario in India, including networks. They describe the information centres functioning under the UGC and the database creation activities of these centres. Salgar (1997) discusses the computerization and networking of libraries in India and describes briefly government data networks such as ERNET, NICNET, I-NET and GIAS. He also discusses the network-based services available. Jain and Rai (1997) present an overview of various networks in India such as NICNET, ERNET, INFLIBNET, SIRNET, INDONET and OPENNET. Francis (1997) lists their objectives. He evaluates the INFLIBNET programme and suggests necessary deviations in a future plan of action, including the establishment of regional networks for pooling and sharing of resources.

Malwad *et al.* (1996) have done a useful job in bringing together Indian thought on digital libraries. Thirty-one papers deal with electronic publishing, data capturing and filtering processing, electronic access, information professionals for digital libraries, achievements, implications, problems and prospects of digital libraries in India. Srivastava (1996) presents an overview of use of digital technology and communication systems in petroleum information management access and seeking patterns in India. He elaborates on the existing and planned facilities at different specialist digital libraries. Goyal (1996) discusses the TECHLIB-plus tool for building and operating electronic libraries. This is to be introduced by the National Informatics Centre (NIC), New Delhi. He reports that NIC is the value-added reseller in India of BASIS plus, BASIS Desktop, BASIS WEB Server and TECHLIB, plus software products from IDI, USA.

Preparing (1995) contains 67 papers on computer culture, resource sharing and networking, community information systems, role of government and non-government agencies, and the role and responsibilities of library and information professionals. The themes reflect the need for more funds, awareness, resource sharing via networks, developing community information resource centres, library legislation, and continuous professional education and training. Government departments generate as well as need information on descriptive, financial, and statistical aspects. The time lag between the collection and processing of data is very high. However, the increasing use of computers and standardization of formats by the Government of India has enabled a gradual reduction (Seetharambai, 1996).

Taneja and Murthy (1997) describe the role of DESIDOC in promoting information technology for library and information services in India. Tariq Ashraf (1994) describes the role of information technology. He discusses the infrastructure, human resources, telecommunications, research and development in IT in the Indian context. He highlights features of the liberalization policy of the government, software policy of 1986, development in networking and the growth of the IT industry. He visualizes major changes in IT in India due to the present policy of liberalization. Kesavan and Sharma (1996) stress the need to promote indigenous databases and local library networks (LLNs) for self-sufficiency. They assume that there is a lot of scope for LLNs to market their products and services in the industrial and academic sectors. Gaddagimath and Parvathamma (1997) discuss the efforts of INFLIBNET and other agencies towards library automation. They describe in detail the strategy for designing and developing a database and highlight the bottlenecks, such as lack of flexible policies, unskilled manpower, bureaucratization and lack of profit orientation. Ramesh Babu and Rao (1995) foresee CD-ROM as a viable medium of communication in libraries and information centres in India. They also discuss the problems and prospects of integrating CD-ROM products in Indian libraries and information centres. Biswas and Daga (1995) report the first indigenous database of the full text of the Sanskrit epic Mahabharata in original Devanagari characteristics. They believe that this machine-readable text will help in developing software for interpreting Sanskrit grammar.

A collection of 39 articles pertaining to manuscripts, books and data centres representing humanities, social sciences and generalia, covering language, religion, folklore, mythology, education, politics, public administration, history and socio-cultural development are good reading for those interested in area studies. These institutional and documentary resources represent Andhra Pradesh, Madhya Pradesh, Maharashtra, Tamil Nadu, Rajasthan, West Bengal and Kerala (Gupta and Mohamed Taher, 1996).

Fernado (1991) describes the role of small newsletters in disseminating information to local communities in local languages. Not all the problems of information development in Sri Lanka are at the grass-roots level. Prasher (1997) (ed.) has compiled 90 papers on various aspects of librarianship and information work worldwide.

Training and education

Mangla (1994) reviews formal library and information science programmes at postgraduate level offered by university departments, documentation centres and research institutions in India, Pakistan, Bangladesh and Sri Lanka. Besides a brief historical background, a detailed account of LIS education for each of the four countries is given under the following headings: library scene, courses, admission requirements and duration, enrolment , main features of the curricula, and teaching faculty. Devarajan (1995) takes note of the proliferation of library and information science courses in India and underlines the irrelevance and uselessness of the majority of these courses in the changing context. He traces the history of library and information science education and research and describes the levels of the courses and also brings to light the recommendations and resolutions of different seminars held in India. In view of the increasing output in the form of research and trained manpower, he stresses the need for a survey of staff requirements in different types of libraries to avoid the high rate of unemployment in future. He underlines the need for more research in the area of library manpower. Parekh (1997) presents the current status of the Bachelors and Masters programmes in Library and Information Science in India and discusses the challenges faced by the library schools in developing information professionals. Guruswamy Naidu (1997) examines constraints and challenges of LIS education in the developing countries. S.P. Agrawal (1997) depicts the present position of LIS education in India. He also offers some practical suggestions for improvement, advising that there is a need to experiment with different models and to select one that fulfils the needs and improves and strengthens the existing infrastructure.

Sahoo (1997) discusses teacher–student ratios and information about headships, buildings, professional activities, book banks and library facilities, and quality of products in Orissa. Prasher (1997) provides information about LIS education in Madhya Pradesh. Konnur (1997) discusses requirements for library and information work, the role of library education, LIS curriculum and its development, teaching of IT and research in library science. Gopinath (1996) provides a modular structure for learning through computer-based information systems. Kamaiah (1997) puts forward a case for using the Internet in education and research and discusses the services available through NICNET and the VSNL Gateway. S.S. Agrawal (1997) suggests that employers adopt a liberal attitude towards continuing education of professionals, so as to enable them to update their knowledge and skills. Kalra (1997) stresses the need for including non-traditional subjects in the continuing education programmes for improving the managerial capabilities of LIS professionals, and advocates inclusion of entrepreneurial management. National (1994), Bansal (1997) and Jagtar Singh (1997a) stress the need for accreditation of library and information science education programmes in India, including standards and criteria for accreditation. Jagtar Singh and Trishanjit Kaur (1997) point out that the picture of library and information science education is not rosy. The course contents of many library and information science programmes have become partially irrelevant and there is a strong need to integrate information technology and networking components into these programmes. Restructuring of library and information science programmes and their quality control through accreditation are immediately needed. Networking and learning should be the top priority in the near future. Navalani (1996) underlines that the whole education system suffers from uncertainty and is increasingly divorced from real human resource needs. Library and information science education is no exception. Sharma (1995) prepares an inventory of 51 correspondence schools and five open universities in India which impart education through correspondence. Out of these, eleven schools offer LIS courses. This article is a good source of information about LIS correspondence courses. Raghvan (1995) addresses the implications of technological changes occuring in the information sector on the education and training of information professionals. He proposes a model structure of curricula and courses.

Chatterjee *et al.* (1995) present an analysis of trends in PhD level research in library and information science and related topics in Indian universities since the award of the first PhD in 1950. The most popular subject has been academic libraries in India and the LIS department of Karnataka University is the most productive in the field. Malhan (1997) examines contemporary issues and future requirements for research in LIS. He suggests that the UGC should develop an appropriate infrastructure for conducting research in LIS departments in India. NISTADS, INSDOC and DRTC should collaborate and cooperate in joint research and all major research findings should be made available for policy framing. Satija (1997) traces the history of LIS research in India. He laments the decline in quality which, in his view, has been constant and at times rapid.

Ahmad (1994) highlights the growth and development of libraries in Bangladesh and stresses the need for trained library workers. He suggests a nationwide policy network of library systems and expansion of current library education. The same author (1991) examines study courses of studies offered in Bangladesh. He identifies the lack of adequate objectives, scarcity and insufficient education programmes, dearth of competent teaching faculty and learning resources, lack of cooperation, strategic planning and support, stereotyped courses, lack of expansion programmes and lack of leadership as the main problems of professional education in Bangladesh. He puts forward a number of suggestions for the expansion and development of libraries and information science education in Bangladesh, since the number of library schools in Bangladesh is unable to provide adequate human resources for the country. Ahmad (1997) and Khan (1997) provide useful information about LIS education in Bangladesh.

Lankage (1997) discusses the growth and development of LIS education in Sri Lanka. The Universities of Ceylon, Kelaniya and Colombo have been running diploma and degree courses. Information is provided regarding admission requirements, courses and curricula, research programmes, faculty facilities and manpower needs. Kamaldeen (1991) traces the history and development of library education in Sri Lanka over the past 31 years. He reports the dearth of professional staff in the senior librarians' grades because of limited opportunities of gaining professional and postgraduate qualifications, while the cost of pursuing higher studies abroad is prohibitive. Mangla (1994) discusses the state of the art in Pakistan; little else on the Pakistani situation was to be found. Nepal has no library school, but professional librarians are trained abroad and the Tribhuvan University Central Library organizes training courses for working librarians. There is virtually no provision of training and education in Bhutan and the Maldives.

Management

Geethananda (1993) provides a perspective on information marketing using the Development Information Network for South Asia (DEVINSA) as a case study. She concludes that budget cuts, coupled with increased costs involved in the application of technology in information processing and dissemination, have forced libraries and information centres to turn to information marketing.

Lahiri (1995) underlines the need for active participation of information users, individuals and institutions responsible for product development, distribution and investment in order to build up a modern information market. This market should encourage Indian users to access the world of knowledge and foreign users to access Indian information. India should organize an indigenous primary and secondary infrastructure for national and international competition. He insists on improving the quality and timeliness of primary publications and linking up of Indian institutions with global database producers for Indian or partial database input support. He suggests that the proportion of government investment in information activities should decrease and the non-profit organizations and private enterprises should take on increased responsibilities. Kaula (1996) identifies three major information worlds: the literature world of libraries and archives; the information and document world of information centres, clearing houses, documentation centres and record centres; and the data world of computers, telecommunications and automated information systems. At present the librarian as a manager is faced with accelerating change in both external environment suprasystems and internal organizational subsystems which affect the managerial process. The professionals as managers are required to maintain an equilibrium between the need for organizational stability, continuity and the need for adaptation and innovation.

Minnatullah (1994) presents a conceptual framework for management information systems (MIS) in water and sanitation agencies, with particular reference to the situation in Pakistan and other South Asian countries. He explains the need for MIS and identifies their characteristics. He describes the planning process in water supply organizations and the information needs of such organizations, and presents proposals for developing MIS for water supply agencies in three phases, outlining a plan of action for the first phase. Moir (1990) surveys the administration, care and accessibility of district records in Pakistan. He puts forward possible solutions to the problems of dealing with the records and makes recommendation for both long-term and immediate action by the Pakistan authorities.

Preservation

Akhtar (1996) deals with traditional manuscript collections in India with special reference to the National Library of India. Prajapati (1995) presents a short historical sketch of Indian manuscripts, their origins and the distinctive features and factors to be taken into account while dealing with their identification, processing and storage. Senapati (1993) discusses the need for education in preservation and conservation (PAC) of library materials. He elaborates on the courses of study and training in different institutions and puts forward a few suggestions for awareness and popularization of PAC programmes among library professionals in India. Senapati (1994) attempts to find out about the growth and development of the National Museum Library in relation to its collection, users, services, budget and manpower. He suggests a future plan of action to satisfy the needs of the public, academics and decision-makers for the promotion of the cultural heritage of India. Joshi (1995) describes the significance of the collection of one of the world's largest sound archives of All India Radio, New Delhi. Trishanjit Kaur (1997) prepares an inventory of preservation and conservation education and training programmes, along with the practical work being done in different types of libraries in India to preserve rare and endangered documents.

Senadeera (1991) describes a non-traditional approach to microfilming which reflects the necessity for all libraries in Sri Lanka to safeguard their collections in the present unsettled and highly volatile situation in the country. Librarians have to face threats, both deliberate and accidental, to the security of library buildings, collections and staff. These threats may encourage other libraries in the country and outside that face similar dangers to introduce safety measures.

Conclusion

The countries in the South Asian region display a wide range of disparities, which add to their socio-economic problems. Unemployment, poverty, illiteracy, inflation and regional inequality are the lingering problems of South Asian countries which cast shadows on the growth and development of the library and information infrastructure. Even India has not so far adopted any national policy on library and information systems. The National Library of India has not fully internalized the concept of library automation and networking, at a time when India needs to provide leadership as the largest country in this region. There are wide variations between and within the different countries and institutions. There is a perceptible gap between rural and urban settings as far as the provision of library and information resources and services is concerned. Whereas the number of library schools in India is far more than required, in Bangladesh the situation is totally the reverse. Nepal, Bhutan and the Maldives have no library schools to make trained personnel available to cater for their information needs.

The position of academic and special libraries is much better than that of school, public and government libraries. The lack of resources and political will is the main hindrance in the establishment, development and maintainence of public libraries under the clear mandate of law in these countries. Even in India, so far, only ten states out of 26 have enacted library legislation to provide comprehensive public library services to urban and rural people. The concept of library automation and networking is being adopted by academic, particularly university libraries, and special libraries in India. There is an immediate need to coordinate and consolidate the resources and services of different types of libraries in South Asia to enhance people's access to quality information in this region. INFLIBNET is an ambitious programme in India to realize the concept of resource sharing via networking. There is a clear trend towards library automation and networking in India, Pakistan, Sri Lanka and Bangladesh. The by-products of information technology are now visible in the form of indigenous databases. There is also a trend towards electronic publishing. NISSAT, INSDOC and DESIDOC in India have really made perceptible progress in their resources and services. Similar work is being done by PANSDOC (Pakistan National Scientific and Technical Documentation Centre) and BANSDOC (Bangladesh National Scientific and Technological Documentation Centre) in Pakistan and Bangladesh respectively. Although a modern technological information system has yet to be realized in Sri Lanka, the Sri Lanka National Library Services Board does have the responsibility for planning, coordinating and providing services.

The position of library and information infrastructures in Pakistan, Sri Lanka and Bangladesh is perceptibly better than in Nepal, Bhutan and the Maldives. Lack of trained manpower, insufficient funds and inadequate materials are the basic hindrances in the expected development in library and information services in all the South Asian countries.

Acknowledgements

The author is deeply grateful to his colleagues, H.P.S. Kalra and Trishanjit Kaur, without whose timely help in collecting and processing the relevant literature it would not have been possible to write this chapter.

References

Agrawal, S.P. (1997) Library and information studies in India. In: Prasher, R.G. (1997) (ed.), vol. 1, pp. 88–104.

Agrawal, S.P. and Sharma, P.R. (1992) *Communication, information and librarianship in India: an introductory guide to the publication based on a survey of libraries in the capital city of India.* New Delhi: Concept. (Concepts in Communication Informatics and Librarianship, CICIL, no. 34).

Agrawal, S.S. (1997) Continuing education of library and information science professionals. In: Prasher, R.G. (1997) (ed.), vol. 1, pp. 272–281.

Ahmad, N. (1991) Problems and prospect of library education in Bangladesh. *Herald of Library Science,* **30**(1/2), 46–50.

Ahmad, N. (1994) Personnel requirements in the libraries of Bangladesh. *International Information and Library Review,* **26**(4), 315–326.

Ahmad, N. (1996) Genesis of library education: its advent to Indian subcontinent. In: P.N. Kaula *et al.* (eds) *International and comparative librarianship and information systems.* Delhi: B.R., pp. 415–422.

Ahmad, N. (1997) Library education in Bangladesh. In: Prasher, R.G. (1997) (ed.), vol. 1, pp. 153–166.

Ahuja, M.L. (1995) ISBN: its use and significance. *Indian Book Industry,* **24**(4), 27–28.

Akhtar, M.S. (1996) Manuscript collections in Indian libraries with special emphasis on National Library. In: B.M. Gupta (ed.) *Handbook of libraries, archives and information centres in India, vol. 14: Social science & humanities information centres and sources.* New Delhi: Segment, pp. 131–141.

Amarasiri, M.S.U. (1991) The national library of Sri Lanka and the national library system. *Information Development,* **7**(4), 196–203.

Amarasuriya, N.R. (1991) Scientific journals of Sri Lanka. *Information Development,* **7**(4), 204–207.

Anis Khurshid (1987) Library development in Pakistan in the mid-1980s. *International Library Review,* **19**(1), 61–71.

Bansal, G.C. (1997) Accreditation of LIS schools in India and US: a proposal for collaboration. In: Prasher, R.G. (1997) (ed.), vol. 1, pp. 245–251.

Barman, R.K. (1994) Networking of university libraries in N.E. Region: problems and prospects. In: *Papers of sixteenth national seminar of IASLIC on networking of libraries: problems and prospects, Bombay, 19–22 December 1994,* eds M.N. Nagaraj *et al.* Calcutta: Indian Association of Special Libraries and Information Centres, pp. 39–40.

Beena, S. (1996) Book publishing in Malayalam: a bibliographic approach. *Library Science with a Slant to Documentation and Information Studies,* **33**(4), 191–199.

Bhatt, R.K. (1995) *History and development of libraries in India.* New Delhi: Mittal, pp. 172–294.

Bhutan (1995) *World of Learning 1995.* 45th ed. London: Europa, p. 171.

Biswas, S.C. and Daga (1995) The Mahabharata database project: a note. In: S.C. Biswas (ed.) *Global trends in library and information science.* New Delhi: Gyan, pp. 481–488

Boost (1996) for Indian book exports, A. *Publishing in India,* **17**(12), 3.

Chandel, A.S. (1996) Public libraries in Himachal Pradesh: past and present. In: B.M. Gupta (ed.) *Handbook of libraries, archives and information centres in India, vol. 16: Library development in India.* New Delhi: Segment, pp. 188–199.

Chatterjee, A. *et al.* (1995) Research trends in library & information science in India. *Annals of Library Science and Documentation,* **42**(2), 54–60.

Chawla, C.M. (1996) Book distribution in India. *Indian Book Industry,* **26**(2), 15–16.

Cholin, V.S. and Prakash, K. (1997) Status of computerisation and networking of university libraries in India. In: A.L. Murthy and P.B. Mangla (eds.), *Information technology applications in academic libraries: papers presented at the fourth National convention for automation of libraries in education and research (CALIBER-97).* Ahmedabad: Information and Library Network Centre, pp. 5–9.

Corea, I. (1991a) Feeding hungry minds: grassroots library services in Sri Lanka. *Information Development,* **7**(4), 220–226.

Corea, I. (1991b) (ed.) Information development in Sri Lanka. *Information Development,* **7**(4), [special issue] 188–190.

Dasgupta, K. (1995) The role of the national library as a bibliographic centre in a multi-lingual situation: the Indian context. In: S.C. Biswas (ed.) *Global trends in library and information science.* New Delhi: Gyan, pp. 286–297.

Datta, D. (1995) Publishing of children's books. *Indian Book Industry,* **24**(3), 21.

Deb, M. and Bhagwan Das. (1994) Planning and designing petroleum information network in ONGC: challenges and prospects. In: *Papers of sixteenth national seminar of IASLIC on networking of libraries: problems and prospects, Bombay, 19–22 December 1994,* eds M.N. Nagaraj et al. Calcutta: Indian Association of Special Libraries and Information Centres, pp. 9–16.

Devarajan, G. (1995) *Library science education and manpower.* New Delhi: Ess Ess.

Dutta, N. and Mitra, R. (1996) Impact of information technology in business houses in Calcutta: an evaluative study. In: *Papers of seventeenth national seminar of IASLIC on meeting the information challenge for development and self-sufficiency, Calcutta, 10–13 December 1996,* eds M.N. Nagaraj *et al.* Calcutta: Indian Association of Special Libraries and Information Centres, pp. 139–142.

Fernado, V. (1991) Newsletters and development communication. *Information Development,* **7**(4), 227.

Francis, A.T. (1997) Regional information networks: necessary thrust area for INFLIBNET to establish integrated information system in India. In: A.L. Murthy and P.B. Mangla (eds) *Information technology applications in academic libraries: papers presented at the fourth national convention for automation of libraries in education and research (CALIBER-97).* Ahmedabad: Information and Library Network Centre, pp. 102–106.

Gaddagimath, R.B. and Parvathamma, N. (1997) Design and development of indigenous databases. In: A.L. Murthy and P.B. Mangla (eds) *Information technology applications in academic libraries: papers presented at the fourth national convention for automation of libraries in education and research (CALIBER-97).* Ahmedabad: Information and Library Network Centre, pp. 54–58.

Ganesan, S. (1992) *Indian publishing industry: an analytical study with special reference to publishing in regional languages.* New Delhi: Sterling.

Geethananda, H. (1993) Marketing development information in South Asia. *Information Development*, **9**(1,2), 44–51.

Ghai, S.K. (1994) Scholarly publishing in South Asia. *Indian Book Industry*, **24**(1), 17–20.

Ghai, S.K. (1995) Institute of Book Publishing. *Indian Book Industry*, **24**(4), 19.

Girija Kumar (1996) Indian publishing: a critical look. In: P.N. Kaula *et al.* (eds) *International and comparative librarianship and information systems.* Delhi: B.R., pp. 393–406.

Gopinath, M.A. (1996) Development of a curriculum for digital information systems: a learning package for library and information professionals. In: N.M. Malwad *et al.* (eds) *Digital libraries: dynamic storehouse of digitized information.* New Delhi: New Age International, pp. 153–163.

Govil, R.C. (1996) Book publishing in India: a bright future. *Printing Times*, (1), 63–66.

Goyal, R.K. (1996) Electronic library management systems for Intranets. In: *Papers of seventeenth national seminar of IASLIC on meeting the information challenge for development and self-sufficiency, Calcutta, 10–13 December 1996*, eds M.N. Nagaraj *et al.* Calcutta: Indian Association of Special Libraries and Information Centres, pp. 93–97.

Gulati, A. and Manjunath, C.K. (1996) OPACs on Internet: Indian scenario. In: *Papers of seventeenth national seminar of IASLIC on meeting the information challenge for development and self-sufficiency, Calcutta, 10–13 December 1996*, eds. M.N. Nagaraj *et al.* Calcutta: Indian Association of Special Libraries and Information Centres, pp. 67–70.

Gupta, A. (1994) *Government of India libraries: their growth, development and services.* Delhi: B.R. Publications.

Gupta, B.M. (1994) (ed.) *South Asia bibliography and documentation, vol. 7.* New Delhi: Segment, vii–xli, 180–277.

Gupta, B.M. and Mohamed Taher (1996) (eds) *Handbook of libraries, archives and information centres in India, vol. 14: Social sciences and humanities information centres and sources.* New Delhi: Segment.

Gupta, D.K. (1997) Library as support service in distance education: a viewpoint. In: Prasher, R.G. (1997) (ed.), vol. 1, pp. 352–359.

Guruswamy Naidu, N. (1997) Library science education in developing countries: constraints and challenges. In: Prasher, R.G. (1997) (ed.), vol. 1, pp. 83–87.

Haider, S.J. (1989) Acquisition of scientific literature in developing countries: Pakistan. *Information Development*, **5**(2), 85–98.

High (1996) literacy, yet no good public library, *Tribune*, 27 December, 1,4.

India: (1994) a reference annual. New Delhi: Publications Division, Ministry of Information and Broadcasting.

Indian (1995) standards of documentation, information and graphic technology. *Indian Book Industry*, **34**(4), 25–26.

Isaac, K.A. (1995) University libraries in India. In: S.C. Biswas (ed.) *Global trends in library and information science.* New Delhi: Gyan, pp. 338–348.

Jagtar Singh (1997a) Accreditation of library and information science programmes in India. In: Prasher, R.G. (1997) (ed.), vol. 1, pp. 252–257.

Jagtar Singh (1997b) Restructuring of MLISc course: issues and implications. In: Prasher, R.G. (1997) (ed.), vol. 1, pp. 203–213.

Jagtar Singh and Kalra, H.P.S. (1996) Digital libraries: new mechanism for horizontal and vertical integration of information. In: N.M. Malwad *et al.* (1996) (eds), pp. 41–48.

Jagtar Singh and Trishanjit Kaur (1997) Vicissitudes in networking and learning: are we ready to meet the challenges? In: A.L. Murthy and P.B. Mangla (eds) *Information technology applications in academic libraries: papers presented at the fourth national convention for automation of libraries in education and research (CALIBER-97)*. Ahmedabad: Information and Library Network Centre, pp. 82–86.

Jain, V. and Rai, A.K. (1997) Education and research networks in India: a brief note. In: A.L. Murthy and P.B. Mangla (eds) *Information technology applications in academic libraries: papers presented at the fourth national convention for automation of libraries in education and research (CALIBER-97)*. Ahmedabad: Information and Library Network Centre, pp. 91–93.

Janak Raj (1996a) Library movement in Haryana. In: B.M. Gupta (ed.) *Handbook of libraries, archives and information centres in India, vol. 16: Library development in India*. New Delhi: Segment, pp. 175–187.

Janak Raj (1996b) State Central Library, Haryana. In: B.M. Gupta (ed.) *Handbook of libraries, archives and information centres in India, vol. 16: Library development in India*. New Delhi: Segment, pp. 286–292.

Joshi, H.M. (1995) Sound archives in All India Radio. In: S.C. Biswas (ed.) *Global trends in library and information science*. New Delhi: Gyan, pp. 152–156.

Kalra, H.P.S. (1997) Entrepreneurial management for information professionals: a timely theme for continuing professional education. In: Prasher, R.G. (1997) (ed.), vol. 1, pp. 261–271.

Kamaiah, P. (1997) Internet and university libraries in developing education and research. In: A.L. Murthy and P.B. Mangla (eds) *Information technology applications in academic libraries: papers presented at the fourth national convention for automation of libraries in education and research (CALIBER-97)*. Ahmedabad: Information and Library Network Centre, pp. 159–162.

Kamaldeen, S.M. (1991) Library education in Sri Lanka. *Information Development*, 7(4), 213–219.

Karisiddappa, C.R. and Kumbar, B.D. (1996) Library movement in Karnataka. In: B.M. Gupta (ed.) *Handbook of libraries, archives and information centres in India, vol. 16: Library development in India*. New Delhi: Segment, pp. 200–207.

Kaula, P.N. (1996) Information technology: legal, policy and management issues. *University News*, 34(42), 8–11.

Kesavan, R.V. and Sharma, R.S. (1996) Promoting local library networks towards self sufficiency: strategies and techniques with special reference to ADINET. In: *Papers of seventeenth national seminar of IASLIC on meeting the information challenge for development and self-sufficiency, Calcutta, 10–13 December 1996*, eds M.N. Nagaraj *et al.* Calcutta: Indian Association of Special Libraries and Information Centres, pp. 99–104.

Khalid Mahmood (1996) Library and information services in Pakistan: a review of articles published in foreign journals. *International Information and Library Review*, 28(4), 383–405.

Khan, M.S.I. (1997) Preparing the libraries and librarians of Bangladesh for the 21st century: the case of library education. In: Prasher, R.G. (1997) (ed.), vol. 1, pp. 167–175.

Khanna, S.N. (1996) Delhi Public Library: past, present and future. In: B.M.Gupta (ed.) *Handbook of libraries, archives and information centres in India, vol. 16: Library development in India*. New Delhi: Segment, pp. 236–249.

Konnur, M.B. (1997) Education for librarianship: some pertinent issues. In: Prasher, R.G. (1997) (ed.), vol. 1, pp. 186–192.

Kulkarni, S. (1994) A scenario of major libraries in Bombay. In: *Souvenir: XVI IASLIC Seminar 1994.* Bombay: Central Library, IIT, pp. 20–27.

Lahiri, A. (1995) Initiatives to facilitate access to S & T information in India. In: S.C. Biswas (ed.) *Global trends in library and information science.* New Delhi: Gyan, pp. 89–104.

Lahiri, A. (1996) Information market scenario in India. *Information Today and Tomorrow,* **15**(1), 17–30.

Lankage, J. (1987) The use of microcomputers in libraries with special reference to problems encountered in developing countries. In: K.D. Lehmann and H. Strohl-Goebel (eds) *The application of micro-computers in information, documentation and libraries.* Amsterdam: North Holland, pp. 557–563.

Lankage, J. (1997) Growth and development of library education in Sri Lanka. In: Prasher, R.G. (1997) (ed.), vol. 1, pp. 144–152.

Libraries (1997) and ninth plan. *IASLIC Newsletter,* (3–4).

Majid, S. (1993) Strengthening agricultural libraries in Pakistan. *International Information and Library Review,* **25**(4), 233–245.

Majumdar, U. (1996) Automated library operations at India's National Library, Calcutta. In: *Papers of seventeenth national seminar of IASLIC on meeting the information challenge for development and self-sufficiency, Calcutta, 10–13 December 1996,* eds M.N. Nagaraj *et al.* Calcutta: Indian Association of Special Libraries and Information Centres, p. 178.

Maldives (1995) *World of Learning 1995.* 45th ed. London: Europa, p. 1005.

Malhan, I.V. (1997) Contemporary issues and future requirements for research in library and information science. In: Prasher, R.G. (1997) (ed.), vol. 1, pp. 292–297.

Malhotra, D.N. (1994) Copyright: awareness and enforcement. *Indian Book Industry,* **24**(2), 5–7.

Malhotra, G.C. (1995) Library, reference, research, documentation and information services to members of parliament in India. In: S.C. Biswas (ed.) *Global trends in library and information science.* New Delhi: Gyan, pp. 163–185.

Malviya, R. and Rajan, S. (1996) Online services for library and information centre. *DESIDOC Bulletin of Information Technology,* **16**(5), 3–9.

Malwad *et al.* (eds) (1996) *Digital libraries: dynamic storehouse of digitized information.* New Delhi: New Age International.

Mangla, P.B. (1993) India. In: R. Wedgeworth (ed.) *World encyclopedia of library and information services.* 2nd ed. Chicago: American Library Association, pp. 361–364.

Mangla, P.B. (1994) Library and information science education in South Asia: India, Pakistan, Bangladesh and Sri Lanka. *Education for Information,* **12**(4), 399–427.

Manorama (1997) *yearbook.* Kottayam: Malayala Manorama, pp. 215–276.

Mehla, R.D. and Singh, P. (1995) Health science databases on CD-ROM and their relevance to Indian libraries. In: *Papers of twentieth All India Conference of IASLIC on information technology products of 1990s and libraries and information centres, Lucknow, 26–29 December 1995.* Calcutta: Indian Association of Special Libraries and Information Centres, pp. 51–56.

Minnatullah, S.M. (1994) Management information systems for water and sanitation agencies: a conceptual framework. *Information Development,* **10**(2), 96–101.

Mishra, S. (1986) Nepal. In: R. Wedgeworth (ed.) *World encyclopedia of library and information services.* 2nd ed. Chicago: ALA, pp. 595–596.

Mobile (1996) library for rural Nepal. *UNISIST Newsletter,* **24**(1), 23–24.

Mohamed Taher (1996) Functions of the state libraries: a case study of A.P. State Central Library, Hyderabad. In: B.M.Gupta (ed.) *Handbook of libraries, archives and information centres in India, vol. 16: Library development in India.* New Delhi: Segment, pp. 250–257.

Mohamed Taher (1997) Development of academic library: a state-of-the-art. In: L.S. Ramaiah *et al. Information and society.* New Delhi: Ess Ess Publications, pp. 64–73.

Moir, M. (1990) Administering and preserving district records in Pakistan. *Information Development*, **6**(3), 144–148.

Murthy, S.S. (1995) Information technologies in libraries: a futuristic perspective. *ILA Bulletin*, **31**(1/2), 27–33.

Murthy, S.S. (1996) Library networks in India: an overview. *DESIDOC Bulletin of Information Technology*, **16**(2), 3–9.

National (1994a) Book Trust. In: *India 1994: a reference annual.* New Delhi: Publications Division, Ministry of Information & Broadcasting, pp. 105–107.

National (1994b) seminar on accreditation of library and information science schools in India, Nagpur, 7–10 March, 1994. *ILA Bulletin*, **30**(1–2), 46–60.

Navalani, K. (1995) National information policy and the third world countries. In: S.C. Biswas (ed.) *Global trends in library and information science.* New Delhi: Gyan, pp. 349–362.

Navalani, K (1996) Library and information science education in India. *CLIS Observer*, **13**(3,4), 3–10.

Nepal (1995) *World of learning 1995.* 45th ed. London: Europa, p. 1047.

Noise (1996) pollution keeps readers away. *Tribune*, 25 December, 1, 6.

Ohdedar, A.K. (1996) State Central Library, West Bengal. In: B.M.Gupta (ed.) *Handbook of libraries, archives and information centres in India, vol. 16: Library development in India.* New Delhi: Segment, pp. 327–340.

Oldest (1997) CSL fights for survival. *Tribune*, 2 January, 1, 5.

Padhi, P. and Panda, K.C. (1996) Harekrushna Mahtab State Library, Orissa: an appraisal. In: B.M.Gupta (ed.) *Handbook of libraries, archives and information centres in India, vol. 16: Library development in India.* New Delhi: Segment, pp. 307–320.

Parekh, H. (1997) Education and training of information professionals: the challenge ahead. In: A.L. Murthy and P.B. Mangla (eds) *Information technology applications in academic libraries: papers presented at the fourth national convention for automation of libraries in education and research (CALIBER-97).* Ahmedabad: Information and Library Network Centre, pp. 174–177.

Powar, K.B. (1996) Information technology and higher education: the Indian context. *University News*, **34**(48), 11–14.

Prakash, K. and Cholin, V.S. (1997) Development of databases at INFLIBNET for accessing electronic information. In: A.L. Murthy and P.B. Mangla (eds) *Information technology applications in academic libraries: papers presented at the fourth national convention for automation of libraries in education and research (CALIBER-97).* Ahmedabad: Information and Library Network Centre, pp. 59–62.

Prasher, R.G. (1997) LIS education in Madhya Pradesh. In: Prasher, R.G. (1997) (ed.), vol. 1, pp. 123–143.

Prasher, R.G. (1997) (ed.) *Library and information science parameters and perspectives: essays in honour of Prof. P.B. Mangla.* 2 vols. New Delhi: Concept. (Concepts in Communication Informatics and Librarianship (CICIL), no. 74).

Preparing (1995) libraries for the 21st century: seminar papers: fortieth all India library conference, Goa University Library Goa, January 5-8, 1995 (Book Review). *ILA Bulletin,* **31**(1/2), 39–40.

Preeti (1996) A study on awareness and use pattern of electronic information material among providers, generators and users. In: *Papers of seventeenth national seminar of IASLIC on meeting the information challenge for development and self-sufficiency, Calcutta, 10–13 December 1996,* eds M.N. Nagaraj *et al.* Calcutta: Indian Association of Special Libraries and Information Centres, pp. 131–138.

Raghvan, K.S. (1995) Education in information science: some basic issues. *DESIDOC Bulletin of Information Technology,* **15**(6), 5–9.

Ramaiah, B.B. (1997) A movement to fulfil the aspirations of people. *Economic Times (International Times),* 12 May, 1.

Ramaiah, L.S. (1997) Communities in search of library and information services in India. In: L.S. Ramaiah *et al. Information and society.* New Delhi: Ess Ess Publications, pp. 17–28.

Raman Nair, R. (1997) Automating agricultural university libraries: need for standards and guidelines. In: A.L. Murthy and P.B. Mangla (eds) *Information technology applications in academic libraries: papers presented at the fourth national convention for automation of libraries in education and research (CALIBER-97).* Ahmedabad: Information and Library Network Centre, pp. 24–29.

Raman Nair, R. and Francis, A.T. (1996) Information needs of agricultural scientists. In: *Papers of seventeenth national seminar of IASLIC on meeting the information challenge for development and self-sufficiency, Calcutta, 10–13 December 1996,* eds M.N. Nagaraj *et al.* Calcutta: Indian Association of Special Libraries and Information Centres, pp. 121–126.

Ramesh Babu, B. and Rao, V.K. (1995) CD-ROM as a media of communication in library and information centres in India: problems and prospects. In: *Papers of twentieth all India Conference of IASLIC on information technology products of 1990s and libraries and information centres, Lucknow, 26–29 December 1995,* eds M.N. Nagaraj. Calcutta: Indian Association of Special Libraries and Information Centres, pp. 47–50.

Ramesh, D.B. and Sahu, J.R. (1996a) Need of library & information services for socio-economic development: a study on local government decision makers in Orissa. In: *Papers of seventeenth national seminar of IASLIC on meeting the information challenge for development and self-sufficiency, Calcutta, 10–13 December 1996,* eds M.N. Nagaraj *et al.* Calcutta: Indian Association of Special Libraries and Information Centres, pp. 21–23.

Ramesh, D.B. and Sahu, J.R. (1996b) Use of digital libraries available on national and international networks: its status and relevance. In: N.M. Malwad *et al.* (eds) *Digital libraries: dynamic storehouse of digitized information.* New Delhi: New Age International, pp. 140–152.

Rare (1996) books fall prey to white ants. *Tribune,* 29 December, 1, 5.

Rare (1997) volumes dumped on floor. *Tribune,* 1 January, 1, 6.

Rauf Meah, M. A. (1994) Agricultural Libraries in Gazipur (Bangladesh): a survey report. *Annals of Library Science and Documentation,* **41**(3), 102–109.

Ravichandra Rao, I.K. (1997) Automation of academic libraries in India: status, problems and future. In: A.L. Murthy and P.B. Mangla (eds) *Information technology applications in academic libraries: papers presented at the fourth national convention for automation of libraries in education and research (CALIBER-97).* Ahmedabad: Information and Library Network Centre, pp. 1–4.

Report (1994) of the expert committee on college libraries. *ILA Bulletin*, **30**(3/4), 109–117.

Report (1996a) of the Sub-group on public library system of the Working Group on Libraries and Informatics appointed by the Planning Commission for the Formulation of Eighth Five Year Plan (1990–95). *CLIS Observer*, **13**(1-2) 27–43.

Report (1996b) of the working group of the Planning Commission on Libraries and Informatics for the Eighth Five Year Plan (1990–95). *CLIS Observer*, **13**(1/2), 7–25.

Riazuddin, S. (1991) Trends in the development of librarianship in Pakistan. In: Niammuiddin Qureshi and Zahiruddin Khurshid (eds) *Trends in international librarianship: a festschrift honouring Anis Khurshid*. Karachi: Royal, pp. 89–104.

SAARC (1996) Documentation Centre. *DESIDOC Bulletin of Information Technology*, **16**(4), 36.

Sahoo, K.C. (1997) Status of library legislation in India. In: Prasher, R.G. (1997) (ed.), vol. 1, pp. 379–386.

Saiful Islam, K.M. (1990) Public library systems and services in Great Britain and Bangladesh. *Herald of Library Science*, **29**(3,4), 163–172.

Salgar, S.M. (1997) Network services for libraries. In: A.L. Murthy and P.B. Mangla (eds) *Information technology applications in academic libraries: papers presented at the fourth national convention for automation of libraries in education and research (CALIBER-97)*. Ahmedabad: Information and Library Network Centre, pp. 78–81.

Salgar, S.M. and Doctor, G. (1994) Networking of university libraries. In: *Papers of sixteenth national seminar of IASLIC on networking of libraries: problems and prospects, Bombay, 19–22 December 1994*, eds M.N. Nagaraj *et al*. Calcutta: Indian Association of Special Libraries and Information Centres, pp. 31–34.

Sasikala, C. *et al*. (1994) Audiovisual materials for Indian libraries. *ILA Bulletin*, **30**(1,2), 38–45.

Sastry, R.S. (1994) Public libraries – modernisation and development. *ILA Bulletin*, **30**(1,2), 3–7.

Satija, M.P. (1997) LIS research in India: a historical perspective. In: Prasher, R.G. (1997) (ed.), vol. 1, pp. 285–291.

Satyanarayana, K.B. (1996) NBT and the book fairs. *University News*, **34**(5), 1–3.

Schools (1992) sans educational facilities. *Statesman*, 21 September.

Seetharama, S. (1996) Information strategies for socio-economic development. In: *Papers of seventeenth national seminar of IASLIC on meeting the information challenge for development and self-sufficiency, Calcutta, 10–13 December 1996*, eds M.N. Nagaraj *et al*. Calcutta: Indian Association of Special Libraries and Information Centres, pp. 1–12.

Seetharambai, N. (1996) HRD information: problems of accessibility. In: *Papers of seventeenth national seminar of IASLIC on meeting the information challenge for development and self-sufficiency, Calcutta, 10–13 December 1996*, eds M.N. Nagaraj *et al*. Calcutta: Indian Association of Special Libraries and Information Centres, pp. 43–44.

Sen, B.K. (1996) Role of Internet in national development. In: *Papers of seventeenth national seminar of IASLIC on meeting the information challenge for development and self-sufficiency, Calcutta, 10–13 December 1996*, eds M.N. Nagaraj *et al*. Calcutta: Indian Association of Special Libraries and Information Centres, pp. 55–62.

Senadeera, N.T.S.A. (1991) Microfilming for the safety of library materials. *Information Development*, **7**(4), 208–212.

Senapati, S.K. (1993) Education in preservation and conservation of library materials in India. *ILA Bulletin*, **29**(1/2), 39–46.

Senapati, S.K. (1994) Growth and development of National Museum library as a model of museum libraries in India. *ILA Bulletin*, **30**(1/2), 25–30.

Shah, P.C. (1995) Friendship without marriage: public library development without library legislation. *ILA Bulletin*, **30**(3/4), 67–72.

Shah, P.C. (1996) Global textile information. In: *Papers of seventeenth national seminar of IASLIC on meeting the information challenge for development and self-sufficiency, Calcutta, 10–13 December 1996*, eds M.N. Nagaraj *et al.* Calcutta: Indian Association of Special Libraries and Information Centres, pp. 45–48.

Shahid Pervez, M.D. (1994) National Library (Calcutta). *ILA Bulletin (ILA Magazine)*, **30**(3/4), 19–21.

Sharma, D.K. (1995) Library and information science courses by open universities and correspondence course institutes in India. *CLIS Observer*, **12**(3/4), 21–24.

Shaw, G. (1995) The history of printing in South Asia: the state of current and future research. In: S.C. Biswas (ed.) *Global trends in library and information science*. New Delhi: Gyan, pp. 105–125.

Sherikar, A. (1996) Gulbarga University Library's computer-aided information retrieval and INFLIBNET related activities: a study. In: *Papers of seventeenth national seminar of IASLIC on meeting the information challenge for development and self-sufficiency, Calcutta, 10–13 December 1996*, eds M.N. Nagaraj *et al.* Calcutta: Indian Association of Special Libraries and Information Centres, pp. 117–120.

Siddique, A.B. (1989) Acquisition of scientific literature in developing countries: Bangladesh. *Information Development*, **5**(1), 15–22.

Singh, D.V. (1997) CD-ROM Network. In: A.L. Murthy and P.B. Mangla (eds) *Information technology applications in academic libraries: papers presented at the fourth national convention for automation of libraries in education and research (CALIBER-97)*. Ahmedabad: Information and Library Network Centre, pp. 87–90.

Sole (1996) public library not made public yet. *Tribune*, 30 December, 1, 4.

Sorry (1997) state of libraries. *Tribune*, 4 January, 1, 10.

Srivastava, A.K. (1996) Evolving digital library of petroleum: efforts and achievement of Indian petroleum industry with special reference to ONGC. In: N.M. Malwad *et al.* (eds) *Digital libraries: dynamic storehouse of digitized information*. New Delhi: New Age International, pp. 261–266.

Srivastava, A.K. and Tyagi, S.K. (1994) Information policy and networking strategy: a model for petroleum libraries and information network. In: *Papers of sixteenth national seminar of IASLIC on networking of libraries: problems and prospects, Bombay, 19–22 December 1994*, eds M.N. Nagaraj *et al.* Calcutta: Indian Association of Special Libraries and Information Centres, pp. 1–8.

Staff (1996) stagnancy, vacancies hit services. *Tribune*, 28 December, 1, 4.

Strengthening (1997) SAARC in its second decade. *Economic Times (International Times)*, 12 May, 4.

Subba Rao, V.S. (1997) Identifying and informing potential end users: a case study of information services by network at IIT-Bombay Central Library. In: A.L. Murthy and P.B. Mangla (eds) *Information technology applications in academic libraries: papers presented at the fourth national convention for automation of libraries in education and research (CALIBER-97)*. Ahmedabad: Information and Library Network Centre, pp. 94–96.

Suchak (1994) on CD-ROM. *University News*, **34**(17), 22.

Sugunavathi, C. (1989) Sharing of information resources in South Asia. *Lucknow Librarian*, **21**(4), 147–152.

Sukhdev Singh (1996) History of library movement in Punjab. In: B.M. Gupta (ed.) *Handbook of libraries, archives and information centres in India, vol. 16: Library development in India*. New Delhi: Segment, pp. 208–224.

Sunil Kumar (1993) Changing role of school library in present scenario. *ILA Bulletin*, **30**(3/4), 124–127.

Suresh Chand (1996) Children's book publishing. *Indian Book Industry*, **26**(2), 25–26.

Suseela Kumar (1995) Libraries and library science in India. In: S.C. Biswas (ed.) *Global trends in library and information science*. New Delhi: Gyan, pp. 323–338.

Taneja, S.K. and Murthy, S.S. (1997) DESIDOC as a promoter of IT for library and information services (LIS) in India. In: Prasher, R.G. (1997) (ed.), vol. 2, pp. 205–213.

Tariq Ashraf (1994) Information technology: the policy making in India. *ILA Bulletin*, **30**(1,2), 21–24.

Trishanjit Kaur (1997) Preservation and conservation: a professional limbo in LIS programmes in India. In: *Papers of the Seminar on library management and operations, Patiala, 10–11 January 1997*. [unpublished].

Upadhaya, P.V. (1997) Information technology and academic libraries. In: A.L. Murthy and P.B. Mangla (eds) *Information technology applications in academic libraries: papers presented at the fourth national convention for automation of libraries in education and research (CALIBER-97)*. Ahmedabad: Information and Library Network Centre, pp. 43–45.

Upkeep (1996) funds don't even meet power bills. *Tribune*, 26 December, 1, 15.

Varma, A.N. (1996) Export of Indian language books: prospects and problems. *Indian Book Industry*, **26**(2), 19–20.

Venkatappaiah, V. (1996) Connemara (State Central) Public Library, Madras. In: B.M.Gupta (ed.) *Handbook of libraries, archives and information centres in India, vol. 16: Library development in India*. New Delhi: Segment, pp. 321–326.

Verma, L.N. and Aggarwal, U.K. (1994) (eds) *Public library services in India*. Udaipur: Himanshu.

Vyas, S.D. (1997) Current issues in Indian academic libraries. In: L.S. Ramaiah *et al. Information and society*. New Delhi: Ess Ess Publications, pp. 57–63.

Where (1996) 'malis' run reading rooms. *Tribune*, 31 December, 1, 4.

Where (1997) readers face simian invasion. *Tribune*, 3 January, 1, 7.

Epilogue

Once again the most common theme in *Librarianship and Information Work Worldwide* is change: not just consolidation or adjustment, but fundamental, all-embracing change. The world changes and librarianship and information work are changing with it. Sometimes the professional change is grudging or tentative, but, more often, information professionals are seeking wholeheartedly to direct their activities towards new realities which centre on the electronic availability of information and the increasing business orientation of the information environment. Often, the only restraining factor is the availability of finance to introduce new systems, retrain personnel, and involve user communities in new patterns of information provision. The speed of change can be disheartening to those who feel a need to retain a hold on the long-established props of professional life.

Almost everything that was familiar now seems open to question. The concept of legal deposit, for instance, underpins national library activity and national bibliography. Extending legal deposit to cover electronic documents is difficult, but far from impossible. Yet, how far can any electronic publication truly be considered part of the intellectual patrimony of any one country? The concept of publication is no longer the same thing as when one could identify a specific press in a specific country as the origin of a printed document. Although an electronic document may emanate from a specific server, with an identifiable geographical location, to what extent can that be said to signify that the document is 'published' in that location? The revisions of long-accepted approaches called for by this, and a host of other changes, lead to the suggestion, made in this book, that libraries must become the opposite of what they are now if they are to survive. This is undoubtedly terrifying to many. Yet change is not just a threat, it also opens exciting prospects. A suggestion that written collection development policies become so swiftly out of date as to be a waste of time, is followed in the same article by an exciting vision of the OPAC as not just a means to find local resources, but an interface between the library's users and resources from both within and without the library. This type of juxtaposition is typical of what the contributors see happening around them, and what the literature reveals to be happening beyond their immediate vision.

Although the diversity of information professionals' reactions and responses to change is enormous, there are some common themes which recur, whatever the sector or specialization that is discussed. A business/market orientation is increasingly natural to librarians, with a growing acceptance that information, in some formats at least, can be marketed and sold like any other product, even in otherwise very traditional information institutions. Associated with this there is also a user/customer focus which has altered the relationship between librarians and users in all but the most curatorially minded institutions. The threats and the demands created by change also continuously raise the profile of co-operative responses, within sectors of librarianship, across sectors, and linking public and commercial organizations. Talk of collaboration, partnerships, consortia, and joint enterprises of many kinds is to be heard everywhere, and the experience of such activities is reflected in many parts of this book.

The vocabulary of the discipline also changes to accommodate practical changes. Thus we have increasing reference to 'convergence' signifying a number of related things. Ways in which it is used include the coming together of libraries, computer services, audio-visual and other services in the academic context. The word is also used for the emergence of new professional profiles, symbolized by the discussions in progress in Britain during 1997 between the Library Association and the Institute of Information Scientists about a merger between the two organizations, or more likely, a new association for information professionals. What to call these new professionals is an issue not resolved by the occasional use of the clumsy 'Modern Information Professionals' or MIPs. A second term heard quite frequently is 'dis-intermediation', referring to the way in which the user is increasingly empowered by information technology to access information without the assistance of a human intermediary. The disturbing implications of this for librarians and other information workers are, however, somewhat relieved by the appearance of references to 're-mediation', presumably by the intervention of modern information professionals.

A final term that is worth mention, from what could easily be a lengthy list, is 'knowledge management'. Although, like the more widely used 'information management', this term is often used when all that is meant is the management of information technology, in its fullest sense it refers to the most positive vision of the future of our professional area. It is the activity that marshals knowledge resources, whether in the form of print, electronic information or the human capital of highly educated and experienced personnel, for the most complete and effective intellectual arming of the organization or individual to meet all the challenges the world offers. Knowledge management would be a calm which would emerge from the current information maelstrom, if it were conceivable that there will be any final outcome of the interaction of social, economic and technical forces which have so disrupted and energized librarianship and information work worldwide.

Perhaps the only thing that we can count on is that, not only has change been the dominant theme of our authors in this volume, it will quite certainly be equally dominant in the forthcoming volumes of this series. Fasten your seatbelts, librarians and information workers, further turbulence is predicted.

Subject index

Note: Entries appear under separate countries and regions, with the exception of the United Kingdom and the United States of America, for both of which the references are too numerous for page numbers to be useful.

.

Author index

Note: The following practices are adopted for the filing of vowels in some European languages in alphabetical sequences:

å is filed as aa
æ and ä are filed as ae
ø and ö are filed as oe
ü is filed as ue
Mac, Mc and M' are all filed as Mac
St is filed as Saint